I Bow to the Buddha in You

I Bow to the Buddha in You

DHARMA TALKS AND WRITINGS OF
THE MOST VENERABLE NICHIDATSU FUJII

TRANSLATED BY
Yumiko Miyazaki

NIPPONZAN MYŌHŌJI

Nipponzan Myōhōji Publications
1127 Glenwood Ave., SE
Atlanta, GA 30316 USA

First Edition
Printed in United States of America

Printed on acid-free paper certified by The Sustainable Forestry Initiative®
Book cover paper is Green Seal® Certified

Publisher's Cataloging-In-Publication Data
(Prepared by The Donohue Group, Inc.)

Fujii, Nittatsu, 1885-
I bow to the Buddha in you : Dharma talks and writings of the most venerable Nichidatsu Fujii / [Nichidatsu Fujii] ; translated by Yumiko Miyazaki. -- 1st ed.

p. : ill. ; cm.

Includes bibliographical references.
Text translated into English from the original Japanese.
ISBN: 978-0-9791298-1-0

1. Fujii, Nittatsu, 1885- 2. Peace--Religious aspects--Buddhism. 3. Nonviolence--Religious aspects--Buddhism. 4. Mahayana Buddhism. 5. Nipponzan Myōhōji (Sect)--History.
I. Miyazaki, Yumiko. II. Title.

BQ4022.F85 2009
294.3 2009927692

Book cover calligraphy by the Most Venerable Nichidatsu Fujii.

Cover design and book layout by Paul Lazzari
Photographs by Seto Kunihiko and Fukuda Tokurō. Used by permission.
Portrait of Mahatma Gandhi by Shri Upendra Maharati.
Used by permission of artist's daughter, Gopa Ratan Maharathi.

Contents

Foreword

Tangyō-raihai is the true name of this book, a Japanese Buddhist term that can be explained but for which there is no equivalent in the English language. The title, *I Bow to the Buddha in You,* reflects a measure of the spirit of *tangyō-raihai.* But *tangyō-raihai* is not a simple declarative sentence; rather it is a single-minded, dedicated practice of bowing in veneration to the Buddha in others. The Most Venerable Nichidatsu Fujii, founder of Nipponzan Myōhōji and the author of this book, spoke often of *tangyō-raihai* as a profound truth and the very essence of world peace, and that without *tangyō-raihai,* peace of any kind was unattainable.

Like Mahatma Gandhi with Satyagraha and *ahimsa* and Martin Luther King, Jr., with nonviolence, Venerable Fujii, or Guruji as he is more often called, not only preached *tangyō-raihai,* he lived it and by living it inspired others to see a higher, more noble potential for humankind. While nonviolence practices are often used as a technique for social and political change, *tangyō-raihai* is an act of nonviolence and reverence that seeks a much deeper revolution: the transformation of the heart and mind of not only the person performing *tangyō-raihai,* but also the one being venerated.

The concept of *tangyō-raihai* comes from Chapter XX of the Lotus Sūtra, *Bodhisattva Never Despise.* In that chapter, Śākyamuni Buddha tells the story of a certain Bodhisattva who lived as a humble monk in an age characterized by powerful, arrogant monks. Whenever this monk encountered another monk, nun, layman or laywoman, he would bow deeply to them and say the following: "I deeply revere you. I dare not slight or despise you. For you will all go about and practice the Bodhisattva way and are to become Buddhas." Rather than change their hearts and minds, such veneration angered those who heard it, and they hurled insults, stones and sticks at him. Yet Bodhisattva Never Despise continued to bow, not to the ignorance and arrogance but because he could see the Buddha nature, which is intrinsic to all sentient beings. And eventually these arrogant people awakened to their own Buddha nature and comprehended the Bodhisattva's great power and compassion and were able to achieve enlightenment.

In an age when nuclear weapons, climate change and other products of human ignorance, greed and arrogance threaten total life extinction, Guruji understood that only *tangyō-raihai*, even at the risk of one's life, could break the endless, downward spiral of violence and open the path to salvation. He embodied the practice of *tangyō-raihai* by following a unique calling to walk throughout the *Jambudvīpa*, this world, beating the drum and chanting Na Mu Myō Hō Ren Ge Kyō for world peace and established an order of monks and nuns, Nipponzan Myōhōji, for this same purpose. He also built stūpas or Peace Pagodas throughout the world to serve as beacons to guide all beings to a world of peace. His life and mission brought him to almost every corner of the globe, and his assiduous practice led him to encounter many great world leaders, including Mahatma Gandhi. Such a life leaves a legacy rich in so many ways, not the least of which is his Dharma talks and writings.

For the second time in recent years, Nipponzan Myōhōji has collaborated with Yumiko Miyazaki to bring some of Guruji's voluminous writings into English. Ms. Miyazaki in her translations has been remarkable in her attention to accuracy and detail and has brought a passionate devotion and deep reverence to the task of translating Guruji's words into English. Her work is made all the more extraordinary by the fact that the countless hours she has spent on this project have been her selfless offering. It is humbling to acknowledge that no amount of appreciation could ever compensate for the enormous debt owed.

The first book published in 2007, *Tranquil Is This Realm of Mine*, was a translation of a compilation, *Tenku Yomōnshū*, that had been made seven years after Guruji passed away on January 9, 1985 at 100 years of age. Those writings were mostly short pieces, many of them excerpts from longer Dharma talks, and offered an introductory guide of sorts into the practice and mission of Nipponzan Myōhōji. That translation was daunting enough, but a far easier task than this second book.

For *I Bow to the Buddha in You*, there was no roadmap. Some of the writings contained here were suggested by members of Nipponzan Myōhōji, but most of them were chosen by Ms. Miyazaki, who tried to find pieces that would convey the enormous breadth of Guruji's work as well as the depth of thought and vision behind his mission. Often when the book appeared close to being done, another writing of Guruji's would be offered as a means of making the collection more complete. In the end, it proved impossible to give a complete overview. Guruji's life was simply too big.

But within these pages are writings that span more than a half century, beginning with *Shishin-kaku,* a moving tribute to his spiritual master, Nichiren Daishōnin, and to his mother, written on the eve of Guruji's departure for *Saiten-kaikyō,* his vow to fulfill Nichiren Daishōnin's prophecy and return Buddha's teachings to *Saiten,* the Western Heavens, an ancient name for India, and from there it would spread to the entire world. His first encounter with Buddha relics in Sri Lanka, his stay at Gandhi's ashram in Wardha, the first Peace Pagoda built in post-war Japan, reflections on militarism, the arms race, the peace movement, Native Americans, the practice of nonviolence are just some of the topics contained herein, and they served as speeches and Dharma talks in Tōkyō, London, Vienna, New Delhi, New York, Washington, D.C. and East Berlin, to name just some of the places. At the heart of every talk by Guruji, regardless of when or where, was the same compassion expressed by the Buddha in Chapter XVI of the Lotus Sūtra:

> At all times making this my thought:
> "How shall I cause all the living
> To enter the Supreme Path
> And speedily attain Buddhahood?"

In other words, he spoke on the central motivation of *tangyō-raihai.*

The times we live in are challenging, and Guruji never minced words when it came to speaking truth to the evils of militarism, materialism and the political regimes that perpetuate those evils. Though *tangyō-raihai* is a practice of reverence towards all, even the wrongdoers, policies of state that are leading the people astray must be corrected, and Guruji worked tirelessly to the end of his life for the salvation of all and in the interest of world peace.

Within this book, style choices were made that differed from *Tranquil Is This Realm of Mine* to better reflect Guruji's own writing and the Japanese culture from which he came. For example, Japanese names follow that culture's tradition of placing the family name first, with the exception of Guruji's own name since books previously have been published under the name of "Nichidatsu Fujii," and consistency was a concern. Also, Guruji sometimes wrote his name at the end of a writing and sometimes not. He varied his signature style and these variations were included with footnotes to explain words specific to Japanese Buddhism or to Sanskrit. Likewise, Ms. Miyazaki has made a heroic effort to research the Buddhist terms and concepts, many quite scholarly and no longer in common usage. The best effort was made to try and explain these terms in the footnotes.

The footnotes deserve a special mention for they are numerous and frequently so detailed that they have almost become a book within a book. Although the length and number sometimes leads to an odd layout where a page contains more footnote than text, it is hoped that their running commentary provide an easy reference to give readers a fuller understanding of the historical and religious context of each piece.

Research was also done to try and find the original date and place when the Dharma talk was made or writing published. This effort was successful most of the time, but on occasion an article has been reprinted so many times in Japanese that the original publication date could not be determined.

Selections for the book, explanation of Buddhist terms and other guidance was offered by a host of helpers over the last four years. Rev. Nanba Kōshō of the Nichiren School Honyōji Temple in Ikeda City was extremely generous with his time and advice on the doctrinal interpretations of Nichiren Daishōnin's citations, and his help greatly contributed to information included in many footnotes. Rev. Yamaguchi Toshihiro of Nichiren School's Bukkōji Temple was the spark who started the entire translation process. From Nipponzan Myōhōji, Rev. Shugei Tenshin provided context to the original texts and insights to Buddhist terminology; Rev. Takeda Takao was generous in supplying financial support; Rev. Kurihara Gyōkō offered valuable counsel on content; Rev. Sasamori Gyōshu facilitated communications with Rev. Shugei; Rev. Asai Mikio gathered information on Nipponzan's history; Rev. Nagase Gyōrō helped research Dharma talks from the U.K.; Rev. Utsumi Gyōshu helped to select some of the writings, chose the photographs and reviewed the overall composition of the book; Rev. Clare Carter proofread the final copy, offering valuable corrections and suggestions; Rev. Denise Laffan proofread through the revision process. Bob Jennings, valued friend and devotee of Nipponzan Myōhōji and engineer of the New England Peace Pagoda, was a most gracious and able proofreader. Paul Lazzari, good friend and supporter of the Great Smoky Mountains Peace Pagoda, was generous in the time he offered to designing the cover of this book and creating its layout.

The final proof was also read by Kazuko Scott, Kosuga Miwa and Miyazaki Hirokazu, who caught typos and glitches that were missed by other eyes. For all of this invaluable assistance, we are grateful.

Nipponzan Myōhōji Publications
July 2009

Translator's Note

One of countless opportunities to interpret for Guruji came during the United Nations Special Session on Disarmament in June of 1982. It was six years into my nine-year association with the Most Venerable Nichidatsu Fujii at a time when I served as interpreter for the Japanese NGOs. Guruji had been brought to the venue—the Church Center for the United Nations, across the street from the UN—in a chauffeured-car graciously offered by a resident of New York City. She may have been keen to hear a venerable Buddhist master speak on meditation or took for granted the popular notion that Buddhism was a religion all about making people feel peaceful. What she and everyone else got was a penetrating analysis of the nuclear arms race that did not mince words when it came to holding the superpowers accountable for their policies. His solution to a world held hostage to this nuclear madness was strong and clear and founded on his discipleship of Lord Buddha and Nichiren Daishōnin: strict adherence to the precept against taking life and taking refuge in the Ineffable Dharma. Peace and tranquility for the individual is impossible so long as peace does not prevail in the world at large, he declared. With his Dharma talk thus concluded, the woman with the chauffeured-driven car was nowhere to be found.

Her disappearance became, quite literally, my good fortune. Needing transportation for a then 97-year-old Guruji, we hailed a cab and Guruji's attendants suggested I sit next to him. As the taxi crawled through the congested streets, Guruji offered to read my palm. I eagerly held out my hands. He examined my palms and said I had good lines. "The lines suggest longevity. Wouldn't it be fun to live as long as I have and to do the work of relieving the suffering of the people? Wouldn't that be a good life?" His Dharma talk that evening had offered harsh words as the good medicine to bring a mad world to its senses, while his words to me were both playful and nurturing. In every case, Guruji saw the capacity of the person or persons in a way that made every contact an act of compassion to bring out the best in people.

More than 30 years later, I have the opportunity to give back to the world. I am grateful to use my training to be part of Guruji's legacy in my own small way, though I know my translation cannot do justice to Guruji's profound teachings. The Foreword acknowledges the many people who have helped me along the way. I wish to personally thank Rev. Nanba Kōshō of Honyōji Temple and Rev. Denise Laffan of Nipponzan Myōhōji. Rev. Nanba is a disciple of Dr. Kubota Shōbun, former vice president of Risshō University and a scholar for whom Guruji had the highest respect. In Guruji's final years, Rev. Nanba served as interlocutor in many of Guruji's significant Dharma talks, listening and responding to a variety of issues on doctrine. His advice not only drew on his extensive knowledge of Nichiren doctrine but was also steeped in a deep appreciation for Guruji's teachings. It proved invaluable for this translation. Rev. Laffan and I went through draft upon draft, revisiting some sections innumerable times trying to best express Guruji's words in English. She was an able, resourceful and patient partner (though I know she has almost given up on me after the 100th revision). Without help from these two, this book would never have made it to completion.

This book is also a tribute to my parents, Miyazaki Hisako and Goro, who by bringing me into this world gave me the invaluable gift of being able to meet Guruji in his lifetime; to my brother Shige, a paragon of filial piety who has taken care of my parents on behalf of the two of us; and to my son, Joel, who has given me joy and insight into the debt of gratitude I owe my own parents.

Yumiko Miyazaki
June 2009

Nichiren Daishōnin [1222-1282]

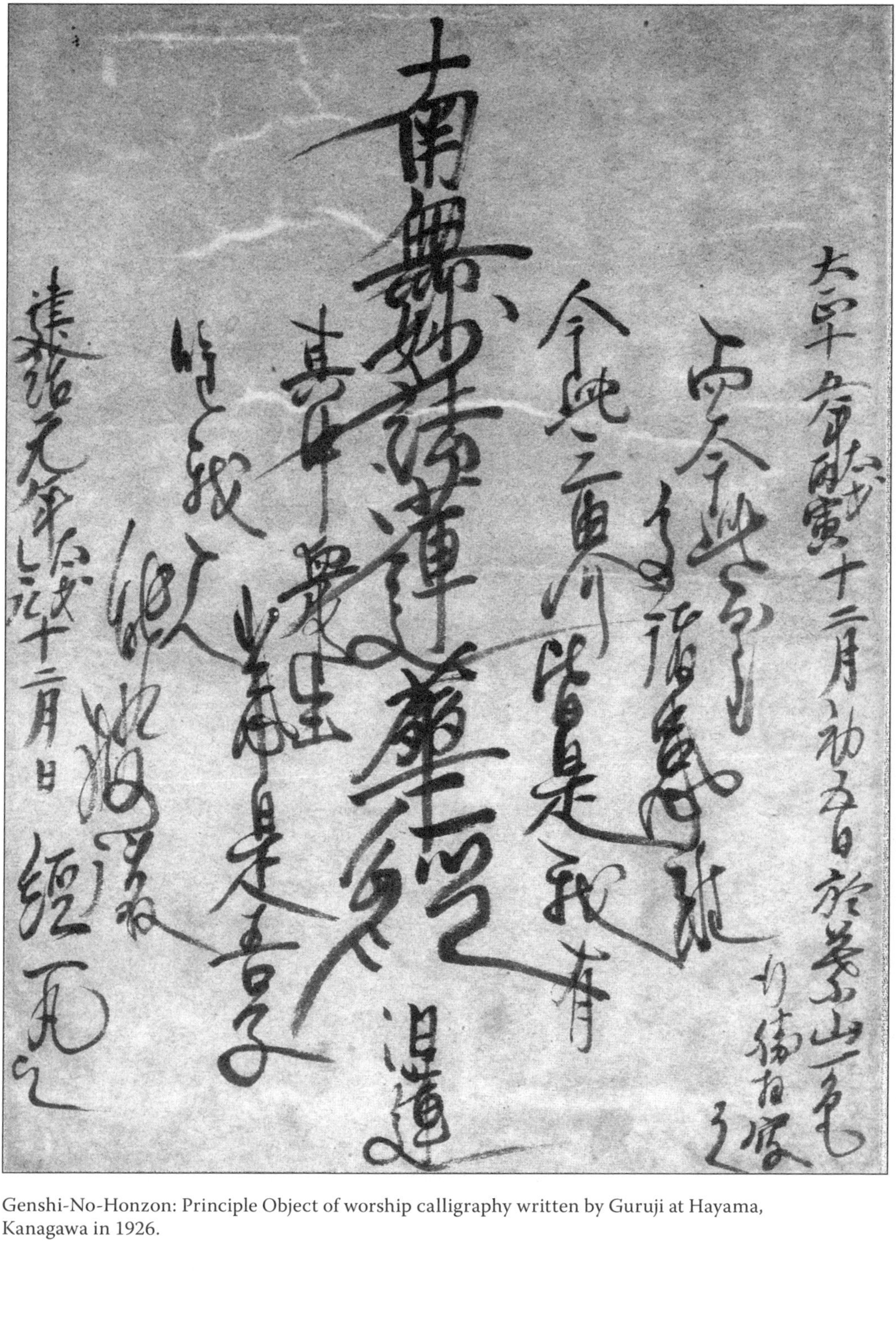

Genshi-No-Honzon: Principle Object of worship calligraphy written by Guruji at Hayama, Kanagawa in 1926.

1

Shishin-kaku
Vow to Return the Dharma to the Western Heavens

July 10, 1930
A hermitage in Jissōji-yama, Beppu, Japan

Careful examination of our great founder, Nichiren Daishōnin's lifelong teachings and guidance in the path to enlightenment reveals that he manifested and illuminated the three merits of the sovereign, teacher and parent.[1] He exemplified the principled path for those realms of humans and deities[2] that are close at hand and whose delusions bind them to the cycle of transmigration; and he taught the tenets of faith, reverence and refuge in the Buddha, who resides afar in the ultimate sacred state of enlightenment free from delusion.[3]

He beat the drum of remonstration[4] by inditing *Risshō-ankoku-ron*[5]

---

1 Nichiren Daishōnin emphasized the three merits of Buddha Śākyamuni as sovereign, teacher and parent based on the Lotus Sūtra's passage "Now this triple world/ All is my domain/ The living beings in it/ All are my children/ But now this place/ Abounds with distress/ And I alone /Am able to save and protect them. [Chapter III, *A Parable*.] Here Guruji is saying that Nichiren Daishōnin assumed these merits as a disciple of the Origin Buddha in his work to fulfill the Buddha's vow to emancipate all sentient beings.

2 The world is divided into ten realms of existence [*jikkai* 十界]: hell, hungry spirits, animals, *asuras*, humans, heavenly beings, sravakas, pratyekabuddhas, Bodhisattvas, and Buddhas. In the six realms from hell to heavenly beings, the lowest three are referred to as the three evil paths 三悪道, and the higher three are called the three good paths 三善道. These six realms are realms of delusion and transmigration. Deities are also part of the six realms of delusion, for while they have supernatural powers, they have not received the Buddha wisdom and are not free from passion.

3 *Gokka-muro-no-shōkyō* 極果無漏の聖境.

4 Synonymous with *dokku* 毒鼓, the poisonous drum. See footnote 24.

5 立正安国論. [Treatise on Giving Rise to the Genuine Dharma to Bring Peace and Tranquility to the Land]. Nichiren Daishōnin's religion is said to have started and ended with *Risshō-ankoku-ron*, a treatise of remonstration against the government. It brought the wrath of the shogunate and marked the beginning of his life under persecution, a life of the practitioner of the Lotus Sūtra. *Risshō-ankoku* is a teaching that when the people in the Era of Final Dharma practice faith in the Lotus Sūtra, as enjoined by Lord Buddha, the physical environment in which the people live [*kokudo-seken* 国土世間] becomes a tranquil Pure Land. It is a world created by the thoughts harbored by an individual, yet is also the true physical environment where the body dwells. This is called *ichinen-sanzen*. However,

as an offering of gratitude to the sovereign, reposed the soul of his master by writing *Requital of Gratitude*[6] and shed tears of longing from atop Mount Minobu in gratitude for the benevolence of his parents during his nine years of residence.

Some may not be moved to tears by the ordeals he endured during three years of exile at Ito in the region of Izu;[7] nor by the assault by swords and arrows suffered at Matsubara in the region of Tōjō;[8] would not shed a tear for the narrowly escaped beheading at the execution grounds in Tatsunokuchi, Katase, in the land of Sagami;[9] and would

---

"tranquil is this realm of mine" materializes only when the single thought of the people becomes one and the same as the single thought of Lord Buddha. In his final discourse on *Risshō-ankoku-ron* on his deathbed at Ikegami, Nichiren Daishōnin directed his disciples to continue the work of *Risshō-ankoku* and fulfill his legacy by reading the Lotus Sūtra with their body and lives.

6 *Hōon-jō* 報恩鈔. Written on July 21, 1276 at Mount Minobu after receiving notice of the death of his master, Dōzen-bō.

7 One of the four major persecutions endured by Nichiren Daishōnin. After presenting the shogunate with *Risshō-ankkoku-ron,* Nichiren Daishōnin was captured by the shogunate and exiled to Itō 伊東in Izu Penninsula [current Shizuoka prefecture] on May 12th of the first year of the Kōchō 弘長 period [1261]. Nichiren Daishōnin was abandoned at Mana-ita Reef [Butcher's Block], a tiny spur of rock, which was almost submerged by the incoming tide. Although the people of Itō were forbidden to shelter or look after Nichiren Daishōnin, Yasaburō 弥三郎, a fisherman, approached in a small boat and rescued him. Yasaburō took Nichiren Daishōnin to his humble hut. Out of concern for the safety of the fisherman and his wife for aiding a criminal, Nichiren Daishōnin declined to stay with them. The couple, with sorrow in their hearts, led Nichiren Daishōnin to a small grotto near the beach and brought him food and water in the secrecy of night to sustain his life for the following months. A pardon was issued on February 22, 1263. Biographical information based on *Nichiren, Leader of Buddhist Reformation in Japan* by J.A. Christensen.

8 Nichiren Daishōnin's party of approximately ten disciples and devotees was ambushed on November 11 in the first year of the Bunei period [1264] while en route to visit the Lord of Amatsu 天津, Kudō Yoshitaka 工藤吉隆. The night was drawing near when they entered Komatsubara 小松原, "Pine Forest," where the dense canopy overhead further blocked the light. They were assaulted by a troop of well-armed warriors led by Lord Tōjō Kagenobu 東条景信, an ardent Nenbutsu believer infuriated over the teachings of Nichiren Daishōnin. Lord Kudō came to the rescue, but was outnumbered by the assailants. Disciple Kyōnin-bō 境忍坊 was killed on the spot, two others fatally wounded, and Lord Kudō also died later from his wounds. Lord Tōjō, seeing Nichiren Daishōnin isolated from the rest, dashed forward to behead him. Nichiren Daishōnin stood quietly with his palms pressed together, holding his prayer beads. Legend has it that Lord Tōjō's horse was spooked by a sudden flash of light reflected from the prayer beads and lifted its hooves dropping Lord Tōjō from his saddle.

9 On September 12 of the 8th year of Bunei 文永 [1271], at the age of 51, Nichiren Daishōnin was captured by the Kamakura shogunate and then mounted on a saddle-less horse like a common criminal and marched through the streets to the execution grounds at Tatsunokuchi 竜の口, Katase 片瀬 as the crowd mocked and jeered him. His devotees knelt along the way crying, but his disciples were all imprisoned and could not bid farewell

remain unmoved by the four years[10] of privation, particularly at the Sanmai-dō in Tsukahara,[11] Sado Island. But who could hold back tears when reflecting on the heart of filial piety that compelled Nichiren Daishōnin, at more than 60 years of age, to climb the precipitous, six-kilometer path to gaze in the direction of his parents' grave? Nothing could be more telling of the constant regret in his heart than the words uttered en route to Tatsunokuchi as he faced his last moments: "I, Nichiren, born a mendicant who walks the path of poverty,[12] fell short in filial piety towards my parents."[13] Confined in the depth of snow at Tsukahara, he pined for his parents saying, "May circumstances enable me to see my parents' grave just one last time." At Mount Minobu he spoke

---

to their master. At Tatsunokuchi, Nichiren Daishōnin dismounted the horse and made his way to the straw mat where his beheading was to take place. He knelt and pressed his palms together, chanted Na Mu Myō Hō Ren Ge Kyō and bent his head before the lifted sword. According to Nichiren Daishōnin's own account, suddenly the midnight sky was ablaze with fire. "A ball of light as bright as the moon, flew from the southeast to the northwest, and all the people became visible, although the moon of the twelfth day had already set." The executioner's sword fell to the ground and shattered. After the unsuccessful execution, Nichiren Daishōnin was soon banished to Sado Island.

10 The actual time span was October 1271 to March 1274. In counting this as four years Guruji is following Eastern tradition and including each calendar year.

11 In October 1271 the order for exile to Sado Island was carried out, and Nichiren Daishōnin arrived at Tsukahara 塚原 in Sado Island 佐渡島 on November 28, 1271. A dilapidated 6x6 feet square remains of a temple called Sanmai-dō 三昧堂 in the middle of a wasteland became his abode. Tsukahara was the dumping grounds of criminals' corpses. An ardent Nenbutsu samurai, Abutsubō 阿仏坊, initially approached Nichiren Daishōnin to kill him, but turned into a believer of the Lotus Sūtra. He and his wife, Sennichi-gozen 千日御前, secretly brought offerings of food, clothing and firewood. When learning of Nichiren Daishōnin's arrival, several hundreds of Nenbutsu and Ritsu School monks and laity gathered and conspired to kill him. Lord Honma Shigetsura 本間重連 issued orders not to kill Nichiren Daishōnin but instead to challenge him in debate. Monk scholars from around the nation gathered to challenge Nichiren Daishōnin, but were all refuted. Nichiren Daishōnin's reputation spread far and wide.

12 貧道. *Hindō*. Literally, "one who walks the path of poverty." It is a reference to a practitioner of the Lotus Sūtra who is poor and without worldly influence as a result of practicing according to Buddha Śākyamuni's command in *The Final Commission*.

13 In the passage previous to this quote from *The Various Conducts of the Master* 種々御振舞御書, Nichiren Daishōnin talks about his previous lives. So rather than bemoaning his poverty, Nichiren Daishōnin is expressing deep gratitude that in this lifetime he is living his mission as a practitioner of the Lotus Sūtra. His regret regarding filial piety is that he believes it to be inadequate for a disciple of Lord Buddha. The full quote reads, "I, Nichiren, born a mendicant who walks the path of poverty, fell short in filial piety towards my parents nor did I possess the ability to requite the debt of gratitude to my country. May the merits of sacrificing my life for the Lotus Sūtra this time be an offering to the souls of my parents."

longingly, "Even the breeze that blows from the east[14] draws me out to the yard; its touch against my skin comforts my longing." His sentiments for his parents, akin to that of an infant yearning for its mother's bosom, carried over to their grave and the land yonder under the sky where they rest. This innate sentiment, true and without pretense, is the very source of Buddha Dharma. Later, men paid tribute by building a temple on the grounds naming it *Shishin-kaku*, [the shrine of yearning for one's parents]. This name truly befits who the Venerable Master really was, and it is the essence of the Lotus Sūtra.

In part to bid farewell [to Nichiren Daishōnin] before embarking on my mission abroad, I carried the relics of my late mother, Maha Bhiksunī Gyōain Nisso, on my back and paid homage at Mount Minobu. Reverend Kaijō Komatsu of Takei-bō and Reverend Nichiun Uchino of Shimizu-bō,[15] who have always been kind, must have particularly sympathized with my sentiments at leaving in solitude with little more than the clothes on my back for a land far beyond the wide ocean to spread the five and seven characters of Myō Hō Ren Ge Kyō,[16] a mission I am ready to lay down my life for. Feeling pity for my recent loss and for the fact that I would leave her grave behind as I set out for a distant land from which I may never return, they allowed me to bury a part of my mother's ash by erecting a tomb in the grand grounds of *Shishin-kaku* atop Mount Minobu, and perform a commemorative service.

If not for the inexplicable compassion of our great Teacher, Nichiren Daishōnin, how could I ever be favored with such grace? Can there be any other expedient that clearly substantiates the enlightenment of women? Benefiting from our great founder's overflowing virtue of filial piety, I was able to accomplish a fraction of his virtue of filial piety. The sacred grounds of *Shishin-kaku*, where our great founder pined for the grave of his parents, have become the sacred grounds of *Shishin-kaku*, where I yearn for my mother's grave. The three characters of *shi*,[17] *shin*,[18] *kaku*[19] have opened the great path for enlightenment for the

---

14 Direction of his homeland of Bōshū 房州. Nichiren Daishōnin climbed the six-kilometer, treacherous path to the peak of the mountain from his hermitage just to look in the direction of his homeland.

15 小松海浄師、内野日運師、武井坊 清水坊. *Bō* signifies a residence for monks, and these are names of monks' residences at Mount Minobu.

16 妙法蓮華経の五字七字.

17 思. Evoke a heartfelt remembrance.

18 親. Parent(s).

19 閣. Shrine or temple.

holy and the ordinary alike.

On March 14, I visited Mount Minobu to bid farewell before my mission abroad. I visited Mount Minobu for the second time on July 15. With my third and final visit coming August 25,[20] I will leave my mother's ash in the care of the great founder and finally embark from Mount Minobu for my journey abroad to spread the Dharma with nothing to hold me back. Though there is lingering sadness to bid farewell, I shall sever all personal sentiments for the sake of spreading the Buddha Dharma. May you [Nichiren Daishōnin] have pity on my overreaching vow and allow me to achieve it.

May I be the harbinger of the Buddha Dharma of Japan, ushering its return to India, in the Western Heavens.[21] May I overcome the 62 distorted views[22] to regenerate the spiritual civilization of Asia. May I emancipate all living beings equally from the inferno of delusion that is replete with strife and hostilities perpetuated by Europe and the United States, that realm of *asuras*,[23] that civilization of murder. Follow me, one after another, to beat the poisonous drum[24] in the snow-capped Himalayas and pour the

---

20 When Guruji bid farewell three times at Mount Minobu, it followed the rites depicted in Chapter II, *Expedients* 方便品, and Chapter XVI of the Lotus Sūtra, *The Eternal Duration of the Life of the Tathāgata* 如来寿量品, in proclaiming the vow thrice to the Buddha.

21 Nichiren Daishōnin's *Kangyō-hachiman-shō* 諫暁八幡抄 *Admonishing Bodhisattva Hachiman* contains the prophecy that just as the Buddha Dharma migrated from India to Japan, the Buddha Dharma of Japan will return westward to India.
Saiten-kaikyō 西天開教 is Guruji's vow to return Buddha's teachings to *Saiten*, the Western Heavens, which was also the fulfillment of Nichiren Daishōnin's prophecy. *Saiten* includes *Tenjiku* 天竺, an ancient name for India. At the time Guruji set out for the Western Heavens in 1930, the British colony of India covered a vast geographical area spanning from the Himalayas bordering on Tibet in the north to the Indian Ocean in the south, including Sri Lanka and part of the Malay Peninsula, and spanned westward to Hindu Kush Mountains.

22 *Rokujūni-ken* 六十二見. Originally, they were the 62 non-Buddhist schools of philosophy and metaphysics at the time of Buddha Śākyamuni. They are roughly divided into two categories: the view that everything is permanent and the view that death is the end of all existence. They can be further subdivided into 62 thoughts.

23 *Asura* originally is a Hindu god, an evil spirit, who is constantly fighting with Indra. In Buddhism it is a demigod, generally considered an evil and fearsome spirit fond of fighting, but some are considered to be good spirits and protectors of Buddhism. *Asura* is a state of existence where strife and battles abound.

24 *Dokku* 毒鼓 is the poisonous drum as opposed to *tenku* 天鼓 the celestial drum. The sound of the Dharma drum can be either the celestial drum for those who are joyous upon hearing it or the poisonous drum for those who are averse to hearing it, depending on their karmic connection to the Dharma. The poisonous drum draws out anger in the heart of the recipient, thereby extinguishing delusion, and becomes a cause for eventual attainment of Buddhahood for both the faithful and the slanderer. As stated in *The Eternal Duration of the Life of the Tathāgata* chapter, the ultimate salvation is to "finally awaken and come back to their right minds."

August 25, 1930 at *Shishin-kaku*, Mt. Minobu before departure to India on the mission of *Saiten-kaikyō*.

Dharma rain into the stream of the Ganges.

If this Dharma is not returned to the Western Heavens, the prophecy of our great founder becomes smeared in mud. If this Dharma is not returned to the Western Heavens, our Bodhisattva practice will not hold true. If this Dharma is not returned to the Western Heavens, living beings of this *sahā* world will long be condemned to the gaol of strife and bloodshed. Therefore devas and good protector kings who lend power to the long-cherished aspiration of our great founder, may you graciously grant protection and guard over our practice.

Na Mu Myō Hō Ren Ge Kyō
Na Mu Myō Hō Ren Ge Kyō
Na Mu Myō Hō Ren Ge Kyō

Gyōshō,
Keibyaku [With humility][25]

---

25 敬白. A term used at the end of a written petition to a deity or Buddha. In this case, it is a petition to Nichiren Daishōnin and protector deities.

2

Disperse the Gloom of the Living

January 7, 1951
Excerpt from *World War III*
Kobe Buddhist Association Hall, Japan

Chapter XXI of the Lotus Sūtra, *The Divine Transcendental Powers of the Tathāgata*, says:

> Just as the light of the sun and moon
> Dispel the darkness,
> So this person where he goes about in practice,
> Shall disperse the gloom of the living

Darkness, once exposed to the light of the sun and moon, cannot but vanish. Darkness also exists in people's collective life on earth, as well as in the hearts and minds of each human. Such darkness is hard to expel, even with the light of the sun and moon.

Only those compassionate individuals who take on hardship and suffering through their invaluable sacrifice of blood and tears can dispel the darkness in society and in the hearts and minds of human beings. Those who stepped up to sacrifice themselves in this way would be India and her people—the country that gave birth to Buddha Śākyamuni, Nagarjuna[1] and Vasubandhu;[2] and Japan and her people, who received the teachings left by the Tathāgata and who uphold the True Dharma in the Era of Final Dharma as the great light for people afflicted by

---

1 Nāgārjuna is one of the chief philosophers of Mahāyāna Buddhism and the founder of Mādhyamika School. He was born in a Brāhmana family in South India around the 2nd or 3rd century.

2 Vasubandhu was born in Purusapura of Gāndhāra in the 5th century. He studied Theravāda and criticized Mahāyāna but later converted to Mahāyāna.

the five pollutions.[3]

India's noble mission is to reject war on earth and to protect the lives of the people. The noble mission of Japan is likewise to reject war on earth and to protect the lives of the people. The precept against taking life, which is practiced through nonviolence and nonresistance, deters evil. The practice of *tangyō-raihai* [the sole practice of bowing in veneration to the Buddha in others] is the precept that creates good.

Take not life even at the expense of giving up your own life. Venerate out on the streets rather than worshipping in temples and monasteries. Venerate fellow human beings instead of Buddha statues.

The act of killing the wicked does nothing to stop their ignoble minds. Bowing towards and reverence offered to wicked people has the power to transform their wicked minds. This religion that focuses solely on the practice of veneration toward others is what will bring emancipation to the Era of Final Dharma.

3 Panca Kāsāyah. The five pollutions of the present world are: i) a period of war, natural disasters, pestilence; ii) a period in which heresies flourish; iii) a period in which passion is strong; iv) a period in which people are physically and mentally weak; v) a period in which the life span is short.

3

Wondrous First Connection with Lord Buddha's Relic

Busshari-engi[1]
September 1, 1933

One hundred years after Buddha's Parinirvāna, Ashoka the Great came into this world and united the *Jambudvīpa* [world]. He built 84,000 stūpas[2] and widely disseminated the Buddha Dharma. His son, Prince Mahinda, was ordained a bhikshu and traveled to Ceylon[3] to spread the Dharma. In the outskirts of the then royal capital of Anuradhapura[4] stands Mount Mihintale,[5] a notable, solitary peak where, according to legend, the Preceptor Buddha Śākyamuni visited and delivered the

---

1 仏舎利縁起. *Wondrous First Connection with Lord Buddha's Relic* was first published in September 1933 as a booklet. This is a translation based on the text reintroduced in 一閻浮堤 *Ichien-budai* [*Jambudvīpa*] published by 大法輪閣 Daihōrinkaku in August 1972. Guruji arrived in Colombo in May 1932 from Bombay, and made extensive pilgrimages throughout Ceylon initially with the Maha Bodhi Society offering its *vihara* as his home base. He later practiced out of a cave he found midway up Sri Pada, a sacred mountain known for Buddha's footprint, in the summer of 1932. August 23 of that year, after the daily prayer service at sunrise at the peak of Sri Pada, he stopped by a waterfall to bathe, as was his custom, on his way down to the cave dōjō. There he found a ring with three gemstones and rejoiced that it could be an auspicious omen for his mission of *Saiten-kaikyō*.

2 The number 84 is quite common in Indian numerology, occurring either alone or as 84,000 or 840,000. It is seen in Buddhist as well as Hindu and Jain traditions. Some sources say it indicates a large, imprecise number while others say it has mystical connotations. According to the *Asokavadana* [*Annals of Ashoka*], King Ashoka opened ten of the original stūpas, divided these relics and vowed to erect 84,000 stūpas.

3 Former name for Sri Lanka until 1972. At the time Guruji wrote these entries, Ceylon was a colony under British rule which stretched from 1815 to 1948.

4 First historic capital of Sri Lanka, located 128 miles from Colombo, the current capital.

5 During the Poson season [June], thousands of devotees ascend the 1,840 stone steps to the top of the Mihintale hill to pay their respects to Arahat Mahinda, whose relics are said to be enshrined in the Ambasthala stūpa. This stūpa was created by King Mahadathika Mahanaga on flat land just below the peak where Mahinda and the king were supposed to have met and talked.

Dharma. It was there Bhikshu Mahinda met King Tissa,[6] who was out hunting, and led the king to the Buddha Dharma. With this encounter the entire country quickly became a land of the Buddha. This original transmission of Buddhism has been celebrated [in the form of a stūpa] with reverence and offerings to this day. The introduction of Buddha Dharma marks not only the beginning of Ceylon's civilization, but of its history as a nation as well. According to its historic records, 2,475 years are said to have passed [following Buddha's Parinirvāna], and closer to 3,000 years, according to Mahāyāna Buddhism.[7] In that time, the seat of the imperial capital relocated several times. Neither it nor the nation itself was immune to the rise and fall of fortune throughout the ages. With the desolation that descended on the city of Anuradhapura came destruction upon destruction of stūpas, temples and monasteries; the unparalleled great stūpa[8] became enshrouded in dense vegetation, neglected and used mainly as a den by troops of monkeys. Nevertheless, reminiscent of the throngs who enlivened this place in days gone by, Buddhists from around the country still converge year after year for this great festival.[9] People gather in untold numbers in and around the ancient ruins of the palace and fill the thicket surrounding the stūpa like an army of ants, each one offering lotus flowers, lighting votive lights and burning incense. Clouds of incense curl up to the heavens, and strewn flower petals cover the ground. Railways issue half-priced tickets, and special trains run to accommodate the crowds.

Last year we traveled by train to participate in the festival. This year we set out to travel both ways on foot and left the dōjō in Colombo[10] early in the morning of May 25. By way of Kandy and Matale stations [towns], we made pilgrimage to noted mountains and ancient temples along the way and arrived in Anuradhapura about five days later, covering a little more than 150 miles. On June 25 I left alone on a walking pilgrimage to

6 Tissa, later Devanampiya Tissa [307-267 BCE], was one of the earliest consecrated kings of Sri Lanka based at the ancient capital of Anuradhapura. He was also said to be a close friend of India's King Ashoka. King Tissa created 68 rock cells at Mihintale for Mahinda and his retinue, who officially introduced Buddhism on a full moon day in the month of Poson.

7 Due to differences in counting systems, there is a discrepancy of approximately 500 years in the date for Buddha's Parinirvāna between Theravāda and Mahāyāna Buddhism.

8 Ruwanwelisaya, also known as the "mahā stūpa," was constructed by King Dutugemunu in 137 BCE with a circumference of 950 feet and rose to a height of 300 feet.

9 Esala Perahera is held during July or August each year in honor of the tooth relic.

10 The dōjō Guruji is referring to may not have been a dōjō built by Nipponzan Myōhōji, but Guruji considered any place where monks reside to practice the Dharma as a dōjō.

initiate the longstanding mission of spreading the Dharma in the ancient seaport of Galle.

On July 25 we left Colombo outfitted for pilgrimage on foot in order to take part in the processions of the grand festival honoring the Temple of the Tooth Relic[11] in the ancient city of Kandy. In the weeks before and after the main celebration of the great festival, spectacular processions traverse the city every night featuring a majestic elephant carrying the casket for the tooth relic on its back. Palm torches are lit, instruments make music and dancers dance. Several tens of elephants, both large and small, caparisoned in silver and gold are a main part of the processions. In truth, this grand festival could be called The Procession of Elephants.

We participated in this festival for the first time last year, hoisting the *gendaiki*[12] and beating the Dharma drum. This year we joined the procession by raising the deep purple *gendaiki*, a donation from Kobe, and beating the 1 *shaku* 8 *sun ōdaiko*[13] donated from Tōkyō that was carried on the bed of a vehicle. Participation by Buddha's disciples from Japan added to the festival's vibrancy.

The festival ended on August 10. The following day, early on the morning of August 11, we left Rev. Dhammaruchika's *vihara* in Karukale, which was our lodging while in Kandy. The four of us[14] walked about 12 miles and prayed at the ruins of the ancient capital Gampola.[15] Two disciples who were heading back to Colombo stayed behind for the night, while two of us parted and set out on a pilgrimage to Sri Pada[16] by walking along the motorway that leads through the mountains to Hatton Station. Silence and desolation prevailed, broken only by the popping sounds of rubber tree nuts. We passed two or three stations in the mountains heading to Ginigathena Station at the junction of Colombo Road to spend the night. The setting sun in the western ridges had descended close enough seemingly to touch my head. Wishing the sun could linger a

---

11 Sri Dalada Maligawa.

12 玄題旗. A banner with the Odaimoku, Na Mu Myō Hō Ren Ge Kyō.

13 A large drum, 54 centimeters or 21¼ inches in diameter.

14 In addition to Guruj, Rev. Nagai Gyōji [永井行慈], who later spread the Dharma in Burma, Rev. Miki Jikyō [三木慈教], who practiced in Ceylon until the end of WWII, and Rev. Imai Gyōkō [今井行孝], who returned to Japan in 1937.

15 A town near Kandy in the central province of Sri Lanka. Gampola became the capital city of the island under King Buwanekabahu IV in the mid 14th century.

16 A 2,243 meter [7,359 ft] conical-shaped mountain located in central Sri Lanka where Buddha's footprint is enshrined. It is also known as Adams Peak and is a sacred mountain not only to Buddhists, but also to people of other faiths.

little longer, we hastened down the sloped path. After passing four or five houses, a shout from behind urged us to stop in. We followed him and learned that he was the master of the house and a mason who had built a bridge over the Seetagangula[17] at Sri Pada; he was a pious *upāsaka* [lay devotee] who had offered sweets to me in the past. He had built a guest house on the premises exclusively for men,[18] and used it to accommodate the Sangha. He urged us to stay for the night and leave early the next day, and most cordially offered to serve supper as well as breakfast the following morning. We accepted the hospitality for the night. Mahaweli Ganga is the main river of four that flows out from Sri Pada, but alongside the house it is yet but a forceful rapid gushing through a narrow gorge. A young bodhi tree planted on the premises had offerings that were made to it. This place has the atmosphere of a solitary mountain monastery. A wondrous and pure dream visited me at daybreak.

A seated image of Śākyamuni Buddha carved from unfinished aromatic white sandalwood was flanked by standing buddhas and bodhisattvas in attendance like a gathering of clouds.[19] These statues were encased in a miniature shrine. In front of the shrine, two heavenly beings closely attended it, making offerings. The heavenly beings, though likewise the size of *hina* dolls,[20] moved freely. I thought to myself, though *Ittō-ryō-son*[21] was revealed as the most crucial representation of the Honzon[22] [principle object of veneration], the Honzon here is a representation of *Yuiga-ichinin*.[23] After venerating the Honzon, I closed the shrine door and locked it from within, at which point I woke from the dream. When

---

17 The parent stream of the Mahaveli-ganga.

18 Women are prohibited from staying at monks' quarters in Sri Lanka.

19 譬如雲集. "Like a gathering of clouds" is a phrase in the Lotus Sūtra, Chapter XXI, *The Divine Transcendental Powers of the Tathāgata*. Clouds made up of innumerable water drops are an analogy of an aggregate involving a huge number.

20 雛人形. *Hina-ningyō*. Dolls representing the Emperor, Empress and their court that are placed on a special step-altar to celebrate *Hina-matsuri* 雛祭り [Doll Festival] on March 3. It is as also celebrated as a festival for girls.

21 一塔両尊. The representation of a stūpa suspended in mid-air with the inscription of Na Mu Myō Hō Ren Ge Kyō in the center flanked by Buddha Śākyamuni and Buddha Prabhūtaratna [Abundant Treasures] on either side, signifying the preaching by Buddha Śākyamuni from within the stūpa suspended in midair as told in the Lotus Sūtra, Chapter XI, *Beholding the Stūpa of Treasures*. It is the most important Honzon representation presented by Nichiren Daishōnin.

22 Here Guruji is referring to the Honzon in the Nichiren School.

23 唯我一人. "And I alone." This Honzon representation enshrines only Buddha Śākyamuni, the Preceptor, based on Chapter III of the Lotus Sūtra, *A Parable*, which states, "Now this triple world is all my domain; the living beings are all my children. But now this place abounds in distress; and I alone can save and protect them."

morning came I told Rev. Nagai of my auspicious dream and described it to him. He responded, "Well, perhaps [Śākyamuni Buddha] shall open the door and once again appear at a time of critical importance."

August 21, 1933

The people of the house kindly prepared simple snacks and tea early in the morning. After receiving the offering, we headed out. A two-mile climb uphill along the river got us to Ginigathena Station. From there, it is 64 miles to Colombo, and 36 miles to the peak of Sri Pada; altogether a hundred-mile trek from Sri Pada to Colombo. We walked quickly as possible to be sure to reach the cave dōjō[24] in Seetagangula at Sri Pada no matter how late we would arrive that night. Last night's mason spoke of a small temple recently built at Ginigathena Station and said the head monk is a good one. Though pressed for time, the temple was on our way, so we climbed the stairs to pay homage. One corner of a tea plantation, which stretched to the skies, had been cleared to build a *dharmashala* [guest house], a small *vihara* [temple] and monks' quarters, which were rather shabby. The bodhi trees, too, looked like fragile saplings, not more than a few years old. Our drumbeat brought the head monk out from the monks' quarters. The temple grounds were an offering from a European patron, who supports and frequents the temple. The head monk told us that the benefactor's grand residence is near the Watawala Station along this road. He asked us where we took lodging last night and whether we had had breakfast. Ginigathena being a 30-mile walk, we took our leave after a brief chat and hurried on.

August 25, 1933

Departure to Anuradhapura, Galle, Kandy and the like have happened always to fall on the 25th of the month. Owing to wondrous karma, three years ago on August 25th, I was able to erect and hold a dedication ceremony of a memorial stone stūpa inscribing the seven characters of the Odaimoku, Na Mu Myō Hō Ren Ge Kyō, as a token of filial piety for my late benevolent mother, Maha Bhiksunī Gyōain Nisso, near *Shishin-kaku*, which is a paragon of filial piety whose very name connotes the longing for one's parents and is likewise the interior

24 A little beyond the present Sri Pada Stūpa alongside the narrow, mountainous pilgrimage road to the peak of Sri Pada is a huge boulder that sticks out like a canopy. Guruji fashioned it into a provisional dōjō.

sanctuary of Mount Minobu in Kōshū, the hallowed grounds where founding master Nichiren Daishōnin rests. At this last Dharma work in Japan, I pronounced my aspiration for *Saiten-kaikyō*,[25] bidding farewell to founding master Nichiren Daishōnin and stepped out with Mount Minobu as my starting point on the seemingly endless journey to India in the Western Heavens. Every year the disciples and devotees of the order commemorate this day by climbing Mount Minobu and paying homage to the stūpa, gaining merit in performing a token[26] of filial piety on my behalf, which I am unable to fulfill. Thus, my thoughts were with them, who again this year practiced *gyakku-senryō*[27] yesterday and today[28] at Mount Minobu and who probably talked about us in the distant Western Heavens. Gripped by a lonesome melancholy, we both spoke repeatedly of what those back home must be doing.

Although Ceylon has been the most enjoyable and comfortable place for me to live next to Japan, an opportunity has presented itself to part from the Buddhist island of Ceylon and travel to another land. Hence, on this day of August 25, I have used as a starting point Sri Pada, the Mount Minobu of the Western Heavens, to set out on a journey for the next land. The first day of this journey of departure from Ceylon was a 30-mile walk to Sri Pada's Ginigathena Station. We fasted 2 nights and 3 days until the 22nd, paid veneration at the peak of Sri Pada on the 23rd, and worked to waterproof the cave dōjō on the 24th; once we cleared the work site and left the Seetagangula cave dōjō on the morning of the 25th, it was already 10 a.m. No matter how much we picked up the pace, it seemed unlikely we would reach our destination before nightfall and cover the 30 miles after starting at 10 a.m. with bodies fatigued from fasting and laden with

---

25 Refer to *Shishin-kaku* footnote 21 p. 5. "If this Dharma is not returned to the Western Heavens, the prophecy of our great founder becomes smeared in mud. If this Dharma is not returned to the Western Heavens, our Bodhisattva practice will not hold true. If this Dharma is not returned to the Western Heavens, living beings of this *sahā* world will long be condemned to the gaol of strife and bloodshed."

26 The term token is used because no matter how much is done, there is no end to filial piety.

27 擊鼓宣令. Proclamation of the Dharma through the beating of the drum and chanting the Odaimoku. This term appears in *Devadatta*, Chapter XII of the Lotus Sūtra. In a previous life of Buddha Śākyamuni, he was a king who renounced the throne, handed the government over to his crown prince, and walked in all directions in search of the Dharma, "beating the drum in open proclamation." Guruji, on the other hand, walked in all directions beating the drum to bring the Dharma of Na Mu Myō Hō Ren Ge Kyō far and wide, a practice in Chapter XIII, *Exhortation to Hold True.*

28 Clergy and laity of Nipponzan Myōhōji pay homage at Mount Minobu each year on August 24 and 25.

heavy loads on our backs. Yet, we continued to walk without stopping for a single cup of tea or any snack. Journey on foot is basically also a practice of fasting. Along the way we passed by more than ten lizards, frogs and a 30-centimeter long snake crushed by tires, spattered with darkened blood. It was particularly unpleasant for someone walking barefoot.

A downpour started before we even walked halfway. Baggage and the hems of our robes[29] were soaked, making us feel wretched; even the pale sun that shone dimly through the clouds seemed to be setting in the western sky. Rain continued intermittently. Just when it seemed to stop, dark clouds loomed, and it rained, rained and rained. We were walking through an area with the highest amount of rainfall in Ceylon. I hear that the dry season lasts just three months out of the year. Though it was just a matter of course to be met by rain passing through the high plains during the rainy season, the gloom and dampness became hard to bear. There was no time to spare even to sit down by the roadside to rest. I wondered whether the situation was a portent for my future, yet encouraged myself and hurried on. Let it rain, let the wind blow; I clenched my jaw and mustered the resolve to remain steadfast in my destined path. Yet, the rain increased in intensity, and dusk arrived. Darkness fell and we could barely make out the single path winding its way through the many ridges that emerged in view through a rift in the clouds. By chance we came across a grass cutter and asked how many more miles we had left to go. He told us six miles. The thought of six more miles in the rain, wind and dark down a hill almost made me lose heart. Walking and chanting the Odaimoku, I worried about the possibility of stepping on a venomous snake with bare feet if one were to slither across the road. The last three miles or so, the path wound back and forth along a steep precipice. It felt precarious in the dark. Finally we reached the temple at Ginigathena at 8 p.m. For the barefooted, the soles of the feet bled from cuts made by shards of glass; and footwear, once removed, found the feet covered in blisters.[30]

Outside the monks' quarters, we called out for the resident monk. He opened the door and ushered us in with a western lamp in his hand. The Reverend roused the temple helper, who was already asleep, and had him make a fire. Since it was late at night, I felt bad to bother him

29 At this time Guruji still wore the traditional black monk's robe similar to the ones worn by Japanese monks of other Buddhist schools. He returned from *Saiten-kaikyō* to Japan in a saffron robe.

30 Most likely Guruji was wearing sandals made of hemp, and Rev. Nagai was barefoot.

and decided to go to bed on an empty stomach, except for some hot tea. Seeing how wet and cold we were, the resident monk built a fire to warm us. He sent out the temple hand to a devotee's house for hot water to cleanse our hands and feet, and requested breakfast to be delivered by 6 in the morning. We sat by the fire, took our tea and appeased our hunger somewhat.

We agreed to leave the temple soon after daybreak the following morning so that we could walk some 40 miles on the downhill motor road while the sun's rays were still mild before stopping for the night; we then decided to retire for that night. The resident monk took out two palm leaf mats and started to instruct the temple helper to place them in the assembly hall where traveling monks are customarily put up. But other lodgers, possibly vagrants or maybe fellow travelers, were already occupying the hall. We said it was unnecessary for us to sleep in the hall, that a spot next to the entrance on the monastery's earthen floor covered in dried cow dung would suffice. The mats were placed directly on the dirt floor. We covered ourselves with a seven *jō*-size[31] monk's robe called *cīvara*, and hoped to get some rest using our arms as pillows. I then noticed that beyond the single-panel door separating the rooms was the resident monk's sitting room. Yet, it was extremely small and untidy to call it a sitting room, and seemed merely an extension of the damp earth floor. The humble room had a few book cases opposite a narrow desk and chair with a single cot in between.

The resident monk approached us and started talking about his pilgrimages to sacred sites and stūpas in various parts of the country, and about the history and lineage[32] of the Preceptor, Buddha Śākyamuni's relics and their types enshrined in the stūpas in these ancient temples and celebrated mountains. Hearing of the various stūpas that have been erected in Ceylon to enshrine the many relics, *byakugōsō*[33] and the like of the Tathāgata, I rejoiced in the deep karmic connection this country has with Buddha Dharma.

---

31 七条. The outer mantle or robe of a monk comprised of seven pieces. The patched stole comes in primarily two sizes, *shichi-jō-gesa* [seven-piece stole] and *gojō-gesa* [five-piece stole].

32 Buddha Śākyamuni's relics, initially enshrined in the Ten Stūpas of the *Jambudvīpa* [footnote 34], were collected by King Ashoka around 200 years after Buddha's demise. He built 84,000 stūpas throughout his empire to enshrine them.

33 白毫相. One of the 32 marks of physical excellence of Buddha. It is a white, treasure-like curl of hair [Skt. *urnakesha*] on the mid-brow that curls tightly clockwise. When pulled

I privately pondered on the sacred Buddha relics that were equally distributed to the five regions of *Tenjiku* [ancient Chinese name for India][34] following the Parinirvāna of the Tathāgata and then enshrined in stūpas. But invasions from India's northwest border brought people of a different ethnic group and faith who oppressed and persecuted Buddhism, destroying stūpas and damaging stone pillars and Buddha statues. Pious kings, prime ministers, ministers, princesses and the like fled from harm to other countries, carrying with them precious, esteemed objects of the Tathāgata, including sacred relics concealed in their hair buns or garments. Ceylon, separated from India only by a narrow strip of water, is a pure Buddhist land where an entire nation's faith in and veneration of the Buddha Dharma has been continually renewed since its introduction. Those fleeing from harm in India settled here, erected stūpas widely to enshrine Buddha's relics and made offerings. Dharma works of erecting stūpas and enshrining the distributed relics reached other countries like Burma, the South Sea Islands and the Indonesian Islands, but their geographic distance and ease of travel to and from India could not compare with Ceylon. From the golden era of Buddha Dharma to the Era of Final Dharma, Ceylon, by far, stands out in the number of Buddha relics introduced. At the very end of the conversation, the resident monk told us he had studied in Maligakanda, Colombo, during the Great War in Europe. At that time he offered sūtras in Pali to as many as 500 Japanese soldiers who disembarked there. He believed some karmic connection made him particularly fond of Japan. He said he was extremely pleased that monks from Japan came for a night's stay at his temple, and that he could not possibly express his gratitude.

The Reverend then confided that treasured relics have long been in his safekeeping. He offered us the honor to behold them that night.

---

from its tip, it extends a huge distance, and when released, it tightly recoils. It is often represented by a crystal on Buddha statues and in some case a wooden bead. Chapter I of the Lotus Sūtra, *Introductory*, describes the six auspicious signs that manifested in the *sahā* world and all other worlds before Buddha Śākyamuni started to preach the Lotus Sūtra, one of which is a ray emitting from the white curl of hair between his eyebrows that illuminated 18,000 worlds, the entire universe, from the highest of heavens to the deepest of hells.

34 天竺、五天竺. The five regions of ancient India were divided into east, west, south, north and middle India at the time of Buddha Śākyamuni's passing in Kushinagar. His cremated remains were equally divided and bestowed on eight kings who each erected a stūpa to enshrine the relics in their kingdoms in India. Small amounts of relics remained in the container used for dividing the relics as well as ash at the cremation site. Stūpas were also built for these relics and for the ash.

He cleaned the room, readied the desk with adornments and presented the relic. We washed ourselves from the top of our head to the tip of our toes with the hot water brought in by a devotee to ready ourselves for the encounter with the relic. Though Buddha Dharma thrives in Japan, the Land of the East, given the countless miles of ocean and mountains that separate it from the Western Heavens, it is not surprising that no school of Buddhism arose that views the straightforward and duly reverent worship of Buddha Śākyamuni as having great importance. Some schools enshrine the Preceptor of another realm[35] and chant the title of Buddha Amida; some worship the Dharma Body Tathāgata, reciting sūtras in Sanskrit; others are absorbed by the various devas and good protectors of Buddhism and pray to them to satisfy their worldly five desires.[36] Crown Prince Shōtoku, who was born with a single Buddha relic clenched in his hand, enshrined it at the top of the five-tiered stūpa; however, subsequent introductions of Buddha's relics to Japan have been fairly limited.[37]

More recently, the relics presented by the Siamese royal family[38] are said to be enshrined in Kakuōzan, Nagoya. For these reasons, we have not had the karmic connection to personally venerate and make offerings to Buddha's relics. Boundless joy welled in our hearts like cumulous clouds filling the entire arch of the sky at the thought of being able to behold and venerate Buddha relics right here this night.

---

35 Buddha Amida, the Preceptor of the Western Pure Land, who preaches the Lotus Sūtra to those who transmigrate to the Western Pure Land instead of in the *sahā* world.

36 五欲. Desires that arise in connection with the five senses of form, sound, scent, taste and touch. Also desires for wealth, sex, food and drink, fame and sleep.

37 鑑真. Chien-chen [687-763] from China, who founded the Japanese Ritsu School, reached Japan after five attempts in 754. He is said to have brought 3,000 relics with him, which are still enshrined in the 唐招提寺 Tōshōdai-ji Temple he founded, of which several were enshrined in Nipponzan's London Peace Pagoda in 1985. This was the first time the relics left Tōshōdaiji. It is possible Guruji did not mention the relics at Tōshōdaiji since they are not enshrined for wide veneration by the public through the erection of stūpas. In addition, 空海 Kūkai [774-835], the founder of the Japanese Shingon School, is said to have brought back 80 relics and 円行 Engyō [799-852], another Shingon monk, 3,000. The whereabouts of many of these relics is not clear. The Shingon School that worships Mahāvairocana, the embodiment of the reality of the universe, used Buddha Śākyamuni's relics for incantation more than as an object of veneration.

38 Relics contained in an urn engraved with ancient letters from 3 BCE were excavated in Northern India in 1898 by a British archaeologist. The relics were identified as Buddha Śākyamuni's after deciphering the letters. The relics were ceded to the Buddhist country of Siam, current Thailand, by the British Empire that ruled India. Some of these relics were donated to the people of Japan by Siamese King Ram V [1853-1910], also known as King Chulalongkorn the Great in the west. These relics were enshrined in a small stūpa at 覚王山日泰寺 Kakuōzan Nittaiji Temple [Buddha Relics Japan-Thai Temple] in Nagoya, which was newly built in 1904 as a repository for the relics.

He opened a gold stūpa of Buddha Prabhūtaratna [Abundant Treasures], the size of a half-finger length. A single relic nestled in a golden lotus was revealed. With profound reverence we prostrated ourselves thrice, recited the *gāthā* from the *Ojigage*[39] in the Lotus Sūtra on making offerings to the *śarīa*,[40] chanted the Odaimoku, beat the drum and were steeped in the bliss of the Dharma. We were in the presence of a memento of Buddha Śākyamuni in the flesh, whose Brahman voice[41] had sonorously expounded the Lotus Sūtra at Sacred Eagle Peak. Moreover, the small relic came from his finger, on which is said fingerprints appear. Joy overflowed from my heart and welled into choking tears with the thought that it was from the very finger that stroked the crown of Bodhisattva Superior Conduct's head when he was entrusted with the dissemination of the Odaimoku.[42] Is this not a dream? Is it a dream? How could there possibly be such wondrous karmic connection? Awestruck, I was in a state of rapture. Spirit and flesh seemed cast into a vast ocean of infinite joy. The

---

39 御自我偈. Reference to the *gāthā* in *The Eternal Duration of the Life of the Tathāgata* that starts, "Since I attained Buddhahood" and ends with "And speedily accomplish their Buddhahood?" Buddha Śākyamuni reveals his eternal nature in this *gāthā*.

40 *Śarīa* are the relics of the Buddha. 為度衆生故　方便現涅槃　而実不滅度　常住此説法 我常住於此　以諸神通力　令顛倒衆生　雖近而不見 衆見我滅度　広供養舎利　咸皆懐恋慕　而生渇仰心 衆生既信伏　質直意柔軟　一心欲見仏　不自惜身命. "In order to save all sentient beings/ by tactful methods I manifest nirvāna/ yet I am not extinct/ but forever here preaching the Dharma./ I forever reside here/ with all my transcendental powers/ so that all perverted sentient beings/fail to see me though I'm near./ Sentient beings seeing me seemingly extinct/ widely make offerings to my *śarīa*/ all cherishing tender longings/ and beget thirsting hearts of adoration./ When all sentient beings have believed and obeyed/ upright in character, gentle in mind/ wholeheartedly wishing to see the Buddha/ not sparing their own body and life/ "

41 梵音. The divine voice of buddhas and bodhisattvas preaching the Dharma, equipped with five kinds of purity. One of the 32 major marks of a tathāgata. It is said to be divine because it delivers elegant speech, brings delight, is like the voice of the *kalavinka* bird, and can be thunderous like a heavenly drum.

42 In the Lotus Sūtra Chapter XXII, *The Final Commission*, the Chinese translation by Kumārajīva 鳩摩羅什 uses the character 摩, which is not simply laying a hand, but stroking the crown of the head. The commissioning of the Odaimoku to the Bodhisattvas Who Emerge from the Earth for dissemination in the Era of Final Dharma takes place in the Lotus Sūtra Chapter XXI, *The Divine Transcendental Powers of the Tathāgata*. The stroking of the crown is a rite when there is a transmission of great importance. Nichiren Daishōnin likewise makes reference to this rite in *Letter to Soya-nyūdō* 曹谷入道許御書, citing that master Suryasoma 須梨耶蘇摩 held the Lotus Sūtra in his left hand, stroked with his right hand the crown of Kumārajīva's head and commissioned him to spread the Lotus Sūtra to the land in the northeast. He translated the Lotus Sūtra from Sanskrit to Chinese in the 5th century, and to this day it is considered to be the preeminent and authoritative translation of that sūtra. Although not spelled out in Chapter XXI, Guruji took it on faith that due to the profound significance of the commission, this rite must have taken place between Buddha and Bodhisattva Superior Conduct.

resident monk joined us and curled over into a ball below the desk that was lit by a single candle and chanted, "*Sadhu*! *Sadhu*!" [Excellent! Excellent!]. He related to us that heeding an earnest plea, one of two relics [on which fingerprints occasionally appear] had been presented to a teacher, the former principal of the school in Maligakanda, who he adored like a parent. Only he had ever received one of the two small white relics that initially were in this monk's care. No one else, regardless of who pleaded, was ever entrusted with the remaining relic. Perhaps seeing us in a state of ultimate bliss, the Reverend asked when we would again visit and offered to bestow on us the relic at that time. He said he was strangely and immediately moved to make the offer that night. If we passed by again the next day, he assured us, he would offer the relic then. Due to our inadequacies with the language, we wondered if we had heard him right on the proffer of the relic, yet retired to lie down, sharing our joy.

The monk reappeared from the room to show us a plan for a *mahavihara* [great temple] he hoped to build here. It was modeled after a *vihara* built by some great king in the ancient capital of Polonnaruwa,[43] though all that remains now is its foundation. It was a project on a grand scale to enshrine this relic in a stūpa with a seated Buddha image in the front and a roof on top. How, I wondered, had a chief monk of a small remote temple come to make a vow to build such a massive structure, and how was he going to achieve it? Matter-of-factly, the monk told us that visiting ruins in Polonnaruwa during his pilgrimage had inspired him all the more to rebuild the [ancient] *vihara*. He had long cherished the hope of one day building a similar *vihara*, and ultimately found himself in this place here. This monk's indomitable perseverance must cause the frivolous and flighty to die of shame. He went on to say that the visit tonight by Buddha's Japanese disciples overwhelmed him with joy. He invited us back to his room for he wished to make the offering of the relic now. We did not hear him wrong! The relic was actually about to be bestowed on us! Returning to the monk's room, my mind immediately became occupied with the question of what vessel to safe keep the millet-size relic in so as not to lose it on my journey. With the single

43 Polonnaruwa became the residence of Ceylon kings in 368 and was known as the "country residence of royalty." Anuradhapura was the formal, administrative capital, but when the Cholas of South India looted and burned it in 993, they made Polonnaruwa the new capital. The Cholas were then conquered by Sinhala King Vijayabahu I in 1070, who kept Polonnaruwa as the new capital. It continued to serve as the capital until sometime in the 12th century.

candle serving as a votive light, the gold stūpa was again taken out. [The monk] tore a piece of red silk to wrap the white sliver of relic and replaced it in the golden lotus within the gold stūpa. I watched the relic being thus wrapped, and the stūpa containing the relic was placed on my palm. I handed it to my attending disciple and wondered aloud what we should do with the stūpa since we understood just the relic was being presented. Meanwhile, the disciple receiving the gold stūpa bowed repeatedly and exclaimed his joy at holding the Buddha's relic for the first time in his 28 years. The chief monk said he had a piece of carved-out ivory in which to store other relics in his care. For 13 years, he carried and served this gold stūpa without ever letting it leave his person, not even for a day. Under no circumstances had he thought of offering it to anyone. However, this night his ever growing joy moved him to present the stūpa, as well. Please guard it with care, he said. Words of gratitude escaped us. Feeling like it was a dream, we accepted the relic with the stūpa and relayed that our great vow has been to erect a stūpa at Seetagangula on Sri Pada, and that there we shall enshrine this relic. Whether the relic is enshrined in a stūpa here or at Seetagangula, in either case it would be a Dharma work within the region of Mount Sri Pada.[44] Can this be anything but an expedient by the Tathāgata to distribute his relics far and wide and offer them for veneration?

I pondered on this epiphanic experience. We were just strangers from another land seeking a place to stay for the night. Though calling ourselves monks, we were mere travelers bathed in perspiration, soaked by the rain and laden with heaps of bags like common hirelings. It was already the dead of night when it's best to be discrete on the topic of relics that are in one's care. Yet, we not only had the opportunity to behold a relic, but were eventually granted it along with an antique stūpa that [the Reverend] kept on his person for many years. All this took place between persons who had yet to even exchange names. The joy that seized the chief monk's heart likewise must be lingering. After he retired and closed the door to his room, his lone voice could be heard reciting a sūtra.

Is this proof that the Buddha Dharma of Japan that was transmitted to me to be disseminated is in accord with the true intentions of the Tathāgatha? Is this a mandate for Buddha's Japanese disciples to restore Buddha Dharma in the Western Heavens? If this is not a wondrous

44 Seetagangula is part-way up the mountain of Sri Pada. Ginigathena is located about 30 miles away.

phenomenon, what is? Had I been in his place of protecting Buddha's relics, I believe my heart would never have been inspired to grant them to monks from another land who just happened to be taking shelter at my hermitage. Could something like this ever happen in a temple in Japan, even once in a thousand years? How else to describe this occurrence other than wondrous?

The resident monk said Buddha's relics are the Tathāgata in the flesh. From now on, Buddha Śākyamuni in the flesh is beside you. Do not hesitate in the face of unbearable hardship, do not fear any hindrances by *māras*.[45] Since this relic came into my possession, I have come face to face with savage beasts deep in mountains as well as with wild elephants, but each time I escaped unharmed. A thief attempted to steal this relic one night, but was likewise unsuccessful. It is due to the wondrous virtue of Buddha's relics. He said if I safeguard it in faith, I, too, will experience the wondrous power it manifests. As I stowed away the Buddha's relic in a hiker's pouch, I remembered a strand of coral prayer beads among the set of altar fittings and articles for worship I carried on the mission of *Saiten-kaikyō*. I took it out and offered it as an expression of my gratitude. Though initially hesitant,[46] the Reverend eventually accepted the gift saying even these precious coral prayer beads can be purchased, but Buddha's relics cannot be bought or made. Noting that he had honored us with the relic, perhaps it was likewise good for him to accept the coral beads. Once accepting the beads, he rejoiced in wearing them around his neck. In that way my strand of prayer beads played a token role in the great Dharma work. It is noteworthy that today is August 25, the monthly return of the date marking my benevolent mother's passing; and it is the third anniversary of my departure for *Saiten-kaikyō*, the day on which I reported [to Nichiren Daishōnin] the dedication of the memorial stone stūpa and offered my sentiments of filial piety to my mother. Now, three years later on this same day, which now marks my journey of departure from Ceylon to another land, I was given this profound karmic connection to the Tathāgata here in Ceylon.

---

45 *Māra* is the personification of evil. Māra sent three daughters, Tanha [desire], Rāga [lust] and Arati [aversion] to seduce Siddhārtha into breaking his concentration and vow not to move until he found a way to eradicate all suffering by achieving Enlightment. Māra is the ruler of desire and death, the two evils that chain humans to the wheel of ceaseless rebirth.
46 Prayer beads are not generally worn by Theravāda Buddhist monks. Their possessions comprise of a few simple items like three robes and an alms bowl.

The resident monk brought a piece of paper with his family name printed on it. It read N. Piyaratana,[47] and the name of the temple, Abinawaramaya, at a place called Ginigathena. Having no card with which to respond, I signed my name in his visitor's book. We finally came to know each other's surnames. Following the Dharma work of granting and receiving the Buddha relic came the human exchange of greetings between fellow monks.

I placed the hiker's pouch with the relic on the desk and turned down the flame of the temple's western lamp that we were using to offer it as an all-night votive light; I then laid down to rest in front of it, my palms pressed together. It was already past midnight, but I did not feel sleepy. 1 a.m., 2 a.m., 3 a.m.; time kept passing. Sheer joy filled my heart, and I felt like stomping my feet in jubilation with my arms dancing in the air. The scene of receiving the gold stūpa as it was placed in my palm remained vivid, as though gazing at a painting. Neither of us could fall asleep. Daybreak approached. In a light sleep at dawn, I saw a dream. The two of us were on our knees bowing in veneration, palms pressed together. Buddha's relic was about to be bestowed. Saying I would receive it first, I opened up my palms. Though I had washed my hands and feet, I realized something was on my robe around my hips, and I used one hand to brush it off. Awake or asleep, the scene of receiving Buddha's relic permeated my heart and mind throughout the night.

August 26, 1933

In the gray light of dawn, the first rays of the rising sun seeped in through the cracks. We arose and went to the assembly hall to beat the drum and chant the Odaimoku. The resident monk came out after a while and opened the *vihara* door. It was a cramped place, about the size of a roadside shrine. While we were inside chanting and beating the drum, the devotee from last night had already arrived with the breakfast offering as requested.

When we returned to the monks' quarters, breakfast had been laid out with milk, tea, bananas, sweets and lots of rice. The resident monk

47 N. Piyaratana Thero was known for being the custodian of a number of Buddha relics in Sri Lanka. He offered many other Buddha relics on subsequent occasions to Guruji through Nipponzan disciples such as Reverend Miki Jikyō, Reverend Yagi Tenshō and Reverend Nagai Gyōji.

again approached us bearing a tiny gold offering bowl on his palm. He wanted to present the bowl, which had been used over the years for mealtime offerings, to accompany the Buddha relic. For example, tea would be offered in the morning, rice at lunch and fruit juice at supper. He wished to provide it for our convenience so that we could serve and make offerings to the Buddha relic.

Though unable to properly judge the age, the somewhat coarse, hammered gold appeared to be an antique. I struggled to find the words that would express our appreciation, and the phrase *chōjō-anata*,[48] a Higo[49] expression of gratitude, came to mind. It was the most perfect phrase to express our thanks to the resident monk. He was the donor of not one sacred treasure, not two sacred treasures, but three sacred treasures. Without a speck of reluctance or attachment, he offered a variety of sacred treasures that miraculously had come into his life and that he had cared for. Truly, he is *chōjō-anata*.

Not accustomed in the art of rhetoric, our gratitude could only be expressed in smiles[50] and "thank you." Yet, our faces must surely convey astonishment and joy every time we reflect on the wondrous karmic connection. Above all else, our tears speak most eloquently of what lies in our hearts. The resident monk accompanied into the room the devotee who donated breakfast and related the story of what happened the night before. He told of the great joy that overcame him when he took in for the night the Buddha disciples from Japan, and how he unreservedly offered Buddha's relic, a gold stūpa and a gold offering bowl. "The Japanese monk presented me with a strand of coral prayer beads that he had brought from Japan," he said, "And that only served to double my joy." He then brought out the coral beads to show the devotee and wore them around his neck. The devotee likewise rejoiced. Who could possibly refrain from joy upon

48 重畳あなた. A person one feels grateful to for kindnesses piled one upon another. *Chōjō* means piled in many layers.
49 肥後. An old province in Japan, current Kumamoto Prefecture on the island of Kyūshū.
50 破顔微笑. *Hagan-mishō* is a face breaking into a broad smile in heart-to-heart communication, an allusion to the famous story on the founding of the Zen tradition. Amidst an assembly of one million at Sacred Eagle Peak, Buddha Śākyamuni spoke no words but simply twirled an *udumbara* flower and blinked. No one except for Mahākāśyapa understood the truth and Buddha's heart. He broke into a broad smile, beaming with joy. Thereupon Buddha said, "I hold the eye treasury of right Dharma, the subtle mind of Nirvāna, the true form of no-form, and the flawless gate of teaching. It is not predicated on words and phrases. It is a special transmission outside tradition. I now transmit it to you, Mahākāśyapa."

The sacred relics of Buddha Śākyamuni offered to Guruji by N. Piyaratana Thero at Abinawaramaya Temple, Sri Lanka in 1933.

hearing of the karmic connection in relation to the transmission of any Buddha relic? The single Buddha relic that passed from a Ceylon monk to a Japanese monk was in truth a historic encounter for the Buddhism of both countries, in which the Buddha relic was bestowed and received through a miraculous phenomenon of the heart and mind. It was the greatest joy I have ever experienced in my life. Between nameless monks from countries so very far apart, Tathāgata Śākyamuni in the flesh exercised great expedience out of infinite compassion, and in the form of a single Buddha relic, revealed the merit of the eternal Triple Jewel.[51] Through the eternal Jewel of the Sangha, the wonders of the eternal Buddha Jewel can also manifest.

Through the eternal Jewel of the Sangha, the Jewel of the Dharma exists; and through the turning of the wheel of the Dharma, the pervading

51 The Triple Jewel of the Buddha, Dharma and Sangha.

five impurities[52] that sink sentient beings into the three evil paths[53] are shattered. Though it seems that the Buddha Dharma of Ceylon has already served its purpose,[54] venerable monks of great virtue such as this one, fearless in their concentration and unflagging in their zeal, practice the *six pāramitās*[55] while hidden in the cloud-covered mountains.

Pilgrimage on foot is a practice of the Sangha. It is an expedient to seek out *zenchishiki* [good and virtuous friends][56] throughout the worlds in the ten directions[57] to benefit from them in the practice of the Buddha Way. If there are those who seek the Dharma in places where people gather like towns or villages, we immediately bring ourselves to them as teachers to proclaim and preach the Right Law of the Tathāgata according to their capacities to comprehend the Dharma. If not for the practice on foot, I never would have known of the existence of this dōjō, even if I had climbed Sri Pada hundreds of thousands of times over. Owing to the karmic connection created through the practice on foot, I sought lodging at this dōjō, met a monk of high virtue, and ultimately was vouchsafed with the karmic connection of Buddha's relic, the gold stūpa and bowl. The merit of the practice on foot was the expedient for encountering and receiving the Buddha relic. The merit of the practice on foot is the zeal for *Saiten-kaikyō*. The merit of the practice on foot is the path for awakening to the ever abiding Jewel of the Sangha. The merit of the practice on foot is to put these words into action: "After my extinction/ in stealth, preach to even one person."[58] The merit of practice on foot is to have faith in and comprehend both in mind and body the eternal and ever present

---

52 *Gojoku* 五濁. The five defilements or impurities are: 1) defilement of the period; an era of turmoil characterized by war, epidemics and starvation; 2) defilement of views; 3) defilement by evil passions [delusions or afflictions of covetousness, antipathy, ignorance, arrogance and doubt]; 4) defilement of the communities of sentient beings; and 5) defilement of a diminished lifespan.
53 三悪道. The three evil realms or states of existence of hell, hungry spirits and animals.
54 In the Era of Final Dharma, Buddha taught that the Lotus Sūtra is the one and only good medicine to relieve people's suffering.
55 六波羅蜜. Six Perfections. The six kinds of practice by which a bodhisattva attains Buddhahood: charity, observing precepts, perseverance, zeal, contemplation and wisdom.
56 善知識. Virtuous persons or teachers who lead one to the Buddha Way.
57 十方世界. The four cardinal points [north, south, east and west], the four intermediate directions [northeast, southeast, northwest and southwest], up and down, which are understood to be the places where sentient beings live. Each world in the ten directions has the pure lands of the buddhas, and these pure lands are called "pure lands in the ten directions."
58 Chapter X of the Lotus Sūtra, *The Teacher of the Law.*

nature of the Response-body[59] of the Tathāgata. The merit of practice on foot tests us and makes us fearless to walk throughout [the worlds in ten directions]. The merit of practice on foot enables us to see that all the worlds in the ten directions are one and the same Buddha Realm.

The founding of Nipponzan Myōhōji is a testament to the merit of practice on foot. Failing to understand this, an increasing number of those claiming to be disciples and devotees of this order have situated themselves at a particular temple, justifying their actions as temple caretakers but living a life that varies little from those at temples of the more established schools. The merit earned from such a life equals less than one one-thousandth of the karmic obstacles that this same life creates. These people are only good at deeds that cause the decline of Buddha Dharma in Nipponzan's name. Those inclined towards deeds that obstruct Buddha's true teachings are comfortable just to stay at one temple. What terrible shame! We are deeply indebted to our Preceptor, Buddha Śākyamuni, who entered Parinirvāna in Kushinagara, and to our venerable master Nichiren Daishōnin, who passed in Ikegami, for exemplifying the merit of practice on foot. Revere and have faith!

Sri Pada is the platform for teaching on the merit of the walking practice. What is called *jinzū-yūke*[60] [to possess transcendental powers of unimpeded existence and go about leading others to the Dharma with a heart of joy] is the free and unimpeded merit of practice on foot. Through the dedicated walking practice, I shall fulfill the great vow at hand of *Saiten-kaikyō* and ultimately fulfill the even greater vow of leading the entire *Jambudvīpa* to take refuge in the ineffable Dharma. An auspicious omen has now manifested.

The Dharma work I aspire to will be achieved. No matter if it is the suspicion leveled at us by British authorities[61] or the enmity and envy of

---

59 The three bodies of Buddha are hosshin 法身 Dharma-body, *hōjin* 報身 reward-body, and *ōjin* 応身 accommodative-body or response body. The Dharma-body is described as truth, the reward-body, wisdom, and the accommodative-body, compassion. The reward-body is a body received as the result of meritorious practices. The accommodative-body is manifested in correspondence with the needs of living beings. The emanative Buddha's [*shakubutsu* 迹仏] Dharma-body is without beginning or end; the reward-body with beginning and no end; the accommodative-body with beginning and end. However, all three bodies of the Origin Buddha are eternal without beginning or end.

60 神通遊化.

61 A reference to the colonial government which viewed monks from Imperial Japan as spies.

the Japanese Consulate,[62] both are akin to wild boars polishing gold with their tusks.[63] They can only enhance the single source of light emitted by our great and cherished vow. Those who shoot arrows at the sun are truly these scoundrels at home and abroad, the army of Lord Māra of the Sixth Heaven.[64] You who are convinced that your deeds sanctioned by the powers-that-be are just, how little you know; justice is the antithesis of power and exists on the other shore. Those unable to awaken to justice, ensnared in the illusion of power, beware the judgment of history one hundred years hence. History will reveal whether the key to friendly relations between the Western Heavens and Japan rested in your hands or in this order. Are not those who torment the Western Heavens and those who misguide Japan the real scoundrels, the army of Lord Māra of the Sixth Heaven, abusing power today with their wicked ideas? Nipponzan, which presses forward on the great noble path of *Saiten-kaikyō*, bears the mandate bestowed by the one and only Buddha Śākyamuni. Your criticism, which resembles the gibberish of drunkards, merits no attention.

If you find this truth unacceptable, wait. Wait for the day when you will see the holy vision of the Western Heavens and Japan, the Far East, reveal they are in reality a single Buddha Realm in which the worlds of sentient beings and non-sentient beings are pure and tranquil.

The wondrous attainment of Buddha's relic is a validation of the remonstration drum of *Risshō-ankoku-ron*, the Buddha Dharma of Japan. The wondrous attainment of Buddha's relic is the seal bestowed on the messengers who were prophesized and sent by Buddha [in Chapter XVI of the Lotus Sūtra] to save the children who had lost their senses. Belittle me not, though I am an ordinary monk, for my whole being shoulders the profound and grave injunction [from Buddha] that was not entrusted even

---

62 The Japanese Consulate often took a dim view of Nipponzan's activities and sometimes refused to issue passports to Nipponzan monks, believing their clothing and behavior compromised Japan's dignity.

63 The expression literally translates, "wild boars scrubbing gold mines." It's an expression used when an act meant to do harm has the unintended consequence of doing good. In this case, those who would thwart Nipponzan's work are powerless to do so and the end result only serves to reveal Nipponzan's integrity. The wild boars charging a gold mine in order to destroy it end up polishing the gold with their tusks and making it shine.

64 天子魔軍. The *māra* army in this heaven is the most powerful in tempting and hindering practitioners of the Buddha Way. The Sixth Heaven is the Heaven of Free Enjoyment of Other's Creations, the sixth and last heaven in the realm of desires.

to Nāgārjuna,[65] Vasubandhu,[66] the four ranks of Bodhisattva teachers [in the Era of Genuine Dharma].[67] Call me arrogant or delusional, I shall not falter until the Pure Land is realized, the complete perfection of Buddha-fruit[68] through *ji-no-ichinen-sanzen*.[69] I shall realize *Risshō-ankoku* [to give

---

65 竜樹 [150-250]. An eminent Buddhist logician instrumental in the early establishment of Indian Mahāyāna philosophy and founder of eight Mahāyāna schools.

66 Also known as 世親 Seshin. First Theravāda philosopher in the 4th century who later converted to Mahāyāna. Both Nāgārjuna and Vasubandhu spread the Lotus Sūtra in the Era of Genuine Dharma.

67 四依の薩埵. There are four reliances respectively for learning Dharma 法四依 and Persons 人四依 who one can rely on in seeking guidance. Here it is a reference to the four reliances or four ranks of Bodhisattva teachers who protect the Genuine Dharma and benefit sentient beings after Buddha's Parinirvāna. Different lists of four reliances exist. Nichiren Daishōnin used the four categories of Theravāda, Mahāyāna, Trace Teaching [*shakumon* 迹門] and Origin Teaching [*honmon* 本門]. 1) The four reliances of Theravāda teachings appeared in the first 500 years of Era of Genuine Dharma and are those like Kāśyapa and Ānanda. 2) Four reliances for Mahāyāna teachings appeared in the latter 500 years of Era of Genuine Dharma, such as Aśvaghosa, Nāgārjuna and Vasubandhu. They engaged in the Bodhisattva practice of seeking enlightenment as well as guiding others. 3) The four reliances who spread the Trace Teaching of the Lotus Sūtra 迹化の菩薩 appeared primarily during the 1,000 years of Era of Semblance Dharma and a few toward the beginning of Era of Final Dharma and include Tendai Daishi and Dengyō Daishi. 4) The four reliances of the Origin Teaching of the Lotus Sūtra 本化の菩薩 are the Bodhisattvas Who Emerge from the Earth prophesized to appear at the beginning of Era of Final Dharma to benefit the world by spreading the origin teaching, the true intent of the eternal Buddha. The Trace and Origin Teachings refer to different sections of the Lotus Sūtra. In the 28 chapters of the Lotus Sūtra, the first 14 arc referred to as the trace teaching expounded by the historical Buddha, the accommodative body of the Origin Buddha. At this point in the sūtra certain Bodhisattvas are instructed to spread the sūtra's teachings in the Eras of Genuine Dharma and Semblance Dharma. In the second half of the sūtra, Buddha's true nature, his eternal life, is revealed and the teachings given are by the Origin Buddha, therefore it is known as Origin Teaching. The dissemination of these teachings is taken up by the Bodhisattvas Who Emerge from the Earth, who receive the mandate to administer the good medicine, the Odaimoku, to bring salvation to the Era of Final Dharma.

68 仏果 *bukka*. The meaning of Buddha-fruit, the result brought about by Buddha-cause differs between the emanative Buddha and Origin Buddha. In the former, Buddha-fruit is the attainment of Buddhahood as a result of the practice seeking Enlightenment, which is the Buddha-cause. In the latter, Buddha-fruit is eternal life as a result of guiding other sentient beings for the sake of emancipating them.

69 一念三千. *Ichinen-sanzen* is the teaching of "three thousand existences contained in a single thought-moment." Each of the *jikkai* 十界, ten worlds of existence [i.e. hell, the world of hungry spirits, animals, *asuras*, human beings, world of deities and heavenly beings, the world of *shamon*, *engaku*, bodhisattva, and Buddhas] includes the other nine in itself. Tendai Daishi established the religious practice of *ichinen-sanzen* through introspection into one's mind-essence, *kanjin* 観心. This is known as *ri-no-ichinen-sanzen* [理の一念三千], which is based on the ten suchness-aspects described in the Trace Teaching of the Lotus Sūtra, specifically, Chapter II, *Expedients*. On the other hand, Nichiren Daishōnin's teaching of *ichinen-sanzen* is based on the Origin Teaching of the Lotus Sūtra, *The Eternal Duration of the Life of the Tathāgata* chapter, and is known as *ji-no-ichinen-sanzen* 事の一念三千. In short, the former is a world that originates in the single thought-moment, the wholehearted

rise to the Genuine Dharma for the sake of bringing peace and tranquility to the land] in India, *Risshō-ankoku* in Ceylon, *Risshō-ankoku* in Burma, *Risshō-ankoku* in Great Asia, and ultimately *Risshō-ankoku* in the entire *Jambudvīpa*. I shall realize *Risshō-ankoku* from the depths of deepest darkness caused by the five impurities that shroud the 10,000 years of the Era of Final Dharma. It is precisely the prophecy of Buddha Śākyamuni in the Lotus Sūtra and the true reason for our founding master Nichiren Daishōnin's appearance in the Era of Final Dharma. Though I am an unworthy disciple, my faith in Buddha's Golden Words is profound and runs deep, and my faith in this vow likewise is immeasurable.

August 25, though of different month, is the monthly return of the date of the passing of my benevolent mother, Maha Bhiksunī Gyōain Nisso. August 26 in the lunar calendar is July 6, the same number as the day on which I was born, though of a different month. On the night of the monthly return date of my mother's passing and on the morning of the date of my birth in the lunar and solar calendars, a watershed event occurred, an omen wondrous and auspicious was bestowed on me for the Dharma work of *Saiten-kaikyō*, for the Dharma work of bringing the world under one sky, surrounded by four oceans to find refuge in the wondrous Dharma, for the Dharma work of uniting the *Jambudvīpa*. Is it a manifestation of my mother's compassion? Is it some grace enabling me to pay a small portion of filial piety? Despite the insults and slanders of the ignorant, even from Japanese beginning with those at the consulate, and in the midst of this mendicant life of dire poverty, I have obtained merits as prodigious as Sumeru[70] through my practice of spreading [the Odaimoku].

Immersed in bliss, gratified, hopeful in this vision and conviction, a pure breeze wafting out of the Land of Eternal Tranquil Light[71] rises from beneath my feet, which are firmly planted on the ground. What joy! What joy!

---

desire of ordinary humans seeking the Buddha realm, and the latter originates in the vow of the Origin Buddha of universal emancipation [At all times making this my thought: "How shall I cause all the living/To enter the Supreme Path/And speedily attain the Buddha-body?"]. It is a realm of "Tranquil is this realm of mine/ever filled with celestial being" brought about by ordinary beings awakening to this vow and who practice the chanting of the Odaimoku.

70 須弥山. A towering mountain at the center of the universe according to Buddhist cosmology.

71 *Jōjakkōdo* 常寂光土. The Land of Eternal Tranquil Light is the realm of the Dharma-body Buddha, the highest of the Pure Lands.

4

Excerpt from the Wardha Diary[1]

Sevagram Ashram, Wardha, India

October 4, 1933

Several women including Mrs. Gandhi came out to greet us when we arrived at the ashram. The Venerable's[2] room was on the second floor. We were led upstairs.

In the front of the room, a partially-clad Gandhiji was spinning yarn. A number of disciples and Bajaji sat on either side of him. Facing them sat journalists and others who had requested to see Gandhiji. We were ushered in front of the visitors, almost directly across from Venerable. We bowed in salutation, chanted Na Mu Myō Hō Ren Ge Kyō thrice with palms pressed together. Rev. Okitsu[3] introduced me to Venerable, and I presented him with gifts of a tin of *arare* [rice crackers] and a fan. The rice

1 There are several different versions of the Wardha Diary in Japanese, edited by various disciples with easier kanji characters and expressions to assist with reading. This rendition is based on the December 16, 1993 reprint 藁田日記 1, 2,藁田消息, which is a compilation of the *Wardha Diary I* [entry from October 2, 1933 to October 9, 1933, first published on April 11, 1934] and *Wardha Diary II* [October 10, 1933 to December 13, 1933, first published on August 11, 1934] as well as *Letters From Wardha*, correspondence between Guruji and his disciple, Rev. Maruyama Gyōryō 丸山行遼上人 [November 13, 1937 to January 24, 1938, first published August 16, 1938].

2 The Japanese term used here is *ou* 翁, a venerable male elder. Guruji uses this term throughout the journal entry when referring to Mahatma Gandhi.

3 興津忠男師. Reverend Okitsu Tadao left Japan on January, 8, 1932, exactly a month after his ordination, to join Guruji in India. He stopped in Shanghai en route to India and, upon arrival Feb. 22, became the bearer of the sad news of the Shanghai incident to Guruji who was practicing alone out of a shed next to a crematory in Bombay. According to the Shanghai Mainichi Newspaper article cited in the 2nd issue of *Geppō* 月報 [Nipponzan Myōhōji's monthly bulletin, a predecessor to *Tenku*], in February 1932, five members of Nipponzan Myōhōji's clergy and laity were attacked by a mob of several hundred during their practice at dusk on the streets of Shanghai on January 18. Rev. Tenzaki Keishō [21] 天崎啓昇上人, Rev. Mizukami Hideo [32] 水上秀雄上人, and Gotō Yoshihira [43] 後藤芳平 were critically injured. Rev. Tenzaki later recovered, joined Guruji in India and practiced at the Wardha ashram with Gandhi, who called him "Keishō-bai." He was one of three disciples sent by the Most Ven. Kawai Nisshin 河合日辰猊下 [22nd Chief Abbot of Nichiren School and 54th Chief Abbot of Myōkenji Temple] to practice with Guruji in India.

crackers had been offered to me the other day from Mr. Sasakura, who lives in Bombay, and the fan was a gift sent by a devotee in Kōbe.

Venerable looked more youthful than the time I saw him at Bombay's Victoria Pier upon his return from the London Roundtable Conference. His face, so carefree and expressive, seemed ready to break into a smile at any moment conveying innocence much like a child. My greatest concern for Venerable is his health. His longevity is invaluable not only for the Indian people, but to us as well. Today's meeting makes me joyous, like I am holding a priceless treasure.

Tears welled up and rolled down my palms pressed together in veneration, moved by the thought that this very person, so easily breaking into innocent laughter while spinning yarn, is the same one who carries the pain and suffering of 370 million Indians on his shoulders, who offered himself up for the invaluable sacrifice of incarceration and upon whom was imposed a life of punishment in his latter years. Moments like these always move me to tears. What is it about this humble labor of spinning cotton that he finds so enjoyable? Would it be possible to find such profound joy in the rewards of this labor without having noble and selfless aspirations and a father's tenderness toward his destitute kin, seeking to clothe the naked and cover their humiliation? The charkhā to Gandhiji is not a thing that spins yarn, but a close friend ceaselessly spinning out his boundless compassion and copious tears.

The picture of the charkhā in the first book I read on Gandhiji did not stir any interest in me. But as I read more about him, I grew increasingly intrigued by the charkhā. Today when I looked beyond its physical form, I felt an exalted light coming from the charkhā. Unwavering faith perhaps exists as light, which makes one oblivious to its physical form.

Venerable was delighted with my gifts, and in his delight he addressed us. "All things Japanese are beautiful and inexpensive. Still, they are fairly expensive. Is Japan intending to conquer India with them?"

Rev. Okitsu had my written greetings in front of him. There was no time for him to translate it. He had to improvise on the spot. "By which path?" he asked in return.

"By its products," said Venerable, coming right to the point.

India's abundant natural resources have been exploited relentlessly by Great Britain, reducing it to its miserable depths of today. No matter how high the cost of inconvenience, Venerable, who grieves India's state of destitution, cannot tolerate any more of its wealth escaping the country.

"We are bhikshus and are totally unfamiliar with business," replied Rev. Okitsu, deftly dodging the question. He then explained himself by saying, "The biscuits are not a sample product but a token of our hearts."

Venerable appeared convinced that the two beautiful Japanese gifts were not secret envoys coming to conquer India. Maybe not all Japanese are merchants?

"I see. Is this edible, too?" Gandhiji removed the beautiful *noshi* [a strip of red and white paper wrapped around a gift to signify a happy occasion] from the rice crackers box.

"No, that is only for decoration. It's not to be eaten."

"Is this part of the biscuits?" He held up a modest russet-colored cotton cloth with an arabesque design used to wrap the box. Gandhiji looked doubtful about the biscuits' elaborate presentation.

"No, it is cotton simply used for wrapping, and it is not edible," responded Rev. Okitsu, who then switched the subject and introduced me.

After hearing that I have been in the Western Heavens for three years, Venerable asked if I could speak English. Graciously he sought a way to communicate directly, even if it were a word or two. Rev. Okitsu explained that I disliked speaking English.

"You don't like speaking English? That's fine. What about Sanskrit or Pali?" Venerable asked again. Rev. Okitsu candidly confessed that I knew neither.

"Most Japanese Buddhist monks who come to India ordinarily study Sanskrit or Pali." Venerable was perplexed by our audacious ignorance of the languages.

Rev. Okitsu explained the lack of linguistic knowledge by saying, "My master studied Buddha Dharma entirely in Japanese. The study of Sanskrit and Pali can be left up to the scholars. We must devote ourselves to religious work."

"What about Hindi?" Venerable continued.

"He spoke Hindi when he was first in India. But during his year and a half or so stay in Ceylon, he completely lost his Hindi," replied Rev. Okitsu.

"Study Hindi. We shall talk in Hindi." Venerable kindly encouraged me to learn Hindi.

"What have you there? Where do you beat it?" Venerable noticed the drum and opened up a new subject.

"This is a symbol of the Buddha Dharma of Japan. We beat it

wherever we are, whenever we can," was Rev. Okitsu's response.

"I see. I have also heard rumors that Japanese Buddhist monks are walking throughout Bombay every night beating the drum." Venerable indicated that he was familiar with our practice. He then advanced the discussion, "Which school beats the drum?"

"It is called Nichiren School founded by Nichiren Daishōnin in Japan 700 years ago."

"Does everyone at Nichiren School beat the drum?"

"No, some in the Nichiren School are business oriented, and these people do not earnestly beat the drum. Our master has taught us to beat the drum with all our hearts and chant Na Mu Myō Hō Ren Ge Kyō. We have grown into a Sangha with many disciples and devotees."

It was already past 4:20 p.m. Venerable smiled and informed us that we had exceeded the time allotted and that today's meeting must come to an end. All this time, I had my palms pressed together in veneration and eyes closed in gratitude for this extremely rare opportunity. I did not expect to gain anything from the dialogue, but only wished to capture who Gandhiji really is. I was not trying to seek out his opinion nor gain his understanding on any subject. The Indian newspapers all reported that I was chanting the Odaimoku and praying during today's entire 20-minute meeting. Truly, truly, the 20 minutes slipped by while tears ran down my face.

With affection and seeming reluctance to part, Gandhiji said, "Because of the large number of visitors who come to see me, these meetings naturally have to be time limited. An exception cannot be made for one person."

"My master also has much more he would like to share with you." Rev. Okitsu likewise expressed our abiding sentiments.

Venerable slowly turned the charkhā, and his laughter seemed to roll with it as he started to speak again. "Until recently I led a life of a prisoner with no free time of my own. The warden controls a prisoner's time. It is like I am still in jail here. Bajaji is my warden, and I am back to being a prisoner. Bajaji decides everything, whether I see someone, when I go to sleep or wake up. If Bajaji tells me I can meet with someone for fifteen minutes, I meet him for fifteen minutes. If he says I have 30 minutes, I meet for 30 minutes. If he says I can meet someone for an hour, I meet with that person for an hour. So, you should talk with Bajaji. Bajaji should kindly make convenient arrangements for our next meeting." Venerable opened the opportunity for our next meeting.

"My master is unable to speak freely with you." Rev. Okitsu appeared to be more concerned about my inability to speak the language than the time restriction.

"Write down what you would like to say. Writing should be easier for you than speaking." He was opening all gates so as to accept our hearts. It was well past the time allotted, and both sides were extending it without end. I felt it was time to bid farewell. We bowed in profound reverence and chanted the Odaimoku thrice. Venerable also took his hands off the charkhā and pressed his palms together in front of his mouth. His penetrating eyes, gazing intently at us over the rims of his spectacles, gradually moistened. I was a visitor from a distant land who could not utter a single word. It was a meeting of merely 20 minutes. I was joyous and sad at the same time. Tears were all that welled up in me. Were we bound to meet by our karmic connection from previous lives or were we newfound friends in this lifetime?

Once we returned to the bungalow, reporters were waiting to hear our story. Rev. Okitsu started with the Japanese biscuits story. I listened by his side. I advised him that the question should have been answered, "If the word 'conquer' is to be used, we feel we must conquer India with Buddhism from Japan. It was India that conquered Japan 1,300 years ago with Buddhism, from which all civilization in Japan developed. To return the blessings that Buddhism brought us, it is our duty today to bring Buddhism back to India from Japan."

"Indeed," said Rev. Okitsu, and translated this for the reporters. They were amused and wrote it down.

If Gandhiji had asked whether Japan was trying to conquer India with Buddha Dharma, the answer would have been an immediate "yes." However, since Japan never came to India for spiritual purposes, no wonder Venerable assumed, as Japanese, that we might be representing some business interest, though we stood before him as Buddha's disciples. To entertain an unfair conjecture, he could have imagined that we were espionage agents for those who would exploit India. Buddhism, which has been handed down over thousands of years, still thrives in Japan, even though it stands at the height of a civilization based on materialism. Not only that, I believe the entire world under one sky will eventually be led to find refuge in the single phrase of the ineffable Dharma.[4] The

4 Here Guruji is reiterating the purpose of his mission. 一天四海皆帰妙法. [*itten-shikai-kaiki-myōhō*] comes from the writings of Nichiren Daishōnin. "One heaven, four seas,

bold proposal to return Buddhism to the land of its origin must be like a bolt out of the blue, an unlikely proposition that would not readily come to mind. The current mandate driving Japanese civilization is to sell cotton textile to India. The Japanese delegation now attending the Simla Conference,[5] with self-styled heroic resolve, would rather die than return home without successfully promoting Japanese cotton goods. The Japan-India Association[6] and the Japanese General Consulate are also concentrating their efforts toward a worthy outcome for the conference in Simla. Is this what they should be doing? If one listens calmly to what is being said, it is even more embarrassing than the British. Japan possesses one thing that ought to be exported abroad. It requires no freight nor is it subject to tariff. Not a single penny would be exploited from the buyer. It is the time-tested crystal of Japanese civilization, a wondrous elixir that regenerates a fallen nation, the principle to unite the East, a bomb that could conquer the world. Japan was not founded for the purpose of promoting cotton textile sales. Why not take a day off from materialism and have a second look at India? As its name implies, the India under discussion in Simla is given as much regard as a lifeless village to be taken advantage of. [Here Guruji is making a play on words because *simla* 死村, as he wrote it in Japanese, refers to a dead or lifeless village.] Its very name is inauspicious in the first place.

Dusk approached the highlands. A nearly full moon rose atop the full-grown cotton in the field across from the bamboo grove. The cotton field is mixed with corn, which is likewise starting to come into ear. The nocturnal view resembles Manchuria somewhat. As we started out to the ashram for the evening service beating the drum, we were offered a ride since time was drawing near. The service takes place in the courtyard of

---

everything seeks refuge in the ineffable Dharma." This idea originates in the charge by Buddha Śākyamuni in Chapter XXIII of the Lotus Sūtra to Bodhisattva Medicine King: "I commit to you, in the last 500 years after my extinction, proclaim and spread it abroad in *Jambudvīpa*, lest it be lost." [嘱累於汝 我滅度後 後五百歳中 広宣流布 於閻浮提 無令断絶] Nichiren Daishōnin awakened to the mission to bring salvation to the Era of Final Dharma with the ineffable Dharma and started chanting Na Mu Myō Hō Ren Ge Kyō. In *Admonishing Bodhisattva Kangyō* [諫暁八幡抄 *Kangyō-hachiman-shō*], he prophesized that Na Mu Myō Hō Ren Ge Kyō would spread widely to China, India and throughout the world. Guruji found his calling in bringing Nichiren Daishōnin's prophesy to fruition.

5 Simla is an Indian city in the state of Himachal Pradesh, located in the northwest Himalayas. In 1864 it was declared the summer capital of the erstwhile British Raj in India. It was the venue of a conference between the British Empire, India and Japan to resolve the trade war that had broken out between them regarding the import of cotton.

6 Founded in 1903 to promote broad exchange and friendship between Japan and India.

the ashram quarters. The courtyard was full of people, men in the front and women behind them. In the middle was a stool with a cushion for Gandhiji.

A blanket was placed for us to sit near Venerable. We hesitated to accept the special seat and sat behind the blanket so that others might use it. Gandhiji's granddaughter came. I hear she had to be treated for tonsillitis. We inquired about an acquaintance of Rev. Okitsu's whom he had met in Ahmedabad.[7] We were told anyone who is not here is most likely in jail. The word jail is used most casually here. Perhaps it is understood simply as a place where one can practice what he or she believes. Children crowded around us. They just stood around gazing at us without any distracting clamor. When the bell sounded, a half-clad Gandhiji came, following a lamp that illuminated his way. He walked with an unsteady gait, his arms resting on the shoulders of two attending women. When he took his seat we caught his eye. He placed his palms together in greeting, then whispered to Bajaji, who was attending him, to tell us to move forward onto the blanket.

As someone recited, others followed. The prayer meeting lasted about 30 minutes. As the moon rose higher, moonbeams slanted across the wide highlands, shining cool and clear in the night, the heat of the day all but forgotten. No greeting was exchanged by those who gathered and found their seat on the ground in an orderly fashion. In all, several hundred men and women had assembled. I wondered where they came from. A roll-call of ashram members followed the service. Venerable rose from his seat and returned to his room. After Gandhiji, the women's group stood up and left. Male members then slowly started to leave. They headed towards where we were seated. Perhaps to prevent the crowd from stepping on us, three or four young men joined their hands to shield us. It was also time for us to leave.

We briefly met with Gandhiji's third son. We parted after promising to visit him tomorrow morning. With the moonlight on our backs, we returned to the bungalow, beating the drum. There were still many people behind us. We arrived at the bungalow, passing several groups of women who left before us. Having no appetite, I skipped supper. But people worried and insisted I take milk or fruit. I agreed to have some milk.

7 The largest city in the state of Gujarat, located on the banks of the River Sabarmati.

October 7, 1933

On October 7, 1933, at the satyagraha [grasping the truth] ashram in Wardha, located in the middle of India's central plains, the long-cherished vow of *Saiten-kaikyō* was expounded for Mahatma Gandhiji, the peerless sage of all times and the supreme leader of the Indian freedom movement. Rev. Okitsu translated what I wrote down in Japanese. As it so happened, it was the time of the full moon, and some nights we worked almost till daybreak by the lamp and moonlight. I cannot fathom how hard it must have been for Rev. Okitsu to translate, much harder than my preparation of the text. When Rev. Okitsu finished translating, he said in tears, "Now that I accomplished the greatest work of my life, I don't mind even if I die of fever disease." His immersion in this work was such that he gave all he had. Bajaji's secretary helped Rev. Okitsu with the translation. A young English Literature scholar was asked to read the draft, and he felt the English did not read well and took the liberty of completely rewriting it. Rev. Okitsu thought it over and wondered what good a refined English text would be if our heart did not come through? He suggested we submit the literal translation with its Japanese-flavored English; Venerable would surely see our hearts through the awkwardness of the text. He thus declined the revision. I wrapped the letter in *fukusa* [a small silk wrapping cloth] to present to Gandhiji.

We again left around 4 p.m. today, as it started to cool down once the sun sank low in the sky. When we arrived at the ashram, a disciple of Venerable came out to stop our drumming and explained that "Bapuji" was being examined by a doctor in a room downstairs. We were taken first to the sitting room upstairs.

We did not have to wait long before the half-clad Venerable entered and took his seat with ease while pressing his palms together and bowing back to us. His whole face was a smile. I read in a sūtra[8] that a holy arhat never fails to greet others with a smile. An unreserved smile cannot come naturally when facing a stranger if the heart is clouded. Although I have always been mindful of this, it is a revered state of mind that does not come easily. As agreed, Rev. Okitsu extended our greetings by saying, "We are deeply grateful to have seen you the other day. My master has written

---

8 増一阿含経. Increased by One Discourses of the Āgama Sūtras [Sk. Ekottara Āgama] is one of the four of the Āgamas [阿含 agon], which are collections of early Buddhist scriptures. Translated by 瞿曇僧伽提婆 Gautama-samghadeva in 397.

a letter since he is unable to freely converse with you. You might find it difficult to read because of the poor English. Your response would be greatly appreciated."

I handed the letter to Rev. Okitsu, who passed it to Gandhiji. "You translated it?" Gandhiji asked.

Rev. Okitsu embarrassed, responded, "It's awkward English." The single-minded desire to somehow convey our hearts must have given him the courage to present Venerable with a letter in such crude English.

"Good, good, excellent!" Venerable respectfully accepted it with a smile. "This is a long letter. I will be on my weekly day of silence starting tonight until tomorrow night, and I will not be able to talk with you. My response might have to wait two or three days. Would that be alright? When are you leaving?"

"Two or three days are not a problem. Master is thoroughly enjoying his stay."

"Well, then make yourselves at home. Have you been able to eat Indian food?"

"Yes, it's delicious." Bajaji, who was sitting by, gave a frank report as host that the master had skipped several meals.

"Are you feeling alright? Is anything wrong?"

"No, there is nothing wrong with my master. He was a little tired. Perhaps his mind is over stimulated. He is taking milk and fruit."

"Good, all I take is milk and fruit, too. Let Bajaji know if there is any food you'd like to have." Venerable noticed Rev. Okitsu's cotton drum bag. "I see your bag is torn."

"A mouse chewed it." Rev. Okitsu's response in Hindi brought everyone in the room to laughter.

"Your belongings are falling out from the hole. Can I offer you a bag?" A member of the ashram thought maybe it needed to be made of Japanese cotton.

Rev. Okitsu said, "No, I prefer handmade Indian cotton."

Today's meeting was set for five minutes. It was time to excuse ourselves. Venerable also carries this type of bag during his pilgrimages on foot. The same is true of his disciples. A white cotton bag is worn across the right shoulder and hangs under the left arm. The cloth on the flap extends slightly to be tied with a string. Likewise, cotton is used in briefcases, handbags and such, rather than leather. I shall send one to the people in Japan.

October 8, 1933

We will be seeing Gandhiji at the ashram at 4 p.m. for his response. It was only at 4 p.m. yesterday that we presented him with my letter. It must have been quite a task amidst his busy schedule to read through the lengthy letter. It also must have been the clumsiest English letter out of the countless letters Gandhiji receives. I assume the difficulty for the reader was compounded by its unusual length. When the letter was presented yesterday and Rev. Okitsu mentioned that the translation was inadequate, Venerable flipped the pages and asked if he translated it. Rev. Okitsu said "yes," but later confided to me that a cold sweat suddenly ran down his spine.

Gandhiji looked very pleased and commended the troubles of translating it by saying, "Did you? Well done!"

After the evening service on the 5th, Gandhiji, who was about to stand from his seat, whispered into Bajaji's ear, "What are the Japanese monks doing with their time?" To which Bajaji replied, "They are writing a letter to you." "Oh," said Venerable, and saluted us, who were sitting right next to him, with palms together and left his seat. More than just wondering what we might have to say, I suspect he felt like he was waiting with all ears for the first song of a bush warbler.

An unexpected friend came from a land far away, led by a longing that grew over the years. But he could only convey the trueness of his heart through an unfamiliar tongue. The luster of a gem is not lost even when wrapped in rags. I believe what shines in a person's heart is the mirrored reflection of the heart of another. Venerable was on his weekly practice of silence where he spends time in meditation and contemplation. His response was a thankful surprise since I did not expect it for the next two or three days. For everything, I am so grateful.

A school stands en route to the ashram on the road cars take. Many congregated in the vicinity of the school today. I have no idea where they came from, but many ox-drawn carts were hitched in the shade of the trees. Just like "the ants' pilgrimage to the Kumano shrines,"[9] an endless stream of local people converged. They came to listen to Gandhiji speak at 6 p.m. We got out of the automobile and, as usual, entered the ashram gate beating the drum. We were led to the room upstairs and were told that the

---

9 蟻の熊野詣. A metaphor describing the numerous pilgrims who travel along the Kumano Kodo pilgrimage routes to pay homage at the Kumano shrine complex in the Kii mountain in central Japan.

doctor was examining Gandhiji downstairs. By now we are acquainted with many of Venerable's multitude of disciples present in the room. Before long, Venerable entered and returned our greeting with palms pressed together as he took his seat. Venerable said, "I have written my response. Let me read it to you first." He read it out loud and made changes along the way. He gave a copy to his secretary, who incorporated the changes. Venerable wrote down my name on the envelope confirming each letter in the spelling of my name. Through Rev. Okitsu, I first thanked him for his response and then asked if we might make the letter public. "Yes, of course you may make it public."

"When will you be leaving?" asked Venerable.

Rev. Okitsu replied, "We will stay another two or three days since my master is very happy here."

"Then come again tomorrow. Every day at 4 p.m., I have come to really look forward to hearing the valiant sound of your drum. I, too, am fond of the sound of the drum."

The reverberation of Nipponzan's *gyakku-senryō*[10] [drumming and proclamation of the Dharma, Na Mu Myō Hō Ren Ge Kyō] found a kindred spirit in the greatest sage of modern times, the chief commander of India's freedom movement, a representative of the people descended from the lineage of Buddha Śākyamuni, and the one whose joyful acceptance resonated with the sound of the drum. At long last! The long-cherished vow of *Saiten-kaikyō* found the one person with the capacity to receive it in accordance with the time.[11] The sweet joyous utterance that escaped Gandhiji's lips at this ashram in Wardha was the joyful voice of 300 million people responding to the Dharma sound of our drum. The wondrous practice of *gyakku-senryō* did not find a kindred spirit among the countless monks in Buddhist Ceylon. The more earnestly I offered it, the greater I was held in contempt. Some, like the Japanese

10 Please refer to *Wondrous First Connection with Lord Buddha's Relic*, footnote 27, p. 14.

11 教機時国鈔. *Treatise on Teaching, Capacity, Time and Country.* Written by Nichiren Daishōnin on February 10, 1262 during exile in Izu, it teaches the five aspects involved in disseminating Buddha Dharma: the teaching [Na Mu Myō Hō Ren Ge Kyō] to be spread; the people's capacity; the time; the country; and the sequence of propagation. Guruji's statement refers to the teaching [Na Mu Myō Hō Ren Ge Kyō] in this writing as well as a prophecy made by Nichiren Daishōnin in *Admonishing Bodhisattva Hachiman* 諫暁八幡抄. Nichiren Daishōnin predicted "an auspicious omen of Buddha Dharma of Japan returning to India, the country of the moon," and Guruji believed both teachings were fulfilled on October 8, 1933 [time] through Gandhiji [who had the capacity to receive the teaching] in India [the country].

Consulate General in India, regard Nipponzan as an objectionable presence internationally, and have taken every possible measure, even at times illegal, to oppress us. The average Indian on the street, if not ridiculing us, has been totally indifferent. I have thus ascertained first-hand that no one possesses the kindred spirit capable of receiving this Dharma proclaimed with the drum other than the leader of India's freedom movement. The prayer for *Risshō-ankoku* is not a sound that can be heard by those resigned to slavery in a fallen country nor by the non-virtuous and arrogant who have profited through treachery by selling out their country in order to revel in extravagance. When they hear the drum, they grow frantic and tormented and cannot help but slander the Dharma.

It is not surprising that the true character of our *gyakku-senryō* would not be understood by diplomats pursuing fame and fortune or by Buddhist scholars who lack the sincere heart needed to comprehend the spirit of Buddhist teachings and so intellectualize them and end up writing intently about superficial issues of translation for third-rate magazines. If this were the kind of Dharma readily comprehended by such people, it would soon be trampled underfoot by the British police. How could the reverberation of this great prayer for *Risshō-ankoku* not create a response in the one truly seeking independence for India, oblivious of the cost to life and limb? For one who grieves the people's anguish, who laments the decline of the motherland, is it possible not to believe in and receive this prayer for *Risshō-ankoku* with an open heart?

When I heard Venerable's delight, that he "looks forward to hearing the sound of our Dharma drum" of *gyakku-senryō*, I, who have not found one kindred spirit in this three-thousand great thousandfold world,[12] knew in my heart that "this is the very one, this is the very person."[13]

---

12 *Sanzen-daisen-sekai* 三千大千世界. Often used to describe the whole universe. A thousand worlds make a small one-thousand world [*shōsen-sekai* 小千世界]. A thousand of them make a medium one-thousand world [*chūsen-sekai* 中千世界]; a thousand of them make a great one-thousand world [daisen-sekai]. Because of this triple multiplication by a thousand, it is called "three-thousand great thousandfold world."

13 For the mission of *Saiten-kaikyō* to materialize, thus fulfilling Nichiren Daishōnin's prophecy and thereby the prophecy of Buddha Śākyamuni as well, a person [in fact, a Bodhisattva disciple of the Origin Buddha 本化] with the capacity to receive the Odaimoku was indispensable. Guruji understood Gandhi to be this person. Seen in the light of Chapter II, *Expedients*, of the Lotus Sūtra, "Only a buddha together with a buddha can fathom the Reality of All Existence." 唯仏与仏 乃能究尽 諸法実相. Therefore, this person would be one who would share in the mission to bring emancipation to the Era of Final Dharma. The spiritual relationship between Guruji and Gandhiji can be understood in the context of Chapter II.

Who other than this person, the rightful one, could I possibly expound this teaching of India's *Risshō-ankoku* [the teaching to bring peace and tranquility to India through the Genuine Dharma]. The prayer for *Risshō-ankoku*, the Dharma sound of *gyakku-senryō* now has undoubtedly been transmitted to the Western Heavens. When Gandhiji beats the Dharma drum of Na Mu Myō Hō Ren Ge Kyō, and when the disciples of Buddha Dharma of Japan reside with his disciples, India's independence shall inevitability come in the near future. At long last! On this day in the Era of Final Dharma in the Western Heavens, the momentous mission shouldered by our master, Nichiren Daishōnin, born in Japan, has been fulfilled. Despite all those who despised or disparaged me, who can deny that I have fulfilled a humble part of the mission in the Western Heavens as "messenger sent back to inform"[14] as described in the *Eternal Duration of the Life of the Tathāgata* in the 6th scroll[15] of the Lotus Sūtra? Years of unswerving faith under adversity had been more than rewarded by Gandhiji's single remark. I have beaten my drum, the Dharma of *gyakku-senryō*, in the vast expanse of the three-thousand great thousandfold world searching for this person. He was, as I expected, that very one. Gandhiji was truly that person. Gandhiji was, as I expected, the Gandhiji I was looking for. Venerable, who perceived even sweet Japanese biscuits, a beautiful fan and cotton goods as bitter foes of India, not to mention his aversion to all Japanese state policy, had today without suspicion immediately believed and embraced as a peerless friend in his life of faith the music of an ancient Japanese instrument which dates back to the age of the gods,[16] the sound of the Dharma drum of Na Mu Myō Hō

14 遣使還告. In *The Eternal Duration of the Life of the Tathāgata* chapter of the Lotus Sūtra, the Tathāgata, the father in the analogy, sends home a messenger to inform his children, who have lost their minds by poison and refuse to take the superb medicine of the father, that their father has passed away. Upon hearing this, the children "finally awaken and come back to their right minds." [心遂醒悟] The messenger sent is a disciple of the Origin Buddha. "To inform" is to bring the message that the Eternal Buddha, as an expedient, manifested Parinirvāna for the sake of emancipating sentient beings. Upon final awakening of sentient beings to this fact, the disciple of the Eternal Buddha administers the superb medicine of Na Mu Myō Hō Ren Ge Kyō for them to take. This is how emancipation in the Era of Final Dharma is described to take place.

15 In scroll form, the Lotus Sūtra is encased and consists of 8 scrolls, 28 chapters and 69,384 kanji characters. 一帙八軸四七品　六万九千三八四　一一文文是真佛[法華経一部八巻] *The Eternal Duration of the Life of the Tathāgata* chapter is at the beginning of the 6th scroll.

16 The drum is also the first instrument that resounds before Buddha Śākyamuni starts to deliver the Lotus Sūtra.

Ren Ge Kyō, the prayer for *Risshō-ankoku*. The reverberation of the Dharma drum of Buddha Dharma of Japan was, likewise, the ineffable sound of the celestial drum that fortifies Venerable's ideals and conviction here at Wardha in the Western Heavens. The war drum of India's independence movement was the wondrous sound of a single fan-drum that Gandhiji beat as he burst into peals of laughter. When Venerable rejoices in the true purpose of Nipponzan's *Saiten-kaikyō* and joyously embraces the wondrous practice of Buddha Dharma of Japan's *gyakku-senryō,* and when India, thus, attains independence, perhaps for the first time, the frivolous will begin to discuss the role I played for the sake of my country, Japan, and Buddhism in Japan.

The two of us were drawn into Gandhiji's laughter, and we also burst into laughter and rejoiced. My happiness was such that I wondered if it were a dream. "Are you fond of drums? May I present you with one?" Rev. Okitsu stepped forward and offered Venerable a used, *shaku-sun*-sized, round hand drum[17] that had been offered to me by Mr. Miyamoto[18] when I left Japan on my mission of *Saiten-kaikyō* and had since been exposed to the elements.

Venerable's laughter rang out, and he accepted it. "Are you giving me a drum too? I shall beat it too. Ha, ha."

I lifted my drum, placed it in front of me and began to beat it. As I beat the drum chanting, "Na Mu Myō Hō Ren Ge Kyō, Na Mu Myō Hō Ren Ge Kyō," Venerable, still wearing a smile, started to beat his drum, uncertain as he tried to recall the chant written in my letter.

Rev. Okitsu became even more enthusiastic and said, "I'll teach you." His remark is most favorably described as being to the point, but how short it fell in decorum! I wonder if it were customary in the arrogance of English, so deficient in modest grace, to audaciously address even someone like Venerable with such words? How lacking in deference he must have appeared. I blushed with the thought. Oh no!

"You'll teach me? Good. Ha, ha." Venerable laughed and was enjoying beating the drum. Could Rev. Okitsu not grasp the invaluable

---

17 団扇太鼓. *Uchiwa-daiko* is a round drum with a wooden handle. *A shaku* [尺一寸] is approximately 30.3 cm, and sun is 3.03 cm. About 13 inches.

18 Miyamoto Unosuke 宮本卯之助, the 5th generation proprietor of Miyamoto Unosuke Shōten founded in 1861, which makes *taiko* drums as well as other festival instruments and *mikoshi* portable shrines.

guidance offered in this sage's response, which sought to bring out the best in others through his self-effacing humility? By the time I realized the unseemliness, the moment to intervene had already passed.

An attendant by Venerable's side doubtfully asked, "Tomorrow is your day of silence, and you won't be able to speak. You don't mind these people coming here?"

"I won't be able to speak, but we can sit here and see each other smile. I enjoy the monks coming here beating their drums." This kind of affection, when directed at his 370 million countrymen and women, drew forth the unified response of the Indian people, "Bapuji! Bapuji!" "Father! Father!" an honorary title befitting this sage. In the Lotus Sūtra, Lord Buddha repeatedly states that the Tathāgata is the parent of us sentient beings. This boundless parental affection had been inherited by this person.

"Stay as long as you like. Come here every day beating your drums while you are here." Our visit is now in a category that can be extended without limit. The Dharma sound of *gyakku-senryō* has tied us together with a thread of common joy. Ahh! Profound gratitude overwhelms me for the magnitude and wondrous workings of *gyakku-senryō*, whose merits far exceed my capacity. We decided to return to the bungalow momentarily and then head out to the school for the speech, gathering after 5 p.m. The audience, in an orderly manner, filled the expansive schoolyard, which gave the appearance of a drill field, and then overflowed out into the road. A stage was set up on the veranda above the entrance hall. We were both led to the stage. There was still 20 to 30 minutes left before the program opened. We stood on one side of the podium, faced the audience and wholeheartedly chanted the Odaimoku, beating the drum.

Gandhiji made his appearance after 5:30 p.m. and took his seat. He bowed to us with palms together as he took his seat. "Where is your drum?" he asked Rev. Okitsu. That drum had been placed in Venerable's hands about an hour ago. Bajaji declared the meeting open. Prayers and tributes of admiration were offered in accordance with the program. After 6 p.m., just about when the sun sets, Gandhiji was scheduled to give a speech for as long as 20 minutes. However, his speech was read by a young male disciple. After the speech, some started to head home. We stayed when it was decided the evening prayer would take place here. Lights were on by the time Gandhiji left at the end of evening prayer. We stood up and saw him off, chanting and beating the drum. The audience gradually thinned out as if untangling twisted thread.

Bajaji prompted us saying, “Let’s go home.”

As we started to walk down the staircase we ran into Venerable’s secretary, Kaka Kalelkar,[19] from whom I had parted uncomfortably after a disagreement we had on the train regarding the precept against taking life. He courteously greeted me and Rev. Okitsu respectively saying, “That was a very fine prayer.” Even for those who may not see eye-to-eye when it come to the precept against taking life, the ineffable sound of *gyakku-senryō* brings all together in one joyous state of mind.

Today was the day the Dharma drum was bestowed on Gandhiji. Today was the day the great Dharma drum was beaten on Gandhiji’s stage. It was the day the celestial drum in prayer for *Risshō-ankoku,* an offering from Japan, resounded in India’s revolutionary movement. All that is needed in *Saiten-kaiyō* from hereon is an extension of this day. Perhaps today can be said to be the precise time of “final awakening"[20] for the Indian people. The darkness of the long night that has shrouded India shall start to clear.

---

19 A close associate of Mahatma Gandhi, a great prose-writer, editor of *Sarvodaya* periodical and freedom fighter, Dattatreya Balakrishna Kalelkar [1885-1981] was lovingly known as Kakasaheb Kalelkar in Gujarat and all over India. Guruji met Kaka [uncle] or Kakasaheb on the train to Wardha when he first visited Gandhiji and ever since cherished a life-long friendship. Among all of Gandhiji’s associates, Guruji had the closest association with Kakasaheb. He attended various Dharma works of Nipponzan Myōhōji throughout Japan as a guest, and several members of Nipponzan Myōhōji and Sarvodaya studied under him.

20 心遂醒悟. Lotus Sūtra Chapter XVI, *The Eternal Duration of the Life of the Tathāgata*. Please refer to footnote 14.

5

Letter to Gandhiji [1]

October 4, 1933
Wardha, India

Na Mu Myō Hō Ren Ge Kyō

I am a disciple of the Preceptor, Buddha Śākyamuni, born in Imperial Japan.[2] My name is Fujii Gyōshō.[3] Since the introduction of Buddhism some 1,300 years ago and until recent years, my country, Imperial Japan, professed faith in Buddhism from the top on down. While China's Confucianism and Taoism were also introduced, what they taught us did not go beyond aspects of literature, philosophy and ethics in a civilization. As for religion,[4] it can be said that Japan is a purely Buddhist nation. There is no Japanese civilization[5] to speak of which was not influenced by Buddhism. Buddhism, which originated in India, is truly the womb for

1 This is an excerpt of the letter Guruji presented to Gandhiji on October 7, 1933.
2 大日本帝国. *Dainippon-teikoku*, officially Empire of Greater Japan, more widely known as Imperial Japan, was a political entity that existed from the promulgation of the Constitution of the Empire of Japan on 1889 until its defeat in WWII in 1945, which spanned over the reigns of Emperors Mutsuhito 睦仁, Yoshihito 嘉仁 and Hirohito 裕仁, now known by their posthumous names corresponding to their eras of Meiji, Taishō and Shōwa.
3 藤井行勝. Gyōshō means "practice is foremost supreme".
4 Here Guruji is defining religion to mean first, *Honzon*, the principle object of veneration; second, the people who are emancipated by the *Honzon*; and third, the teachings expounded by the *Honzon*, which are the methods to bring salvation. Shintoism, which is indigenous to Japan, lacks any formal doctrine regarding salvation, and the noumenon of Honzon is not clearly defined. Furthermore, what is meant by human beings becoming gods is not clear. Warriors or public figures have been posthumously enshrined as deities. Enemies of state power that are destroyed have also been enshrined as gods to appease their grudges and to prevent their spirits from wreaking vengeance. Therefore, from the perspective of Buddhist doctrine, Shintoism does not fulfill the prerequisite of a religion.
5 "Civilization is not about installing electric lights, having airplanes or producing nuclear weapons. What defines civilization in its entirety? It is not to kill; not to destroy; not to wage war. It is about people holding one another in mutual affection and respect. There is nothing else that defines a viable human civilization." From *Deeply Venerate the Triple Jewel*, found in *Tranquil is This Realm of Mine*.

Mahatma Gandhi portrait by Shri Upendra Maharati.

all civilizations of Japan as a people. From the perspective of our spirits edified for 1,300 years and more by Buddhism, Buddhism can be said to belong as much to Japan as to India. From the standpoint of Buddhism, wherever its teachings spread, the people are, without exception, Buddha's disciples and the country Buddha's abode.

When we, Buddha's disciples from a Buddhist nation, arrived at the land of its origin, all that greeted us at the abandoned, desolate sacred sites of Buddhism were the wild shrieks of monkeys. Among the 300+ million Indians, we met none with whom we could share Buddha's stories. As travelers crossing the sea from a distant country, we wondered whether the India we stepped foot on for the first time was the same India we have come to know through Buddha's scriptures. Our doubts arose not only from Buddhism being extinct in India, but everything—the government, society, education and industries—made us wonder whether this was the same India which once gave birth to Buddhism.

India, the country that gave birth to Buddhism, and Japan, the country which nurtured Buddhism, ought to easily understand one another, if so desired. In holy Gandhiji, I hope to find the real India that I have come to know through the Buddhist sūtras. For the sake of restoring the Indian civilization, for the happiness of the Indian people, I hope to find the real India in the people who accept humiliation and hardship for truth's sake at the cost of things in the world most difficult to put aside, such as treasure, wife and children, honor and social standing. At the same time, we wish to reveal the true purpose of Japan through the transmission of the Buddha Dharma of Japan.

When one's sincere, wholehearted love of country springs from one's religious belief, and, by the same token, when one's religious belief is an embodiment of the utmost devotion to the country, a country's survival is determined by the rightness or wrongness of its beliefs. The relative excellence and profundity of any given religion do not lie in the realm of philosophy, but are determined by how that religion actually influences the rise or fall of a nation. That being the case, Nichiren Daishōnin stated, "A nation prospers by the Dharma; and the Dharma's reverence manifests through the people."[6] In order for the country to prosper, the teachings put into practice by religion must be correct. His words mean that through the wholehearted faith of the people, the virtue and power of the right teachings will manifest.

Myōhō in the chant I do—Na Mu Myō Hō Ren Ge Kyō—is a translation of *Saddarma*, signifying righteous truth. It is a religious teaching for humans to profess faith in. *Renge* is *pundarika*, a metaphor for the adorned land. *Kyō* is "sūtra," signifying the complete immutability of the truth of this teaching, unaltered by the vicissitudes of time, the advent of sages or attempted destruction by demons. It is the name of the sūtra authenticated as Buddha's teachings. In the [eight] scrolls of the sūtra named *Myōhō-renge-kyō*,[7] Buddha expounded and revealed to the fullest the congruence between faith in truth and love for one's country that creates the adorned land. *Namu* is a phonetic representation of the ancient Indian term *namaskar*, which offers salutations to truth, salutations to the land, and salutations to the sūtra. Bowing is an expression of piety. Chanting Na Mu Myō Hō Ren Ge Kyō is a cry of utmost sincerity

---

6 Citation from *Risshō-ankoku-ron*.
7 *Saddarma-pundarika-sūtra* in Sanskrit.

in devotion to one's country, an expression of joy in grasping the truth, a proclamation of Buddha's gospel to the world, and a salutation offered in humble abidance.

The beating of the drum is frequently referred to in Buddha's scriptures, particularly in the Lotus Sūtra. Out of some 70,000 [Chinese] characters that comprise the Lotus Sūtra,[8] characters relating to the drum are found in more than 30 places. Also there is a Japanese legend that relates to the drum. Legend has it that a period of prolonged darkness shrouded the world. Various gods and deities converged in one place in order to lure the goddess of the sun from a rock cave whose entrance was blocked by a huge boulder.[9] Cocks were gathered to crow; and a young goddess danced and beat the drum. Its sound is said to have drawn the sun goddess out, piercing the long night with light. For this reason, a drum to pray with is always placed in front of altars enshrining Japanese gods. Anyone young or old, female or male, of high social status or low can beat the drum to pray. The sound of this instrument embodies the heart and mind of the Japanese people seeking light. It gives voice to the prayer of the Japanese people seeking escape from sorrow and suffering. It symbolizes our search for light in which the actual world of suffering is transformed into a Pure Land of peace. The sound of the drum is an expression of the workings of God hoping to awaken the people, who are trapped in an eternal slumber of darkness as opaque as lacquer with no hint of when dawn might come. The sound of this instrument represents the mind and heart that enunciates the simple chant of Na Mu Myō Hō Ren Ge Kyō.

---

8 Translated into Chinese by 鳩摩羅什 Kumārajīva [344-413] in 406.

9 *Kojiki* 古事記 or *Record of Ancient Things* is Japan's oldest extant chronicle compiled in 712. It tells the story of 天照大御神 Amaterasu-ōmikani [the goddess who shines in the heavens], who was the ruling goddess of the Higher Celestial Plain 高天原, and who was born from the left eye of the primeval being Izanagi. She represents the sun and is considered one of the gods from whom the Japanese Imperial family descended. Her younger brother, 素戔嗚尊 Susanoo-no-mikoto [god of wind, storms, oceans and snakes] was born from Izanagi's nose and was assigned to rule the sea. Wanting to descend to the underworld in order to see his mother, Izanami, Susanoo flew into a fit of rage which caused tremendous damage to heaven and earth and resulted in his banishment from heaven by his father, Izanagi. He decided to bid his sister farewell before leaving. Amaterasu, suspicious that he came to take over, proposed a challenge: each of them was to transform an object of the other's into people. Amaterasu created three women from Susanoo's sword while he created five men from her necklace. When she claimed the men were hers because they were born of her necklace, Susanoo destroyed Amaterasu's rice fields, hurled a flayed pony at her loom and killed one of her attendants. In fury and grief, Amaterasu, hid inside the heavenly rock cave [天岩戸 Ama-no-iwato], and the world was thrown into darkness for a long period of time.

Nichiren Daishōnin, founder of the Buddha Dharma of Japan, entitled the most crucial of his numerous treatises *Risshō-ankoku-ron.* He admonished the then-governing regent three times with this writing. On every occasion he was either sentenced to death by beheading, banished to a remote island or assaulted by mobs. *Risshō-ankoku-ron* states that the way to prevent calamities from befalling a country and to ensure lasting peace and comfort in mind and body for the people is to choose the most supreme and genuine of all the religions that exist. More specifically, the *Myōhōrenge-kyō* [The Sūtra of the Lotus Flower of Wondrous Dharma] has been regarded as supreme among all the teachings of the Buddha. Nichiren Daishōnin urged that this supreme teaching, *Myōhōrenge-kyō,* be embraced and upheld wholeheartedly, discarding all others. There are as many as 84,000 discourses[10] expounded by Buddha, but Nichiren Daishōnin ultimately arrived at the single phrase of Myō Hō Ren Ge Kyō as the crystallization of the Japanese people's love of country and a way to save it from impending danger and to bring lasting tranquility. In this sense, it is the flip side of militaristic patriotism, which drives the development of weapons of greater sophistication and power in order to defend the nation.

Unfortunately, no one in Japan, starting with the ruling regent at the time, initially believed in Nichiren Daishōnin's *Risshō-ankoku-ron.* Not only did the people doubt the teaching, they ridiculed, abhorred and were enraged, regarding it as one would an enemy who caused a parent's death. As a result, not only was Nichiren Daishōnin's life characterized by persecutions and ordeals so brutal as to be incomparable in the 3,000 years history of Buddhism, but his disciples and devotees, likewise, had to endure persecution, incarceration and death.

From that time onto today, some 700 years later, the history of his order has been stained with blood. Regrettably, this strong love of country of the Japanese people has resulted in a history marred by this horrendous brutality and woven by differing points of view as to which religion the country ought to profess faith in. But after a very long period of oppression and ordeal, today Japan has come to believe in Nichiren Daishōnin's *Risshō-ankoku-ron.*

I do not expect the Buddha Dharma of Na Mu Myō Hō Ren Ge Kyō founded by Nichiren Daishōnin will be easily believed and accepted

10 Chapter XI of the Lotus Sūtra, *Beholding the Stupa of Treasures.*

by the Indian people. In the past three years since my arrival in India, I know of no Indian who found faith in it. It is due not only to my lack of virtue, but because the profundity of *myōhō*, the ineffable Dharma, makes it, by nature, "difficult to believe and difficult to comprehend."[11] Buddha himself taught how incredibly difficult it is to have faith in this wondrous Dharma, more challenging even than crossing the Pacific Ocean with the Himalayas on one's back. Nichiren Daishōnin said that "if anyone were able to easily believe and accept this ineffable Dharma, it could not be anything but shallow."[12] Even if it takes ten, a hundred, 200 or 700 years, I will not grow weary in my aspiration to return Buddha Dharma of Japan to India. As clearly as seeing daylight, I believe the Indian people will believe in the Buddha Dharma of Japan when true tranquility and comfort come to India.

The Lotus Sūtra tells the following parable.[13] A father, who is in fact the eternal and ever-present Buddha, temporarily went abroad to another land. In his absence, the many children he left behind were deceived into taking poison.[14] They were unable to breathe, coughed up blood and rolled around on the ground in agony. "Where has our father gone? Hurry, someone help us!" they cried out loud, clawing the air. Upon his return, the father was startled to see his children writhing in agony. Because the father was a good doctor, he immediately gathered fine medicinal herbs, dispensed the most efficacious medicine and administered it to his children to detoxify the poison. The children who took this good medicine were healed and delivered from suffering; but others, whose body and mind were deeply affected by the poison, refused to take the good medicine. Their bodies were deeply stricken, and they had lost their minds. Led by compassion, the father conceived of a way to have these children take the good medicine. He was compelled, once again, to leave his suffering children and go elsewhere where he could not be seen. The children continued their tantrums, refusing to take the good medicine, but once the father was gone, they found no one to complain their pain to. As their pain intensified, they screamed out for their father's return. Choosing the right moment, the father first sent a messenger on

---

11 Citation from the Lotus Sūtra, Chapter VII, *The Parable of the Magic City*, and Chapter X, *The Teacher of the Dharma*.

12 観心本尊抄 *Kanjin-honzon-shō*.

13 Chapter XVI, *The Eternal Duration of the Life of the Tathāgata*.

14 Chapter XVI of the Lotus Sūtra, *The Eternal Duration of the Life of the Tathāgata*.

his behalf to administer the good medicine he had prepared.[15] At the urging of this messenger from a foreign land, the children finally took the good medicine that their father dispensed for their sake. Their bodies were relieved from the protracted suffering, and their minds awakened from delusional frenzy.[16] At this time, the father rushed home in headlong flight back to his beloved children. The sūtra preaches this as "comes back to his home."[17] Buddha Śakyāmuni, who has gone to another country up to this day, must now return to the country of his birth, to the country of his descendants. "I shall return, I shall return, to my country, to my home."

Proclaiming it as his mission, Nichiren Daishōnin deeply believed that it was he and his disciples, Buddha's disciples of Japan, who would one day administer the superb medicine that the father prepared and serve as his messengers to the Indian people, who are suffering from the poison as described in this sūtra. In numerous places throughout the Lotus Sūtra, it is clearly stated that the era designated for Buddha's messengers to be sent to India is 2,000 years after the Parinirvārna of the Preceptor, Buddha Sakyāmuni. The era designated is about to pass. The moans of 300 million Indian people reach the farthest corners of the earth. Nevertheless, somehow no one comes, from Japan or from any other Buddhist country, as Buddha's messenger to India to exhort the taking of the great medicine of *Myōhorenge-kyō*. If Buddha's golden words are not false, I believe before long the messenger will come to India without fail. I also believe when that time comes, the Indian people will take the good medicine and be delivered from their current suffering. I have cited this prophecy of the Buddha in the hope that the arrival of Buddha's messenger from Japan will come as soon as possible. Believing in this prophetic sūtra, I can easily believe in the day when the Indian people will chant Na Mu Myō Hō Ren Ge Kyō in one voice.

Oh Lord Buddha with boundless compassion, the promised era for the Tathāgata's return home to the country of India is about to pass. May you hastily return to India! This single phrase of prayer is the faith of Japanese Buddhist disciples and, at the same time, the unquenchable longing of the 300 million Indian descendants of the Tathāgata.

---

15 遣使還告.
16 心遂醒悟.
17 還来帰家.

6

THE PURPOSE OF ERECTING A STŪPA AND MAKING OFFERINGS

PROSPECTUS FOR BUILDING A STŪPA IN HANAOKAYAMA, KUMAMOTO PREFECTURE

Autumnal Equinox, September 1947
2,607th year of the Imperial reign[1]

Tranquil is this realm of mine,
Ever-filled with celestial beings
Gardens, groves, all kinds of temples and splendid buildings
With every kind of gem adorned.
Jeweled trees abound in blossoms and fruit,
A place where all the living play with glee
The devas strike the celestial drums,
Constantly making music,
Showering mandārava flowers
On me, the Buddha, and the great congregation.[2]

WITH THESE 10 SŪTRA VERSES, [Buddha Śākyamuni] revealed and taught aspects of the Buddha Realm Pure Land, the abode of the various Buddhas and Bodhisattvas. The greatest attribute of the Buddha's Pure Land is tranquility—the heavens and earth exist without natural catastrophes, societies are free from the fear of war, famine and plague, and the arts and sciences are conducive to peace, tranquility and pleasure. The land in which humans live is called the defiled land, a place where human life is threatened constantly by every kind of anguish, fear and affliction. When fear storms like bone-quaking thunder, suffering swells in a drowning flood and anguish engulfs like an impenetrable smog, who wouldn't constantly dream and yearn for a land free of fear,

---

1 皇紀. *Kōki*. A calendar based on the year of Emperor Jinmu's 神武天皇 accession as first emperor of Japan [660 BCE].
2 Chapter XVI of the Lotus Sūtra, *The Eternal Duration of the Life of the Tathāgata*.

a life without suffering and a community unburdened by misery. Religion is a response to the pressing issues of life. In the Pure Land, religion is not necessary, only in the defiled land. Religion is necessary for those who suffer, not for the peaceful and tranquil. Some point to the Land in the West[3] as a world free from suffering, and others to Heaven as a place of eternal life.

The aforementioned Lotus Sūtra makes no distinction between the defiled land consumed by conflagration where the people live and the Pure Land of tranquility and joy where the Tathāgata resides. Between the defiled and Pure Land, the realm's intrinsic nature is the same without distinction of purity or defilement. The Pure Land manifests where the Tathāgata resides and is the same land as the defiled land that manifests where the people reside. The difference between the Pure Land and the defiled land, in the final analysis, depends on the pureness or contamination in the heart and mind of those who reside there, according to the sūtra. Following the sūtra's teaching, "Even when all the living see, at the kalpa's end/[4] the conflagration burning/ Tranquil is this realm of mine" are the ten verses already mentioned and then the teaching that "This Pure Land of mine is never destroyed/ Yet, all see it as being consumed by fire/ Rife with grief, fear and various afflictions as such."

Society's greatest anguish and affliction is the calamity of a conflagration that burns everything down to the ground. In a time of war, our entire nation, too—men and women both old and young—experienced the horrors of a conflagration that raged both day and night. Buddha Dharma teaches that the cause of fear originates in the hearts and minds of those living in this realm. Although the flames of war have been extinguished, there is no way of knowing when the sufferings brought by war will cease. The lingering suffering has turned this land of ours into a stage on which the people must act out the tragedy of a downfall. Anyone seeing the karma of a defiled land manifesting in the torment

---

3 西方. The Western Pure Land of Amida.

4 An eon, a world-period, the longest period of time in the Indian cosmology. The universe is said to go through a repeated cycle of formation and destruction which consists of four eons [四劫]: 1) 成劫 kalpa of formation; 2) 住劫 kalpa of existence; 3) 懷劫 kalpa of destruction; and 4) 空劫 kalpa of nothingness. A complete cycle of these four is called a mahākalpa 大劫 or great kalpa. In the kalpa of formation, the natural world 器世間 as well as sentient beings 有情世間 come into existence. The kalpa of existence is when the formed world abides in peace. The kalpa of destruction is when the natural world and world of sentient beings are destroyed. And the kalpa of nothingness is a period of nonexistence.

of the people even after the flames of war have been extinguished would ponder on ways to relieve the suffering and bring it to an end. Bringing relief to the people's plight can happen in many ways. A host of relief facilities are required. However, if the defilement of the land is the singular result of delusions of the heart and mind, and the Pure Land the product of enlightenment of that heart and mind, would it not follow that Japan's path to liberation from all anguish and suffering is, in essence, to guide the people's hearts and minds in cultivating the karmic seeds of virtue and merit? If so, what can be done to bring peace, pureness and tranquility to a human heart and mind? The Lotus Sūtra's teaching is clear. Chapter XVI of the Lotus Sūtra, *The Eternal Duration of the Life of the Tathāgata* says:

> When living beings see me as extinct,
> And make offerings to my relics far and wide,
> All cherishing longing adoration,
> Thirsting in their heart to seek me out,
> Thus, all living beings surrender in their faith,
> Upright in character and gentle,
> Wholeheartedly wishing to see the Buddha,
> Not sparing their body and life
> Then together with all the Sangha,
> I once again appear on the Sacred Eagle Peak.

This passage expounds that following the Parinirvāna of the World Honored One, the Tathāgata, when stūpas tall, spacious and splendid, adorned with seven gems are built to enshrine the true body relics of the Tathāgata, and offerings are made, the suffering people will see these stūpas as places to take refuge. Their hearts will thirst for and seek the great compassionate vow of [the Tathāgata], and they will voluntarily shed their arrogance. They will become upright in character and gentle, at which time their realm is nothing other than the Pure Land, the abode of the Tathāgata. Japan, now a place of hardship, is not destined to remain a defiled land. Tomorrow it can be a Pure Land, a place where people live untroubled and content, a manifestation that comes from the merits of building a pure land, which materializes through the single working of the mind of those who reside there.

Chapter II of the Lotus Sūtra, *Expedients*, says:

Or if those in open plains,
Make Buddha shrines out of mounds of earth,
Or children who play
Gathering sand to make stūpas.
Persons such as these
Have all attained the Buddha Way.

It means that even a child's play of making stūpas from sand gathered at the roadside becomes the seed of realizing the Pure Land, and that child will attain unsurpassed awakening.

Chapter VI of the Lotus Sūtra, *Assurance of Future Enlightenment* says:

After the buddhas are extinct
He will erect stūpas of seven precious jewels,
And, also with flowers and incense,
Make offerings to their relics;
In his final bodily existence[5]
He will obtain Buddha-wisdom,
And attain Perfect Supreme Enlightenment,[6]
His land will be pure.

The above citation is Buddha Śākyamuni's prophecy of future enlightenment for his four principle disciples.[7] From the first awakening of the mind to the Buddha Dharma practice until the state of final bodily existence, the practice prescribed by the Buddha that leads to enlightenment is the construction of stūpas and the making of offerings to the enshrined Buddha relics. Numerous other references on erecting stūpas and making offerings are found in the sūtra. Guiding the human mind ought to be given the highest significance in building the Japanese culture, and erecting stūpas and making offerings is taught to

5 最終身.

6 等正覚. *Tōshōkaku*. The phonetic representation of *anuttara-samyak-sambodhi*, i.e., perfect supreme enlightenment.

7 迦葉 Mahā Kāśyapa, 須菩提 Subhūti, 迦旃延 Kātyāyana and 目連 Mahā-Maudgalyāyana. Also referred to as the four major voice-hearers 四大声聞, direct disciples of Buddha who heard his voice. Before the Lotus Sūtra was preached, these disciples believed they could never achieve Buddha wisdom. However, Buddha corrects this misunderstanding when expounding the Lotus Sūtra.

surpass all other practices in enlightening the human heart and mind. Obtaining Buddha-wisdom, attaining Perfect Supreme Enlightenment and making the land pure are integral to the merit of erecting stūpas and making offerings. The lesson of these sūtra verses is not for Kātyāyana[8] alone. I wish to erect a stūpa on Hanaokayama using the above sūtra verses as a foundation. When Buddhism was introduced to Japan, an imperial mandate decreed the rise of the Triple Jewel[9], and a charter was laid down that emphasized the wholehearted veneration of the Triple Jewel.[10] Many pagodas enshrining Buddha relics were constructed and offerings made, including Hōkō-ji Temple by Emperor Suiko, Shitennō-ji in Nanba along with others built by Crown Prince Shōtoku, and the academic temple attached to Hōryō-ji Temple. These works resulted in the culture of peace that prevailed in the Asuka and Nara periods. India's Ashoka the Great[11] was a great king who built a grand empire of culture, the like of which has never before or since been seen in the 5,000 years of Indian history. He erected 84,000 stūpas in his lifetime,[12] enshrined Buddha relics, and made offerings of relics to places far and wide throughout the world. Many stūpa ruins exist to this day. Both the golden words of the Tathāgata in the sūtra and the remains of history leave no room for doubt that when stūpas adorned with seven jewels to enshrine Buddha relics are erected and offerings made,

---

8 The aforementioned verses from Chapter VI were specifically addressed to Kātyāyana, prophesying his future attainment of enlightenment.

9 興隆三宝の詔勅. The Triple Jewel is the Buddha, Dharma and Sangha. According to documentation on the origin of Gangō-ji Temple 元興寺縁起, King Seong [Song 523–554] of Baekje sent a mission to the Japanese court in 538 during the reign of Emperor Kinmei 欽明 [552 according to Nihon Shoki] with an image of Buddha Śākyamuni and several sūtras. This has traditionally been considered the official introduction of Buddhism to Japan. In February 594, the 2nd year of the reign of Empress Suiko 推古, the imperial decree to facilitate the flourishing of the Triple Jewel was issued.

10 Crown Prince Shōtoku 聖徳太子 [574-622] brought Buddhist teachings into the center of Japanese government. He was the son of the 31st Emperor of Japan, Yōmei, and became Regent for Empress Suiko. He is credited with bringing peace and harmony to the Japanese nation, which was a quagmire of warring factions in this period, through the proclamation of the Seventeen Article Constitution, Japan's first constitution. That constitution, based on Buddhist teachings, prescribed the philosophical and religious principles on which Japanese government was based for 1,500 years.

11 Ashoka the Great [304-232 BCE] was an Indian emperor of the Mauryan Dynasty who ruled from 273-232 BCE. He is cited as one of India's greatest emperors. More is said about King Ashoka in *Inaugural Speech of the Kalinga World Peace Pagoda*, p. 179, and in *Land Purifying Ceremony of Lumbini*, footnote 16, p. 188.

12 Please refer to *Wondrous First Connection with Lord Buddha's Relic*, footnote 2, p. 9.

the world becomes peaceful and its people joyous. In other words, a Pure Land that enables life to prosper manifests. Since ancient times, the sacred writings of Buddhism have been called wondrous scriptures that guard the nation.[13] Guiding the hearts and minds of the people ultimately enables a nation to thrive and soar. I hereby vow to build a Buddha stūpa as a beacon for the rebuilding of Japan.[14]

Na Mu Myō Hō Ren Ge Kyō

Nipponzan Myōhōji
Nichidatsu

---

13 鎮護国家の妙典.

14 The Hanaokayama Peace Pagoda, the first one built by Guruji, was dedicated April 8, 1954 after seven arduous years of construction in the destitution of post-war Japan. The relic offered by N. Piyaratana Thero of Sri Lanka to Guruji, as described in *Wondrous First Encounter with Lord Buddha's Relic*, p. 9, was enshrined two days prior to the inauguration ceremony on April 6 under the *kurin* 九輪, also known as *kūrin* 空輪, the nine jewel-shaped wheels or rings at the peak of the pagoda. On the day of the ceremony, ten pieces of Buddha's sacred relics offered by India Prime Minister Jawaharlal Nehru were presented by Kakasaheb Kalelkar, and one was enshrined under the *kurin*. The remainder were bestowed to disciples and representatives of major cities in Japan and one was brought to Hawaii. Furthermore, the second World Pacifist Conference was convened at the dedication of the Hanaokayama Peace Pagoda. The first World Pacifist Conference had been held at Gandhi's ashram in Wardha in Dec. 1949, and it was decided to make Hanaokayama the venue for the second conference.

7

Tangyō-Raihai is the Law for World Peace

March 14, 1953
A message to the Peace Constitution Defense Rally
Kumamoto, Japan

Na Mu Myō Hō Ren Ge Kyō

It is universally true that living beings must consume other creatures to sustain their own lives. This is called survival of the fittest. Those preyed upon cannot resign themselves to such a fate. Here is the origin of struggle. To prevail in this struggle, it becomes necessary to assume a fierce and gruesome appearance or employ methods of deception and brute force. Every detestable and horrifying phenomenon originates from this struggle. In the struggle for survival, intraspecies struggles such as snake versus snake or cat versus cat, is even more tragic than a snake swallowing a frog or a cat gnawing on a mouse.

In Papua New Guinea, cannibal tribes known to consume human flesh still exist. They are abhorred and feared and called barbarians. Human beings see themselves as the master of all creation, and are considered the most evolved species, not because they are victors in the struggle for survival, but, on the contrary, because they have been gradually liberated from such a notion and have the ability to lead a life apart from it. From this life apart emerged religion and morality, setting forth noble goals to strive for in human life. Politics and economics were intended to be means to achieve these more lofty objectives.

The Old Testament in the Bible states that various birds, beasts and sea creatures, just like vegetables, were created for people to partake of and sustain themselves. Tragic as it may be for humans to devour cattle or whales, there may be a rationale that it cannot be helped for the sake of human survival. However, even the God Jehovah does not sanction humans consuming other humans for sustenance. Humans devouring humans would be an intolerable tragedy, even in the eyes of God Jehovah.

If survival of the fittest is a law of the biological world, cannibalism for sustenance might be an acceptable rationalization when seen from the cold theory of evolution. However, merciless and needless murders of other humans who ardently wish to live is a tragedy that deviates even from evolution's survival theory, which recognizes the need for self-sustenance, and marks the tragedy of modern society's barbarity with acts far worse than cannibalism.

When cannibals eat the flesh of other humans, it is said that several tribal members work together to kill one and share the meat among themselves. What is known as the modern states, in other words, a sovereign state or a defense state,[1] is a massive institution developed to maximize the cannibals' model of collaborative killing. The military specializes in research and training to develop the technology and skill to kill humans. Tragic as it may be to kill another human being for food, the number of people killed still would be limited. Yet, when the military engages in war, there is no limit to the number of people that can be killed. Not only is the number limitless, development in war over the years has been egged on by requirements to kill the greatest number of people as quickly as possible with as much brutality as possible and with the greatest possible efficiency. Atomic bombs satisfy all of these requirements.

In today's world in which war's objective is to senselessly murder massive numbers of people rather than killing others for sustenance, one can easily foresee that once the military is created and becomes involved in war, a situation develops where the weak and the strong are both destroyed and human beings can no longer live on the face of the earth.

---

1 Possibly a reference to a policy for the Advanced Defense State 高度国防国家. After the breakout of the Sino-Japanese War, the campaign to establish a new order was promoted starting in 1940 by Prime Minister Konoe Fumimaro 近衛文麿 [1891-1945] during his second cabinet. Military power was considered an important national strategy, and the campaign for the new order was an attempt to establish a centralized state structure with supporting ideologies to reinforce the nation's military capacity. The state structure was to integrate various systems, including political, social, financial, economic and strategic. An advanced defense state was its goal. To establish new order and thereby resolve domestic issues and defend Japan from the threat of the United States, Konoe felt the need for a powerful political organization and founded the Imperial Rule Assistance Association 大政翼賛会 in 1940.

The new president of the United States, Dwight Eisenhower, called atomic bombs weapons that protect peace. The new premier of the Soviet Union, Georgy Malenkov,[2] boasted during a speech given at, of all places, the funeral of his predecessor, the late Joseph Stalin, "Our sacred duty is to strengthen, in every possible way, the powerful Soviet Armed Forces. We are to keep them at the alertness for a crushing rebuff to any assault of the enemy."[3]

Whether it is an invention of a new weapon or a reinforcement of existing arms, these tools are ultimately used to perpetuate war, never to prevent war. Both the people of the United States and the Soviet Union were victors in the previous world war and gained enormous profit as a result. Relishing the profits that war brings has heightened their militaristic state of mind, and in this state of exhilaration they have become increasingly reckless, even at the risk of war. They see other nations as nothing more than potential adversaries and make repeated diatribes against the purported immorality of these perceived adversaries, threatening invasion, massacre, plunder and destruction.

In light of all this, the prospect of averting World War III appears dim. If we cannot prevent World War III, this world of ours will be engulfed by conflagrations like those of Avici hell,[4] condemning humanity to violent death, the ultimate punishment of being burned alive. If evolution's "survival of the fittest" is developed to the point where it undermines the security of the people rather than protecting life and causes the destruction and ruination of the world and of humanity, we must search for another law for the sake of our own security and, ultimately, for peace in the world.

Humanity no longer faces the threat of being easy prey to other species that inhabit the earth. If only we can stop humans from killing other humans, our personal security will be assured and peace will prevail in the world. Without the military institutions created to kill other human beings, mass killing cannot take place in the world.

Instead of imagining potential adversaries
Let us imagine a potential Heaven.

---

2 Became premier of the Soviet Union from 1953 to 1955 after Joseph Stalin's death.
3 English translation from the original Russian by Professor Alexander Konkretny.
4 Hell of incessant suffering, the worst hell of all.

Instead of suspecting others to be potential enemies
Let us believe they are children of God with innate Buddha-nature.
Instead of harboring mutual contempt,
Let us hold mutual respect.
Let each engage in *tangyō-raihai*, one to another.
At worst our lives may be taken,
Even so, let us perform *tangyō-raihai*.

Tangyō-raihai is the first step that opens the path for us to amicably come together, transforming the most bitter resentment and rancor. The single thing modern society has far too much of is struggle, while ruefully lacking the single act of *tangyō-raihai*. From the perspective of science, humans may be defined as those who engage in struggle. Regardless of the reality of struggle in human life, struggle is never the noble objective of humanity. Peace is humanity's noble objective. And it is religion that teaches us the path of *tangyō-raihai* [the single practice of bowing in veneration to the Buddha in others] that enables us to reach that goal. There is no religion that does not teach veneration. When we contemplate on our own security and peace in the world, we must step onto the true path of religion.

8

Requisition of Land[1]

July 27, 1953
Otaru, Japan

Na Mu Myō Hō Ren Ge Kyō

When the U.S. aid policy on Japan was reported by the papers on [June] 22, Director Young[2] was quoted as saying:

> Improvement in Japan's defense capability will allow for the incremental withdrawal of U.S. forces, thereby eliminating the friction that always occurs when foreign troops are stationed on sovereign territory.

The referred to friction that always occurs is nothing other than a host of immoral and overbearing crimes committed by foreign soldiers stationed here. According to the *White Paper on Crimes by Foreign Troops* published by the National Police headquarters, the number of crimes during approximately a year from April of last year when the Peace Treaty took effect until May of this year was 3,382 cases, which comes to a monthly average of 282 cases and a daily average of 9.4. Of the total number of crimes committed by foreign servicemen, those perpetrated by U.S. soldiers constitute the majority, ranging from murder, robbery,

---

1 Ahagon Shōkō 阿波根昌鴻 [1903-2002], known as the Gandhi of Okinawa, was a devout Christian and spiritual pillar of the nonviolent movement against U.S. military bases in Okinawa. He confided to Nipponzan's Rev. Utsumi Gyōshū 内海行洲 during a peace walk in Okinawa that he always carried this manuscript by Guruji on his person as a bible of nonviolent resistance. Ahagon was one of the residents of Ieson 伊江村 in Iejima 伊江島 whose home was seized at gunpoint by U.S. soldiers in 1955. All the families were evicted, and the village completely torched and bulldozed.

2 Most likely a reference to Director of Northeast Asian Affairs Kenneth T. Young of the State Department. Quotation is translator's rendition from Japanese.

rape, assault and infliction of bodily harm to fraud and others crimes, all of which are shameless acts.

Books like *Children of the Base*[3] or *Chastity of Japan*[4] are making headlines in the publishing industry. Aside from the crime statistics already mentioned, these books chronicle the breakdown in public decency and morality, which are being trampled by the stationed troops. The successful sales of this type of book attest to the awakening of the Japanese, who at last are trying to see the true colors of the Japan-U.S. Security Treaty.

The issue of permanent requisition of land in Uchinada village, Ishikawa Prefecture for a U.S. firing range occurred recently.[5] Some say Uchinada will develop into a political issue, but the failure to address the underlying political issue is what developed into the Uchinada incident. Even if the Uchinada issue is somehow resolved, unless the root political issue is addressed, innumerable similar incidents will follow throughout Japan. The government tried to persuade

---

3 基地の子. *Children of the Base*, compiled by Shimizu Ikutarō 清水幾太郎. A compilation of essays by school children living adjacent to U.S. military bases.

4 日本の貞操-外国兵に犯された女性達の手記. *Chastity of Japan—Memoirs of Women Violated by Foreign Soldiers* by Itoi Shigeko 糸井しげこ. Memoirs of four women raped by U.S. soldiers.

5 内灘村事件 [1952-1953]. The Uchinada incident was the first anti-U.S. military base campaign in post-WWII on mainland Japan. Struggles against U.S. bases were already taking place in Okinawa. As a result of the special demand for munitions arising from the Korean War in December 1952, and based on a request from the United States, the Yoshida cabinet decided to requisition the sand dunes and designated areas of the Japan Sea at Uchinada, a small fishing village in Ishikawa Prefecture, 200 miles northwest of Tōkyō. The requisitioned land was to be a site for a U.S. firing range to test Japanese artillery, which was being purchased in $1 million lots. People of the Uchinada village started their resistance under the banner, "Money lasts only years; land forever." Opposition by the prefectural assembly made negotiations difficult, but an agreement was reached on a limited requisition for artillery drills starting in March 1953 and continuing until May. Fish catches decreased in that time. When the government decided to extend the term indefinitely in June 1953, opposition intensified and firing was temporarily suspended. It resumed on June 15. Rev. Nishimoto Atsushi 西本敦 and two other Nipponzan Myōhōji monks started an indefinite fast and prayed at the impact area, while Rev. Nagai Gyōji 永井行慈 set up a makeshift tent in front of the Diet in Tōkyō to lead a concurrent fast. More than 30,000 local citizens and supporters sat in protest at the impact area, and the Hokuriku District Railway Workers Union refused to transport U.S. resources. The Weekly Sankei magazine reported in its August 16, 1953 issue that the reverberations of the hand drum by the monks were tormenting U.S. forces, and one officer was said to complain that he wanted the drumming to stop since it reminded him of Indian attacks. The U.S. military did withdraw from land specifically requisitioned for the Korean War, such as in the cases of Uchinada and Myōgi, but other major bases, including those in Okinawa, Kure, Yokosuka and Sunagawa, expanded.

villagers to give up their land but was unsuccessful in the face of unyielding opposition from local and prefectural citizens. Meanwhile, the United States remained intransigent, insisting on a June 15 date to commence firing exercises, demanding sternly that Japan settle all negotiations on the requisition no matter what measures it takes before then. Finding itself between a rock and a hard place, the Japanese government brazenly chose to extricate itself from this predicament by dismissing local opposition, ignoring public opinion and enforcing a takeover through state power. It started by whittling away at the opposition in order to erode the solidarity of the local community. It took the position that refusal to negotiate would leave the government with no choice but to enforce expropriation of the necessary land pursuant to the provisions of Article 3 of the Japan-U.S. Security Treaty, and that this enforced requisition could result in expulsion from the land without any compensation. Rather, the government suggested, it was far more sensible to negotiate and receive a hefty compensation. When a handful of greedy, opportunistic Liberal Party[6] assembly members got wind of the government's threat to expropriate the land by force, they started to secretly undermine the opposition's united front. It almost seemed as if the government's coercion might succeed. Promptly on June 15 at the appointed time, U.S. soldiers unreservedly began live artillery drills in Uchinada without any consideration for the citizens who sat in protest.

Uchinada is not the only example of forced permanent requisition in Japan by the United States. Its unbridled demand for land includes the foothills of Mt. Fuji, Mt. Asama, Mt. Myōgi and Mt. Aso. The total area seized by the United States thus far is so extensive as to be the equivalent of the entire Shikoku Island comprised of Iyo, Tosa, Awa and Sanuki regions.[7] When the Japan-U.S. Security Treaty was first signed,[8] the Yoshida Cabinet was derided as a traitor cabinet. While vari-

6 自由党. Conservative political party founded in 1945 by Hatoyama Ichirō 鳩山一郎[1883-1959], who served two terms as prime minister in the 1940s and 1950s. In 1955 it was joined with the Democratic Party to become the Liberal Democratic Party.

7 Shikoku is one of the four major islands comprising mainland Japan. Presently, the four prefectures of Shikoku are called Ehime, Kōchi, Tokushima and Kagawa. The total area is approximately 18,000 square kilometers.

8 The Japan-U.S. Security Treaty 日米安全保障条約 was initially concluded on September 8, 1951. On January 19, 1960, Article 1 was amended and the new Japan-U.S. Security Treaty, Treaty of Mutual Corporation and Security Between Japan and the United States of America 日米相互協力及び安全保障条約, was concluded.

ous parts of Japan are being sold off one right after another rendering them forever off-limits to Japanese nationals starting with Uchinada, it remains to be seen whether mandatory requisition will succeed, as some politicians optimistically scheme.

Moreover, why did the United States announce its intent to initiate test firing on June 15 without regard for the Japanese government, knowing of the deep-seated opposition among the local village community, prefectural assembly and, more broadly, the entire Japanese nation? The mission of the United States should be to guarantee the safety of the peaceful village as it engages in farming and fishing on a narrow strip of ancestral land and sea under the auspices of the Peace Constitution; and we wonder where this contrary, psychological mindset comes from that promotes the un-peaceful purposes of war by using its power to steal the land and sea from farmers and fishermen, depriving them of their means of livelihood.

In *A Study of History*, Professor Arnold J. Toynbee[9] explicates on this Western psychology.

> When we Westerners call people "Natives," we implicitly take the culture out of our perceptions of them. We see them as trees walking, or as wild animals infesting the country in which we happen to come across them. In fact, we see them as part of the local flora and fauna and not as men of like passions with ourselves; and, seeing them thus as something infra-human, we feel entitled to treat them as though they did not possess ordinary human rights. They are merely natives of the lands which they occupy; and no term of occupancy can be long enough to confer any prescriptive right. Their tenure is provisional and precarious as that of the forest trees which the Western pioneer fells or that of the big game which he shoots down.

9 Arnold J. Toynbee [1889-1975] was a British historian who is most famous for his 12-volume *A Study of History*, written from 1934 through 1961. In it he sought to examine history on a global scale, writing of the rise and fall of civilizations rather than adhering to the more common and accepted method of study of nation-states or ethnic groups. He saw the rise of every civilization as a creative response to physical and social challenges. Toynbee was unusual among historians because of his emphasis on the role religions played in civilizations over other aspects of society. Toward the end of his life he is quoted as saying, "The coming of Buddhism to the West may well prove to be the most important event of the Twentieth Century."

Professor Toynbee then poses a rhetorical question:

> And how shall the "civilized" Lords of Creation [naturally limited to Westerners[10]] treat the human game [this is a reference to Asians and all other ethnic groups of people], when in their own good time they come to the possession of the land which, by right of eminent domain, is indefeasibly their own?

The Lords of Creation [limited to Westerners] have given the answer to this question over an extensive period of time:

> Shall they treat these "Natives" as vermin to be, or as domestic-able animals to be turned into hewers of wood and drawers of water?

From ancient times, various ethnic groups have inhabited land throughout the world. The Yamato [Japanese] people live in Japan. Some 2,600 years are said to have passed since the Yamato people built a nation on Japanese land. However, in the eyes of Americans, the Japanese do not have any prescriptive right to Japanese territory. Just like birds, which from the ancient past have made the crown of trees their abode but are not considered to have prescriptive rights to the crown of trees nor foxes to their foxhole, likewise, Americans can expel Japanese people who have long lived on Japanese land simply because they so desire. U.S. war objectives become supreme commands for the Japanese. At any time, the United States can issue a supreme order and expropriate land.

In the days of the Sino-Japanese War, the Japanese Kwantung Army summoned representatives of Manchurian and Korean farmers to Hsinking[11] in order to impose the obligatory delivery of their crops. The army loudly insisted that the farmers' cooperation with the Japanese war was a supreme order. Now it is Japan's position to be subject to supreme orders from the United States. Karmic retribution has manifested in

---

10 Translator's note: The insertions in brackets appear to be by Guruji.

11 Xingjing or Hsinking 新京. In 1932, when the independence of Manchuko was declared by the puppet government installed by the Japanese military, the capital was renamed Xingjing. After Japan's defeat it reverted to its original name Changchun and is now the capital of Jilin province in the People's Republic of China.

this lifetime.

If the "Natives" hold on to the land they occupy and dare to refuse permanent expropriation by the United States, without exception they will be regarded as vermin living on that land. And because they are seen as vermin like rats or snakes, they must be expelled. Communists top the list of vermin, followed by socialists, intellectuals and various pacifists. These are people who provoke animosity in the United States.

Others—like professional killers who serve the United States by hunting down vermin, such as the National Security Force,[12] along with Democratic and Liberal party members and the cabinet who willingly take on the role of cajoling the people, as well as cooks, cleaning staff, prostitutes and young *pan-pan* girls [prostitutes catering to American soldiers during the Occupation]—are obedient to U.S. orders and are harmless. These docile and domestic-able animals can be trained to understand English to the extent of obeying orders. Topping the list of domestic-able animals are the members of the Yoshida Cabinet, followed by members of the Democratic Party, Reform Party,[13] the National Police bureaucrats, National Police Reserve, National Security Force, proponents of rearmament and anti-communists. For the time being their upbringing rewards them with subsidies. That being said, even the life of a domesticated animal is tenuous; it is never unconditionally guaranteed. It is like swine and chicken that are fed and housed in a pen or a coop but are not necessarily guaranteed a long life by the master. We must bear in mind that the same holds true for us.

The Western civilization is also called the Christian civilization. Western religion is largely Christian. Christianity's distorted views lie at the root of the Westerners' view of the world. Let me attempt to summarize Germany's Ludwig Feuerbach's[14] opinion as an example.

---

12 保安隊. A ground force of approximately 110,000 that was founded in 1952 to replace the National Police Reserve 警察予備隊. It is the forerunner of the Self-Defense Forces, which comprise of the three services on land, sea and air, established in June 1954.

13 Reform Party 改進党 [1952-1954] was led by Shigemitsu Mamoru 重光葵 [1887-1957] and Secretary General Miki Takeo 三木武夫 [1907-1988]. It joined forces with Hatoyama Ichirō's group 鳩山一郎 and formed the Japan Democratic Party 日本民主党 in 1954.

14 Ludwig Feuerbach [1804-1872] was a German philosopher and anthropologist. He studied under Georg Wilhelm Friedrich Hegel, a German philosopher who represented German idealism. He later became part of the Young Hegelians, a radical offshoot of Hegelian philosophy, which criticized Hegel's metaphysical assumptions yet used Hegel's dialectical method. In *Essence of Christianity*, Feuerbach argued that God was a human invention, a projection of human ideals.

> Thought and disposition found in Christians are the same as in the Israelites. [That is to say, the purpose in creating the world was for Israel alone. The world was created for the sake of the Israelites, the fruit of the world; other nations are like husks of the world.] Christians inherited this thought and claim [that all creation exists for humans, humans exist for Jesus Christ and Jesus Christ exists for God. God created the world for the chosen people. There is no purpose in God's creation other than that which serves the Church.] The origin of Christian thought furthermore holds that Christians are masters of the Earth, and the world is in accord with God's justice; so, by the same token, the immoral or heathen ownership of their own country goes against God's justice.[15]

A distorted religious view exists that American world domination serves God's justice because they are Christians, and communist nations, such as the Soviet Union, built by the depraved or the irreligious, are illegitimate entities, which do not meet God's justice.

On the other hand, communist nations possess a distorted view arising from their belief in science. The misguided view on science inevitably arises from the theory of social evolution that is predicated on Karl Marx's dialectical materialism, which subscribes to perpetual armed revolution until the realization of a world governed by communist regimes following the overthrow of capitalistic rule. The distorted religious view of Christianity in the United States and the distorted view of science in communism in the Soviet Union have created a menace to humankind. This menace to world humanity comes from their possession of weapons of the greatest brutal killing power and destructive force.

Whether talking about religion or science as developed in the West, the ingrained myth that sees violence as omnipotent and affirms murder has caused the West invariably to fall into the crisis of mutual slaughter and destruction. Differently put, this goes to show the lack of a religion of peace or pacifist thought in the West.

If we are to successfully prevent war between the Soviet Union

---

15 Parts of this translation were taken from *Essence of Christianity,* translated into English by Marian Evans, 3rd edition, Kegan, Paul, Trench Trubner & Co, 1893, p. 298-299 of Appendix 10. Bracketed portions appear to be Guruji's paraphrasing of Feuerbach.

and the United States, we must, on one hand, bring change to the egoistical purpose and sentiment found in the American belief of creation, and, on the other hand, bring an end to the delusions instigated by the communists of animosity, struggle and vengeance. Instead, we must work so that a spiritual life based on trust, benevolence and compassion is embraced. This deep-rooted calamity cannot be resolved short of a spiritual revolution in the West at large.

According to Professor Toynbee, his earlier description not only characterizes what Westerners have done over the centuries, but also what they intend to continue doing today as their innate, rightful prerogative.

Emigration policy for settlements abroad adopted in Britain in fact resulted in complete displacement of native peoples in various parts of the world. Likewise, the forced expropriation in Uchinada casts a shadow of apprehension on the Japanese about our future; we, too, sooner or later may have to face eviction from our country or annihilation due to initiatives taken by Caucasians to implement their own settlement policies. Japan ruled Korea in a similar fashion but failed. Japanese bought land belonging to Koreans cheaply, and then drove them out of Korean land. These people had to leave their homeland, harboring resentment in their hearts. Some moved to Japan and others to Manchuria. Groups of young Japanese agricultural settlers trained at Uchihara, Ibaragi Prefecture,[16] were sent out to purchase and cultivate Manchu land. Manchurian farmers were expelled from the land of their ancestors' graves and fled into the woods. As soon as the Japanese rule collapsed, they returned from the woods to kill male settlers and trample infants to death. Women and girls were forced to toil as servants, barefoot in the cold, and were made to give birth to Manchurian offspring. We must realize the extent of enmity and rage among the people incurred by power politics

16 満州開拓青少年義勇軍内原訓練所 Uchihara Youth Brigade Training Center for Developing Manchuria [1938-1945]. The center gave approximately 87,000 youth between the ages of 15 and 19 basic military and agricultural training before sending them to rural areas in Manchuria. Although the stated goal was to train the youth in farming to facilitate harmony between Japan and Manchuria, in time the youth took on aspects of colonial troops and were used to maintain order and military preparedness against the Soviet Union. Approximately 25,000 lives of the youth brigade were claimed by war, freezing weather and starvation. In 1945 with the entry of the Soviet Union into the war, the majority of settlers were stranded in the regions adjacent to the border with the Soviet Union. Of the 270,000 to 320,000 total agricultural settlers sent, only 110,000 returned after the war.

through legal justifications. Through the actions of the United States, we are about to pay for the bad karma created by the Japanese expropriation of lands in Korea and Manchuria.

Dr. [Radhabinod] Pal[17] discussed Japan's population problem with an American official. The American official offhandedly commented that the solution was quite simple. Dr. Pal asked what should be done, and he replied, "Well, all you have to do is stop sending food to Japan. Then, 20 million Japanese would die of starvation in 45 years." He was not joking. Completely dumbfounded, Dr. Pal's jaw dropped, and he was left speechless. Dr. Pal observed what a diabolic coldness lies at the bottom of Westerners' view of us Asians.

On the 175th anniversary of the Declaration of Independence, U.S. President Harry Truman stated,

> We must remember that Korea is only part of a wider conflict. The attack on freedom is worldwide. And it is not simply an attack by fire and sword. It is an attack that uses all the weapons that a dictatorship can command: subversion, threats, violence, torture, imprisonment, lies, and deceit. . . And we must continue the struggle to overcome the constant efforts of the Soviet rulers to dominate the world by lies and threats and subversion.[18]

We do not need to hear the U.S. censure of the Soviet Union for the raw memory of the Soviet Union's falsehoods, threats, torture,

---

17 Dr. Radhabinod Pal [1886-1967] was a professor of the Law College of the University of Calcutta and judge of Calcutta High Court. He was appointed to the International Military Tribunal for the Far East's trial of Japanese war crimes and delivered one of the three dissenting opinions. While condemning Japan's wartime conduct as "devilish and fiendish," he held that the defendants were not guilty of Class A war crimes. And he believed the tribunal was more a court of retribution and not a court of impartial justice. In his dissent, he wrote, "The Trial held according to the definition of crime now given by the victors obliterates the centuries of civilization which stretch between us and the summary slaying of the defeated in a war. A trial with law thus prescribed will only be a sham employment of legal process for the satisfaction of a thirst for revenge . . . Formalized vengeance can bring only an ephemeral satisfaction, with every probability of ultimate regret; but vindication of law through genuine legal process alone may contribute substantially to the re-establishment of order and decency in international relations." Justice Pal also pointed out the illegitimacy of the use of atomic bombs and that the victors, too, should be brought before tribunals. His dissenting opinion was not allowed to be read at the tribunal.

18 Address at the ceremonies commemorating the 175th Anniversary of the Declaration of Independence, July 4, 1951.

imprisonment and aggression by fire and sword still lies within us. Right-wing organizations in Japan utterly loathe the Communist Party.

Along with this fear of Russian aggression, we have come to see clearly the implications of America's Japan-U.S. Security Treaty. Since the end of WWII, U.S. leaders have been mainly preoccupied with expanding their global influence or even more accurately, to broaden the U.S. sphere of absolute control in order to compete with and combat communist nations. Consequently, people of foreign nations, foreign governments and foreign lands have been constantly subjected to American hegemony and abuse, which is characteristic of power politics. Examples of intimidation are plentiful and came in quick succession in the territories of Amami Ōshima,[19] Okinawa and the Ogasawara Islands;[20] Japan has had to endure pressure on the government to expropriate its former military bases and exercise grounds; coercion to rearm; destruction of people's livelihood in agriculture and fishing; and abuse and oppression of the people's movement in the Okinawa Islands, which seeks to revert to Japanese sovereignty.[21]

As for Okinawa where the entire island has been turned into a military base, not only is the livelihood of its people not guaranteed, even the lives of its people are not assured. Reports say that school facilities on the islands under direct U.S. rule are no better than horse stables, and close to 30 percent of the youth are unable to attend school. The legal basis for this unbridled expansion of U.S. power in Japan and the rea-

---

19 Amami Ōshima 奄美大島 is a major archipelago in the Amami Islands, a group of subtropical islands in Kagoshima Prefecture about 300 km north of Okinawa and about 380 km south of Kyūshū.

20 The Ogasawara Islands 小笠原諸島 is an archipelago of more than 30 subtropical and tropical islands, located about 1,000 km south of Tōkyō. Iōjima [Iwo Jima], one of the islands, is at the southern end of the Ogasawara Islands with a U.S. military base and its staff of about 400.

21 When postwar Japan was first reconstituted under a "Peace Constitution" in 1946 and sovereignty returned to the government of Japan in 1952, Okinawa was excluded from both processes and remained under U.S. military control until 1972. It was the "war state" that made Japan's "peace state" possible. In general, Okinawa suffered immeasurably more than mainland Japan in the war, and that experience generated a deep commitment to pacifism; nevertheless, when the islands were eventually returned to Japan in 1972, the U.S. bases remained intact. Constitutional pacifism and local self-government proved empty promises. When at last the Cold War ended, Okinawans hoped anew that the bases would be removed and that a peace orientation would replace the war orientation. But they slowly learned that Pentagon plans were predicated on retention, even beefing up, the facilities, and that the Japanese government was committed to following the U.S. government's lead.

son why Japan must acquiesce is found in the Japan-U.S. Security Treaty [1951] concluded by the Yoshida cabinet. *Administrative Agreement under Article III of the Security Treaty between the United States of America and Japan* stipulates, "The United States shall have the rights, power and authority within the facilities and areas which are necessary or appropriate for their establishment, use, operation, defense or control." Therefore, the government is obligated to enforce expropriation of land for use by the United States over any opposition by the people, no matter how great, so long as the United States sees the need and deems it appropriate. The job of the Japanese government is no more than that of an administrative agency working on behalf of the United States, which is at liberty to use Japanese land as it will. Once this is understood, any measure taken by the government has no credibility with the people.

The name "security" is a disguise. In truth, it is nothing other than legitimizing, sanctifying and effectively implementing the United States' extortion, lust for power and sense of superiority over Japanese territory. Japanese veterans were purged or driven into the mountains and forests for reclamation work after the war.[22] It is dubious enough when a former belligerent military makes the audacious claim that it now wants to ensure Japan's security, but it goes even further to use security as the pretext to permanently expropriate land freely in more than 700 locations within this land-starved country. The U.S. military has come into farming villages and fishing communities, which are diligently working to create peace, and has destroyed their means of livelihood. Vast areas of land are being devastated by the firing of live ammunition and by a myriad of war games that incite a mind of war. They can call the drills or shelling "necessary and appropriate," but ultimately it is training in murder and destruction. Those frightened by this training in murder and destruction are not the communist nations. The truth is these shots fired for intimidation are a demonstration of force against the Japanese.

Still painful and vivid in our collective memory is the experience that no matter how intense or massive military exercises may be, no matter how extensively arsenals are built up, not only do they fail to

---

22 6.5 million Japanese were left in various places in Asia and the Pacific when Japan was defeated, of which 3.5 million were Army and Navy soldiers. The rest were civilians including women and children of middle and lower class settlers who were sent out to develop the sphere of the empire. The government promoted cultivation of undeveloped land as a way to resolve the food shortage as well as to encourage returnees to take up agriculture as a means of sustenance.

assure peace or security in a nation-state, they provoke apprehension and danger, sacrifice and disgrace. From this realization, Japan has resolutely turned a new leaf, cast away the old myth of security through arms and war, and avowed to step into the uncharted waters of building a permanent pacifist state as a herald of a new age in the history of world nations. Japan's aspiration to create a nation of peace is not following a path well-trod by others due to a global outbreak of peace. Quite the contrary, in a global landscape fraught with the danger of aggression that threatens the tragedy of human extinction, we are the ones determined to press forward in creating an everlasting peace while prevailing over hardship in order to bring salvation to our time. Therefore, Japan as a pacifist nation must refrain from confronting anyone with arms, even aggressors or provokers of war, but instead endure all evil for the sake of these aggressors. We must bear no hatred, enmity or mind of war towards anyone. Collective life in a society built on violence, ruthlessness, hatred, enmity or a mind of war is not sustainable. Only when respect, veneration, gift giving, offering and sustaining others[23] are mutually extended can lasting prosperity of the human species be attained and security of individuals guaranteed.

In all circumstances we must nurture a religious and moral disposition of peace, believe in the ultimate and just victory of the True Dharma and emancipate ourselves from the terror of violence. The most formidable mission shouldered by the Japanese people is to overcome armed aggression with unarmed peace. It is indeed a formidable mission.

Not only were agriculture and fishery destroyed in the name of military exercises, and public morals undermined by the establishment of brothel villages,[24] the National Police Headquarters' white paper on crime reports the crimes committed by U.S. soldiers stationed in Japan and lists every conceivable crime, including murder, robbery, rape, theft,

23 Fuse-kuyō 布施供養. *Fuse* means "gift" [Sk. *dāna*] whether in cash or goods to a person, especially to a monk. *Kuyō* means "offering and sustaining" [Sk. *pūjā*], generally an offering of food, drink, clothes or the like to Buddha, monk, teacher or the deceased.

24 Comfort stations were hastily set up in villages to cater to the Occupation Force along with brothels in the cities nearby the bases. Some sources suggest that these comfort villages and brothels [the *tokushu-ianshisetsu-kyōkai* 特殊慰安施設協会 RAA: Recreation and Amusement Association] were set up due to pressure from the Occupation Force; other sources indicate that they were a voluntary measure from the Ministry of Home Affairs intended as a human bulwark to protect the general female population from being raped. Unlike the comfort stations during the war, women were recruited without being

assault, destruction of property, fraud and embezzlement. Not included are numerous crimes of murder, robbery, rape, assault and destruction by stationed troops that were hushed up and never saw the light of day. Most likely those numbers multiply the statistics by ten times or more, a fact directly experienced by the general public.

The government greatly fears violence by the Communist Party, yet it has never brazenly committed crimes of this magnitude against society. Why does the government not fear the harm to society from these crimes violating law and morals committed by the troops stationed in Japan? Expropriation of the Uchinada village was enforced by the power of the so-called government, a political organization representing a mere fraction of society, without regard for the villagers' opposition, the prefectural residents' aspirations nor for public opinion; the only consideration was for a small minority of constituents and their interests, for example, munitions manufacturers. How can an amicable resolution be made? Without it, the seeds for a domestic uprising have been sown. The source of domestic unrest is never found within the peaceful populace but always comes from an abuse of political power that oppresses the people.

Without a U.S. military presence, the possibility of communist nations exploiting the opportunity and invading Japan as outlined in John Foster Dulles' vacuum theory may not be so farfetched.[25] If communist troops chose Japan as the next target for invasion, we could see a repeat of what happened to the battle lines in Korea, and no doubt they could take on the Japanese Security Force with its scant, junky, obsolete weapons or a few cowardly divisions of the stationed U.S. forces. They have off-handedly declared that in as little as 70 hours they could completely occupy Japan. However, ought we succumb to communist propaganda threatening aggression, either direct or indirect, and thereby tolerate

---

told specifics other than that housing, food and clothes would be provided. Many left after learning what was involved, yet 1,600 women, who either had no other means to sustain themselves or who were coerced into bonded labor, registered. The RAA was officially terminated in January 1946 by the passage of a law which made public prostitution illegal. This law came at the same time as General Douglas MacArthur's order declaring all places of prostitution off-limits, most likely because of the high incidence of sexually transmitted diseases among American soldiers. However, patronage of prostitution did not cease.

25 John Foster Dulles, dispatched to Japan as a special presidential envoy by President Harry Truman, argued for the rearmament of Japan, saying a nation without an armed military was like a vacuum into which foreign invasions can flow, like air fills an empty bottle. Guruji further refutes this argument in his speech, *In Defense of the Peace Constitution*, p. 131.

direct and indirect invasion by the United States?

The definition of a war of aggression has yet to be established by international law, but does not occupation of foreign territory, intimidation of foreign governments, indifferent treatment, control and exploitation of foreign people constitute acts of aggression? Not only do we not need foreign troops throughout Japanese land as part of the Japan-U.S. Security Treaty, but we demand immediate withdrawal of all foreign troops for endangering the country and provoking apprehension among the Japanese people.

We might be tempted to yield to the belief that Japan's plight is desperate if we consider Japan standing firm in defense of its constitution of disarmament and renunciation of war on one side, while on the other side superpowers with massive arsenals and nuclear weapons wantonly display their egoism and lust for power. It is possible that from here on out the Japanese people could be subjected to cruel mistreatment by either superpower, the Soviet Union if not the United States. No matter how cruelly we are treated, there is no disgrace for the nation of Japan, though it cannot be called an honor. Moreover, the Japanese as a people would have done nothing to be blamed for. A nation or state which abuses and affronts a disarmed nation is truly to be blamed, and it is their indelible disgrace. The outcome of countering of arms with more arms and defending peace with war is nothing but piles of corpses and hard feelings. The United States shall return home from the Korean War leaving piles of those who died in vain and having incurred the resentment of women and children. What is constructive and brings ultimate victory in building peace is to stop relying on violence and to refuse to abet the crimes of war and murder. To this end, renunciation of war through demilitarization is imperative.

The enforced requisition at Uchinada is merely the beginning of the Japanese tragedy; and the unlimited and permanent expropriation of the land for military bases and training grounds is only one part of it. The real tragedy for Japan would be a partition of the land to divide-and-rule along with a murderous war that pits Japanese against fellow Japanese. Close to home we have actual examples of this in the Korean War, which was caused by the division of Korea at the 38th parallel, and the continuation of the Chinese Civil War.[26] An example farther away is the division of

26 国共内戦. Literally the Nationalist-Communist Civil War [1927-1949]. It was fought between the Nationalist Party and the Chinese Communist Party.

Fasting and Praying Against War and for Nonviolence, November 3, 1951, Shinbashi, Tōkyō. Other banners read: "Defend the Pacifist Constitution," "Complete the Peace Treaty, Adhere to Neutrality," "Against All Wars and Use of Force," and "Freedom of Speech, Gathering and Association."

Germany into East and West. These are all hostilities between liberalism and communism. When Dwight Eisenhower announced his six-point policy immediately after assuming office, one point was to have Asians fight the wars in Asia. Given the ages-old history of peace among Asian people, and given the absence of any real reason to war upon each other today, war objectives have to be created and principles of war provided to ensure that wars would be fought by Asians. The United States' propaganda states that only liberalism guarantees human happiness; next, humanity must protect liberalism; America, the supreme orthodoxy of liberalism, deserves collaboration in protecting it; therefore, communism, the enemy of liberalism, must be countered collectively by every nation of the free world in every corner of the world; and, finally, countering communism is a sacred war objective of the Asian nations, particularly the Japanese government. Acts of war in Korea, Formosa and other parts of Asia are perpetuated under this notion of shared purpose.

On the other hand, those who question U.S. invasions and the Japanese government's servile foreign policy believe that the U.S.

military presence severely oppresses the Japanese aspiration to build a nation of peace. Hence, proponents of U.S. troop withdrawal are turning to communism as a means of denouncing the United States. Communism advocates the use of violence to undermine the authority of the other under the guise of militant materialism.[27] In order to execute violence, the Japanese Communist Party would have to import weapons from the Soviet Union or Communist China. Testimony provided at the Foreign Affairs Committee of the House of Representatives on the 20th of this month claims the Public Service Investigation Agency has reliable information that the Communist Party already possesses advanced weapons.

If Asians can be made to fight wars in Asia—such as Koreans fighting the war in Korea and Chinese fighting the war in China—and if the Japanese likewise are made to fight wars against each other in different parts of the country, Japan most likely will be divided and ruled just as they took free reign and willfully divided Korea.

Currently, 900,000 Japanese reside in the Ryūkyū Islands.[28] Ryūkyū and the Ogasawara Islands were divided from Japan to be ruled by the United States, just as the Soviet Union divided and assumed control of the Kuril Islands and Sakhalin. However, these territories are not big enough to take on Japan. Therefore, Japan needs a bit more dividing up. The treaty with Japan provides the language for further partition by enabling permanent expropriation of Japanese territory. Thus, it is likely Japan will be gradually neutralized, divided, subordinated and turned into a theater of war.

Who would not wail aloud at the tragic thought of Japanese citizens, who have declared a pacifist nation, engaging in merciless, mutual mass slaughter of their fellow countrymen and women with weapons provided by the Soviet Union and the United States? No matter how much our principles and ideologies conflict, even if we are

---

27 According to V.I. Lenin's *On the Significance of Militant Materialism*, militant materialism seeks to carry on an untiring campaign of atheist propaganda, using both communist and non-communist sources, in order to defeat the "graduated flunkeys of clericalism," a phrase he borrowed from the 19th century socialist philosopher Joseph Dietgen. Lenin's essay was first published March 12, 1922 in *Pod Znamenem Marksizma*, a journal published in Moscow from January 1922 to June 1944 with the purpose of popularizing materialism and atheism.

28 琉球列島. A chain of islands in the western Pacific Ocean at the eastern end of the East China Sea stretching southwest from Kyūshū to Taiwan. They include Okinawa, which is the largest of the Ryūkyū Islands.

divided left and right because of it, we, the Japanese people, must not take to violence and kill each other. Before turning to violence, we must awaken to the revered mission bestowed on us by the divine,[29] a life-affirming mission to be embraced by our people.

Whether financial capital, as in the case of the United States, or production, as in the case of the Soviet Union, the present civilization is founded on the supremacy of material goods. A material-centric view naturally has no regard for things spiritual in life, such as human hope, supplications or imagination. The next war cannot possibly be averted without radical change to this material-centric mindset. The next war means self-destruction of the material civilization. We must overcome the reprehensible civilization that sanctions murder and plunder through wars of invasion arising from materialism, and become proponents of a spiritual civilization of peace. We must transform materialism, a belief in the supremacy of economic forces which has long been the guiding principle of western institutions, and offer a religious complexion by apprehending the great unity among world nations and community life based on mutual assistance, that is to say, spread the practice of *tangyō-raihai* [bowing in veneration to the Buddha in others] as well as the practice of gift offering and sustaining. The happiest and most delightful activity for humans is to produce. Western societies exploit workers' productivity through restrictions or coercion. And this exploitation forms the foundation for the social organization. From this phenomenon comes the onus of paying taxes. Also in Japan, what is referred to as "the cyclone of tax collection" is driving entire families to commit suicide. When our activities to produce are neither restricted nor coerced but are done purely out of joy and service to society, it is called reciprocity. The practice of *fuse-kuyō* [gift-offering and sustaining others] expounded in Buddhism teaches that the joy of giving is greater than the joy of receiving. Like the difference between heaven and earth, clouds and mud, there is a world of difference between the nature of *fuse-kuyō* and what is called charity. Great unity among humans through reconciliation requires an understanding of others, which means

29 "The revered mission of the divine" is salvation of sentient beings by the Eternal Buddha, a mission commissioned to his disciples. It could be understood as Guruji's belief that the nation, which experienced the first atomic bombings, has the karmic connection of engaging in the Bodhisattva practice of preventing it from being repeated through adherence to the precept against taking life.

humanity at large. How are we to understand the other? When we understand that humanity at large possesses the true nature that becomes the Tathāgata, The World Honored One of supreme dignity, or God, and that each is capable, if so desired, to engage in the task that makes him or her Buddha or one with the Divine, then we can adopt the religious rite of bowing in veneration with palms together to Buddha, the World Honored One, the principle object of veneration, and apply it to the human society we live in and pray for peace by bowing in veneration towards others. No matter what kind of violence arises, we respond by bowing in veneration. Violence may bring people into submission, but it can never unite people. Bowing in veneration may not be able to bring people into submission, but can bring amicable understanding and unite the people.

Nichiren Daishōnin's *Risshō-ankoku-ron*[30] states,

> Promptly mend thy trivial faith[31] and immediately embrace the single good of the Genuine Vehicle. Then the entire triple world is one and inseparable from the Buddha Realm; how can the Buddha Realm ever decline? The worlds in the ten directions are without exception, the Jeweled Land. How can the Jeweled Land ever be destroyed? When the domain is free from decline, and the land[32] free from destruction, our bodies will be safe and our hearts and minds tranquil. Believe in these words and revere them.

With the global crisis at hand, we cannot afford to hesitate. If we remain spectators or dawdle, no other nation in the world may be willing to stand up to the task of rejecting violence to advocate the building of spiritual peace. Transforming material-centric thought means overcoming the outdated ideologies and pronouncements of both the Soviet Union and the United States. We, the Japanese nation, must not fall victim to either communism or the world domination of capitalism.

---

30 Please refer to *Shishin-kaku*, footnote 5, p. 1.

31 "Trivial faith" in *Risshō-Ankoku-ron* is a term that contrasts with "the single good of the Genuine Vehicle". The former according to literal superficial interpretation [一往 *ichiō*] signifies expedient teachings, and the latter, the genuine teaching [The Lotus Sūtra]. According to a deeper interpretation [再往 *saiō*], the former is faith wherein people seek divine favor from Buddha, and the latter, faith wherein Buddha requires people to practice for the sake of others. Differently put, the good medicine according to the former approach is the Lotus Sūtra, while the latter approach regards it as the Odaimoku.

32 Land or the physical environment where sentient beings dwell, *kokudo-seken* 国土世間.

Though left empty-handed and bare-foot from the atrocity of nuclear weapons, we must rise and shine a single ray of light to indicate the dawn of an era of spiritual peace that will overcome the Western civilization of machines.

Is it possible to accomplish this task? Yes, it is. It is the only thing that is possible. The terror facing humanity today is not found in nuclear weapons, unmanned aircraft, guided bombs or massive arsenals. In truth, the source of terror facing humankind today is the decay in religious fervor and moral wit that allows wars to be sanctioned and implemented even at the cost of humanity's annihilation through the reckless use of such weapons and troops at one's command. If humanity at large can restore religious sentiments of lament and fear out of a moral sense of having done wrong toward the mutual mass genocide of fellow humans, no one can possibly unleash an atomic bomb over people one holds no grudge against. Then justice in the international community can be realized, and harmony within the human race can be found. The future of the United States of America is cursed for it has never felt deep remorse within the recesses of its heart. On a recent visit to Japan, Mrs. Roosevelt whitewashed the crime of the atomic bombing, speaking so fallaciously as to offend every moral standard in the world.

The entire world is currently frozen in a military mindset. This military mindset has served no purpose for humanity other than to create fear. Humanity is eagerly searching for an alternative path to alleviate the fear. No matter how arduous and narrow this path may be, there is no other way for humanity to rid the fear but to seek a different path. This alternative path is to universally elevate spirituality and moral values. No matter how small our influences may be, yet all the more because of our inadequacies, we cannot afford to be idle. We must be the vanguard of spiritual advocacy and defenders in creating peace. This is the common goal of humanity and the way to bring emancipation to the modern times. Who can believe that even the harshest winter that hardens everything into solid ice yields to the gentle sprouting of vegetation stirred by the spirit of creation when the time comes? With the quickening of the spirit of creation, ice eventually thaws. This heralds the beginning of spring: the winter solstice.[33] In time, winter solstice will

33 The original term used here is *ichiyō-raifuku* 一陽来復, a term derived from the Chinese I Ching, the *Book of Changes*, meaning the winter solstice. According to the lunar calendar, the spirit of incipient creation starts to stir with the winter solstice.

likewise greet human society.

Just as the height of winter is the prelude to spring, the fear that shrouds humanity can be seen as a harbinger of peace, leading to a sudden upsurge of spiritual vigor sprouting in the hearts and minds of humankind. Only with such spiritual conviction can we overcome the trials we face in this perilous time. Humanity's challenge in the latter half of the 20th century is to choose between extinction and great unity through reconciliation. It is in turn a choice of victory of violence or that of human spirituality.

We, the Japanese nation, have risen to our feet for the sake of humanity's great unity through reconciliation, believing in the victory of spiritual strength. We must stand before nuclear weapons, bowing in veneration with palms together. We must eradicate the iniquity of nuclear weapons from the face of the earth, not by killing others but by offering our lives to others. This is what I understand is the essence of a sacrifice offered to God.

Gasshō [With palms together]

Na Mu Myō Hō Ren Ge Kyō

9

Nuclear Technology and the Future of Humanity

August 6, 1956[1]
Tōkyō, Japan

Nuclear Technology and the Future of Humanity is the title of Yukawa Hideki's[2] article published in the arts and science section of the *Asahi Shinbun*[3] on June 12, 1956. I would like to explore this title in depth, particularly as it relates to the issue of the future of humanity.

According to Yukawa Hideki: "The innate tendency of human beings is to do whatever one imagines can be done. Along with increased capabilities to launch rockets over greater distances came plans to go to the moon or even to Mars. Similarly, with the development of mechanical devices, we were no longer satisfied with substituting them for the functions of human limbs, and moved on to even replacing human brain functions with them. Computers today can run complex calculations at speeds far beyond that of a human."

From ancient times human growth and development, beginning at birth in the mother's womb, has been described by the adage, "Parental love eagerly awaits the child to stand when the child starts crawling, and then to walk when the child stands." This is not merely the parents' wish; it is also the natural development of most infants. It is true that the human tendency to attempt whatever seems possible brings personal growth as well as development to the society. However, as

---

1 This manuscript was completed on July 25, 1956 in Nasu and was printed and distributed for Guruji's 72nd birthday celebration on August 6.

2 Yukawa Hideki [1907-1981] was a professor of theoretical physics and director of the Research Institute for Fundamental Physics at Kyōto University. He published his theory of elementary particles based on the "non-local" field [interactions faster than the speed of light] in his 1935 paper entitled *On the Interaction of Elementary Particles,* a new field theory of nuclear forces predicting the existence of the meson for which he received the 1949 Nobel Prize in Physics.

3 *Asahi Shinbun* is one of the three daily newspapers with nationwide circulation in Japan.

individuals grow and society develops, the consumption of alcohol, indulgence in gambling and engaging in fights are tempting things that could be done. Yet, reckless indulgences in alcohol or gambling or fighting are injurious to the growth of an individual and a society. Hence, there arises a need to prohibit these harmful acts. Embracing a moral code is prerequisite to establishing such prohibitions.

Whether something is done simply because it is possible or because an individual wants to do it, there are some things that should never be done. They are called evil. On the other hand, there are things that unequivocally must be done. They are called good. Things that do not matter either way are called *muki*,[4] neither good nor bad. Distinguishing among these three qualities of good, bad and neither is an exercise largely seen in societies across time and geographic locations. These ideals are held in common, and the aggregate of these commonly held, socially accepted concepts constitutes a moral code. Honorific titles, such as "saint," "sage" and "person of virtue" are conferred on those who practice and live by a moral code. Individuals grow harmoniously, gradually perfecting their humanity, and societies show healthy development in an era where a moral code is honored and upheld. In an era where a moral code is slighted, ridiculed and violated, individuals become corrupt and societies chaotic. The omnipotence of violence is the hallmark of such an era, and murder and destruction are the defining skills of the times. The conditions of such times are described in Buddha Dharma as "concealment of the Genuine Dharma resulting in the prevalence of strife and hostilities."[5] Marital altercations or murders are possible, yet they are largely deterred by the commonly accepted moral ideals of modern society.

No matter how much computers and artificial intelligence advance or whether the program to send man to the moon becomes a reality, the lives of the general public are not particularly swayed towards either joy or anxiety. These matters are neutral in nature, neither good nor bad. However, we live in a time when highly advanced science and technology are inevitably used for murder and destruction. This is the reality. It is highly likely that all scientific inventions, starting with nuclear technology, are becoming the root cause of a human evil capable of committing diabolic crimes. This is the curse of the civilization

---

4 無記. One of the three basic qualities of good, bad or neutral.

5 白法隠没闘諍堅固. *Byakuhō-onmotsu tōjō-kengo.*

of science.

Neither moral code nor religious admonishment has a place in modern international war. Those who staunchly adhere to the moral code or religious belief are branded as traitors and punished. The ultimate judgment in war is solely who the victor is. A truism from ancient days holds that once the war starts, winning the war is the only acceptable outcome. To win the war, a country must kill and wound the greatest number of enemy combatants in the adversary's fighting force. However, in the final stages of World War II, the United States adopted a military campaign known as "strategic bombing," which culminated in the atomic bombings of Japan's Hiroshima and Nagasaki. This indiscriminate, instantaneous and cruel mass slaughter targeting the opponent's most vulnerable population, along with the mass destruction of entire cities, brought victory to the United States. It also brought striking changes to how war is fought. And it marked the origin of an unprecedented fear about war common to humanity today.

Savoring the experience of using nuclear weapons, the United States—even after the war—dedicated its national resources to an all-out effort to produce and stockpile nuclear weapons. The magnitude of the kill force and destructiveness of the hydrogen bomb, tested at the Bikini atolls this May, is known to be roughly five hundred times that of the nuclear bombs exploded over Hiroshima and Nagasaki. The United States is on a course to incessantly explore ways to produce bombs with powers in the thousand-folds, even tens of thousand-folds. The United States does not stand alone. The Soviet Union and Great Britain are on the same track. While science has made amazing strides propelled by the simple human urge to attempt whatever seems possible, once it reached the pinnacle of scientific advancement, the ultimate calamity in human life—the possibility of the total destruction of humanity and its civilization—has become more obvious.

Considering the appalling catastrophe by nuclear weapons, including potential total annihilation of the human race, the people most aghast, most alarmed, most remorseful and frustrated were members of the scientific community who invented and manufactured nuclear weapons in the first place. Albert Einstein's reflection in his latter years, and more recently the statements issued by Bertrand Russell on July 9 of last year[6] and the Lindau[7] statement on July 15 of the same year, all attest to this.

These repeated, poignant statements issued by world-renowned, learned men do not appear to be easing the fear about the use of nuclear weapons in the world. It is because the war plutocracy in Russia, the United States, Great Britain and the like, together with politicians hired by the plutocracy and the professional military, want nuclear weapons to increase in scale, destructive power and extreme brutality, and are exaggerating and acclaiming nuclear weapons. Be it Franklin Roosevelt who sanctioned their development, his widow,[8] Harry Truman who commanded their use, Douglas MacArthur who came to Japan as commander in chief of the occupation force, or even the general American public, not a trace of remorse has been shown after seeing and hearing of these catastrophic disasters, the grave crime against humanity committed in Hiroshima and Nagasaki. Instead, they proudly maintain that the atomic bombings effectively brought an early end to the war.

Yukawa Hideki stated that science could never become a moral code no matter how great its advancement. Likewise, Albert Einstein stated that scientists give all meaning to existence but assign no value to inclination, appraisal, difference or purpose. In the modern civilization, everything, including science, economics, politics or war, is either antagonistic to or critical of moral codes and religious belief. Herein is the dark side of the modern world. Worldly values reign in modern civilization, including science, economics and politics. Everything religion and moral codes strictly inhibited in the past—the momentary pleasures and secular happiness of the five dusts[9] and six

---

6 The Russell-Einstein Manifesto was issued in London on July 9, 1955. It petitioned for the renunciation of war in order to avert human extinction and was written by Bertrand Russell and signed by nine Nobel Prize winners, including Yukawa Hideki and Albert Einstein. It asks: "Shall we put an end to the human race; or shall mankind renounce war?"

7 Lindau is a small town in Germany where Nobel laureates have gathered annually since 1951. On July 15, 1955, eighteen Nobel laureates from that gathering issued The Mainau Declaration, similar in content to The Russell-Einstein Manifesto released six days earlier.

8 Eleanor Roosevelt visited Japan in 1953 as part of the U.S.-Japan Intellectual Interchange Program. She went expecting to talk about women's status and rights, but found that the topics most on the minds of Japanese women were the rearmament of Japan and the presence of U.S. military bases.

9 *Gojin* 五塵. The five objects of sensation and perception corresponding to the five sense organs. They are objects sensed as visual color or form, sound, odor, taste and touch. Since they give rise to desires and thereby pollute the mind, they are called dust.

desires[10]– is given supreme value, driving human endeavor into pointless competition to increase production in order to fulfill desire. According to a materialistic view of life, such fulfillment of desires purportedly rids the world of all social evils and instantly turns this world into a paradise. Hence, true religion, ethics and morals are rejected. Instead, economics and production, in essence, money, once meant merely as a means of exchange, have become prized, worshipped and served as almighty god on earth. This aberrant object of worship is now the subject of devout zeal. Thus, spiritual inversion has gradually taken place without being noticed, and societies of modern civilization, at the height of prosperity, suddenly find themselves confronted with the risk of being reduced to ashes by the flames of eternal hell.

Modern civilization's two favorites, the United States, a free nation, and the Soviet Union, a communist nation, both represent nothing but outright blunt realities of power. There is not a hint of ethos that honors religion and morality, which are the pillars of human ideals. U.S. expansion of military bases in Okinawa, attempted implementation of lump sum payment of land rents by force,[11] compulsory expropriation of former Japanese military bases such as Sunagawa and Komaki, and the Soviet Union's forced labor of Japanese prisoners, war tribunals and the like, are all imperious acts of the greatest barbarity by those who flatter themselves to be the victors. These acts are possible only for those who have completely lost perspective on matters of the mind and spirit. Unless the spirit is infused back into these people, nothing will prevent them from eventually igniting the conflagration of annihilation. The escape path is not in nuclear technology—the science and technology

---

10 *Rokuyoku* 六欲. The six desires arising from sight, sound, scent, taste, touch and the mind.

11 From the end of WWII in 1945 until the 1952 Peace Treaty went into effect, the United States acquired land in Okinawa without paying compensation pursuant to the Rules of Land Warfare. The U.S. military would take land by force, sometimes taking over entire villages, encountering little opposition from Okinawans devastated by war and who were heavily dependent on the U.S. military for food and shelter. The 1952 Peace Treaty separated Okinawa from mainland Japan. Although Japan retained residual sovereignty, Okinawa was directly administered by the U.S. military with a clause suggesting that control eventually be relinquished to a UN trusteeship, which never occurred. Having a civil administration in Okinawa made the use of Rules of Land Warfare extremely controversial, and Okinawans started to protest the continued land expropriation. The U.S. military initially set out to purchase needed land, but was rebuffed by Okinawans who feared the U.S. presence in Okinawa would become permanent. The United States then proposed a lease system in which lump-sum payments would be made for a 16½ year period. Island-wide protests developed, culminating in a rally involving approximately 450,000 people who stood up to protect the homeland, territorial rights and sovereignty.

they possess faith in—nor in economics or politics.

The appalling calamities of atomic and hydrogen war reflect the agonies of an illness of inner darkness that will bring the fall of the civilization of science on its own. Atomic and hydrogen war is retribution on us human beings for leading immoral lives. Atomic and hydrogen war is the great abyss of fire into which we human beings will inevitably fall for leading faithless lives. Yukawa Hideki laments and states: "We are tempted to succumb to despair when considering all this. However, we need not despair yet. No religion or doctrine worthy of faith and acceptance by the multitude affirms mutual mass killing, much less the act of humanity's self-destruction." Yukawa Hideki's despair directed towards the civilization of science is precisely on target and sounds the tolling of the funeral bell for the last days of this so-called modern civilization, also called the civilization of the West or the civilization of machines.

Everything relating to the civilization of science must now step down from leadership in our societies. Should the civilization of science continue to lead, the obvious path is one of self-destruction for the human race. The spiritual civilization is the alternative to the civilization of science, and only its emergence in the latter half of the 20th century can save humanity from the catastrophe of self-destruction. In the end, Dr. Yukawa, a scientist himself, arrived at this supra-logical conclusion, which transcends any theory. It is a direct and realistic remedy that requires no rationalization or justification.

One of the slogans raised at the beginning of modern civilization was "liberty, equality and fraternity." Among the three, fraternity is nowhere to be found in science, economics or politics. There is no room for fraternity to exist where religion and morality are rejected. Here, equality is a demand for liberty by the majority who are ruled by the minority. Hence, the modern civilization is characterized by its intent pursuit and assertion of "freedom". Likewise, science developed to liberate humanity from constraints on freedom. Every idea under the influence of liberalism, including politics and economics, aimed to free people from restrictions posed by religion and morality. The single word "freedom" is regarded as a sacred maxim that surpasses morality and religion. In the realm called freedom, freedom to do good waned due to its association with morality and religion. Freedom to assert and even do evil is reckoned to be true freedom. The surge of freedom unencumbered by the strictures of morality and religion is nothing more than sophistry that heightens vice in the human world.

Whether it is science and technology or politics and economics, in the end all are used to accommodate human wishes and objectives. The more removed our hopes and aspirations become from the constraints of morality and religion, the more we become absorbed in the pursuit of base desires, physical pleasures, comforts, indulgences, power and fame. While we, modern humanity, call ourselves civilized and pride ourselves on the power of science and technology, we concurrently risk regressing back to the greatest savagery. Nuclear war is the epitome of unprecedented savagery not only in the human history of war, but also in the history of struggle among living creatures of the world.

In Chapter XVI of the Lotus Sūtra, *The Eternal Duration of the Life of the Tathāgata*, delivered by the Preceptor, Buddha Śākyamuni, at Mount Grdhrakūta [Sacred Eagle Peak] in Rajgir of the ancient Magadha Kingdom in India, the World Honored One, preached on aspects of this prophesized "modern age," the non-virtuous Era of Final Dharma, which was to come far in the future, and he expounded on the gate for salvation for this era.

> Even when all the living see, at the kalpa's end,
> The conflagration burning,
> Tranquil is this realm of mine,
> Ever-filled with celestial beings
> Gardens, groves, all kinds of temples and splendid buildings
> With every kind of gem adorned.
> Jeweled trees abound in blossoms and fruit,
> A place where all the living play with glee
> The devas strike the celestial drums,
> Constantly making music,
> Showering mandārava flowers
> On me, the Buddha, and the great congregation.
> This Pure Land of mine is never destroyed,
> Yet, all see it as being consumed by fire,
> Rife with grief, fear and various afflictions as such.

The import of this passage of the sūtra is that the accursed time of potential human annihilation was brought on by us human beings.

The calamity of human annihilation was not the Deluge, rather the sūtra prophesizes that it is the conflagration whose flames from eternal hell reach to the face of the earth, reducing everything to ash. Until now a conflagration that engulfs the entire world was inconceivable. But are not today's new weapons, the atomic and hydrogen bombs, precisely that?

A single gate is open for us to escape from the ravages of this conflagration. That is to dispel the delusion of the military and the politicians who view the entire threefold world, i.e., the heavens, earth and underwater, as battlefields for killing and destruction. Instead, we are to believe that this land, the physical world we live in, is inherently a sacred Pure Land, which we make into a solemn ceremonial ground where our thought, word and deed are done out of the pleasure of bringing joy to others,[12] and all the things we produce are a treasure of temples, splendid structures, gardens and groves;[13] in the Pure Land, the Enlightened World Honored One, the people who listen to him preach and the golden words of the Dharma expounded are equally revered,[14] and offerings of flowers never cease. To engage in the Bodhisattva practice of creating the Pure Land without ever leaving this physical world, believing in the intrinsic existence of the Pure Land and the eternal presence and preaching of the Lord of the Pure Land, offers human beings the ultimate and fundamental goal for which to strive. Religion in general encourages devoted pursuit of what is noble and supreme, mindful of eternal life without departing from our reality in this physical existence. This is expressed in the immeasurable compassion and vow of the Eternal Buddha Śākyamuni, the World Honored One, in the chapter of *The Eternal Duration of the Life of the Tathāgata* of the Lotus Sūtra:

> At all times making this my thought:
> "How shall I cause all the living
> To enter the Supreme Path
> And speedily attain the Buddha-body?[15]

12 Here the reference is, as in the citation from Chapter XVI of the Lotus Sūtra, the enlightenment of the realm of sentient beings.

13 The enlightenment of the world of non-sentient beings, the physical world in its entirety.

14 Reverence of the Triple Jewel: the Buddha, Dharma and Sangha.

15 *Busshin* 仏身. The Origin Buddha manifested as the historical Buddha who attained Enlightenment as a human being, and the sūtra describes this as "difficult to believe and difficult to comprehend." The Lotus Sūtra emphasizes that the action involved in the

Out of his wish to encourage people to conduct themselves in a way that gives life value, Buddha laid down different precepts[16] of varying degrees as passive rules; and as active or positive rules, Buddha preached the Dharma of the four great Bodhisattva vows[17] and the six kinds of practice by which bodhisattvas are able to attain enlightenment.[18] In a letter written in response to Lord Saemon-no-jō, Nichiren Daishōnin states:

> Nothing is a greater treasure to sentient beings than life. Thus, those who deprive others of it will inevitably fall into the three evil paths. Wheel Turning Noble Kings[19] are born because of the merit they have earned by observing the precept against taking life, which is foremost among the Ten Good Deeds.[20] Among the Hīnayāna precepts, Buddha first laid down the Five Precepts,[21] and the precept against taking life is the first of the five. It is the first of the Ten Major

---

Buddha's vow to bring salvation to all reveals the oneness of matter and mind. "So this person where he goes about in practice, shall disperse the gloom of the living" [Chapter XXI], teaches that the gloom of the living in the Era of Final Dharma can be dispersed only by those who have a body to manifest Buddha's salvation through action on his behalf. More specifically, it means to become a practitioner who chants the Odaimoku and practices veneration toward others in the tradition of Bodhisattva Never Despise for the purpose of achieving the salvation of sentient beings in the Era of Final Dharma. Chapter XI, also states, "If one is able to keep it, then one keeps the Buddha's body."

16 They are teachings that prohibit harmful acts as rules of behavior to observe inwardly.

17 The four great Bodhisattva vows are: "I vow to relieve all sentient beings, no matter how innumerable they may be; I vow to extinguish all passions, no matter how inexhaustible they may be; I vow to study the Dharma, no matter how limitless it may be; I vow to attain the Buddha-truth, no matter how infinite it may be."

18 *Roku-haramitsu* 六波羅密 *haramitsu, paramita* [Sk.]. The six kinds of practice refers to the crossing over from this shore of birth and death to the other shore of nirvāna. Frequently the practices leading to this objective are themselves termed *haramitsu*. The six *paramita* are the practice of offering [*dāna*], observance of precepts, perseverance in the face of insult and persecution, devotion, meditation [*dhyana*] and to shed light on truth *[prajnā*].

19 Rinnō or Tenrinjōō 輪王. The ideal monarch conceived in India who rules the world with the wheel which he spontaneously obtains at the time of enthronement. In one of the sūtras, *Cakkavatti Sihanada Suttanta*, Buddha laid down the duties of a monarch. The greatest cakkavatti, King Ashoka's Rock Edicts, were inspired by these teachings of Buddha.

20 Ten Good Deeds, *Jūzen* 十善, also known as *jūzenkai* 十善戒. They are : i) *fusesshō* 不殺生 not to kill living things; ii) *fuchūtō* 不偸盗 not to steal; iii) *fujain* 不邪淫 not to commit adultery; iv) *fumōgo* 不妄語 not to tell lies; v) *fuakku* 不悪口 not to speak ill of others; vi) *furyōzetsu* 不兩舌 not to utter words which cause enmity ; vii) *fukigo* 不綺語 not to engage in idle talk; viii) *futonyoku* 不貪欲 not to be greedy; ix) *fushinni* 不瞋恚 not to be angry; x) *fujaken* 不邪見 not to have distorted views.

21 The Five Precepts are: not to take life, not to take what is not given to one, not to commit adultery, not to tell lies, not to consume intoxicants.

> Precepts in the Mahāyāna Brahmajala Sūtra; and the Buddha revealed in *The Eternal Duration of the Life of the Tathāgata* chapter attained ever-present, eternal life through the merits of his compassion to emancipate all sentient beings and his practice of the precept against taking life. Accordingly, the Buddhas of the Triple World shall forsake those who kill, and devas of the Six Heavens of the World of Desire will not lend their protection.[22]

If today's politicians believed that the precept against taking life is an objective truth and a sacred act valuable to humanity, murderous machines like nuclear weapons would never have been produced. Even if produced, they would not have been used in war. Furthermore, had people not discarded the precept against taking life like an old shoe, there could have been no room for manipulation by architects of war. The only salvation for the modern times is to believe and accept that the precept against taking life is what truly has transcendent value. Yukawa Hideki has finally come to this realization. How can this awareness on the truth of the precept against taking life be awakened to resonate in the hearts and minds of all the people? Only the dawning of faith can answer this question. There is no answer in science.

Distorted views negate the innate truth of the precept against taking life, leaving it despised and discarded. A misguided sense of freedom leads to competition, which leads to victory or defeat, which leads to the incorporation of the law of domination of the strong over the weak in human society. Even the act of murder receives moral justification, and wars cast in religious overtones are used to inspire zeal. Recently we again hear terms like "The European Crusades." In the end, the whole society risks bathing in blood and burning in the flames of war. Science lies at the root of these distorted views towards life. The theory of evolution is one such example.[23] Buddha Dharma calls this

---

22 主君耳入此法門免与同罪事. *On Recommending This Dharma to the Lord to Spare Oneself from Complicity in Slandering the Dharma*. Written on September 26, 1274 at Mount Minobu as a reply to Shijō Kingo.

23 In his essay *Kanjin-Honzon*, Guruji presents his view on the theory of evolution as follows: "According to the theory of evolution, human beings evolved from apes. Bestiality is said, therefore, to be inherent in humans. What characterizes the evolved human is not bestiality, but rather the ability to reflect upon, control and free oneself from physical desire and beastliness along with a yearning to discover and venerate the sublime God, which is

kenjoku[24] [defilement of views]. How can the civilization of science ever accept and have faith in the precept of not taking life? It is no wonder that those who believe and embrace the path of the Buddha become gentle, straightforward and honest, and lead peaceful communal lives. The history of peace that prevailed in Japan from the reign of Crown Prince Shōtoku[25] until the end of the Nara period is a testimonial to the precept. Those who do not believe nor accept the Buddha Way, who resent and harbor grudges against it, and even bloodthirsty killers who only seek strife must all be transformed by Buddha Dharma to become upright in character, gentle in mind, enabled to lead peaceful lives within society. This is the kind of deliverance required by the modern times. The chapter of *The Eternal Duration of the Life of the Tathāgata* of the Lotus Sūtra says:

> I know always which living beings
> Practice the way, and which do not,
> And in response to their need for salvation
> I expound various Dharma

How can we dispel the delusions of those who do not practice the Way of the Buddha or who, by choice or ignorance, transgress the precept against taking life or who do not practice offering? In *Kanjin-honzon-shō* [*Treatise on Seeing the Essential Object of Veneration in the Heart and Mind*],[26] Nichiren Daishōnin states:

> We are now at the beginning of the Era of Final Dharma when Hīnayāna teachings are favored over Mahāyāna doctrines and

---

invisible and dormant in one's mind. This act is called faith. Spiritual acts make human life unique. Such acts are not seen in any animal other than human beings. The depth of the pursuit to discover God and truth are what distinguish the measure of progress and development in human society."

24 見濁. One of the five defilements [*gojoku* 五濁; *panca kasāyā* (Sk.)]. *Kenjoku* is the defilement of views, giving rise to distorted views. The five defilements are: i) defilement of the period; ii) defilement of views; iii) defilement by evil passions; iv) defilement of sentient beings and; v) shortening of life.

25 Please refer to *The Purpose of Erecting a Stūpa and Making Offerings*, footnote 10, p. 58.

26 観心本尊抄. Written by Nichiren Daishōnin on the fourth month of Bunei Period [1273] at Sado Island during his exile, it is considered one of his most essential writings. Commonly known by this title, its official title is *Nyorai-metsugo-gogohyakusai-shi kanjin-honzon-shō* 如来滅後五五百歳始観心本尊抄 *Treatise on Seeing the Essential Object of Veneration in the Heart and Mind Revealed for the First Time in the Fifth Five-Hundred Year Period Following the Nirvāna of the Tathāgata*.

> provisional Mahāyāna teachings undermine true Mahāyāna teachings. East is mistaken for West, West for East, and the heavens and earth are confounded one for the other. The four ranks of Bodhisattva teachers, who were to preach the Trace Teaching of the Lotus Sūtra [over the Origin Teaching], have concealed themselves,[27] and gods and good deities have all deserted the country[28] and no longer lend their protection. At this very time, the Bodhisattvas Who Emerge from the Earth appear in the world for the first time to administer the good medicine of the five characters Myō Hō Ren Ge Kyō to the people in their spiritual infancy in the Era of Final Dharma. This is what is meant by "even if they revile the true teachings and fall into the evil paths, they are nevertheless graced with the Dharma, thereby creating cause for eventual attainment of Buddhahood."[29]

The perceived inversion of the heavens and earth is the state of the Era of Final Dharma. As foretold in the Lotus Sūtra, "I [Buddha] disappear from the eyes of perverted people, who fail to see me though I remain near."[30] People lost sight of the true savior, the Preceptor, and instead worship money as God on earth, although it was initially nothing more than a means of trade. An aberration sets in by which people are ruled by money instead of the other way around. Finally, in the stage of financial capitalism, individuals, the state and even the world became shackled by

---

27 According to Nichiren Daishōnin, the four ranks of Bodhisattva teachers who were mandated to spread the Trace Teachings of the Lotus Sūtra for the most part appeared during the 1,000 years of the Era of Semblance Dharma and a few at the beginning of Era of Final Dharma, such as Tendai Daishi, Myōraku Daishi and Dengyō Daishi. For more information, please refer to footnote 67 in *Wondrous First Connection with Lord Buddha's Relic*, p.29.

28 According to the teaching of *zenjin-shakoku* 善神捨国, "the desertion of a nation by good deities," the good deities thrive on the Dharma flavor of the Lotus Sūtra. Therefore, they desert land where the Lotus Sūtra is not believed in or where there are no practitioners of the Lotus Sūtra for they cannot attain enlightenment. Furthermore, the gods' and good deities' mission entrusted to them by Buddha is to lend protection to the practitioners of the Lotus Sūtra, therefore their presence becomes meaningless in a land without practitioners.

29 因謗堕悪必(由)因得益とは是也. The last quote is from Miao-lê in his *Annotations on the Words and Phrases of the Lotus Sūtra*. In it Nichiren Daishōnin replaces the word "由," meaning indirect karmic connection in Miao-lê's quotation, with "因,"meaning direct cause. The result is his assertion that even slander of the genuine Dharma becomes a direct cause for eventual enlightenment.

30 Chapter XVI, *The Eternal Duration of the Life of the Tathāgata*.

money, and true freedom has been lost. The reason Japan has no choice but to follow the United States is due to the fetters of financial capitalism. Workers have become slaves to machines; capitalists have become slaves to the pursuit of profit. Everyone in civilized societies has been enslaved. The sweet wine of civilization brought about such vagaries due to this inversion. Infected with this poison, modern civilization thrashes around in agony. The good medicine left by Buddha Śākyamuni specifically for the Era of Final Dharma is the five and seven characters of Na Mu Myō Hō Ren Ge Kyō.[31] The Lotus Sūtra says:

> This good medicine I now leave here.
> You may take it and have no fear of not being cured.[32]

If we were to simply chant Na Mu Myō Hō Ren Ge Kyō without adhering to the precept against taking life or the practice of offering[33] how could that possibly make us Buddhas or transform this world into a Pure Land? This question would naturally come to anyone's mind. The answer only comes by chanting Na Mu Myō Hō Ren Ge Kyō. We must chant Na Mu Myō Hō Ren Ge Kyō for those who do not chant it to hear. We must constantly chant Na Mu Myō Hō Ren Ge Kyō with great compassion and without neglect also for those who close their mouths, cover their ears and refuse to chant or hear it.

In the *Letter to Soya-nyūdō*,[34] Nichiren Daishōnin says:

> We are now in the Era of Final Dharma when those who received karmic connection to the Lotus Sūtra and to their eventual enlightenment through Lord Buddha's teachings have gradually declined. The people with the aptitude to seek emancipation through both Lord Buddha's expedient and genuine teachings are now no longer. It is now time for

---

31 The great compassion of the Tathāgata is to bring salvation to sentient beings in the Era of Final Dharma. For this purpose, the good medicine, the Lotus Sūtra, was condensed into the Odaimoku, i.e., the five characters Myō Hō Ren Ge Kyō, and was conferred to those in the Era of Final Dharma to be chanted as the seven-character Odaimoku of Na Mu Myō Hō Ren Ge Kyō.

32 Chapter XVI, *The Eternal Duration of the Life of the Tathāgata.*

33 *Fuse-haramitsu* 布施波羅密 *dāna paramita.*

34 曾谷入道殿許御書. Written in 1275 at Mount Minobu.

the Bodhisattva Never Despise to emerge in the Era of Final Dharma and beat the poisonous drum.[35]

The people addicted to civilization abhor the voice chanting Na Mu Myō Hō Ren Ge Kyō and the beating of the great Dharma drum, which they perceive as poisonous. For this reason they slander Na Mu Myō Hō Ren Ge Kyō and hold the sound of the Dharma drum in contempt. Those who chant the Odaimoku and beat the Dharma drum are resented, abused and struck. At this time the three formidable adversaries,[36] one after another, vie in their attack on the practitioners of the Lotus Sūtra. It takes extraordinary compassion to beat the poisonous drum and persevere in the face of attacks from these three daunting enemies. I have been able to chant Na Mu Myō Hō Ren Ge Kyō due to the boundless compassion of Nichiren Daishōnin. And the Preceptor, Buddha Śākyamuni, in his inexhaustible compassion, has wrapped the two Dharma of causal practice and its resulting merit[37] in the five characters of Myō Hō Ren Ge Kyō and offered them to the spiritual infants of the Era of Final Dharma. This is my religious belief.

Even those with distorted views will find no room for argument on the universal salvation brought to sentient beings in this world by Buddha Śākyamuni's golden voice over the vast expanse of time. The voices heard morning and evening from household altars reciting and maintaining the sūtras show that Buddha's teaching is the peaceful guiding light in the spiritual lives of the people. The five characters of Myō Hō Ren Ge Kyō are said to be the ultimate teaching among all the teachings delivered by Buddha Śākyamuni throughout his 50 years of preaching in this world and are the original purpose for the advent of the Buddhas past, present and future in this world. How then could Na Mu Myō Hō Ren Ge Kyō not cure the spiritual ailment of the Era of Final Dharma? The efficacy of this good medicine is obvious, and the diagnosis of the foretold human

---

35 Please refer to *Shishin-kaku*, footnote 24, p.5.

36 The three formidable adversaries are: arrogance in the lay world, including state power; arrogance in the clergy; and arrogance of exalted sages. All three, out of perverted understanding of the teachings, persecute those who practice the Genuine Dharma.

37 *Ingyō-katoku-no-nihō* 因行果徳の二法. The two Dharma of causal practice [*ingyō* 因行] and resulting merit [*katoku* 果徳] are understood as the Origin Buddha's work of bringing salvation to all sentient beings, performed over the eternal past, which is the causal practice; and the resulting merit is the eternal life to continue the emancipation of all. Therefore, those who receive Myō Hō Ren Ge Kyō inherit the merits of Origin Buddha's Dharma of causal practice and Dharma of resulting merit.

aberration proven true. Furthermore, the Bodhisattvas Who Emerge from the Earth, entrusted to spread the Genuine Dharma to bring emancipation in the Era of Final Dharma, have unmistakably emerged. The single phrase of Na Mu Myō Hō Ren Ge Kyō is the one and only promise made to the human world to extricate it from the collapse of modern civilization.

The fact that the precept against taking life and practice of offering and generosity are recorded in the sūtras does not bring emancipation to individuals or societies in and of itself. If people regard this precept and practice of offering simply as words on a page, then they are no different than any provision of law. Neither the precept of non-killing nor the practice of offering and generosity acts as cursory codes; rather they are the working of the mind. This is known as *kaitai*[38] [essence of precepts]. This is the reason why *kaitai* is also referred to as *muhyōshiki* [unmanifest form][39] or *musa* [uncreated, a state of being whose function is yet to materialize in visible conduct].[40] Conduct expressed through the three acts of word, thought and deed, is required to induce and bring to bear the essence of precepts, which is otherwise un-created and yet to take visible form.

Na Mu Myō Hō Ren Ge Kyō is the *kaitai* of the Buddhas of the past, present and future. The Lotus Sūtra states: "Such a one [who keeps Na Mu Myō Hō Ren Ge Kyō] even for a short period of time is named precept-keeper."[41] Na Mu Myō Hō Ren Ge Kyō is the *kaitai* through which all people can attain Buddhahood. It also states:

> This person shall in the Way of the Buddha
> Be resolved and have no doubts.[42]

Nichiren Daishōnin taught that "Na Mu Myō Hō Ren Ge Kyō is neither a word nor its meaning, but the very essence of Buddha's compassion

38 戒體.

39 *Muhyōshiki* 無表色 [*Avijinapti-rupa*]. According to Buddhist traditions, when a vow to preserve the precepts of the Buddha is made, certain invisible Dharma produced in the body becomes instrumental in keeping the precepts and eschewing evil. It is termed non-manifest or un-manifested form because it is not manifested as externally recognizable conduct and cannot be seen.

40 無作.

41 Chapter XI, *Beholding the Stūpa of Treasures.*

42 Chapter XXI, *The Divine Transcendental Powers of the Tathāgata.*

revealed in the Lotus Sūtra, comprised of twenty-eight chapters."[43] Na Mu Myō Hō Ren Ge Kyō, condensed into a single phrase of mystery and entrusted to the human world, manifests the essential substance of Buddha's precepts in our heart and mind, where its intrinsic existence never perishes. Through the manifest, audible act of enunciating Na Mu Myō Hō Ren Ge Kyō, Na Mu Myō Hō Ren Ge Kyō's unmanifest essense of precept is realized. This makes it possible for us to believe in the attainment of our Buddhahood as well as in the realization that "this *sahā* world is one and inseparable from the Land of Eternal Tranquil Light."[44]

Be it highly advanced science and technology or the politics and economics of liberalism or of communism that employ science and technology, the way to prevent humanity from self-destruction is in neither doctrine espoused today or in any new weapon they produce. Moral code and religion were cast aside as superfluous and antiquated by modern civilization. Yet, religion, which transforms and purifies even evil that defies restraint by moral code, is where we find the path to rescue humanity from self-destruction.

Science and technology invented atomic and hydrogen bombs, and a democracy used them in war for murder. A major international debate now questions whether their use was right or wrong. After World War II, the United States invited Prime Minister Jawaharlal Nehru of India to speak. In his address, Mr. Nehru stated that India, with great pride, wishes to let the American people know that India will neither produce nor use atomic and hydrogen bombs. The production and use of atomic and hydrogen bombs are a great disgrace to human civilization. The moral code will denounce this act as an indelible disgrace for the United States.

The Supreme Soviet, the governing body of the Soviet Union, recently announced its support for the Japanese parliament resolution calling for a ban on testing atomic and hydrogen bombs. The British prime minister subsequently expressed similar views. Several months ago, American presidential candidate, Adlai Stevenson, declared the United

43 Citation from *Shishin-gohon-shō* 四信五品鈔, written by Nichiren Daishōnin April 10, 1277 at Mount Minobu. 妙法蓮華経五字非経文　非其義　唯一部意耳.

44 *Shaba* 娑婆. The *sahā* world is one of the four lands distinguished in Tendai doctrine. It is the land where ordinary people and sages live together. *Jōjakkōdo* 常寂光土. The Land of Eternal Tranquil Light is the realm of the Dharma-body Buddha, the highest of the Pure Lands.

States should resolutely engage in a unilateral ban on nuclear testing and urged the Soviet Union and the United Kingdom to follow suit. However, the current administrations of the United States and Japan still dream about the efficacy of nuclear weapons and oppose the testing ban.

It is now evident that the issue of nuclear war is inextricably linked to the moral code, which supersedes the question of victory or defeat in war. The moral code governs people's conduct. Whether it is adhered to or not is ultimately determined by the action or non-action of the non-manifest *kaitai* of the precept of not taking life lying deep within our minds. We must recognize that while morals and religion exist in different spheres, they share a common life. Religious faith is not a personal matter, as maintained by advocates of communism. It is a great beacon that illuminates the darkness of the modern civilization. Purification through the transformation of evil in religion transcends any merits found in competing doctrines. It is the cardinal prohibition against the greatest tragedy of all tragedies in the human world: murder. The absolute and fundamental prohibition of murder is humanity's ultimate civilization, which is yet to be heeded by science, economics or politics. The cardinal prohibition of murder is the paramount issue that extends throughout and beyond politics, economics and science. It is the imperative of all time, one that must be unequivocally embraced for liberating humankind from extinction.

Na Mu Myō Hō Ren Ge Kyō

Nipponzan Myōhōji *Shamon* [45]
Nichidatsu

45 沙門 *śramana* [Sk]. A Buddhist monk, a mendicant.

At Ashoka Stūpa, Sanchi, India, 1956.

10

A Nation under Rule of Law

October 30, 1956
Tōkyō

In the middle of this month, the government's forcible land survey in Sunagawa conducted with an eye to the proposed expansion of the military air base[1] culminated in more than 1,000 casualties among the members of the opposition alliance, various support groups and monks of Nipponzan Myōhōji. After the bloody incident, a public outcry ensued.

The majority of voices denounced the police assault and battery, and yet we also saw and heard admonitions directed against the opposition alliance and its supporters. One argument defended the government's violent assault as possibly justifiable under the circumstances and not at all unreasonable from a logical point of view. Here the rationale is that citizens of a nation under rule of law are required to adhere to the law, and dissent is a disruption of peace and order, giving the government no choice but to exercise its power to remove those who refuse to abide by the law.

In the Nichiren School, the phrase "nation under rule of law" appears in the title of the *Treatise on Nation Under Rule of the True Law* written by Venerable Kuon-jōin Nisshin[2] of the Higashiyama

---

1 During the Korean War, U.S. air missions were carried out from the Tachikawa base in Japan. In 1953 the United States planned the expansion of the Tachikawa base's runway into Sunagawa, which was then a small farming community abutting Tachikawa City. The city was notified of the plan by the Japanese government in 1955. The Sunagawa Confederation Against the Expansion of the Military Base was formed to stop the government's plan. On October 12 and 13, 1956, the confrontation between the surveying squad, which was accompanied by armed police, and the protesters resulted in more than 1,000 casualties. The government announced the suspension of the survey on radio on the night of October 14.

2 久遠成院日親上人 [1407-1488]. He founded the Honpōji 本法寺 denomination of the Nichiren School. He called on the hereditary military dictator to profess faith in the Lotus Sūtra and was imprisoned and tortured but refused to renounce his faith. He is also known as *nabekamuri* Nisshin for the torture he endured when forced to wear a burning pot on his head.

period to remonstrate the policies of Shōgun Ashikaga Yoshinori[3] and, as a result, he endured a gruesome persecution. In the eight years preceding his passing, the World Honored One, Buddha Śākyamuni, expounded the Lotus Sūtra atop Grdhrakūta, and revealed the true reason for his advent. In the final part of the epilogue of the Threefold Lotus Sūtra—the Sūtra of Meditation on the Bodhisattva Universal Virtue—the five repentances were taught for kings, ministers, Brahmins, lay believers, elderly men of wealth and virtue and state officials to heed. Specifically, "Their third repentance is to rule their countries with the True Law and not to unjustly oppress the people. This is called one who practices the third repentance." The term "nation under rule of law" originated here.

Laws must be abided by. Laws which cannot be adhered to are unworthy of becoming law. For this reason, the laws of a nation under rule of law require strict scrutiny. In Buddhism, the term used is not simply "nation under rule of law," but specifically, "nation under rule of the Genuine Law." No natural law, such as water seeks its own level or flames rise in height, is illegitimate, pernicious or unjust. But many laws of human construct are illegitimate, pernicious and unjust. They benefit rulers in power and contain provisions detrimental to all or some of the general public. The greater the detriment, the greater the underlying seeds of revolution. Particularly states established by force enact laws rife with illegitimate and pernicious provisions for murder and punishment. Having said that, let us not forget that from ancient times, the ambitious who aspired to world domination ended their days in ignominy.

In the Sunagawa incident, the Japan-U.S. Security Treaty Administrative Agreement[4] and the Land Expropriation Law are the legal underpinnings for the actions taken by the Japanese government. These

---

3 足利義教 [1394-1441]. The 6th Shōgun in the Ashikaga Shogunate during the Muromachi period.

4 Formally known as the Administrative Agreement under Article III of the Security Treaty between the United States of America and Japan. The Security Treaty was signed the same day [Sept. 8, 1951] as the San Francisco Peace Treaty, which officially ended WWII and the occupation of Japan. The Security Treaty allowed the U.S. to maintain its own bases in Japan without any restriction from the Japanese government. Also, the U.S. had full jurisdiction over American personnel who committed crimes in Japan, and the treaty could only be ended by mutual consent. In return, Japan ostensibly received military protection from the U.S., however, this was not guaranteed. Although later amended to correct some of the more unequal terms of the treaty, it sparked decades of widespread opposition, at times quite fierce, within Japan.

Protesting the expansion of the U.S. Air Force base at Sunagawa, October 1956.

laws were established as a result of war, a product of the admixture of the victor's sense of entitlement and the obsequiousness of the defeated. Each law drips with deceit. They are pernicious, illicit and unjust laws claiming to be just, legitimate and righteous. The occupation force is euphemistically called "stationed troops," and selling U.S. goods to Japan is called "U.S. aid". The Japan-U.S. Security Treaty was the justification for the confrontation and tragic bloodshed that occurred adjacent to the Tōkyō metropolis between the Japanese government and the people, producing 1,000 casualties in merely two or three hours, unheard of in the history of Japanese law enforcement. It is material proof of Japan's compromised state of security and a modern tragedy of the nation. It could be the source of unrest which might undermine security between Japan and the United States. Moreover, just as sure as night follows day, domestic bloodshed will spread far and wide if the government continues to fiercely defend the said treaty and forcibly requisition land in Sunagawa. The new Japanese Constitution has never caused any tribulation or bloodshed in Japan, nor has it created any threat, apprehension or suspicion abroad. Despite that, the government of this nation under rule of law does not intend to defend it at all costs. They contradict themselves concerning the importance of maintaining a nation under rule of law. The words of the constitution underpin every law of the land, yet they are violated by clever and deceptive interpretations. Ultimately, these same people call for revision of the constitution, contending that Japan needs to adopt an "autonomous constitution," employing the chicanery that what exists now was imposed on us by the United States. On the other hand, the Japan-U.S. Security Treaty, which allows for unrestricted foreign military presence on Japanese territory, unheard of for a sovereign nation, is defended and enforced no matter what the toll despite the government's shattered credibility over the bloodshed of its own people. This clearly proves that this treaty is a pernicious law supported by violence.

The sūtra carefully clarifies what is meant by "nation under rule of Genuine Law" with the phrase "not to unjustly oppress the people." Abrogating people's rights, disrupting their livelihood, plundering their fields and paddies without deference to the desires of the people is strictly prohibited. Though the government expects acquiescence in a nation under rule of law as a matter of course, the people shall no longer be deceived into thinking by the government's line of reasoning that they must offer blind, unconditional compliance to an illegitimate, pernicious bilateral treaty, lest they undermine security, law and order in the land.

Those who believe in the Genuine Dharma cannot at the same time believe in unjust laws. Those who adhere to the Genuine Dharma cannot submit to unjust laws. Those who wish to observe the Genuine Dharma must abide in noble spirituality and endure various hardships inflicted by violence constantly employed to enforce unjust laws. Violence has absolutely no place in the Genuine Law.

Blind obedience to vile laws amounts to collaboration with vile acts of the government and causes vile influences to pervade society. Disobedience to the unjust is, in itself, an allegiance to truth, the Genuine Dharma. We must recognize how the emergence of a faction willing to compromise[5] with the government in Sunagawa abetted the government's ignoble intentions and significantly facilitated the state violence.

---

5 It is believed that some people made deals with the government after being given money for their land.

Banner reads, "Stakes can be driven into the ground, but not into our hearts." Sunagawa, 1956.

The discussion of good or evil, pros or cons of a law is not a conceptual argument on morality or philosophy. It is an issue that determines order or chaos in a nation, security or insecurity in a society. This issue cannot be left merely to individual, subjective judgment, but must be guided by religious teachings based on a conviction of faith.

To chant Na Mu Myō Hō Ren Ge Kyō is a vow to give one's life and limb in serving the Genuine Dharma—truth—attested to by the Preceptor, Buddha Śākyamuni, and a vocal proclamation of our resolve not to spare our lives and bodies in creating a tranquil nation and, ultimately, peace for humanity at large. The merit of chanting Na Mu Myō Hō Ren Ge Kyō is attested to by the various Buddhas and is made explicit in the teachings of the World Honored One, Buddha Śākyamuni. Those who chant Na Mu Myō Hō Ren Ge Kyō must never follow any ignoble law which compromises the safety of the country. No matter what kind of law it may be, we ought never to collaborate with any unjust law that perpetuates peril and fear among societies and humanity. We can never take part in preparing or implementing any harm, killing or war, not to mention the preparation for the dreadful atomic and hydrogen wars.

A police officer of the Metropolitan Police Department who was mobilized to Sunagawa left a note and committed suicide at the Kamakura Beach. In accordance with the Administrative Agreement, an unjust law, his superior ordered a charge against passive-resistant workers, students, monks and women, who were seeking to defend the safety of their homeland. He was among the policemen who mercilessly clubbed and injured some 1,000 protesters. He took his own life after reflecting on the profession that made him a slave to pernicious and unjust laws and the perpetuator of rampant domestic strife.

Government authorities, starting with Superintendent General Eguchi of the Tōkyō Metropolitan Police Department, are attempting to evade their crime and maliciously deny the assault by police. In light of this police officer's suicide, the authorities deserve a death of torment and guilt. Even police officers [who commit such violence] are not beasts. Though they may barbarically inflict injuries on good citizens in a manner lower than beasts, would they not suffer pangs of conscience when they eventually leave service and reflect on their disgraceful conduct? The reverberation of Na Mu Myō Hō Ren Ge Kyō shall be the mirror for their introspection, and a robe of penitence that cloaks the hearer.

Na Mu Myō Hō Ren Ge Kyō

Nipponzan Myōhōji *Shamon*
Nichidatsu

Addendum 1:
Letter Presented to Japan's Prime Minister Hatoyama Ichirō

July 8, 1956
Shiobara, Japan

Word has reached my ears of the despicable flattery and deviousness Your Excellency displayed in a personal letter, sent before you assumed office, to curry favor with U.S. Secretary of State John Foster Dulles. Rumor has it that you advocated revising Article 9 of the Japanese Constitution to include a provision for rearmament and upgrade of the Self-Defense Forces personnel to 300,000 strong. This would lead the people astray and once again thrust the nation into crisis.

After assuming the office of Prime Minister, you stated recently in parliament that, "A constitution of peace and demilitarization cannot be adopted." Maintaining Japan's autonomy and peace solely by means of military force necessitated the reprehensible invitation for a foreign military presence, acceptance of unlimited U.S. military bases on our sacred homeland and inevitably forced Japan to collaborate with them.

Ensuring independence and peace by military force has been common in international relations. However, it is risky business, anachronistic in today's world. The disproportionate influence the military wields over U.S foreign policy has sparked opposition in various parts of the world, starting in Europe, and harsh criticism is gradually arising in the United States as well.

Use of military power is destined to become a hopelessly outdated means of achieving foreign policy objectives in the near future and ought to be disposed of as junk in the interest of world peace. Just like Prime Minister Hatoyama's obsolete perspective, it is antiquated thinking that requires our country to possess arms to become a stabilizing force for peace in Asia. The cost for rearmament should instead be allocated toward reeducation of the nation. Those trained in Satyagraha [grasping of truth] and in defending the Genuine Dharma can become disciples for peace who enable the nation to demonstrate the true power of the brave in creating peace in the world and guiding our civilization. As a nation avowed never again to make war, this is the good faith Japan must valiantly demonstrate to the world.

Should Japan recklessly expand its military bases and adopt

policies of arms build-up contrary to this aspiration, not only will it provoke fear and breed mistrust and suspicion among other nations, it will incur calamities of internal coups and foreign invasion, ultimately bringing about the fall of our nation. This is the prophecy of *Risshō-ankoku*.[7] I dare to counsel you out of my concern for the future of our people.

It is imperative that Your Excellency correct the political views of the weak, who favor arms build-up, and sincerely endeavor to create a climate of support and respect that has faith in the justice and compassion existing in the hearts and minds of nations and people of the world.

Regardless of race or ideology, no one is void of affection for one's own family. The affectionate heart for family is universal and has remained unchanged throughout the ages. Fostering tenderness and love towards each other should be Japan's one and only policy to create a peaceful nation; in the same vein it is the ultimate objective of world humanity. To achieve this objective, Japan must remove U.S. military bases at home, which are the source of resentment for farmers and fishermen, and rescind its affiliation with any unilateral international military alliance.

Fujii Nichidatsu
Nipponzan Myōhōji *Shamon*

7 Please refer to *Shishin-kaku*, footnote 5, p. 1.

Addendum 2: Letter to Director General of the Defense Agency

July 8, 1956
Tōkyō

Director General Funada Naka,[8]

The stated purpose of the Defense Agency is to protect the territory of Japan and its people from the ravages of war. The U.S. forces stationed in Japan and their military bases are said to exist for precisely the same purpose. This so-called military purpose has been generally assumed by all nations of the world without question. But the time has come to reexamine these weapons and war institutions and to seek out alternatives for the sake of future peace and security.

War is caused by the human heart and mind. Ultimately, any act of international war is a result of escalating mistrust, suspicion and antagonism that is mutual and fueled by animosity and fear.

The Japan-U.S. Security Treaty is without doubt a treaty that invites war.

> Such forces [U.S. land, air and sea forces] may be utilized to contribute to...the security of Japan against armed attack from without...including assistance to put down large-scale internal riots and disturbances in Japan, caused through instigation or intervention by an outside Power or Powers.[9]

With no large-scale internal riots nor any attacks from "without" looming anytime soon, inviting the U.S. military to be stationed in Japan and unilaterally reinforcing arms only heightens apprehension and confusion at home and abroad. The administrative agreement that governs said treaty allows U.S. land, air and sea forces to freely build countless numbers of bases in and around this small Japanese territory. It provides for cost sharing between the two countries and grants the

---

8 船田中 [1895-1979]. Member of the Japanese House of Representatives. He served as Director General of the Defense Agency from 1955 to 1956, the Speaker of the House of Representatives from 1963-1965, 1970-1971.

9 Article I of the Japan-U.S. Security Treaty, September 8, 1951.

United States free use of transportation, communication and electric power, undermining Japanese sovereignty.

Throughout the nation's history, Japan has never suffered this kind of humiliation. Japanese, as a race of people, have always held reverence for and believed in the sacredness of the land. This agreement violates the sacredness of the land, and the U.S. bases invading farm lands and fishing waters have destroyed the livelihood of farmers and fishermen. Not only were the livelihoods of farmers and fishermen destroyed, morals and customs vital to the social order have been trampled, the women degraded and men held in contempt. As the damage to the community becomes increasingly intolerable, the anguished cries of innocent farmers and fishermen grow ever more loudly throughout the entire land.

Should you continue to cover your ears against the tormented cries of farmers and fishermen and encourage the U.S.'s unrivaled and insatiable invasion of the world, mutual trust between Japan and the United States will suffer, and you will be planting the harmful seeds of mutual enmity.

The sacred duty that accompanies your position requires you, at the very least, to convey the suffering of the Japanese people, to halt the tyranny and inordinate greed of the United States and to be resolute in demanding the return of these bases. Furthermore, modern states are groaning under the increasing onerous burden of the arms race, leading many to propose the convention of disarmament conferences. Japan, on the contrary, caved in to U.S. pressure by covertly arming itself and adroitly sidestepped the confines of the Peace Constitution by calling it "the Defense Agency."

Since then, the government has acted like a den of thieves, spending exorbitant sums of tax money and legitimatizing the plunder of the Japanese people all in the name of national defense.

A true national defense that protects the Japanese land and its people while deterring internal riots and foreign invasion requires the abolition of the Defense Agency. Your resignation from office is a prerequisite.

Nipponzan Myōhōji *Shamon*
Fujii Nichidatsu

11

Denounced as Communists[1]

June 8, 1957
Colombo, Sri Lanka

Na Mu Myō Hō Ren Ge Kyō

The Unites States may passionately espouse "liberty," but there is one freedom it does not have—freedom of peace. Some Christian denominations are wholly engaged in the peace movement and suffer oppression from the government as a result. I hear the government refuses to issue passports to those planning to attend pacifist meetings abroad. "Peace" is alleged to be a communist plot, while atomic and hydrogen weapons are revered as "guardians of peace." The Japanese government is following in these footsteps. When even the communists are calling out for peace, why must proponents of freedom tolerate the absence of freedom of peace? Why not heed the communist call for peace by seizing the initiative in creating actual peace? From the very beginning, Nipponzan's call for peace has drawn relentless criticism. However, members of the Japanese Communist Party have come to appreciate Nipponzan's peace movement since the Sunagawa incident.[2] The first article on Nipponzan's

---

1 Excerpt of a letter Guruji wrote. The General Assembly of the World Peace Council was held in Colombo, Sri Lanka, in June 1957, attended by the leaders of developing countries, nations of the socialist bloc and peace delegates. It adopted an appeal for immediate and unconditional cessation of nuclear testing as well as a declaration of disarmament.

2 In 1956, Nipponzan Myōhōji monks and nuns joined local farmers, students and other activists in protesting the expansion of a military airfield into farmland in Sunagawa by the U.S. military with the backing of the Japanese government. The expropriation of land was done without any consultation with local people and without any compensation to them. The standoff between the local people and the government culminated in a three-day confrontation in which there were more than 1,000 casualties, including several monks of Nipponzan Myōhōji, who were beaten on the head, sustaining serious head injuries while drumming and chanting on the front line of the demonstrators. More on this subject can be found in the previous article, *Nation Under Rule of Law.*

work—*Religious Persecution* carried in *Daihōrin* [*Great Dharma Wheel*]—was written by a communist. It is true that there are communists among the delegation traveling with me. Despite their belief in communism, the majority of these people have come to embrace the ineffable sound of Nipponzan's Dharma drum with joy.

Weapons proponents who hold to the doctrine of "self-defense" along with those who believe in nuclear war are becoming ever more influential in the free nations of the world. Most likely the communist nations will beat the free world in making the first move to suspend nuclear tests. Why won't advocates of liberty awaken from their atomic war dreams? Starting with "Ike," Syngman Rhee,[3] Chiang Kai-shek,[4] Yoshida Shigeru[5] and a whole line of top Japanese officials who came after him, all are in a deep slumber.

Taking Okinawa as an example, the United States attacks anyone responding to the cries of the Okinawans and who stands up for them, labeling them "communists" or "reds." People sympathetic to their plight are likewise called "reds." Only those who go along with, remain a spectator to, or who show leniency towards crimes perpetuated by the United States are immune from attack. If we are not subjected to slander, invectives and attacks by staff and stone, how can we qualify as the practitioners of the Lotus Sūtra? Nipponzan will not be cowed by groundless slander.

---

3 李承晩 [1875-1965]. First president of South Korea [1948-1960] who was considered an anti-communist dictator.

4 蒋介石 [1887-1975]. Head of the Nationalist government in China [1928-1949] and later in Taiwan [1949-1975].

5 吉田茂 [1878-1967]. Japan's prime minister from 1946 to 1947, 1948 to 1954.

12

The Precept Against Taking Life

February 26, 1961
The Hour of Religion, a Nippon TV broadcast

In a letter, Nichiren Daishōnin states:

> There is no greater treasure to sentient beings than life. Those who deprive others of it will inevitably fall into the three evil paths. Wheel Turning Noble Kings[1] are born because of the merit they have earned by observing the precept against taking life, the foremost among the Ten Good Deeds.[2] Among the Hīnayāna precepts, Buddha first laid down the Five Precepts, and the precept against taking life is the first of the five. It is the first of the Ten Major Precepts in the Mahāyāna Brahmajala Sūtra; and the Buddha revealed in *The Eternal Duration of the Life of the Tathāgata* chapter attained ever-present, eternal life through the merits of his compassion to emancipate all sentient beings and his practice of the precept against taking life. Accordingly, the Buddhas of the Triple World shall forsake those who kill, and devas of the Six Heavens of the World of Desire will not lend their protection.[3]

Those inhabiting the earth in modern times are equally shrouded in the utmost anxiety, fear and agony, irrespective of age or gender, because

1 The ideal monarch. Please refer to *Nuclear Technology and the Future of Humanity*, footnote 19, p. 92.

2 Not to kill, not to steal, not to commit adultery, not to tell lies, not to speak ill of others, not to utter words that cause enmity, not to engage in idle talk, not to be greedy, not to be angry, and not to have distorted views. For the original Japanese, please refer to *Nuclear Technology*, footnote 20.

3 Please refer to *Nuclear Technology*, footnote 22, p. 93.

the peril to our most precious possession—our life and limb, which could be instantaneously reduced to smoke and ash—is keenly felt.

Modern civilization is the bedrock of the modern state. Everything from politics to economics to foreign policies, arms, academics and entertainment are constantly being refined and developed to serve and to be subservient to the modern state's ultimate quest: the art of killing culminating in the crime of human annihilation. The arrival of the space age has not removed the menace confronting human beings in the least, rather it has magnified it. Every time world leaders open their mouths, they speak of peace while simultaneously clutching dreadful bombs of murder and destruction in their hands. How tragic the state of modern civilization, whose true identity is the cursed demon king.

All life forms seek to protect themselves by any number of means. This is called self-defense or self-preservation. However, now the heinous atomic and hydrogen war that foreshadows human annihilation is disguised from the world under the stolen name of self-defense. The Self-Defense Forces established in Japan are precisely that. They are in the business of killing and destruction. Not only are they unproductive, immoral and anti-religious, the very name of Self-Defense Forces is immoral in and of itself.

Self-defense originally meant protecting oneself from perils and persecution. If the perils are natural disasters, attacks by ferocious beasts or venomous serpents or pandemics, means adopted to guard against them are not necessarily immoral or anti-religious. Yet, when the threat of danger is deemed as coming from our communities or from another nation, it means neighbors or neighboring countries are perceived as a threat to our lives. This perception harbors mistrust and heightens suspicion and fear among the people and between nations. These negative perceptions destroy the moral feeling that makes peaceful community life possible or allows negotiations to settle international issues amicably. The result is unending research into methods of merciless mass killing and destruction for so-called self-defense, which, in reality, is the preparation and training in modern warfare. The true colors of immorality are precisely and palpably revealed.

In humanity's long history, it is a fact that in some eras the means of war, that is to say murder and destruction, were wrongfully used for self-defense. However, had humanity persisted in this mistake, it would have been annihilated long before the modern era of atomic and hydrogen weapons, possibly during the civilization of the Bronze Age or with the discovery of gunpowder. The fact that humanity has somehow survived and thrived on the face of the earth to this day is because human beings adopted and honored a method of self-defense antithetical to killing and war, namely, the precept against taking life.

For example, in examining Japanese history we learn about the rival clans of Genji and Heike, who defended themselves by making war. In just 45 years after Genji and Heike started to kill each other, both clans perished. Their distant descendants have survived to this day only because their ancestors experienced first-hand the true nature of war with its futility and criminality. They took refuge in mountains and valleys free from war, where they ungrudgingly renounced weapons, turning spears and swords into sickles, and in converting their lives to absolute peace, they transformed the hearts and minds of their foes with love and nonviolence. Testimony to the singular self-defense that spared the Heike remnant from the Genji's punitive forces is found in the lyrics of the folk ballad *Hietsuki-bushi*[4] handed down in the deep mountains of Hyūga[5] on the border of Higo.[6]

Street campaigns were recently launched to prevent juveniles from possessing knives. Horrible crimes of murder, assault and rape are on the rise among juveniles, who act with increased malice. Protective custody by police has had little effect in stemming crime, and so the campaign seeks to pre-empt it by raising society's awareness in order to prevent knives used in crime from getting into juvenile hands. Some young people claim they keep knives to purge the evil that pervades society. Regardless of the motive, once the knife possession is condoned, others, too, can use

---

4 稗搗節. A ballad sung at the time of hulling millet is based on an 800-year-old tale of a remnant group of Heike fugitives at Shiiba 椎葉, whose lives were spared by the commander of the Genji, Nasu Daihachirō. Daihachirō observed their modest life cultivating crops in this obscure land and felt no animosity from them. He reported back to Minamoto Yoritomo [1147-1180], the founder of the first shogunate in Japan, the Kamakura Shogunate, that the mission was accomplished. He decided to remain at Shiiba and built a shrine to Itsukushima, the tutelary deity of the Heike clan. He lived harmoniously with them by teaching farming and later fell in love with Princess Tsurutomi. By the time he was ordered to return to Kamakura, Princess Tsurutomi was pregnant with his child. Daihachirō presented Princess Tsurutomi with his celebrated sword as a token of his relationship to the unborn child and asked her to send the child to him in Kamakura if it was a boy and raise the child in Shiiba if it was a girl. Princess Tsurutomi gave birth to a girl, raised her in Shiiba, and when her daughter married, the son-in-law took the last name of Nasu.

5 Present day Miyazaki Prefecture in Kyūshū, the southernmost island in the Japanese mainland.

6 The present day Kumamoto Prefecture on Kyūshū, northwest of Miyazaki Prefecture.

this pretext resulting in a rise in juvenile crime. To counter this type of reasoning, the campaign calls for abstaining from the use of knives even in a just cause or for self-defense.

The source of terror shrouding humanity today is the frenzied arms race by the developed nations, often called the superpowers. Western superpowers blundered at the outset by making the ignoble law of survival of the fittest a basic policy of the modern state. Furthermore, the formation of the Self-Defense Forces in Japan only added to the arms race by increasing the number of those vying to be the fittest. This only serves to heighten the crisis facing humanity but offers nothing towards Japan's security nor towards the prevention of a national catastrophe.

If we use as a model the campaign to deter juvenile crime by denying access to all knives, even prohibiting possession of a knife for self-defense, and apply it not only to adults but to the international community, then humanity can avert the grave crime of annihilation and rejoice in a life free from agony and fear through a moral development that embraces total disarmament and renounces war in the name of self-defense. In these turbulent times, no one can absolutely deny the possibility of a national crisis unexpectedly befalling Japan. What are we to do in such a case? The Self-Defense Forces are supposedly established in anticipation of such contingencies. However, without careful consideration, one could fall under the illusion that the Self-Defense Forces will provide an assured defense in a national crisis simply by reason of their existence, and that war in self-defense will always prevail. To believe that peace and security of the nation depend absolutely on the Self-Defense Forces is a misconception that becomes nothing more than a delusion that military might is everything. With the establishment of the Self-Defense Forces, commentators on military matters, as part of their job, imagined scenarios in which the Self-Defense Forces are mobilized for war, but never contemplated tragic defeat as a possible outcome in a war of self-defense. This is the height of shortsightedness and imprudence.

From ancient times, the idea that security comes from might is nothing more than an entrenched myth held for the most part by the military profession. The notion found in a Chinese book of military strategy, "Be prepared and have no regrets," is embraced as truth. But based on today's common knowledge, we know the reverse is true: preparation for war, that is the possession of arms, fosters a nation's insecurity. We cannot forget the profound misery and sorrow of the Japanese nation as a consequence of the "sacred war" embarked upon by the loyal, valiant and invincible Emperor's Army, which was believed to invoke the Divine Wind. The capability of new modern weapons is a divine warning of the heavens that the time has come to ban all acts of war. Should this warning go unheeded, and should we unwisely arm and engage in wars of self-defense, it will only lead to engulfing our homeland in conflagration and opening up the abyss of national ruin.

The nation of Japan became a bellwether among nations of the world by enacting a constitution that calls for complete disarmament and renounces the right to war.[7] We must awaken to our mission as messengers of the Tathāgata sent to emancipate the ignoble Era of Final Dharma, the world in perpetual strife and hostility as prophesized by the Tathāgata, and with unequivocal integrity adhere to the precept against taking life laid down by the Buddha. What is at stake is the survival of humanity consisting of three billion and the preservation of the land covering five continents.

On the other hand, if Japan abolishes the Self-Defense Forces, outlaws war and truly becomes a nation without arms, what are we to do if faced with a sudden and unexpected national crisis? At such a time, let the leaders of Japan line up in front of the invader's dreadful weapons with palms together bowing in veneration and negotiate peace. Let the men and women of the nation follow suit. No matter how great the enmity or hostility of the invading forces, they will not be able to recklessly fire on or bomb Japan. The human spirit is too developed for such wanton acts to be readily committed. The basis for humans to believe and embrace the Tathāgata's precept of non-killing is already present in our hearts and minds. Nevertheless, the invaders still may mercilessly shoot or bomb the Japanese leaders, men and women who seek peace lined up with palms pressed together, bowing in veneration. Let us stand side by side and meet death in serenity. It is a sacred sacrifice for building lasting peace in the world. It is a Bodhisattva practice of extricating the afflictions and

---

7 In Japan's Constitution, Article 9, *Renunciation of War*, reads: "Aspiring sincerely to an international peace based on justice and order, the Japanese people forever renounce war as a sovereign right of the nation and the threat or use of force as means of settling international disputes.

"In order to accomplish the aim of the preceding paragraph, land, sea, and air forces, as well as other war potential, will never be maintained. The right of belligerency of the state will not be recognized."

agonies of world humanity.

In the previous World War, the Emperor's Army declared it a war of self-preservation. The people evacuated from their homes to the countryside or hid in air raid shelters, yet roughly eight million were killed. The toll to foreign nationals killed by Japan was even greater. Even if we were to be killed lined up with palms together, the number of deaths could not possibly be more than one-thousandth or one-millionth of that. Furthermore, not a single life from another country would be taken. No matter how much we fear death, death is inevitable in modern war. If we fear death, we absolutely must avert war. To renounce war, we must completely lay down arms, the instruments of war.

Risshō-ankoku-ron written by Nichiren Daishōnin states: "If one wishes to have peace for oneself, first pray for the tranquility of the world." If our vision is narrow, concerned solely with danger for ourselves or our nation, we become prone to the illusion that the Self-Defense Forces are necessary. However, the overriding issue of concern to humanity right now is the imminent danger of annihilation, leaving no nation safe. Let us broaden our vision and recognize that weapons and war by Japan or any nation are the enemies of humanity. For the sake of extricating humanity from the menace of annihilation, we must first eliminate weapons and war. The teaching shows that when we first and foremost pray for the tranquility of the world—in other words, the emancipation of all humanity—then through that prayer, the safety for us as individuals and for the nation of Japan will naturally be realized. If Japan along with three billion fellow human beings of the world ultimately wish to seek a way out of modern civilization's tragedy into peace and tranquility, the only viable option is to believe, embrace and uphold the precept of not to take life laid down by the World Honored One, Buddha Śākyamuni.

Na Mu Myō Hō Ren Ge Kyō

Nichidatsu

13

The Doctrine of the Sword

November 23, 1962
Radio Broadcast Speech on All India Radio, New Delhi[1]

Out of all of Bapuji's[2] works, I was most moved by an article titled *The Doctrine of the Sword*. It inspired a profound faith in India and Mahatma Gandhi for me. Let me quote a passage from it.

> My religion has no geographical limits. If I have a living faith in it, it will transcend my love for India itself.

By virtue of these words, please allow me, though not a citizen of this country, to urge India to embrace the ideas highlighted in *The Doctrine of the Sword* because I believe it is in her best interest.

> I am not pleading for India to practice nonviolence because it is weak. I want her to practice nonviolence being conscious of her strength and power. No training in arms is required for realization of her strength. We seem to need it because we seem to think that we are but a lump of flesh. I want India to recognize that she has a soul that cannot perish and that can rise triumphant above every physical weakness and defy the physical combination of the whole world. [*The Doctrine of the Sword*, hereafter referred as DOS.][3]

---

1 A similar but shorter speech was given at the All India Sarvodaya Conference held in Vedchi, Gujarat.

2 Term of endearment used to refer to Mahatma Gandhi by the Indian people. It means father.

3 The English is as it appears in *The Doctrine of the Sword* by Mohandas Gandhi, *Young India*, Ahmedabad, August 11, 1920.

Participating in the International Conference for the Abolition of Nuclear Weapons, New Delhi, India, 1960.

Gandhiji emphatically rejected arms training as unnecessary for the great political revolution of India's independence. Training in arms is seen as necessary due to simple timidity when we fail to believe in the superiority of our spiritual strength and misconstrue India to be but a lump of flesh. Gandhiji called upon India to challenge the combined physical violence of the whole world and recognize that she has the strength to triumph over it, that she has a soul, which cannot be destroyed by any weapon. What kind of mistake is it to relinquish her spiritual strength and to take to bestial and cruel weapons before the earth covering Gandhiji's grave has even dried?

> The high-souled men, who are unable to suffer national humiliation any longer, will want to vent their wrath. They will take to violence. So far as I know, they must perish without delivering themselves or their country from the wrong. [DOS]

The people of India, a nation of newly acquired independence, were outraged by the heavy-handedness of the People's Republic of

China in the border conflict,[4] regarding it as an intolerable national humiliation, and decided to resort to arms to do away with the tyranny of the People's Republic of China. What a grave misfortune it would be if India's conviction of victory through violence turns out to be a miscalculation or misjudgment. Furthermore, violence is never an easy fix to a border conflict. Once force is used, the issue, which ought to be framed as to what is reasonable and just both spiritually and morally, is instantly degraded to a brutish concept of victory or defeat by violence. Even if India were to prevail through violence, it bestows no honor on her aspiration to be a peaceful nation. If worse comes to worst and victory is not the outcome of war, there will be a tremendous, untold material and spiritual price to pay, which will include causalities, destruction of property, devastation of the land, and bring disgrace to the peaceful Indian nation. War would only exasperate the original border issue. We, the Japanese people, experienced these evils of war first hand at the end of World War II. "If India takes up the doctrine of the sword, she may gain momentary victory. Then India will cease to be the pride of my heart." As these words of Gandhiji show, he went as far as to flatly reject the notion of victory in war for India.

The French Emperor Napoleon Bonaparte, even at the height of his military triumphs, reflected, "The sword will always be conquered by the spirit."[5] He is said to have been prevented from conclusively laying down the sword due to pressure from emperors and kings surrounding him, driving him to continual battle against his wishes.

I firmly believe that the recent act of war by India does not reflect the true intention of its leaders. The declaration and resolutions adopted at the nuclear weapons abolition conference held in June of this year bears this out. It is hard to fathom the great disappointment Gandhiji, the compassionate father of India's independence, would have

4 Indo-Sino Border Conflict or Indo-Sino War broke out between the Chinese Liberation Army and Indian military in fall of 1962 initially over a dispute on the Himalayan border in Arunachal Pradesh, located in northeastern India. China does not recognize the boundary between it and Arunachal Pradesh. The origin of the war was a Chinese attack on the Indian military patrol in the North East Frontier Province. The conflict also later involved Aksai Chin 阿克賽欽, a region administered by China at the juncture of China, India and Pakistan, which India and Pakistan both claim. Aksai Chin was traditionally part of the Himalayan Kingdom Ladakh until its annexation by Kashmir in 1834.

5 "There are only two forces in the world, the sword and the spirit. In the long run the sword will always be conquered by the spirit."

felt when only months later the entire Indian nation took up the doctrine of the sword.

> I believe absolutely that she has a mission for the world. She is not to copy Europe blindly. [DOS]

The world has turned into a huge fortress structured for war, a situation unprecedented since the dawn of humanity. Regardless of any personal aversion to war, we are all trapped in this war machine. It is precisely the age fraught with struggle and strife, as prophesized by Buddha.

The escape route from this system of perpetual war is neither in the materialistic economic policies of the West nor in "isms" or doctrines, but only in the spirituality of the East, religious faith. Bapuji's life was dedicated to the pursuit of India's independence through his faith in the teachings of the precept against taking life, nonviolence, which he believed to be the principal tenet of a religion born among the people of India. This indeed is the only Mahāyāna path open to all to save humanity from the tragedies of the nuclear and conventional arms race.

Simply solving the border issue, which is the tip of the iceberg, is not India's mission. Her mission is to save the world from total destruction. In order to fulfill this mission for the world, India must first instill faith among the peace-seeking peoples of the world in the precept against taking life, nonviolence, the fundamental tenet of a religion born in India. It means to abandon weapons of murder, no matter how intolerable the humiliation may be.

It is much to expect any country to abandon its right to war in an iniquitous age rife with conflict and strife. India is the only country and nation capable of responding to this call. Now is the time for India to be resolved and demonstrate the just essence of her spiritual faith to the grief stricken world afflicted by the "doctrine of the sword," by laying down the sword for the sake of world humanity.

In Bapuji's The *Sword v. Spirit,* he cites a passage in a letter Napoleon addressed to the Emperor of Austria from the battlefield:

> Amid grief and surrounded by 15,000 corpses, I feel bound to give your Majesty an urgent warning. You are far from the scene; your heart cannot be so deeply moved as mine is on

> the spot . . . I implore your Majesty to return our generation to peace and tranquility. Should the people of latter ages be folly enough to start war, they would have to accept peace after years of war and to seek a way to mutually live.

Even in this non-virtuous era of strife and conflict, up to now India has been fortunate to be spared the scourge of modern war, the root of misery and aggregation of evil, owing to the blessings of the precept against taking life and nonviolence, the very heart of religion. However, taking up the doctrine of the sword in the current border conflict has already resulted in 1,500 to 2,500 deaths on the battlefield. There will be no return for these innocent youth of India, which once had a firm faith in nonviolence. The border may eventually be returned to India. However, the souls of those who were lost in war have departed to a place from where they will never return. If India were to further expand and continue the war, its calamities would no longer be limited to India's misfortune but could eventually spark the tragedy of humanity's annihilation. In this broader context, prevailing in a local conflict should not be a matter of national priority.

I, as a Buddhist bhikshu, am resolved to dedicate my life to the service of India, and ultimately to serve the world, through the essential, elemental Buddhist precept against taking life, in other words, the teaching of nonviolence. If my service can take the place of even one young Indian soldier's life, I shall meet my death without regret.

I implore you; allow me to go to the battlefield in the Himalayas so that I may practice my prayers for peace. I have come to India with an unfaltering determination not to spare my life. Two, three, ten, a hundred of my Japanese Buddhist disciples and devotees will follow me to the battlefield to stop the Indo-Sino border conflict. We have vowed to each other to lay down our lives in prayer for nonviolence.

Na Mu Myō Hō Ren Ge Kyō

14

Odaimoku

January 1964
Message to the Japan-India Cultural Association
Patna, India

Na Mu Myō Hō Ren Ge Kyō is the quintessential Daimoku of the Saddharma-pundrīka-sūtra [Myōhō-renge-kyō, the Lotus Sūtra], the true purpose of Buddha's advent in this world as expounded by the Preceptor, the World Honored One, Buddha Śākyamuni at Mount Grdhrakūta [Sacred Eagle Peak] in Magadha Kingdom in Middle India during the last eight years of his life.

The Preceptor Buddha Śākyamuni perfected his guidance to the Dharma in his lifetime, which proved to accommodate all sentient beings of varying capacities in the ten worlds in achieving Supreme Enlightenment. However, out of his pity towards all sentient beings after his Parinirvāna, in particular humanity who would come 2,000 years later in the iniquitous Era of Final Dharma, a time of *tojō-kengo*[1] when the world is steeped in war and killing, the Buddha encapsulated the quintessence of the Saddharma-pundrīka-sūtra in a single phrase to relieve humanity of the fear of war and to provide refuge from the darkness of rampant murder. The disciples to whom it would be entrusted were designated. The good medicine Buddha Śākyamuni left behind for the *sahā* world, replete with distress and affliction, is the Daimoku consisting of the five and seven characters of Na Mu Myō Hō Ren Ge Kyō.

Na Mu Myō Hō Ren Ge Kyō benefits all sentient beings in particular men and women of today when embraced in our hearts and minds, chanted through our mouth and offered to others as a guide to the Dharma. It is therefore superfluous of me to attempt to offer any commentary or lecture on it at this time. That being said, even a child building a stūpa from sand

---

1 闘諍堅固.

is said to be practicing the Bodhisattva Way.[2] With that in mind, in the interest of those who seek the Buddha Way, allow me to briefly address Na Mu Myō Hō Ren Ge Kyō to the best of my ability, guided by the wisdom that ancient sages acquired through profound faith and erudition.

Peace rests in the hands of the World Honored One, the Buddha. It is called *Buppō* [Buddha Dharma]. Buddha Dharma in acclamation is referred to as *Myōhō*[3] [Sublime Dharma]. The Sublime Dharma is likened to the lotus flower. It is a lotus flower in the height of its bloom and glory. This is called *Myōhō-renge*[4] [the Sublime Dharma of the Lotus Flower]. The Sublime Dharma of the Lotus Flower is the immutable Truth, True Dharma, throughout the past, present and future. No Demon King[5] can change it, nor would it be altered in any way even with the advent of a thousand Buddhas. Its changeless nature is called *kyō*.[6] *Myōhō-renge-kyō* is the Dharma of intrinsic reverence, the object of veneration and offerings. This is Na Mu Myō Hō Ren Ge Kyō.

Peace is essentially the intrinsic law of the human heart and mind.[7] It is called *shinpō*[8] [Dharma heart-mind]. The Dharma heart-mind is praised as Sublime Dharma. The Dharma heart-mind is likened to the lotus flower. The lotus flower representing the Dharma heart-mind is a blossom yet to bloom. On rare occasions blossoms will bloom in part. This is called the Wondrous Dharma of the Lotus Flower. This *Myōhō-renge*, the Wondrous Dharma of the Lotus Flower, is never affected nor tainted by evil conduct[9] caused by ignorance[10] and delusions[11] constantly created by humans. This state free from any contamination is *kyō*.

To induce the blossoming of the Sublime Dharma of the Lotus Flower representing the Dharma nature of our heart-mind, we venerate and make offerings to it by invocation through oral enunciation. This is Na Mu Myō Hō Ren Ge Kyō. Na Mu Myō Hō Ren Ge Kyō at this stage still has a strong personal trait.

---

2 Chapter II, *Expedients*, of the Lotus Sūtra.

3 妙法.

4 妙法蓮華.

5 Devamāra-pāpīyas. Demon King of the sixth heaven of desire who attempts to obstruct the practice and prevents one from attaining enlightenment.

6 経.

7 *Shinshō* 心性 *citta- svabhāva.*

8 *Shinpō* 心法 *citta-samtāna.*

9 *Akuśala-karman.* Evil conduct in thought, word and deed.

10 *Avidyā.* Ignorance on the true nature of existence.

11 *Kleśa.* Mental afflictions.

Peace is fundamentally the law that ensures the survival of the realm of sentient beings.[12] This is called *shujōhō*[13] [the Dharma of the realm of sentient beings]. The Dharma of the realm of sentient beings in acclamation is called *Myōhō*. The Wondrous Dharma, the Dharma of the realm of sentient beings, is likened to the lotus flower. It is called *Myōhō-renge*, the Wondrous Dharma of the Lotus Flower. This lotus flower is also yet to open. On rare occasions flowers will open partially, and some will have blossomed. The Wondrous Dharma of the Lotus Flower, the Dharma of the realm of sentient beings is extremely broad in what it encompasses, including the various facets of good and evil, pain and joy, birth and death, concealed and revealed, transmigration,[14] rise and fall. These myriad phenomena of creation within heaven and earth, the entire universe, are facets of the true state[15] of the active forces in pursuit of peace. As such, the law of peace consistently present in all phenomena is *kyō*.

The law of peace must be believed in and embraced in order to bring the Wondrous Dharma of the Lotus Flower, the Dharma of sentient beings, to bloom and actualize peace in the communities of beings. This is Na Mu Myō Hō Ren Ge Kyō. This Na Mu Myō Hō Ren Ge Kyō is the great principle in creating peace in the world. The fruit borne of it is *Risshō-ankoku* [The realm made tranquil through the rise of the True Dharma].

The merits of Na Mu Myō Hō Ren Ge Kyō for *Risshō-ankoku* expand to the state, society, the nation and to the world. When lack of this spiritual constructive component is deemed acceptable in the function of the state, of the society or of the world, then tragedies of strife, war and imminent threat of humanity's extinction ensue. Herein is the agony and darkness of modern states.

Extremely profound is the Buddha Dharma, and almost no one has awakened to it up to this day. The Exceptional One in the human world

---

12 *Shujō-seken* 衆生世間 *Manusya-loka-dhātu*. Sentient beings regarded as a constituent of the world. The three constituents of the world are sentient beings, non-sentient beings and the five skandha or aggregates, which are the five constituent elements of all existences [matter or form, perception, conception, volition and consciousness]. These three constituents comprise all beings, sentient and non-sentient.

13 衆生法.

14 *Samsārita*. Originally it meant flow, i.e., the perpetual repetition of birth and death in the three worlds and the realms of existence.

15 *Jissō* 実相. The real state of all things, the truth; the universal and eternal truth applicable to all things.

who awakened to it is venerated and called the World Honored One, the Buddha. The World Honored One, Buddha Śākyamuni, is the one who awakened to the Buddha Dharma based on his vow to be the One to emancipate all sentient beings. Homage is paid to the World Honored One, Buddha Śākyamuni by calling him Na Mu Myō Hō Ren Ge Kyō. The World Honored One, Buddha Śākyamuni, or in other words, Na Mu Myō Hō Ren Ge Kyō, is both the *Honzon*[16] of world peace in the human world and the object of religious faith. The indivisible relationship between what is called Truth and God espoused by Gandhiji is the Thusness[17] of the one and indivisible Person Dharma,[18] Na Mu Myō Hō Ren Ge Kyō, and is the reason we chant through our mouth and venerate with our bodies.

A metaphor is used to facilitate humans in understanding the Wondrous Dharma of the Lotus Flower, the Buddha Dharma. This is known as the metaphoric lotus. However, Buddha Dharma's Wondrous Dharma of the Lotus Flower is one and inseparable from the existential lotus.[19]

The scope covered by the Dharma of sentient beings is extremely vast. Notwithstanding its vastness, this Dharma, law, does not act in random but is in perfect order. From the galaxies to the nucleus of the atom, everything assumes its assigned place and moves in precise concordance based on cause and effect. The same is true with the society of human beings. History bears witness to the fact that this Dharma—which is behind good and evil, rise and fall, destruction and construction—consistently applies to individuals, to families, to nations and to the entire world. This is called the Dharma of sentient beings. The Dharma of sentient beings is to be followed, respected and paid homage to. This is called Na Mu Myō Hō Ren Ge Kyō.

Time after time conflict and agony are experienced due to the vastness and intricacies of worldly existence. As a lucid illustration for human beings on the inherent purity of the Dharma of sentient beings, it is

---

16 本尊. Principle object of veneration.

17 Tathāgata [Thusness, suchness] refers to the true form of things, reality. It is the absolute reality that transcends the multitude of forms in the phenomenal world. It is regarded as being identical with *Hosshin* [法身 Dharma Body] and cannot be expressed in words or contemplated by the unenlightened.

18 Pudgala Dharma. Pudgala in Buddhism means an individual or a person.

19 *Tōtai-renge* 当体蓮華. It is reference to an individual, i.e., the disciple of the Origin Buddha, who has awakened to the mission of realizing universal emancipation. This mission is carried out by disseminating the Lotus Sūtra through the Odaimoku in this world on behalf of the Origin Buddha.

metaphorically referred to as The Wondrous Dharma of the Lotus Flower. When everyone chants Na Mu Myō Hō Ren Ge Kyō, the metaphoric lotus becomes one and inseparable from the existential lotus. The passage in the sūtra[20] "tranquil is this realm of mine, ever filled with celestial beings" is a description of that.

The Dharma heart-mind of individual human beings is said to encompass three thousand worlds if there is even a trace of the heart-mind. It is not as sublime as the Buddha Dharma or far-reaching as the Dharma of sentient beings. Rather, it is extremely narrow and exists extremely close to us. Moreover, this Dharma heart-mind is connected to the wondrous Buddha Dharma and the vast Dharma of sentient beings. When the Dharma heart-mind of an individual truly blossoms into the flower of Na Mu Myō Hō Ren Ge Kyō, the metaphoric lotus becomes one and inseparable from the existential lotus, and the merit of this transformation provides a foundation for creating universal peace that goes beyond geographic and spatial boundaries. Throughout the ages down to this day, there appeared those who assumed the work [of the Origin Buddha in this world on his behalf], and their merit is unhindered by the constraints of time.

It is said that when a Buddha who attains Enlightenment quietly looks around the Buddha Realm[21] [the existence of the entire universe], everything in sight, from grass and trees to the land, is in the state of enlightenment. The wondrous, ineffable Buddha Dharma,[22] the far-reaching ineffable Dharma of sentient beings[23] and the proximate ineffable Dharma mind[24] are known as the ineffable Triple Dharma.[25] Essentially, the ineffable Triple Dharma is the single ineffable Dharma of Na Mu Myō Hō Ren Ge Kyō. The ineffable Triple Dharma is separately identified to encourage people to believe, embrace and practice the Honzon of the ineffable Single Dharma, Na Mu Myō Hō Ren Ge Kyō.

We must chant Na Mu Myō Hō Ren Ge Kyō in pursuit of peace in our own minds and hearts. We must chant Na Mu Myō Hō Ren Ge Kyō in pursuit of peace in our country and the world. We must chant Na Mu Myō Hō Ren Ge Kyō to manifest the spiritual essence of peace.

---

20 Chapter XVI of the Lotus Sūtra, *The Eternal Duration of the Life of the Tathāgata.*

21 *Hokkai* 法界 *Dharma-Dhātu*. The oneness of the totality of all things.

22 *Buppō-myō* 仏法妙.

23 *Shujō-hō-myō* 衆生法妙.

24 *Shin-pō-myō* 心法妙.

25 *Sanbō-myō* 三法妙.

Writing the calligraphy of the Odaimoku.

15

In Defense of the Peace Constitution

May 16, 1964
Delivered at the Kumamoto Rally to Protect the Peace Constitution
Kumamoto, Japan

Na Mu Myō Hō Ren Ge Kyō

It is an honor to address you here at the rally for the great walk to safeguard the Peace Constitution. For convenience, I will entitle this talk "In Defense of the Peace Constitution."

The Japanese government had set up a study commission on the constitution some years ago.[1] Now eight years later, the commission is expected shortly to submit its findings from the past years of study to the cabinet and the National Diet. The progressive parties have maintained that such a commission was uncalled for, and some even refused to participate. For this reason, the number of progressive members is limited. The conservatives' agenda has been to advocate for an investigation on the constitution in order to amend the constitution based on its findings.[2] They oppose the distinctively progressive features of the current Constitution

---

1 The Constitution of Japan was promulgated on November 3, 1946 and enacted on May 3, 1947. In April 1952, the de facto rule by the Supreme Command of the Allied Powers [SCAP] was terminated after six years and seven months. In 1955, the Liberal Democratic Party Prime Minister Hatoyama Ichirō declared the revision of the constitution as a fundamental party platform policy "to restore Japan to a truly independent nation state." The Constitutional Investigation Law passed in May 1956, and the Commission on the Constitution [憲法調査会] was set up. Between its first meeting in 1957 to the submission of the final report, the commission compiled more than 5,400 pages in findings from more than 130 plenary meetings and even more subcommittee meetings with testimony from 500 individuals who appeared at 50-plus public hearings. Members of the Socialist and Communist parties and experts who opposed revision and did not take part in the commission.

2 On January 20, 2000, the Commission on the Constitution was re-opened and inaugurated its 147th session within both houses of the National Diet. Unlike the 1956 commission, the current commission does not include representatives from academia and other experts.

of Japan, which is unlike the previous constitution.[3]

Proponents who advocate the need for an investigative commission characterize the current constitution written under Allied occupation as an imposed constitution, which they argue does not reflect the true will of the Japanese people. Indeed, since it was drawn up during the occupation, it may not have been possible to go against the intentions of the occupation forces, and the draft must have been subjected to their scrutiny and revision.

However, to argue that the constitution needs to be re-examined and revised at this juncture reflects a narrow, insular sentiment that fails to appreciate the character of the pacifist constitution in modern times. The specific targets of these would-be revisions are the preamble to the Constitution, which provides for demilitarization,[4] and the article on renunciation of war.[5]

It is precisely for this reason that we maintain that the constitution needs to be safeguarded. Out of fear of Japan falling back into militarism, the Allied Powers presumably saw the need to completely disarm Japan and make it accept the renunciation of the state's right of belligerency to maintain future peace in Asia and the world.

However, General Douglas MacArthur's[6] memoirs suggest that the articles of demilitarization and renunciation of war did not come from his instructions, but rather were proposed by the Japanese government.

---

3 The Meiji Constitution, promulgated on February 11, 1889 as part of the Meiji Restoration, provided for a form of constitutional monarchy modeled after the Prussian constitution.

4 "We, the Japanese people, desire peace for all time and are deeply conscious of the high ideals controlling human relationship, and we have determined to preserve our security and existence, trusting in the justice and faith of the peace-loving peoples of the world."

5 Article 9: "Aspiring sincerely to an international peace based on justice and order, the Japanese people forever renounce war as a sovereign right of the nation and the threat or use of force as means of settling international disputes. In order to accomplish the aim of the preceding paragraph, land, sea, and air forces, as well as other war potential, will never be maintained. The right of belligerency of the state will not be recognized."

6 General MacArthur served as Supreme Commander of the Allied Powers [SCAP] in Japan from September 1945 until June 1950. According to MacArthur, the provision was suggested by Baron Shidehara Kijūrō 幣原 喜重郎 [1872-1951], a prominent pre-World War II diplomat and the 44th Prime Minister of Japan [1945-1946]. [Douglas MacArthur, *Reminiscences* 1964, p. 302.] Shidehara admitted to his authorship in his memoirs *Gaikō Gojū-Nen* [*Fifty Years of Diplomacy*], published in 1951. MacArthur himself confirmed Shidehara's authorship on several occasions. However, according to some interpretations, the inclusion of Article 9 was mainly performed by the members of SCAP's Government Section [民政局 *Min-Sei-Kyoku*] in particular, Charles Kades, one of MacArthur's closest associates, and finally approved by the Diet of Japan on November 3, 1946. This article embodied the spirit of the 1928 Kellogg-Briand Pact renouncing war. However, Kades

Commander MacArthur confesses that he was absolutely stunned when he saw these articles. I believe it is because a constitution that provides for disarmament and renunciation of war is without precedent anywhere in the world.

Capitalizing on its 300 or so military bases in Japan, the United States provoked the Korean War. Consequently, it engaged in a disadvantageous war that almost drove it back to the Genkainada,[7] despite paying a heavy price. In recent years the United States is starting to revisit the same folly of the Korean War in Vietnam, Laos, Cambodia and the like. The United States has publicly solicited Japan's assistance in subjugating the South Vietnamese National Liberation Force. As a member of the free world, the Japanese government intends to play a role in exterminating the Vietnamese liberation army. Rearming Japan is deemed necessary towards that end.

The U.S. failure in the Korean War led to the realization that Japanese support in the form of military bases, war supplies and, in particular, its military force, is essential in implementing U.S. policy to control the "Orient." Therefore, Mr. Yoshida Shigeru,[8] upon whom was conferred not too long ago Supreme Orders of the Chrysanthemum,[9] was summoned to the United States to pressure Japan into rearming. Mr. Yoshida Shigeru shielded himself behind Article 9 of the Japanese Constitution and did not give in to this pressure, a rather unexpected disappointment for the United States. Special presidential envoy John Foster Dulles[10] was

---

rejected language that would have prohibited Japan's use of force "for its own security," believing that self-preservation was the right of every nation. The article's acceptance by the Japanese government may, in part, be explained by the desire to protect the imperial throne. Some Allied leaders held the Emperor accountable for Japan's bellicose aggressions in the WWII era. His assent to the "No War" clause weakened their arguments for abolishing the throne or trying the emperor as a war criminal.

7 玄界灘. The sea that extents northwest from Fukuoka Prefecture. Pusan, Korea is situated northwest of it.

8 Yoshida Shigeru 吉田茂 [1878-1967]. A diplomat and politician who served as ambassador to Italy and Britain in the 1930's, and Japanese prime minister five times between 1946 and 1954. He was a key figure in reestablishing Japan politically and economically after WWII. His administration saw a new constitution enacted, land reforms, the end of U.S. occupation and Japan's economic transformation.

9 大勲位菊花章 *daikun-i kikkashō*. Literally it means Grand Order of the Badge of the Chrysanthemums, the highest honor/award in Japan.

10 John Foster Dulles was secretary of state for the Eisenhower administration. Before becoming the secretary of state, he carried out several important diplomatic missions for the Truman administration. He was the architect of the 1951 peace treaty with Japan [San Francisco Peace Treaty]. In 1950 President Harry Truman appointed Dulles as a special envoy to Japan to negotiate a peace treaty with Japanese Prime Minister Yoshida Shigeru.

hastily dispatched to Japan and advanced an absurd "vacuum theory" and "house-lock theory" and eagerly propagandized for Japan's rearmament. According to these theories, a sovereign state without arms is like a vacuum bottle because it can be overrun by foreign invasions just like air immediately fills up a bottle; likewise, a sovereign state without a military is like a house without locks, vulnerable to burglars.

As if that was not enough, Vice President Nixon was dispatched to Japan, where he delivered a speech claiming the U.S. made a "mistake" in disarming Japan and that Japan's rearmament is an imperative.[11] Evidently, Japan's rearmament is what the United States wants, and I call this an imposition by the United States.

Putting aside the issue of whether Article 9 of the Constitution was coercion by the United States, what is secretly underway is the reinforcement of the Japanese Self Defense Forces.[12] Some years ago, Asahi Newspaper carried an editorial on the pros and cons of Japan's demilitarization versus rearmament. An officer of the Defense Agency defiantly declared that a sovereign state defending itself against foreign invasion is as natural and instinctive as blinking to keep debris out of the eyes or raising an arm to block an oncoming stone or wood chip, and that this is an issue even more fundamental than the constitution. The audacious phrase "even more fundamental than the constitution" became a short-lived buzzword. The provisions of the Constitution do not seem to be much more than a piece of tissue or toilet paper to a career officer like him.

---

11 At a special meeting of the Japan-America Society in Tōkyō on November 19, 1953, Vice President Richard Nixon said: "Now if disarmament was right in 1946, why is it wrong in 1953? And if it was right in 1946 and wrong in 1953, why doesn't the United States admit for once that it made a mistake? And I'm going to say something that I think perhaps ought to be done more by people in public life. I'm going to admit right here that the United States did make a mistake in 1946. We made a mistake because we misjudged the intention of the Soviet leaders." Quoted in Kajima Heiwa Kenkyūjo, *Nippon Gaikō Shuyō Bunsho II*, Hara Shobō, 1983, pp.598-599.

12 With the start of the Korean War in 1950, U.S. infantry was pulled out of Japan and sent to the front lines in Korea, leaving Japan with no armed protection. General MacArthur ordered the creation of a 75,000-strong National Police Reserve 警察予備隊 to maintain order and ward off foreign invasion. The NPR was given U.S. Army surplus equipment, but to avoid possible constitution violations, these items were renamed. For instance, tanks became "special vehicles." A suit was brought by the leader of the Japan Socialist Party, Suzuki Shigesaburō 鈴木重三郎, challenging the constitutionality of the NPR, but the case was dismissed. Four years later, the NPR became the Japan Self-Defense Forces [SDF], and by that time its numbers had swelled to 164,500. By 1980, there were 295,500 men and women in the SDF, making it one of the stronger military forces in the world.

The goal of this commission on constitutional investigation is not only expressly to expand and incorporate provisions in the constitution but to establish unequivocally in the minds of the public this so-called "right to self-defense" as instinctual and a privilege of a sovereign state. Let us examine whether "self-defense" or "national defense" is viable in the first place for a state that prepares for war through military build-up. Japan's rearmament, driven by the notion that it is "instinctual" and as such "even more fundamental" to the constitution, will most likely result in "self-destruction" rather than providing for "self-defense."

All countries of the world have developed arms, in particular modern weaponry, for the purpose of "national defense." However, when nuclear bombs were dropped on Hiroshima and Nagasaki in Japan during the last World War, decimating these two cities and indiscriminately incinerating women, children and infants, voices in the U.S. military called out, "This is not right;" "This should be the last time;" "Never should this be repeated." President J.F. Kennedy declared, ". . . modern weapons—ten million times more powerful than any that the world has ever seen" are "only minutes away from any target on earth." He continued that "a nation's security may well be shrinking even as its arms increase."[13]

Today scientists, generals, politicians and military critics all agree on the following:

1. Modern weapons have wiped out the possibility of national defense.
2. There exists no defense against modern weapons now or in the future.
3. The very use of the term "defense" as it relates to modern weapons is just one extreme example of how words are manipulated to deceive the people.

"Defense" is a fallacy. It is nothing more than a fraudulent name that will not hold water.

U.S. Secretary of Defense Robert McNamara said the following regarding domestic defense: A first strike by the USSR would most likely kill 50 million Americans instantaneously and cause another 20 million serious casualties. However, he added, 10 to 15 million lives might be saved if people could evacuate to secure shelters. This means only a fraction

13 Address before the General Assembly of the United Nations, New York City, September 25, 1961.

could survive. Is it still worth going to war?

Mr. Peterson[14] opposed a $15 million renovation in New York City to accommodate subway stations as shelters for civilian defense arguing that if New York City's skyscrapers collapsed in a nuclear attack, 75 to 100 feet of rubble would cover the ground, and citizens evacuated to shelters would suffocate to death from the debris piled over them. He further stated that even if all 170 million Americans had places to evacuate, at least half the lives would be lost to enemy surprise attacks. In his the final analysis, no nation in the world is fully prepared for thermonuclear war.

The British Ministry of Defense had the following to say on their status of national defense. "We must take the present situation into consideration. Regardless of how effective our defense program may be, if half a dozen nuclear bombers invade, a single attack by them would result in countless deaths and devastation of a vast region. Moreover, we are now entering a new phase where we are immediately subjected to ballistic missile attacks. Those who suggest that prompt and effective defense measures can be taken against this kind of attack must be out of their minds."[15]

The British would laugh and say that those in Japan who assert that elevating the Defense Agency to a Defense Ministry or that incorporating a clause in the constitution to rearm makes for an effective defense are "out of their minds." The British observe that their civilian defense during the last world war was not useful other than coping with the aftermath of fire, and that it is as clear as day that no effective defenses today exist

---

14 Frederick Valdemar Peterson [1903-1983] was Governor of Nebraska and later Administrator of the Federal Civil Defense Administration during the Eisenhower Administration [1953-1957]. During the Truman Administration, Congress enacted the Federal Defense Act of 1950, placing the burden for civil defense on the states, and it created the Federal Civil Defense Administration to formulate national policy to guide the states' efforts. Under Truman, the FCFA led shelter building programs, established an attack warning system, stockpiled supplies and started a national civic education program. However, President Eisenhower's approach to civil defense differed from his predecessor. The enormous expense to develop weapons undermined funding for expensive civil defense programs. In 1953 the Soviet Union detonated its first hydrogen nuclear bomb, and shortly after that a report on the effects of the initial U.S. hydrogen bomb test was released to the American public. The effects of these new fusion nuclear weapons were so destructive that many experts argued that American cities would be doomed in the event of a nuclear attack, regardless of sheltering efforts. As a result, new FCDA administrator Fredrick Peterson urged Congress to scale back or completely eliminate the shelter program. [Civil Defense and Homeland Security: Short History of National Preparedness Efforts, Homeland Security National Preparedness Task Force, September 2006, p.9.]

15 Translator's rendition based on Japanese translation.

against this kind of hostile attack.

If the United States cannot defend itself and the UK cannot defend itself, what about the Soviet Union? The Soviet Union has an even greater geographical advantage than the United States. Its vast territory allows it to decentralize the population, heavy industries, air force bases and other defense installations. On top of that, they possess a massive nuclear arsenal. Its short and intermediate range missiles are second to none. Despite this, NATO Supreme Commander General Norstad[16] says that the West has more than 255 bases surrounding the Soviet Union with nuclear weapons poised against the USSR from every angle which could completely wipe out its combat potential. This nullifies the Soviet Union's defense.

Examination of all the above brings to light the fact that none, be it the Soviet Union with the most powerful defense capabilities in the world, the United States or Britain are able to offer any viable military defense against nuclear weapons delivered by modern aircraft, guided missiles or ballistic missiles. Notwithstanding this, we are told that if we desire to effectively defend a nation through military means, there is one way to do this, namely, an "offensive defense."

What this means is to preempt the adversary with massive use of nuclear weapons and to engage in indiscriminate mass slaughter of an adversary's citizens, young and old alike. This is most likely the reason why the world fears a surprise attack. Are the Japanese Self Defense Forces confident that they are prepared to do this? How absurd!

If the governments of the world today are willing to protect their nations' interest by use of these nuclear weapons, it means that the state will be committing a collective massacre of humanity and its societies. It is painfully clear today that all civilization would be completely wiped out overnight.

In addition to imposing the potential tragedy of nuclear weapons on the world, military superpowers are researching various alternatives that could also annihilate humanity. During the last world war, 83,000 men, women and children in Tōkyō were burnt to death in a single night by incendiary bomb raids. A young student soldier who ran about removing

16 General Lauris Norstad, Supreme Commander of NATO and a major U.S. Air Force leader during the defining years of the Cold War. Except for Dwight Eisenhower, he was the most prominent of all the Supreme Allied Commanders Europe [SACEUR] since that position was established in early 1951. He was one of the earliest advocates of flexible response.

the corpses survived the attack to tell the gruesome story.

A former U.S. chief of staff stated, "If the Air Force used poison gas bombs, they would make extremely effective weapons. Their use on major cities like London and Paris can easily kill several million civilians over a short period of time. In an attack like that, it's impossible to protect civilian non-combatants."[17]

In addition, preparations for biological warfare are also underway. In a 1954 disarmament subcommittee, Mr. Mock[18] said, "Some modes of the already devised biological warfare are even more dangerous than atom bombs, their production cost cheaper and their manufacture much easier. They could kill many more people, and they could bring harm beyond words." Major General Chisholm[19] said, "I will repeat that we do not have any method of defense against them." It is also known that Japan was preparing for biological warfare in the suburbs of Harbin, China during World War II.[20]

United States President Dwight Eisenhower asserted that war in our time has become an anachronism; whatever the case in the past, war

---

17 Source unknown.

18 The translator could not identify Mr. Mock, and the spelling of the name is uncertain. Citation is translator's rendition.

19 Possibly George Brock Chisholm, psychiatrist and medical administrator [1896- 1971]. In 1948 he was appointed first director general of the World Health Organization, a position he held until 1953.

20 Officially called "Epidemic Prevention and Water Purification Department of the Kwantung Army," Unit 731 was a covert military medical experimentation unit of the Imperial Japanese Army led by Lieutenant General Ishii Shirō 石井四郎. It researched biological warfare and other matters through human experiments on Chinese, Koreans, Russian and U.S. prisoners and Chinese civilians during the Second Sino-Japanese War and World War II [1937-1945]. A major facility was in Pingfang near the city of Harbin in northeastern China, then part of the puppet state of Manchuria. As early as 1949, the Soviet Union held a week-long trial at Khabarovsk on Japanese war crimes for biological warfare. Among thousands of Japanese prisoners of war repatriated from Siberia, some belonged to Unit 731. Together with Japanese POWs detained in China, they were tried in a special court at Shenyang [Mukden] in June 1956 as well as at other trials. However, in 1945 MacArthur granted immunity to a large number of Unit 731 members, starting with Ishii Shirō, in exchange for test data. In *Factories of Death*, Sheldon H. Harris writes, "The value to the U.S. of Japanese BW [biological warfare] data is of such importance to national security as to far outweigh the value accruing from war crimes' prosecution. The BW information obtained from Japanese sources should be retained in 'top secret' intelligence channels and not be employed as war crimes evidence and not be fallen into the Soviet hands." Former members of Unit 731 became leading figures in post-war medical circles, and some, who played a central role in establishing and managing Midori-jūji Corporation [Green Cross Corporation]. Initially called Japan Blood Bank, Midori-jūji was later accused of selling unheated blood products, which caused hemophiliacs to contract HIV, and of failing to recall them after production was suspended.

in the future can serve no useful purpose, that it is akin to playing with fire.[21] Governments, both large and small, unanimously agreed with this statement.

If it is obvious that all arms are useless to national defense and that all wars serve no useful purpose, then why are countries, above all Japan, arming and preparing for war? Professor Ravi[22] responds to this question by saying, "The various facts pertaining to modern warfare, its criminality and the resulting tragedy are not fully appreciated. This applies equally to all leaders of the world. Not the governments nor the joint chiefs of staff nor the people of the respective countries understand the implications of modern weaponry to humanity."

In the final analysis, we must resolve how to live together on this planet Earth instead of how to kill each other. Otherwise, we are doomed to perish by modern weapons. Governments, the military and people of the world not only fail to consider the meaning of nuclear war, but have forgotten the tragedy of Hiroshima and Nagasaki and are incapable of envisioning what they were like.

At such a time, we, the Japanese people, more than anyone else, have the power to constantly remind the people of the world what nuclear wars mean in light of what happened at Hiroshima and Nagasaki and to help the world to envision the horror and misery of nuclear weapons. More than any other nation, the Japanese people have an obligation to strive to eliminate these senseless weapons and to bring an end to the crimes of war on Earth.

This duty of the Japanese people to eradicate arms and war provides us with the opportunity to make a monumental contribution to humanity. To save Asia, and ultimately the entire world from the imminent catastrophe of nuclear war, we must staunchly adhere to and protect the articles of complete disarmament and renunciation of war as stipulated in the Japanese Constitution.

Na Mu Myō Hō Ren Ge Kyō

---

21 Research could not determine if or when President Eisenhower made this statement. A similar statement was found that was attributed to the British philosopher Bertrand Russell.

22 The translator could not identify Professor Ravi. Citation is translator's rendition from the Japanese text.

16

For the Foundation of World Peace

December 27, 1964
Welcome reception at the Japanese Consulate General
Calcutta, India

I first came to India more than 30 years ago. At that time, Gandhiji had been incarcerated for the Salt Walk after launching the freedom movement against the British.

Nichiren Daishōnin has prophesized that "Buddha Dharma of Japan will be returned to the Country of the Moon"[1] in an era when the world is plagued with conflict and strife.[2] He taught that during an era characterized by war, Buddha Dharma of Japan, a teaching that creates peace, will spread in India. Deeply inspired by these words, I came to India as a person of faith with a single prayer drum.

Back then Japan was prospering as one of the world powers. Britain was not pleased with Gandhiji's freedom movement and banned all contact between Japanese nationals and Gandhiji and his people. However, I went to see Gandhiji, convinced that his movement was just. I prayed there believing that my prayers for the success of this movement were in accord with Ososhi-sama's[3] true intent. My prayer was to simply beat the Dharma drum. I beat the drum wherever I went, whether at Congress[4] meetings or anywhere else. This practice produced a karmic connection that resulted in a temple being built in Calcutta solely through the generosity of the affluent Birlaji.[5] The same was true with the temple in Bombay.

---

1 月氏. Gasshi or Tenjiku. A general reference to ancient India.

2 闘諍堅固 *Tōjō-kengo.*

3 御祖師様. Founding master, Nichiren Daishōnin.

4 The oldest Indian political party, the Indian National Congress, was formed in 1885 and was the most powerful force behind the country's struggle for independence. It also held power for several decades after independence in 1947.

5 Jugar Kishore Birla was a relative of G.D. Birla. The members of the Birla family are well known philanthropists in India, and it was G.D. Birla who bankrolled the freedom

We have finally embarked on the restoration of Rajgir.[6] This is where the most crucial Mahāyāna sūtra in the life of Buddha Śākyamuni was preached, the sermon ground where the Lotus Sūtra was expounded for eight years. My prayer for India's independence was expressly the restoration of Rajgir. For this reason, most of my time in India was spent in Rajgir. We had no temples back then, and for several years we practiced out of the Burmese or Hindu temples or out of pilgrim's lodges.

In those days Mr. Ishibashi [who later joined Nipponzan Myōhōji and became Rev. Ishibashi Gyōjū], was manager of Nichimen[7] and lived in Calcutta. One day by chance, the issue of purchasing some land came up. We later finally found a site for the temple in Rajgir, and Mrs. Ishibashi spent her life savings to buy it for us. This is how the current, modest temple came about. I made the bricks for the temple with my own hands and baked them. Mr. Ishibashi donated the entire cost. Not only that, he commuted to Rajgir every weekend from Calcutta and oversaw the construction and facilitated its progress.

Every morning we plowed our way through the jungle to Grdhrakūta,[8] the Sacred Eagle Peak, to get there before sunrise.[9] We also performed several *Rōhachi-sesshin* sessions[10] [at Grdhrakūta] and continued our sunrise prayers over the years. Sacred sites of the Buddha, like Bodhi Gaya and Lumbini, greatly improved after India's independence, but there was much to be desired at Rajgir. While parts of Rajgir improved, they were limited to the vicinity of New Rajgir built by King Ajātaśatru, son of King Bimbisāra.[11] After independence,

---

movement and advised Gandhiji on economic policies. The funds to build the Nipponzan temples in Calcutta and Bombay were donated by J.K. Birla.

6 During the lifetime of the Buddha, Rajgir was the capital of the powerful Magadha kingdom ruled by King Bimbisāra. Rajagriha, as it was known in the past, was a picturesque place [the name literally means the abode of kings], surrounded by the meandering river Banganga and five hills. The hills and caves surrounding Rajagriha were home to spiritual teachers, ranging from the materialism of the early Charavaka school to the metaphysics of Upanishad philosophers.

7 Nichimen Corporation is a Japanese trading firm.

8 The hill where Buddha delivered the Lotus Sūtra.

9 The morning prayer sessions were held in time to greet the rising sun.

10 A week-long fast performed from December 1-8 in commemoration of the meditation and fast by the Lord Buddha before reaching Enlightenment under a bodhi tree.

11 King Bimbisāra was the first royal patron of the Buddha and the founder of the Magadha kingdom. It is said that he sent 500 carts of food and other necessities daily as offerings to Lord Buddha and the newly-created order of more than a thousand monks.

At New Delhi with Dr. Rajendra Prasad, first president of India, February 1956.

Prime Minister Nehru began a number of projects there, including construction of a government-operated lodge.

Three or four years ago, the International Conference for Nuclear Abolition was held in New Delhi. Former President Dr. Rajendra Prasad[12] attended despite his poor health. On that occasion Dr. Prasad stated, "Nuclear weapons are a woe to the whole of humanity. Removing

12 Rajendra Prasad [1884–1963], first president of India. In 1917 he began working with Mohandas K. Gandhi, and in 1920 he joined the Indian National Congress and served several times [1934, 1939, 1947–48] as its president. Mr. Prasad became president of India in 1950, when the republic of India was proclaimed, and held office until 1962.

them would be one thing, but they represent a problem that is merely the tip of the iceberg. As long as military power exists, killing is an undeniable possibility. Therefore, to eliminate war, the military must be eliminated above everything else. India's true mission is to lead and be the first in the world to put it into practice."

World leaders gave their respective views on the issue at the conference. When I was asked to speak, I told them that I had listened to the various ideas for abolishing nuclear weapons, and that I shared the same commitment to work to eliminate them. On that single point, I was in complete agreement with every opinion expressed at the conference. However, I stated that none of the opinions raised were decisive solutions. As a person of faith, I felt that the ultimate solution rests with the heart and mind. If one endorses war in the mind, no other opinion, no matter how fine it may be, is good enough. Change will not come unless the sentiments of the people affirming war are transformed. We must believe that "humans must not kill other humans." Religion exists for the very purpose of transforming the hearts and minds of the people. People must be taught that "humans must not kill other humans." The prime example of this teaching is the precept of not taking life, the first of the Buddhist Five Precepts. There is an old Japanese term known as *sesshō*.[13] The kanji characters mean "to kill life," and a commonly used epithet to describe a cruel, heartless person includes the characters for *sesshō*. We must ponder what this means. Refusal to engage in war is an essential part of the teachings of Lord Buddha. Lord Buddha did not resort to force and had to watch his Śākya clan perish.[14] Similarly, Crown Prince Shōtoku's[15] clan was also massacred.

Faith in Buddhist teachings calls on us to offer our lives as a sacrifice to end war. There is no authority that can stop war other than the wide dissemination of the Buddha Dharma as expounded by Buddha Śākyamuni. I appealed to the conference that in order to establish that killing others is completely unacceptable from the standpoint of faith, the restoration of Buddha Dharma is indispensable. That was the gist of my statement. When I concluded my remarks, Rajaji[16] took my hands and

13 殺生.

14 The Śakya clan and the city of Kapilavastu were destroyed by the rival king Vaidraka.

15 Please refer to *The Purpose of Erecting a Stūpa and Making Offerings*, footnote 10, p. 58.

16 Chakravarthi Rajagopalachari [1878-1975]. Known as Rajaji or C.R., he was an Indian lawyer, writer, statesman and a Hindu spiritualist. In 1948 when Indian independence

said, "What you just said is the ultimate solution." In line with these words, the Rajgir Restoration Committee was installed with Prime Minister Jawaharlal Nehru as its chairman. I also became a member. I believe the current Prime Minister, Mr. Lal Bahadur Shastri,[17] is a member as well. The project has been moving forward based on my recommendations, and a concrete plan for the restoration of Rajgir was finally completed.

On my next visit to India, Prime Minister Nehru made his desires known to me. "Let us create the foundation of world peace through the restoration of Rajgir. India must set the example. It must be restored even beyond what it was in the times of King Bimbisāra. Let's create a lake at the site of old Rajgir and construct the largest park in the world; hills will be forested to provide a place where people can enjoy themselves. We will build a university that offers a course on the Lotus Sūtra. We will build a hospital. There will be a library where people of the world can research the teachings of the Tathāgata. Lodgings and a Japanese garden would also be part of it. We will dig new hot springs, build a stūpa and provide a cable car for access. I would like Japan to take care of the cable car. We will do what we can on the rest." This was the heart of the discussion, and Patna Commissioner, Mr. S.V. Sohoni, wrote up the plan. The construction is now underway.

We have been continuing the practice of paying daily homage at Grdhrakūta, about three miles from the temple, for thirty years. We have been faced with many obstacles in India; nevertheless, my disciples, led by Rev. Yagi Tenshō,[18] started to open up the jungle with spades and sickles. Upon seeing this, the Indians were galvanized into a response, knowing they should not stand idle. It was former Indian Ambassador to Japan, Sir C.P.N. Singh, who made the appeal to not allow the Japanese monks to toil by themselves and challenged India to stand in the forefront in this effort. That is how we were able to see the beginning of the construction today.

Restoration of Rajgir is the restoration of Buddhism. I wish for

---

was recognized, he replaced Mountbatten and became the only Indian Governor-General of India and served until 1950. With the new constitution in January of 1950, the governor-general post was eliminated and replaced by the office of president.

17 Lal Bahadur Shastri [1904-1966] succeeded Jawaharlal Nehru as Prime Minister of India in 1964.

18 八木天攝. Ordained in Japan around 1935 while Guruji was in India, he left for India in 1937 and aspired to practice with Guruji. The majority of his life as a monk was spent in India. He passed away in 1987 at 75 years of age.

Rajgir to play a pivotal role in resolving the Sino-Indian war,[19] and towards this end I have sent invitations to China. I hope to bring people like Kuo Mo-jo[20] and Zhao Puchu.[21] In time, Buddhists and pacifists from around the globe will gather here. Based on the peaceful history of Buddha Śākyamuni, restoration of Rajgir will provide the principal dōjō, the source for creating peace in human history. This hope was also shared by Gandhiji and Prime Minister Nehru.

Gandhiji once requested Rev. Maruyama Gyōryō[22] to translate Nichiren Daishōnin's *Risshō-ankoku-ron*[23] to be incorporated as a pillar of the freedom movement, and said he would bear all necessary expenses for its publication. Gandhiji also contacted me about it. We tried to keep our promise, but Rev. Maruyama was eventually sent to jail for his involvement in the independence movement, and the promise remained unfulfilled. Those words of Gandhiji's, out of his prayers for peace, have borne fruit today. There shall come a day when lectures on the tenets of *Risshō-ankoku-ron* are given at a Buddhist University [in Rajgir].

In their search for peace, the people of the world struggle on where to find the ultimate beacon of peace. One such example of this struggle

---

19 Unable to resolve the disputed territory along the 3,225-kilometer Himalayan border, China attacked India on October 20, 1962. At the time of this speech, nine divisions from India's eastern and western commands were deployed along the border with China.

20 Kuo Mo-jo [1892-1978] was a Chinese poet, dramatist, historian, archaeologist and revolutionary activist. Because of his commitment to and involvement in revolutionary politics, he was compelled to flee from China in 1927 and sought refuge in Japan. He later returned to China and served as a prominent government official from 1949 until his death. During the period referred to in Guruji's talk, he was serving as the bridge between China and Japan and contributed greatly to friendship between the two nations.

21 Before 1949, Venerable Zhao Puchu [1907-2000] was a local leader in Buddhist and charitable circles in Shanghai. After the founding of the People's Republic of China in 1949, he became a national Buddhist leader and a leading activist in promoting Sino-foreign relations and exchanges. Zhao was an honorary chairman of the 10th Central Committee of the China Association for Promoting Democracy [CAPD]. The people of China were deeply impressed by Nipponzan's peace movement, in particular the nonviolent resistance of beating the drums during the Uchinada struggle—the 1952 land-requisition by the U.S. military for its firing grounds—and the Sunagawa struggle in 1956 when the U.S. planned to expand its Tachikawa military base in Tōkyō. During an official visit to Japan, Venerable Zhao visited Guruji to pay his respect.

22 Rev. Maruyama Gyōryō 丸山行遼, a disciple of Guruji's, ordained in 1926 and practiced in China, southeast Asia and India. His longtime practice in India during the independence movement led to a special relationship with Gandhiji, who called Rev. Maruyama "Ananda-bai." His deep bond with the freedom fighters in India later led him to serve as a bridge between India and Japan after independence. He passed away in 1967 at 66 years of age.

23 Please refer to *Shishin-kaku*, footnote 5, p. 1.

is the Japanese movement against atomic and hydrogen bombs. Against the wishes of the people, a rift developed within the movement against A&H bombs and today it exists as a divided movement.[24] The breakup is extremely troubling for a movement that has been a major driving force in creating world peace. Various university professors are now suggesting a grand religious ceremony to restore the movement. It is the first time the anti-nuclear movement has sought a spiritual core. Before my departure for India, Mr. Yasui Ken[25] and Dr. Moritaki Ichirō[26] came to see me. I would like to invite these people to Rajgir as well.

Genuine peace will prevail when we approach the imperative of world peace by centering on the teachings of Buddha Śākyamuni. Peace prevailed wherever the doctrines and teachings of Buddha spread. This is evident when comparing the histories of East and West. People of the world are beginning to realize that there were no international wars in

---

24 The crew of the Japanese fishing boat, Daigo-fukuryū-maru 第五福竜丸 [Fifth Lucky Dragon], was exposed to radiation fallout from the U.S. nuclear testing in the Bikini Atoll, Marshall Islands, March 1954. In Japan a nationwide campaign quickly developed calling for a ban on hydrogen bomb tests as well as a ban on all military use of nuclear energy. This grassroots effort received support from the Japanese Diet, local governments, academia and labor. The momentum led to the first World Conference Against A&H Bombs in Hiroshima in1955. It combined both the movements against A&H bombs and aid to hibakusha, A-bomb survivors. The executive committee adopted the name Gensuikyō [Japan Council Against A & H Bombs]. In 1958, a rift started to develop in Gensuikyō over various issues. To promote unity in the movement especially in the interest of hibakushas, Rev. Nishimoto Atsushi 西本敦, a Nipponzan monk, along with a Mr. Kurachi 倉知, a representative of the Japan National Railways Workers' Union, initiated a 1,000-km Peace Walk from the Hiroshima Peace Memorial to Tōkyō. A total of 700,000 people participated along the way. By the time the walk crossed Tamagawa River into Tōkyō, the walk surged to 10,000 people. A hibakusha and anti-war poet, Madam Sadako Kurihara, described the scene "like a river ablaze in flame sweeping through Japan." In 1961, a second walk took place, this time from the Fifth Lucky Dragon to Hiroshima; it was led by another Nipponzan Myōhōji monk, Rev. Ōki Gyōji 大木行治 , marking the beginning of the annual peace walk from Tōkyō to Hiroshima. Disagreements within Gensuikyō remained, and in 1961 some groups broke away and formed Kakukin-kaigi [National Council for Peace and Against Nuclear Weapons]. In 1963 another split occurred over the resumption of Soviet nuclear testing leading to the establishment of Gensuikin [Japan Congress Against A&H Bombs]. Guruji sent disciples to both Gensuikyō and Gensuikin and worked to bring a united World Conference Against A&H Bomb, which happened in 1977, 17 years after the split.

25 Yasui Ken 安井謙 was Speaker of the House of Representatives.

26 Professor Moritaki Ichirō 森滝市郎 was a survivor of the Hiroshima bombing and became one of the leading figures in the anti-nuclear movement and later served as chairman of the Japan Congress Against A&H Bombs. The atomic bombing is believed to have caused his death in 1994, 49 years after the attack. Mr. Moritaki, like many other atomic-bomb survivors, died of cancer.

Asia [where Buddhism thrived].

In creating peace, we must reevaluate the teachings that created 2,500 years of peace. It shall be the ultimate course for humanity's future. My vow to restore Rajgir is based on this belief. Prime Minister Nehru of India, the land of Buddhism's origin, was a leading proponent of peace in his time. My ardent wish is for Prime Minister Shastri to continue in his footsteps and lead the endeavor to forge global peace. On the other hand, the people are the driving force in the creation of world peace. I would like to see the people of Japan and India collaborate in building the foundation for global peace in Asia.

It may be a self-serving dream on my part, but this belief is what I hold true. A handful of disciples who work here have endured hardship and remain committed despite all difficulties. Their unfaltering practice against all odds will form the heart for creating world peace.

The movement against atomic and hydrogen bombs in Japan will be restored when *Risshō-ankoku-ron* is incorporated at its heart. Peace will prevail when the world's peace movements seek guidance in the teachings of Nichiren Daishōnin. That is what I believe in, and it is what keeps me going.

17

The Path for Humanity's Survival[1]

July/August 1967 edition of *Sarvodaya*

Ever since the United States became mired in the morass of the Vietnam War, it has been impetuously using all its major military bases in Japan,[2] including those in Okinawa, Ogasawara, Sunagawa, Yokosuka, Sasebo and Itazuke, in a desperate attempt to win the war. The planned expansion of the [Tachikawa] base into Sunagawa is also intended for that purpose.

We will do everything in our power to stop it. Facilitating U.S. war efforts goes against the desires of the peace-loving peoples of the world and conflicts with the ideals of the peaceful nation that Japan aspires to be. The best solution is for the United States to voluntarily cease acts of war, yet this is unlikely since these acts of war are profit driven by a state-sponsored arms trade. In recent years when war was imminent between the Arab states and Israel, the United States seized the opportunity to sell arms. Rather than saying war broke out in the Middle

---

1 This is an oral response by Guruji to Dr. Tokoro Shigemoto's criticism of Nipponzan Myōhōji's peace movement. Guruji also made a more elaborate written response, *The Lotus Sūtra and Pacifist Thought*, which appeared in the March 1968 issue of *Daihōrin* 大法輪 [*The Great Dharma Wheel*].

2 When the United States began occupying Japan after World War II, it used Japan's former military bases as its frontline bases in the Cold War. During the 1950-53 Korean War, these bases were used intensely as attack posts, directly supporting the U.S. war front. From the very beginning, the use and expansion of U.S. military bases met vigorous opposition from local communities, students and trade unions in Japan. These alliances successfully prevented some major base expansions, including Uchinada, Myogi and Tachikawa in the 1950s. Also in the 1950s, local farmers began the movement against U.S. and Japan's live shelling exercises at the base of Mount Fuji, and that opposition continues today. Today there are approximately 90 U.S. military facilities throughout mainland Japan and Okinawa, occupying an area of about 1,200 square miles, 75 percent of which is in Okinawa. According to statistics from 2001, about 52,000 U.S. troops were stationed at those bases, 26,000 in the mainland and 25,000 in Okinawa. *U.S. Military Bases in Japan-An Overview*, Ichiyō Mutō, People's Plan Study Groups, January 2, 2004.

East, it is more accurate to say that U.S. weapons sales to its business partners in the region perpetuated conflict. Arms trade has become the business of major powers. Those in need of weapons purchase them and, once acquired, use them to kill people. Thus wars erupt. The reason why war will not cease today is because major powers produce weapons for trade. Japan is no exception. Massive amounts of its arms are sold abroad. Weapons production neither feeds nor clothes people. These weapons become profitless stock unless sold, a compelling reason to make war. And that is why both Japan and the U.S. oppose the cessation of war.

The preamble to the Constitution declares that Japan's defense is "trusting in the justice and faith of the peace-loving peoples of the world." However, it is commonly believed that security is guaranteed through military strength, which is a violation of the preamble. There is a notion that Japan cannot survive with inferior military power, making protection under the U.S. umbrella indispensable. This is a pretext. It is a fallacy that Japan's security is assured by weapons from the United States or by selling weapons domestically produced.

Japan went into World War II with the explicit assurance of the Army General Staff Office[3] that Japan's amassed force could not be defeated by any nation of the world. Yet, defeat was the outcome. The price we pay today as a partner of the United States is to have our land lost to requisition, belying the claim that our security is ensured by the U.S. umbrella. Scientific research, which ought to be for the good of humanity, is funded by the U.S. military. Japanese scientists may try to evade responsibility by arguing that their research is not directly involved in killing, yet to say their military-sponsored research would not be used for military purposes is ludicrous. In modern Japan, science and politics blinded by greed pose a danger.

The absolute rejection of the need for war is not only a provision of the Japanese Constitution; it is the common wisdom of the people of the world. Nothing is gained by war. Look at what is happening in Vietnam. Nothing good comes out of war. We are safe so long as there is no war.

Dr. Tokoro[4] recently criticized our order. Some points he raised

---

3 *Sanbō-honbu* 参謀本部 also known as the Imperial Army General Staff Office of Japan. It was created in 1878, modeled on *Die Grösse Generalste*, the German General Staff.

4 Dr. Tokoro Shigemoto's 戸頃重基 [1911-1977]. A doctor of literature who specialized in the history of Japanese philosophy and ethics, he was a professor at Kanazawa University.

are valid, and some are not. I would like to take this opportunity to refute some points raised. On page 239 in *Religion and Nationalism*,[5] Dr. Tokoro states:

> First, Fujii interprets Nichiren's religion to be pacifist in every sense of the word, but is this true? Given the impact of defeat, one can certainly appreciate Fujii's fine religious intentions of wanting to do everything in his power to prevent Nichiren's religion from once again being driven to militarism.[6] However, his good religious intentions in defending the teachings should not compromise historical facts. In light of the historical facts, Nichiren did have a pacifist legacy, as inherited by Fujii; however, at the same time, his thoughts were militant enough to receive the acclaim of pre-war terrorists.
>
> It is necessary to look with a critical eye at Nichiren as he was, taking this duality into account to fully appreciate him. The pious Fujii lacks the spirit of voluntary criticism towards Nichiren. Therefore, regrettably, his interpretation of Nichiren's teachings as pacifist tends to lack cogency since facts that do not suit this interpretation are deliberately withheld. More than anything else, Nichiren was a man of the Kamakura Period [1192-1333]; therefore, he was neither a militarist nor a pacifist in the modern sense of the word.
>
> It is true that Nichiren upheld the precept against killing stating, "The first of the Five Precepts is named the precept against taking life,[7] which teaches to evoke compassion and not to take life. Unreasonable killing is prohibited."[8] If Nichiren maintained the prohibition against killing under all circumstances based on this precept, then Fujii's thought can be confidently based on Nichiren's teaching. However, as I just

5 *Kindai-Nihon-no Shūkyō-to Nashonarizumu* 近代日本の宗教とナショナリズム [*Modern Japan Religion and Nationalism*], 1966, Toyamabō 富山房.

6 Caught up in the worldwide trend of imperialism by world powers, Japan embarked on the road to modernization through militarization after the Meiji Restoration of the 19th century. In line with Japan's increased militarism starting in the 1930's and up to WWII, some Nichiren adherents also embraced nationalism and helped to promote militarism.

7 *Fusesshō-kai* 不殺生戒.

8 *Kaihōmon* 戒法門, *The Teachings on Precepts*, 1243.

quoted, Nichiren says that the precept against taking life is a prohibition of unreasonable killing, but does not go so far as to prohibit reasonable killing. Had even that been prohibited, if the precept were to be followed to the letter, Nichiren would not have been able to accept the *Bandō-musha*,[9] who were called "the wicked who commit murder day and night," as his devotees.

Immediately after the earlier quote, Nichiren states: "Killing one to let live a multitude should be condoned." In other words, Nichiren taught that when the lives of a multitude are at risk because of one person, then they must be saved by taking that person's life. Nichiren does not consider this to be unreasonable killing. He was by no means an advocate of a formalist precept against taking life. For this reason, I cannot accept as originating in Nichiren the principle of nonresistance as advanced by Fujii that calls for standing in front of atrocious weapons of the aggressor with palms joined together in veneration and opting for peaceful negotiation.

In terms of overall tendency, the Lotus Sūtra could be seen as advocating nonresistance in *Exhortation to Hold Firm, Comfortable Practices* and *Bodhisattva Never Despise*. However, *A Parable* describes sanction in Avici hell[10] for those who disbelieve and slander the Dharma. Likewise, *Dhāranīs* preaches that, "those who trouble the expounder of the Dharma shall have their heads split into seven pieces." As these examples show, the Lotus Sūtra is much more militant than the Brahmajala-sūtra.[11] I have pointed out in the past that Nichiren's thought on *shakubuku*[12] is much more heavily influenced by the Mahaparinirvārna Sūtra[13] than by the Lotus Sūtra. At any rate, Nichiren cannot be defined unilaterally

---

9 Warriors from the Kantō region known for their valor and fighting spirit.

10 Hell of incessant suffering, the worst hell of all.

11 Translated by Kumārajīva 鳩摩羅什 in 406. This work is esteemed as the basic canon concerning the discipline or precepts of Bodhisattvas in Mahāyāna.

12 折伏. *Shakubuku* traditionally means a forceful remonstration to defeat evil and manifest good, the opposite of *shōjyu* 摂受, acceptance. However, in his Dharma talk Guruji taught that *tangyō-raihai* is the *shakubuku* needed in this age to guide people to the Dharma.

13 It teaches that the Dharma is everlasting and all human beings possess Buddha-nature.

as an advocate of nonresistance or absolute pacifism. The part of him that says, "Sagami-no-kami[14] is indeed a good friend,[15] and Hei no Saemon[16] is indeed Devadatta.[17] The Nenbutsu believers[18] are like Koka-lika,[19] and Jisai[20] are like Sunaksatra bhikshu,"[21] [*Shuju-onfurumai-gosho*[22]] is undoubtedly a statement by a pacifist. "Those who believe will become Buddha. Those who slander will also become Buddha through the karmic seed administered by the poisonous drum,"[23] [*Hokke-Shoshin-Jōbutsu-Shō*][24] is a passage that reflects Nichiren's desire to overcome hatred with love rather than with hatred. It does not go against reason for Fujii, a proclaimed disciple of Nichiren who has taken on the vow to continue with the mission of his master, to seek grounds for his own pacifism in Nichiren. It is fully possible to regard Nichiren who states, "Being born in this land where the king reigns, he

---

14 Hōjō Tokimune 北条時宗 [1251-1284], was the 8th regent of the Kamakura Bakufu 鎌倉幕府 [Shogunate]. He ruled at the time when the prophesized foreign invasion [Mongolian invasion] became a reality.

15 *Zen-chishiki* 善知識 in Japanese [good or virtuous friend]. It means a teacher or someone who leads another in spiritual progress and to the Way of the Buddha.

16 Reference to Heino Saemonnojō Yoritsuna 平左衛門尉頼綱, who was Hōjō Tokimune's trusted vassal. He was the leading figure in Nichiren Daishōnin's persecution in the Kamakura Bakufu.

17 Devadatta is a cousin of Buddha Śākyamuni. He was initially the Buddha's follower, but later turned against him out of jealousy and attempted to kill the Buddha.

18 Believers of the Jōdo School [Pure Land], Jōdo-shin School [True Pure Land] and others that invoke the name of the Amida in order to be reborn in his Pure Land.

19 A member of the Śākya family who was first Buddha's disciple but later on became Devadatta's follower.

20 Monks who observe strict religious discipline.

21 A son of the Buddha born when Buddha was Prince Siddhārtha and who later became his disciple. He practiced and reached the 4th stage of meditation, yet he fell to false views and renounced the practice. He later went against the Buddha and went to Avici hell alive. Footnotes 18, 19 and 21 refer to people who attempted to either injure the Buddha or Buddha's monastic order. However, Buddha did not expel them. They fell to Avici hell as a consequence of their own actions.

22 種々御振舞御書 *The Various Conducts of the Master.* The title was given by disciples at the time of compiling Nichiren Daishōnin's writings. Originally written in 1275 at Mount Minobu, it chronicles important events in the Daishōnin's life starting shortly before the persecution at Tatsunokuchi, followed by exile at Sado Island and his retreat to Mount Minobu.

23 For those who do not welcome the sound of the celestial drum, it resounds like a poisonous drum. Refer to *Shishin-kaku*, footnote 24, p. 5.

24 法華初心成仏鈔. *On Buddhahood to be Attained Through the Lotus Sūtra by Even the Newly Initiated* was written in 1277 at Mount Minobu.

25 撰時鈔 *Selecting the Opportune Time.* Written in 1275 after the foreign invasion [the

may rule my body but not my mind" [*Senji-shō*][25] as a proponent of nonviolence. However, Nichiren's teachings are not simply monistic. That is the reason why, as stated earlier, on one hand he sees slanderers of the Dharma who persecute him in reaction to the poisonous drum as not only worthy of veneration, but also as respected teachers who lead him to enlightenment through transformation.[26] But, on the other hand, as if corresponding to the citations related to falling into Avici hell described in *A Parable* and the head-splitting into seven pieces in *Dharanīs,* Nichiren writes "Unless all the temples of the Pure Land and Zen Schools such as Kenchōji, Jūfukuji, Gokurakuji, Daibutsu, and Chōrakuji are burned down and their monks all beheaded at Yuigahama Beach, Japan is bound to fall." [*Senji-shō*] Another passage along this line is "Deterring those who act as enemies of the Lotus Sūtra is taught to be the greatest merit. Then how could making offerings to such persons be right? [Before the advent of Buddha Śākyamuni], King Sen'yo[27] put 500 Brahmins to death and Bhikshu Kakutoku[28] killed countless slanderers of the Dharma, and Emperor Ashoka[29] killed 108,000 heretics. These rulers were looked upon as the most worthy kings in the entire *Jambudvīpa*[30] and the monk as the world's wisest of all among the adherents of the precepts." [*Akimoto-Gosho*][31] In these

---

Mongolian invasion] prophesized in the *Risshō-ankoku-ron* came true. To prevent national ruin, Nichiren Daishōnin declared the only way to save Japan was through the Lotus Sūtra, and that Nichiren himself was the practitioner of the Lotus Sūtra entrusted by Buddha Śākyamuni to spread this teaching in the Era of Final Dharma.

26 In *The Various Conduct of the Master,* Nichiren Daishōnin says, "Devadatta was the foremost good friend to Tathāgata Śākyamuni, and the one who enabled him to attain Enlightenment. Likewise in this age, it is not your allies but your formidable enemies who make you a person of character."

27 King Rsidatta [spelling uncertain]. A king in ancient India who was a previous incarnation of the Buddha.

28 Monk Awakened Consciousness. The account on Bhikshu Awakened Consciousness is described in the Nirvāna Sutra.

29 Ashoka the Great [304-232 BCE] was an Indian emperor of the Mauryan Dynasty who ruled from 273-232 BCE. He is cited as one of India's greatest emperors.

30 The *sahā* world, the world of human beings

31 秋元御書 *Letter to Lord Akimoto,* 1280. In response to the traveler's eighth question in *Risshō-ankoku-ron,* Nichiren Daishōnin states, ". . . it was taught prior to the advent of Buddha Śākyamuni that slanderers of the Dharma were to be killed. However, the present Buddha Śākyamuni teaches not to make offerings to such slanderers . . . Therefore, if the world and the four kinds of Buddhists [monks, nuns, laymen and laywomen] cease to make

> paragraphs he advances a fierce doctrine of condemnation towards those who slander the Dharma. In the event one regards him as a pacifist, how to react towards this fierce condemnation of slanderers should naturally become an issue, yet that is not the case with Fujii.

What I just quoted are Dr. Tokoro's arguments. "To kill one to let live a multitude" is a concept that Nichiren Daishōnin also alluded to. However, this is an armchair theory, a hypothetical exercise more like a drawing board strategy than anything else. Behind the palatable term of "letting live a multitude," the gate to killing is opened. Once the gate is unlatched, "letting a multitude live" is no longer viable. Killing one inevitably leads to the killing of a multitude. This is how war occurs.

War cannot be terminated at one's convenience. War is the reflection of a state of mind that has gone amok, a mind out of control to the extreme due to delusions created by the three poisons.[32] The killing of one person activates delusions of the three poisons that cause one to lose one's senses. Never, from ancient times, has there been an actual example of multitudes saved by the killing of one. When has it ever happened? There is absolutely no killing that is reasonable.

In China, King Wu of Zhou[33] who defeated King Di Xin of the Yin Dynasty[34] killed his sovereign. However, Chinese history characterizes him as one who slew a guilty ruler to carry out the divine will, not one who killed his rightful sovereign. This might be excused as reasonable killing. Yet, killing is commonly committed under the pretext of allowing the multitude to live or justified as acting on the divine will to vanquish the unjust.

Violating the precept against killing is a crime of the utmost gravity. There is no rationalization or excuse for it. The rationale of acting for Providence cannot be sanctioned either. In the days when the tragedy of killing, the most grave crime, was committed on a one-on-one basis, the act of killing one wicked person for the sake of the multitude or

---

offerings to evil practitioners and instead take refuge in the Genuine Dharma, how could we be confronted with calamities or disasters?"

32 Covetousness, anger and delusions.

33 King Wu of Zhou [周武王] or King Wu of Chou was the first sovereign of the Chinese Zhou Dynasty.

34 Also known as the Shang Dynasty [16th - 11th century BCE]. It is the oldest Chinese dynasty with documentary evidence.

committing murder under the pretense of defeating evil to act on the will of the divine might not have been excessively harmful to society as a whole. However, if we were to open the gate of killing today, humanity would be engulfed by the conflagration of annihilation tomorrow. If humanity hopes to avert extinction, the only means of escape is to unconditionally accept and adhere to the precept against taking life. There is no path for humanity to survive other than not to kill others, not to make war.

All killers justify their acts. The several international wars fought by Japan since the Meiji Restoration were all called holy wars, and the nation accepted them as such. Today, starting with Vietnam, the United States is committing indiscriminate carnage and destroying lands around the world. Despite the censure by the people of the world against its unconscionable invasion and murder, the United States remains unfazed and intent on expanding its war. Furthermore, moral reasons are assigned to acts of war, such as "protecting peace in Vietnam" or "defending the freedom of the people of the free world." The Japanese government follows suit and refuses to call the Vietnam War an invasion. It blatantly supports the U.S. war of invasion on the basis of the Japan-U.S. Security Treaty. There is no weapon more destructive in the world than rationalization.

The precept of not to take life transcends all rationalization. The inviolable precept against killing must not be compromised by any rationale. It is a divine path that must be honored and takes precedence over acting on one's interpretation of the divine will. It is intrinsically human.

Then why did Nichiren Daishōnin mention reasonable killing? There are two approaches to a precept from the standpoint of Buddhist doctrine: prohibition and tolerance. One is to prevent an act, the other to allow a degree of flexibility to the precept in extenuating circumstances. This phrase [killing one to let live a multitude[35]] suggests the latter. By no means does it contradict the essential spirit of the precept against taking

35 The Mahaparinirvāna Sūtra preaches the doctrine of *tōjō-shitsuji* 刀杖執持, which sanctions the use of arms against slanderers of Dharma to defend the true Dharma, and the concept of taking the life of one to let a multitude live in order to allow some tolerance to the precept against killing. On the other hand, the Lotus Sūtra preaches withholding alms to slanderers of Dharma rather than resorting to force. As in footnote 31, Nichiren Daishōnin advocated withholding alms to slanderers in *Risshō-ankoku-ron* and honoring the precept against taking life even at the cost of one's life. Passages cited by Dr. Tokoro were written when Nichiren Daishōnin was 22, prior to the founding of his order. His central creed of *tangyō-raihai* is founded in his words, "the essential practice of the Lotus Sūtra is that of the chapter on *Bodhisattva Never Despise*."

life. Killing one for all or reasonable killing is not Nichiren Daishōnin's persuasion. Based on this belief, I disregarded this phrase. I do not feel the need to take up what is not the essential creed of Nichiren Daishōnin.

It is odd to say that our principle of nonresistance cannot have originated in Nichiren Daishōnin because we disregard the phrase of "kill one for the good of all" or "reasonable killing." Quite the contrary, this misconception is caused by disregarding Nichiren Daishōnin's essential creed of *tangyō-raihai* [the sole practice of bowing in veneration to the Buddha-nature in others] and erroneously interpreting the phrase "kill one for the good of all" to be his doctrine.

The essential creed of Nichiren Daishōnin is "to venerate" not "to kill." In a discourse by Nichiren Daishōnin entitled *Ongiku-den,*[36] the grounds for the practice of veneration by the Bodhisattva Never Despise are revealed.[37] It expounds on the 14 bases for veneration. Nichiren Daishōnin states, "The first reason for veneration is known also to scholars of our times,[38] but the remaining thirteen remain obscure to them." It shows how thoroughly Nichiren Daishōnin examined from every angle the reasons for veneration.

When *tangyō-raihai,* not the phrase of "kill one to let live a multitude," is understood as the heart of Nichiren Daishōnin's teachings, the act of placing palms together and bowing in veneration before intruders must be recognized as originating in Nichiren Daishōnin.

---

36 *Record of the Orally Transmitted Teachings* of Nichiren Daishōnin.

37 According to an extant annotation on *Ongiku-den,* the original term used here—住所 *jūsho*—is to be understood as "grounds for, or basis." The first grounds for veneration stated in *Ongiku-den* is veneration demonstrated in the stūpa of Buddha Prabhūtaratna in the Lotus Sūtra. Buddha Prabhūtaratna's stūpa represents the five elements of earth, water, fire, wind and sky, symbolizing veneration towards the Dharma and the whole universe. Nichiren Daishōnin said that the five elements also corresponds with the five kanji characters of the Odaimoku, Myō Hō Ren Ge Kyō

38 Here Nichiren Daishōnin refers to his contemporary scholar monks of Mt. Hie. They were disciples of Tendai Daishi and Dengyō Daishi, the Bodhisattvas of the Trace Teaching 迹化の菩薩, given the mission to spread the Lotus Sūtra in the Eras of Genuine and Semblance Dharma. Nichiren Daishōnin is known as the Bodhisattva of the Origin Teaching of the Lotus Sūtra, who had awakened to the mission of bringing universal salvation in the Era of Final Dharma. While Tendai Daishi and Dengyō Daishi both served their mission in the Era of Semblance Dharma, continuing those teachings in the Era of Final Dharma, according to Nichiren Daishōnin, was "Buddha Dharma whose time had past." [過時の仏法]. Contemporary scholar monks' understanding of veneration was based on *Beholding the Stūpa of Precious Treasures* chapter of the Lotus Sūtra; but Nichiren Daishōnin understood the premier grounds for veneration to be found in Bodhisattva Never Despise's sole practice of veneration of unconditional reverence towards all.

18

The Inevitable Victory for the Vietnamese People

June 17, 1967
Chuō University, Tōkyō

The Vietnamese nation can be traced back to 208 BCE. Since the spread of Buddhism early in its history, the majority of its people have led a pious life of Buddhist faith.

Buddhism, which originated in India, had crossed the Himalayas and was introduced to China, Korea and Japan. This is called *Hokuden-bukkyō*[1] [Buddhism introduced to the North]. Buddhism introduced to countries such as Burma and Ceylon [present day Sri Lanka] is referred to as *Nanden-bukkyō*[2] [Buddhism introduced to the South]. In general, *Hokuden-bukkyō* is called Mahāyāna Buddhism, and *Nanden-bukkyō* is known as Theravāda Buddhism.

Theravāda Buddhism, which places importance on the way of life taught by the Buddha, encourages strict observance of the Five Precepts, the Eight Precepts, the Two Hundred Fifty Precepts, and the like. Mahāyāna Buddhism emphasizes spiritual introspection called *kannen*[3] and tends to take lightly the external life of precept observance. Consequently, there developed an attitude of neglect towards the precepts among the ordained in the Era of Final Dharma,[4] which brought on today's decline of Buddha Dharma in Japan. Vietnam Buddhists preserve and recite the Mahāyāna sūtras, practice meditation and spiritual contemplation. However, just like Theravāda Buddhists, both clergy and laity strictly observe the precepts laid down by the Tathāgata.[5]

1 北伝仏教.
2 南伝仏教.
3 観念.
4 The teachings of the Buddha are taught to spread in three different periods after the passing of the Buddha: the Era of Genuine Dharma, Era of Semblance Dharma and Era of Final Dharma.
5 One of the epithets of the Buddha meaning, "One who has gone thus; one who has followed the path." In Mahāyāna this epithet is taken to mean one who has arrived from and gone to the world of truth, namely, nirvāna.

The United States expects to win the war in Vietnam, counting on its overwhelming superiority in materials, weapons and troops. On the other hand, the Vietnamese people stand firm in their conviction of prevailing due to a spirituality grounded in justice and perseverance. A rare, historic and wondrous outcome to confrontation is unfolding before our eyes as the final judgment to the Vietnam War: a peaceful power predicated on religious faith is triumphing over the barbaric violence of murderous machines.

World public opinion unanimously supports a peaceful settlement to the Vietnam War in line with the Geneva Accords concluded at the 1954 Geneva Conference. The United States has not rejected this either. Representatives of nine countries, i.e., the Democratic Republic of Vietnam, the Republic of Vietnam [headed by Bao Dai], Cambodia, Laos, the People's Republic of China, the Soviet Union, France, Great Britain and the United States convened and participated in the Geneva Conference.

[Let us look at the parties to the Geneva Conference.] First, the Democratic Republic of Vietnam was founded on September 2, 1945 when Ho Chi Minh read the Declaration of Independence of Vietnam in Hanoi. The prestige of this newly-born republic spread throughout Vietnam, and it is said that never before in Vietnam's history had its people been so joyously united in celebrating independence.

Next is the Republic of Vietnam. After Japan's surrender, France returned to reassert its rule on its former colonies in Indochina. It bombed Haiphong on November 13, 1946, occupied Hanoi in early 1947 and, from then until 1954, sent 250,000 troops to subjugate the guerrilla warfare of the Vietnamese people. During this period, France installed Bao Dai, whom Japan backed during World War II, as president of South Vietnam and granted nominal independence. The Republic of Vietnam was given the legal status of statehood by France, but, in fact, it was nothing more than an illusionary state whose sole purpose was to serve France's political objectives. For this reason, it has no credibility with the general Vietnamese people. This is the origin of the current South Vietnamese government.

Cambodia and Laos attended the conference as Vietnam's bordering neighbors in Indochina and as former French colonies. The People's Republic of China and the Soviet Union attended as socialist nations with an interest in aiding Ho Chi Minh's formation of the Democratic Republic of Vietnam.

Great Britain attended because it was present in 1945 when the Japanese surrendered south of the 16th parallel,[6] and the British had released French prisoners who had been charged with collaborating with Japan. This incident indicated Britain's support for the restoration of French rule in Vietnam and was the reason behind Britain's presence at the Geneva Conference.

After occupying Vietnam by force in 1858, France annexed Laos and Cambodia by 1884, thus establishing colonial rule in these nations and suppressing their people through exploitation and punishment. Most notably in Vietnam during the 60 years of colonial rule, only two out of a hundred children received a primary education, and 81 prisons were built. Laos was left in a deplorable condition where only a single doctor was available for the entire country. Heavy taxes were levied on the people. The French held a monopoly on sales of opium, alcohol, tobacco and salt, and excise tax revenue from them funded 50 to 60 percent of the cost to rule the colonies in Indochina. Similar actions were imposed by the Japanese government to exploit the people.

Reports coming out from Vietnam today relate ongoing misery, misery beyond imagination endured by the Vietnamese people. As bad as it is now, it was even worse during French colonial rule when starvation was pervasive, and the streets were piled high with skeletons and corpses. The reports claim that the number of people who died of starvation outnumbered those killed in modern warfare. Farmers who could no longer tolerate their plight rose up in several nationwide rebellions. Every uprising was crushed with unrelenting oppression.

Europe sparked the flame that became World War I. France was also engulfed by its fires. One hundred thousand Vietnamese were conscripted for service and labor in the suzerain state and at battlefronts in Europe. Once the war ended, France reneged on its promise to relax control in Vietnam, and no improvement was brought to the situation. The ruler's arrogance escalated, injustice was rampant and dissent was mercilessly repressed.

---

6 In July 1945, three World War II Allies, the U.S., Britain and Soviet Union, held the Potsdam Conference in Germany following Germany's defeat to plan the post-war world. Vietnam was considered a minor item on the agenda. In order to disarm the Japanese in Vietnam, the Allies divided the country in half at the 16th parallel. Chinese Nationalists were to move in and disarm the Japanese north of the parallel while the British would do the same in the south.

In 1930 and 1931, France cracked down on every democratic political party in the country, resulting in massive incarceration of Vietnamese communists, nationalists and liberals. Several thousands among them were executed on groundless or false charges. One of the collaborators with this oppression was a Vietnamese aristocrat by the name Ngo Dinh Diem, who later was appointed president of South Vietnam by the United States government.

Ten years later in 1940, Japan advanced into Vietnam as an Axis army during World War II and placed Indochina under colonial rule in the name of building a new order. In 1945, immediately before its defeat, Japan backed Vietnamese aristocrat Bao Dai to ascend as emperor and enabled him to rule Vietnam.

Ho Chi Minh secretly formed the League for Vietnamese Independence [Viet Minh] during Japan's occupation. Its slogan read, "Down with the rulers, whether French, Japanese or anyone else. We stand for the independence of Vietnam." August 15, 1945, Japan surrendered. On the heels of Japan's capitulation, on September 2 of the same year, Ho Chi Minh proclaimed the Declaration of Independence of Vietnam in Hanoi. The declaration concludes with the following statement:

> The French have fled, the Japanese have capitulated, Emperor Bao Dai has abdicated. Our people have broken the chains, which for nearly a century have fettered them and have won independence for the Fatherland. . . .For these reasons, we, members of the Provisional Government of the Democratic Republic of Vietnam, solemnly declare to the world that Vietnam has the right to be a free and independent country—and in fact is so already. The entire Vietnamese people are determined to mobilize all their physical and mental strength, to sacrifice their lives and property in order to safeguard their independence and liberty.

On March 6, 1946, France unwillingly agreed to recognize Vietnam's independence within the framework of the French Union. However, France's true intent was otherwise. Its troops advanced into Vietnam to restore colonial rule, and finally occupied Hanoi in the beginning of 1947. The Vietnamese people launched an all-out war for independence through guerrilla warfare. From 1947 to 1954, France fortified its troops to 250,000 to subjugate the guerillas, yet ultimately sustained a major defeat in Diên Biên Phũ. France, realizing that the Vietnamese people would no longer tolerate colonial rule, granted independence to the Republic of Vietnam in 1950 and installed abdicated Emperor Bao Dai as president. It further solicited U.S. aid and weapons, going so far as to request a nuclear attack, and tried to continue subduing the guerrillas. This attempt not only ended in failure, it developed into the current Vietnam War involving the United States.

From the outset the United States had no interest in reinstalling French colonial rule in Indochina. As just stated, France granted Vietnam nominal independence in 1950 and installed Bao Dai as its president in order to use him to serve France's interests. Instead of engaging in an overt war to reestablish control over its colonial holdings, France set up a "free Vietnam" ruled by Bao Dai as its puppet and redefined the war's purpose as defense against communism, in other words, "a crusade against communist invasion." It appointed itself as "the guardian of the free world," and turned Vietnam into a breakwater against communism. This created a divided Vietnam—the north and the south.

At this point, the United States finally sent the Military Assistance Advisory Group[7] and weapons to prevent "free Vietnam" from turning communist. U.S. military aid in support of the French effort was nothing less than hypocrisy. It was merely the first step by the United States towards establishing its own rule in Vietnam in place of France.

On March 29, 1954, Secretary of State John Dulles stated, "It is rich in many raw materials such as tin, oil, rubber and iron ore. . . That region has great strategic value to us. It has major naval and air bases."[8]

On April 4, 1954, U.S. News and World Report carried an editorial with the lengthy title, *Why U.S. Risks War for Indochina: It's The Key to Control All of Asia.*[9]

On August 4, 1953, after the United States decided to appropriate

---

7 Military Assistance Advisory Group [MAAG] refers to U.S. military advisors who trained conventional armed forces in developing countries. Before and during the Vietnam War, there were three of these groups operating in Southeast Asia.

8 *Indochina—Views of the United States on the Eve of the Geneva Conference.* A speech delivered in Manhattan to the Overseas Press Club of America.

9 "One of the world's richest areas is open to the winner of Indo-China. That's behind the growing US concern . . . tin, rubber, rice; key strategic raw materials are what the war is really about. The US sees it as a place to hold—at any cost."

$400 million to aid the war efforts in Indochina, President Dwight Eisenhower said, "[When the United States votes $400 million to help that war], we are not voting for a giveaway program. We are voting for the cheapest way that we can to prevent the occurrence of something that would be of a most terrible significance to the United States of America, our security, our power and ability to get certain things we need from the riches of the Indochinese territory and from Southeast Asia."[10] If France were to win the guerilla war with U.S. military aid, it would have been the cheapest way. However, the 250,000-strong French force capitulated to the Viet Minh, bringing an end to French colonial rule in Indochina.

The United States, the self-appointed guardian of free nations, did not pull out from Vietnam after the French defeat although it was likely to become much more costly than initially expected. Moreover, it is constructing naval and air force bases in strategically significant locations throughout Vietnam including Da Nang and Kam Ranh Bay based on the view that Vietnam is the key to controlling the entire Asian region. These are the nine parties of the Geneva Conference.

The United States is currently fighting a war against South Vietnam's National Liberation Front, which it calls the Viet Cong. Yet, it limits their representative in the peace negotiations with the North Vietnamese government, attempting to ignore NLF'S existence in the south.

In 1954, the aforementioned nine nations gathered in Geneva to deliberate the various political issues following the termination of French colonial rule in Indochina. The conference, attended by countries with totally opposing views, made no headway in its proceedings. In particular, the U.S. delegation made it patently clear that they are absolutely against any kind of settlement that renders independence to a unified Vietnam.

On June 8, the North Vietnamese government offered a substantial concession in hopes of breaking the stalemate and proposed to agree to a provisional partition of Vietnam into north and south. However, this concession was based on three conditions. First, the partition of Vietnam at the 17th parallel should be deemed strictly tentative and not in any way construed as a permanent division. Second, a general election should be held within two years to assure the reunification of Vietnam. Third, neither North nor South Vietnam was to form any international military

10 U.S. President Eisenhower's speech on aid to France's war against Vietnam, given at the Governor's Conference in Seattle, Washington.

alliance or accept foreign military aid during this period. Delegations of all parties except for the United States and the Bao Dai regime of South Vietnam accepted the proposal. This is what is known as the Geneva Accords.

No matter what agreement may come from the Geneva Conference, the U.S. has already set its policy on Vietnam. The conference and its agreements hold no value. For this reason, it refuses to accept the accords. Nonetheless, The United States gave its word to "refrain from the threat or the use of force to disturb" the accords.[11] This promise was short-lived. Two days after the conclusion of the Geneva Conference, Secretary of State Dulles noted that the conference benefited South Vietnam by advancing its position on independence; but that the conference must acknowledge the risk of further "communist inroads" into South East Asia as a result of "the loss in Northern Vietnam" from the free world. That expansion needs to be prevented, he said.

Immediately after the conference the French government likewise announced that the Bao Dai regime will continue to be the sole proprietor of the sovereign Vietnam recognized by France.

During the conference, U.S. Secretary of State Dulles had the French delegation order Bao Dai to appoint Ngo Dinh Diem as Prime Minister. Diem subsequently conducted a farcical referendum and, with the sanction of the U.S., ousted Bao Dai, becoming the president of the Republic of Vietnam while concurrently assuming the positions of prime minister and defense minister. Some say that U.S. leaders made a misjudgment in appointing Ngo Dinh Diem to the presidency. However, as far as the Vietnamese people are concerned, the United States and Diem are kindred tyrants. They are as alike as thieves. The Diem regime started a de facto manhunt. Anyone who did not consent to the despotic rule by the few was killed. We are told that the number of Vietnamese killed by Ngo Dinh Diem surpasses those killed in the Vietnam War to date.

In April 1960, eighteen leaders of South Vietnam warned Diem that the people would be forced to resort to revolution unless they were given more freedom. In November of the same year, officers of the South Vietnamese Army staged a coup. One elderly Vietnamese soldier told

---

11 July 21, 1954, *The American Response to the Geneva Declarations*, SOURCE: Neil Sheehan and others [eds.], *The Pentagon Papers*, pp. 52-53.

an American leader that the suffering under the French was nothing compared to the present sufferings inflicted on them by the Americans.

International media offers extensive coverage through articles and photographs of the atrocities and injustice committed in the Vietnam War. Vietnam has been artificially divided into two nations against the will of the people. The Vietnam War we see today is caused by the armed invasion of the United States, which seeks to make this unnatural partition permanent in violation of the 1954 Geneva Accords. The United States and its puppet Diem regime collaborated in refusing to implement the free election for the reunification of Vietnam prescribed in the Geneva Accords on the grounds that it would likely result in an overwhelming victory for Ho Chi Minh. The U.S. Pentagon is an institution that thrives on war, an institution with the sole purpose of profiting enormously from war.

Sir Bertrand Russell of Great Britain elaborates on this point:

> The U.S. Pentagon is the world's largest military organization, possessing 32 million acres of land at home and several tens of thousand acres abroad. There are 1,400 officers including 261 generals and commanders who are executives of major corporations. General Dynamics has 187 commissioned officers and 27 generals, admirals, and a former secretary of the Department of War on its payroll. Those in power, including the president and the ruling class, are compelled to serve this omnipotent group . . . Thus, democracy in America has lost its soul because the electorate can no longer dismiss the people who rule America. This concentration of power allows gigantic corporations to sustain the arms race for their own interest. Hence, more than 50 percent of U.S. GNP is devoted to military expenditure. For the people in the three continents of Asia, Africa and Latin America, this enormous American military machinery, giant defense industry and their hired media are the major enemies threatening the people's livelihood as well as the root cause of their misery and hunger.[12]

---

12 Translator's rendition from the Japanese translation.

Japan is experiencing an economic boom referred to as the "Vietnam special procurement boom." On July 4 of last year, the Mainichi newspaper reported, "There is a rumor that an additional $1 billion worth of Japanese goods are sold abroad annually due to the Vietnam War. The source of this rumor concerning $1 billion in foreign currency revenue is unknown." On the second day of deliberation at the Asian Pacific Region Ambassadors Conference held from the 14th of this month, Ambassador Nakayama, Japanese ambassador to South Vietnam, observed, "The South Vietnamese people are discontent with Japanese aid, feeling it has a strong overtone of profit-making and that aid, in the true sense of the word, is limited." His observation indicates the attitude of the Japanese government and business toward the Vietnam War.

On July 13, 1965, President Lyndon Johnson flatly stated that the United States has made twelve attempts to negotiate or discuss the conditions of Vietnam so far; the other side, North Vietnam, showed not an iota of interest. This statement gives the impression that North Vietnam is pro-war. Yet, the truth of the matter is the United States has rejected seven approaches to a negotiated settlement to end the war. First, in the fall of 1963, Secretary of State David Dean Rusk refused a French proposal. Second, in July 1964, the United States rejected a proposal by UN Secretary General U Thant. Third, in December 1964, Ho Chi Minh notified France that he was prepared to talk with the United States. The United States scornfully rejected it. Fourth, in February 1965, French President Charles de Gaulle's request to reconvene the Geneva Conference met a U.S. refusal. Fifth, on February 24, 1965, the Soviet Union recommended the reconvening of the Geneva Conference. Sixth, on February 24, 1965, U Thant proposed a preliminary discussion. Seventh, he simultaneously proposed to hold an unofficial conference of seven nations. The United States refused every one of them. Both Hanoi and the National Front for the Liberation of the South are refusing the non-conditional discussions proposed by the United States on grounds that they are intended to force Vietnam into unconditional surrender.

The Japanese government thought so highly of America's peace negotiations that it propagandized the eagerness of the American negotiators and became their agent by sending special envoys abroad. This move was met with a sneer.

The U.S. State Department bulletin of August 31, 1964 stated that the Americans who are keen on expanding the conflict are calling on young Americans to do a job that should be done by young Asians, but U.S. involvement will not solve the real problem in Vietnam. Contrary to this statement, by the middle of 1966, 400,000 young Americans had been sent to take over "the work of young Asians."

The United States will not prevail in the Vietnam War. It has experienced consecutive defeats. The National Liberation Front cites its many victories won so far. On December 23, 1964, the Pentagon predicted that without immediate implementation of decisive measures, America would almost certainly see the greatest defeat in its history. A little more than a year later on March 21, 1966, Senator [Richard B.] Russell said the South Vietnamese army was at the brink of collapse, and he thought it unlikely that they could hold out another month. [Separately] the February 23, 1964 Sunday Times reported that the U.S. military advisors stationed in Vietnam, anticipating such a collapse, were strongly advocating direct U.S. intervention to advance the war beyond the 17th parallel into North Vietnam.

Accordingly, the United States has become a direct party to the war. First the helicopter operation was employed, followed by the Strategic Hamlet Program based on the Stanley proposal. It was predicted South Vietnam would be pacified within eighteen months. The plan called for crowding ten million farmers into 16,000 concentration camps and was considered the backbone of the special war strategy. Eighteen months later, the project had produced nothing but disillusionment. None of what was expected happened. Amphibious troops had been introduced, supposedly to run freely in the paddy fields of the Mekong Delta, but the combat operations in the Mekong Delta also failed to bring victory.

Toward the end of 1965, a plan devised by [U.S. Secretary of Defense Robert] McNamara was launched, placing priority on bombing peripheral provinces in target areas. Brutal and shameless crimes were committed to pacify areas surrounding Saigon and Cholon. Peaceful villages, temples and shrines, schools, hospitals, and markets were indiscriminately targeted. In all, 170,000 civilians were killed; 800,000 people were maimed or injured by torture; 400,000 people were incarcerated in 1,000 prisons; and five million people were contained in strategic hamlets. Tens of thousands of women of all ages, including girls, the elderly and nuns, were raped. Five thousand people were either buried alive or had their stomachs ripped open. Several thousand temples and churches were destroyed, and tens of thousands of devotees were slaughtered.

Next came the defoliation operation.[13] Napalm bombs, poisons and agricultural chemicals are being used to defoliate the jungle. The bombing of North Vietnam had begun. As the war escalated and the number of U.S. troops increased, the already enormous interest groups fattened up further by gobbling up the profits of war. Still, the United States has not won the war.

Prime Minister Ngugen Cao Ky of South Vietnam told a Japanese newspaper that it would take 600,000 U.S. troops to win the Vietnam War. Secretary of Defense McNamara went on a fact-finding tour [in November 1965] to determine what needed to be done. The National Liberation Front in South Vietnam, with as little as 300,000, are defeating U.S. forces consisting of 462,000 troops along with the South Vietnamese armed forces of 600,000.

Shedding a remarkable light on the Vietnam War are Buddhist acts of self-immolation, fasting and veneration before altars set up in the streets. Buddhists monks have enshrined altars in the middle of the main street in Hue where tanks roar through. In front of troops charging with bayonets drawn, they kneel and rise in veneration and recite sūtras. Consequently, the world no longer focuses on who occupies the city of Hue but rather watches the true soldiers of peace and knights of justice.

Chapter XXIII of the Lotus Sūtra, *The Story of the Bodhisattva Medicine King*, states:

> Having made this offering [Bodhisattva Gladly-Seen-by-All-Beings] arose from samādhi, and reflected within himself, thus saying, "Though I, by my transcendental powers have made offerings to the Buddha, yet, these offerings cannot compare to the offering of my body."
>
> . . . he anointed his body with a variety of scented oils, and, in the presence of the Buddha Sun-Moon-Pure-Bright-Virtue, wrapped himself in a celestial, jeweled garment, bathed in scented oils of various kinds, and, by his transcendent vow, set fire to his own body. Its light universally illuminated worlds as numerous as eight hundred billion times the number of the sands in the River Ganges.

13 Initially called Operation Hades, changed to Operation Ranch Hands.

> Buddhas of these worlds simultaneously extolled him saying: "Excellent, excellent, good son! This is true devotion. It is called the offering to the Tathāgata according to the Genuine Dharma."
>
> . . . Having said thus, they all became silent. His body continued to burn for twelve hundred years, after which it was consumed.

The self-immolation of a bodhisattva is void of indignation, enmity or spite. This is clearly communicated to the world by the letter[14] left behind [by its practitioner]. It is a practice in which one's life is given as an offering to the World Honored One, Buddha Śākyamuni. It demonstrates one's devotion and reverence toward the Genuine Dharma. It takes selfless devotion to lay down one's life. Such fearless devotion speaks to society and becomes a prayer for universal peace as well as a vow to emancipate humankind. While the prime precept in Buddha Dharma is the precept against taking life, at the same time we are taught to practice the Genuine Dharma without attachment to our body and life, and to lay down our life for the sake of honoring and making offerings to the Buddha, Dharma and Sangha.

When Nichiren Daishōnin was brought to the execution ground at Tatsunokuchi[15] to be decapitated, he said:

> Many are the places where I, Nichiren, had laid down my life in my past lives for the sake of my wife and children, my land and kin. At times I forsook my life in mountains or oceans, at times in rivers, at seashores and along roadsides.[16]

Young Japanese today still give up their lives in the mountains. Many die in the ocean near Kamakura. Some commit double suicides in rivers or seashores.

---

14 Reference to the letter written by the Most Venerable Thich Quang Duc [1897-1963] from Hue who performed self-immolation in the busy intersection of Saigon. It has come to be known as the Letter of the Heart Blood.

15 Located on the eastern shore of Katase River in Katase, Fujisawa City. It was the execution ground of the Kamakura shogunate ruled by the Hōjō clan.

16 *Shijō-kingo-dono-goshōsoku* 四条金吾殿御消息 *Letter to Shijō Kingo*. Written in 1271 at Echi.

> However, if not for the sake of the Lotus Sūtra, the hardships encountered because of the Daimoku, the lives offered and the persecutions suffered will not benefit the attaining of enlightenment. If not for attaining enlightenment, the ocean and rivers where my lives were lost will not become the Buddha Land.[17]

This means that no matter how many climb mountains and lose their lives, those mountains do not transform into the Pure Land.

> As a practitioner of the Lotus Sūtra, I was exiled to Ito[18] and now face execution here at Tatsunokuchi in Sōshū.[19] Is not Tatsunokuchi the Buddha Land, for my life will be offered for the Lotus Sūtra? The sūtra says that "There is but one Dharma-vehicle throughout the one hundred thousand Buddha Lands." Does not this passage of the sūtra signify this? The One Vehicle expounded in this sūtra is the Lotus Sūtra. There are no other teachings save the Lotus Sūtra in the one hundred thousand Buddha Lands, except for Buddha's teaching of expedience. Thus, wherever I, Nichiren, am faced with adversity, that very place becomes the Buddha Land. Since Tatsunokuchi of Katase located in Sōshu of Japan, is where my life will be offered for the Lotus Sūtra, it is no different from the Land of Eternal Tranquil Light. Could the passage in *The Divine Transcendental Powers of the Tathāgata*[20] of ". . . or in a grove or in a garden or on the mountains or in valleys or in open fields . . . that Buddha entered Parinirvāna" be signifying this?[21]

The place where a person lays down his or her life must transform into the Buddha Realm, the Pure Land. It is hard to fathom the immeasurable power being exerted by the many Vietnamese who offer their lives through self-immolation to bring peace to Vietnam. I believe

---

17 *Shijō-kingo-dono-goshōsoku* 四条金吾殿御消息 *Letter to Shijō Kingo.*
18 A city located in the east bank of the Izu peninsula in Shizuoka Prefecture.
19 Another name for Sagami, currently Kanagawa Prefecture.
20 Chapter XXI of the Lotus Sūtra.
21 *Shijō-kingo-dono-goshōsoku* 四条金吾殿御消息 *Letter to Shijō Kingo.*

Peace vigil against the Vietnam War on June 1, 1968, Times Square, New York City.

the creation of peace in our world tomorrow depends on the rise of Buddha Dharma.

Signs of U.S. defeat are unfolding. Five hundred [U.S.] soldiers recently engaged in collective desertion. People burn draft cards in public. Five hundred thousand people attended a massive march against the Vietnam War. And 2,500 clergy of Catholic, Protestant and Jewish faiths sent an open letter to President Johnson to "stop this war in the name of God."

The South Vietnamese government cannot keep their soldiers after mandatory draft. Two-thirds of the recruits, which is to say the majority, desert. However, what the United States should fear is not the large number of deserters, but rather the Vietnamese soldiers who remain with the government's army. They are waiting for an opportunity to undermine the U.S. forces from within.

The United States of America can afford to spend $400,000 to kill a single member of NLF. The United States of America can spend a million dollars per hour in the Vietnam War. The United States of America can confine Vietnamese peasants in concentration camps surrounded by barbed wire and armed guards, torture, cripple and slaughter them.

The United States of America can violate the Geneva Accords and infringe on any number of laws regarding international war. The United States of America can torture, shoot or bury their prisoners alive. The United States of America can burn defenseless villages and hamlets, kill the Vietnamese people with napalm bombs, yellow phosphorous bombs and poison gas. The United States of America can implement defoliant operations and burn the forest, destroy the jungles and crops. It is also not impossible for the United States to exterminate the Vietnamese people. The United States can take advantage of their military bases in mainland Japan and Okinawa. However, the United States of America cannot prevail in the Vietnam War because it fails to understand the inherent justice and "military" tactics[22] of the Vietnamese people.

The United States does not have a war objective. The initial rationale for the United States in becoming involved in this war was to honor its commitment to send troops, although no such commitment was ever made. It then escalated the war, contending it was preventing the expansion of communism from the north. Evidence shows that none of this is true. A country with "fictitious" war objectives cannot win a war.

The U.S. forces will be defeated by corruption and its own inhumane brutality. Military defeat may be a disgrace to the United States, yet it's not an uncommon disgrace in this world. However, its moral defeat will go down in the history of humanity as the darkest stain for the United States. No other war in history has been the subject of such dishonorable criticism as the U.S. war in Vietnam.

The Vietnamese need not declare their objectives in this war. The entire nation has already stood up. The Vietnamese need not draft their soldiers. The Vietnamese are clad in rags that barely cover them. The Vietnamese people are poor and hungry. The Vietnamese soldiers hide in holes and caves dug in the depths of the mountains. The Vietnamese soldiers are fighting in fields and forests, moving from one house to another, one village to another. The Vietnamese are injured and killed in great number by the state-of-the-art U.S. weapons.

Nonetheless, the liberation army grows day by day, both in the numbers of soldiers and units. The military victory of the Vietnamese people over the United States will be an incredible miracle in the history

22 Here Guruji is referring to the just cause of defending their homeland from U.S. invasion; the use of altars in the streets to prevent the U.S. military's advancement; and self-immolation to defend the authority of Buddhist teachings.

In accord with his deep faith in the Lotus Sūtra and his anguish and compassion for his fellow Vietnamese, the Most Venerable Thich Quang Duc set himself on fire in Saigon on June 11, 1963. The image was captured by Malcolm Browne of the Associated Press.

of humankind. Even more striking is the unbelievable, indomitable spirit of the Vietnamese people, who are willing to lay down their lives one by one, and their lack of rancor in defense of their homeland, their freedom and peace.

The conduct of the Vietnamese people is indeed the Bodhisattva practice preached in Buddhism. It shall shed eternal light in the history of human civilization. The Lotus Sūtra expounds that its light will illuminate worlds as many as 800 billion times the number of grains of sand in the River Ganges.

The ordeal of the Vietnamese people has opened the gate, through which humanity can further elevate itself and enter the Unsurpassed Path. It is a tremendous and noble sacrifice. The Vietnam War is a confrontation between the materialist civilization—which causes human depravity, a dehumanizing civilization of machines, in truth, the American civilization—and the power of the human spirit and endeavor in pursuit of liberty and peace, in essence, the Buddhist civilization.

The outcome of the battle is already decided. The Vietnamese people shall inevitably prevail.

Na Mu Myō Hō Ren Ge Kyō

19

Aspire to Be Champions of the Heart[1]

January 23, 1968
New Delhi, India

Today, countries professing to be Christian states, starting with the United States and Britain, have become specialists in war. In reality, they are anti-Christians cloaked in the name of Christianity.

When Gandhiji was invited to address the British Missionary Conference in Madras, he stated that what was happening in Europe "shows that the message of Jesus of Nazareth, the Son of Peace, has been little understood in Europe and that light upon it may have to be thrown from the East."[2] He was referring to the light of a faith that practices the message of Jesus of Nazareth, the civilization of the East.

Many Japanese researchers in agriculture and the like, as well as young people come to India to do this or that, but relatively speaking, these things are trifles, side issues. They are not issues that determine the rise or fall of India. If we are concerned for India, we must understand that the major issue determining the rise or fall of a nation is in the spiritual realm. Our obligation as Japanese is to collaborate in this effort, but not many understand this. They seem satisfied with just making a living in India.

It is now our turn to follow in Gandhiji's footsteps and lift up the spirit of the great precept of nonviolence, the precept against taking life, among the Indian people as a service to India. It does not matter who does this work, Christians or Buddhists. The underlying concern is whether we act to let others live or to deprive them of their lives. We, as Japanese,

---

1 Japanese Christian youths working in India as volunteers visited Guruji at his lodgings for his advice on the mental attitude needed to serve India. Transcribed from a tape from that occasion.

2 *Collected Works of Mahatma Gandhi*, Vol.13, p. 220, June 6, 1925.

must expound the gospel of peace in this context, be it in the name of Jesus Christ or Buddha. When the scriptures are faithfully expounded, peace is what is taught in every sacred scripture.

Religion becomes useless when people of faith accommodate power and use religion as a tool to make a living. The loss of credibility today for the Congress Party comes as a consequence of losing sight of Gandhiji's true spirit. Working in cooperation with this forgotten spiritual issue is what we must do. Sending rice or money—these things can be left to the United States or U.K., where the money would otherwise fund military campaigns. The other day when visiting Europe, Mrs. Nonomiya Hatsue,[3] a Christian, met with representatives from Vietnam. On that occasion she asked what they desired most from Japan. They answered that there exists a dire need for money, medical supplies and other essentials, but more than anything, they implored Japan not to produce the atrocious bombs that the United States is using on Vietnam. Today Japan is willing to do anything, no matter how egregious, for political objectives, for power or for money. The Vietnamese people are made to suffer as a result. The only wish of the Vietnamese people is for Japan not to make these bombs. There is no reason their wish cannot be heeded. Politics and economy today are responsible for this inhumanity. Despite this reality, youth in Japan happily become politicians or members of the business circle. This is a mistake.

---

3 Vice Chair of the Japan-Bharat Sarvodaya Mitrata Sangha. Sarvodaya is a word coined by Mahatma Gandhi signifying "the welfare of all" or "universal uplift." Its current usage means the "awakening of all." In his 1908 translation of John Ruskin's tract on political-economy, *Unto This Last,* Gandhi used this term, which also reflected his ideal political philosophy. After independence, Gandhi's associate, Vinoba Bhave, developed a social movement under this name striving for self-determination and equality for all strata of India society. In concurrence with Nipponzan Myōhōji's dedication of its first stūpa in Hanaokayama, the World Pacifist Conference 世界平和者会議 was held at multiple locations in Japan, and Bharatan Kumarappa and Kakasaheb Kalelkar were among the guests. Nipponzan disciples Rev. Maruyama Gyōryō 丸山行遼 and Rev. Imai Gyōjun 今井行順 were instrumental in founding the Japan-Bharat Sarvodaya Mitrata Sangha in 1960, much to Vinoba Bhave's pleasure. Guruji served as President of Japan Sarvodaya, which has had prominent figures in the peace movement, religious circles and academia on its board. Mrs. Nonomiya Hatsue 野々宮初枝 [1898-1978], a professor at Japan Women's University 日本女子大学, became its vice president. She was also the director of Women's Peace Association 婦人平和協会, the first women's peace organization founded in Japan in 1921, and president of WILPF [Women's International League for Peace and Freedom] branch in Japan. Ms. Nonomiya met Guruji in 1962 at an All-India Sarvodaya Conference in Vedchi, Gujarat, when he delivered his message *The Doctrine of the Sword* [p. 120] urging India to seek a peaceful settlement in the Indo-Sino War.

Aspire to be champions of the heart! No other solution exists in the world of the nuclear era other than that of the heart and mind. The Japanese people must offer a peaceful solution in this issue of the heart and mind. We must awaken to this great mission. I heard that you are committed to dedicating your lives to India. It is quite laudable. Moreover, if you seek to dedicate your lives not in agriculture, crafts or industry, but to the spiritual realm, work to advance Gandhiji's legacy. As Japanese, when you advocate the heart and spirit of Jesus Christ, do so in a way that you are not exploited by politics; rather, please criticize politics with the Bible. This is the work that you can do as Japanese in India's interest.

His Excellency, the current president of India,[4] is of the Muslim faith. When I met the president the other day, he fondly reminisced about the days when he saw me beat the drum and pray in the morning and evening at Gandhiji's ashram in Wardha. Spiritual work requires no words or anything else. All I did was to pray to Lord Buddha for the success of India's independence. It was understood by the Indian people. I still do not speak the language, but it has not been an obstacle to my work in India. Many religious scholars, Vedantist, university professors come to India, yet are of little service to India. Giving lectures on books or cultivating fields are not related to the core human issue, which is how human beings can live in peace and joy. This was true at the time of Jesus Christ and was also true in the days of Buddha Śākyamuni. It remains true today. There is nothing difficult about it. It all boils down to the single truth that humans must not kill, but instead serve others, bring joy to others. It's that simple. Their joy becomes our joy when we live like that.

Gandhiji was not haughty. I was in India in those days and know firsthand that Gandhiji never took anything but the third-class train compartment. Life at the Wardha ashram was comparable to life at the lowest social stratum. Japan was using terms like first-class country or second-class country, and even young people were assuming an air of importance. That was plain wrong. The United States claims that it will find an honorable solution in Vietnam, but nothing is more dishonorable than murder. Nothing is more disgraceful than using poison or germs. Who would sympathize with the U.S., who would respect it, even if the war were won that way? This is the mistake of acting like a calculator

4 Dr. Zakir Hussain [1897-1969], a known scholar, was the third president of India from 1967 to 1969. He is said to have contributed much to the popularization of the Gandhian scheme for the basic national education.

in modern times while losing sight of religion, spiritual life. It is not acceptable in the human world. The president of the United States said that the U.S. will teach [Vietnam] how costly invasion is; instead they themselves got stuck in a rut, and invasion came with a hefty price for the United States. The next thing [the United States] had to do was to defend the dollar. Awesome are the workings of the heavens! Computers developed by human beings could never calculate it.

India is a land Japan is deeply indebted to. It is the country that transmitted Buddhism to Japan, which has nurtured and cultivated our culture for more than a thousand years. The Japanese people owe it to India to provide spiritual support. No religion exists in Japan today, which also hold true for Buddhism. Buddhism has become a means of making a living. People only make money, talk haughtily as if they know something or play up to others. How petty!

Gandhiji led India's freedom movement, proposing that the future of humanity would be resolved through nonviolence. People might think that it is a dream to believe in a future realized through nonviolence. I, too, think it is a dream. But, it is a good dream to dream. I want you to share this dream. At a time when nuclear weapons threaten the entire world, there is nothing to fear in the spiritual world. Fascinating, isn't it? While you are all still in your youth, you have become involved in matters of spirituality. It was the right thing to do, an even better choice than pursuing crafts or technology.

Should you perish in India working for what you believe, I will come to lay you to rest. Let that be so. It would be gratifying if one or two of you would lay down your lives in India.

20

On the Dedication of the Rajgir Stūpa

October 24, 1969
Ratnagiri Hill, Rajgir, India

The emergence of the stūpa in the sky above Ratnagiri Hill, Rajgir, goes back more than 2,500 years. During the eight years the Lotus Sūtra was expounded by the Great Enlightened, World Honored One at Grdhrakūta, a stūpa enshrining the whole body relics of Tathāgata Prabhūtaratna, who entered Nirvāna in the remotest kalpa past, suddenly appeared above Ratnagiri Hill. Buddha Śākyamuni entered the stūpa and from there preached the quintessence of the Lotus Sūtra, the chapter of *The Eternal Duration of the Life of the Tathāgata*. He then bundled it with the five and seven characters of Na Mu Myō Hō Ren Ge Kyō and left it for the emancipation of sentient beings in the defiled Era of Final Dharma to follow.

Today, in the defiled Era of Final Dharma, amidst the thunderous chant of Na Mu Myō Hō Ren Ge Kyō and the reverberation of the celestial drums, the majestically adorned, monumental stūpa of the Preceptor, Buddha Śākyamuni, has suddenly emerged before our eyes above Ratnagiri Hill, bringing jubilation once again to the hearts of all who witness it, clergy and laity alike.[1]

The emergence of the stūpa in Rajgir is a monument to the birth of a nation of peace, the Republic of India. Had India not won freedom and independence through nonviolence, and had Prime Minister Jawaharlal Nehru not pledged to restore Rajgir, the stūpa would never have appeared on top of this hill.

The stūpa here at the peak of Ratnagiri Hill, Rajgir is a humble offering of reverence by Japanese Buddhists, a requital of gratitude for the infinite blessings and guidance by Buddhism's Preceptor, the World

1 The four assemblies 四衆 of monks, nuns, laymen and laywomen.

Honored One, Buddha Śākyamuni, for building a Japanese nation of progress, peace, and culture over the past 1,300 years.

I am overwhelmed with joy that we were able to perform this unprecedented dedication rite today in the presence of His Excellency, the President of India,[2] and the great leaders of India's freedom movement.

The Eternal Duration of the Life of the Tathāgata of the Lotus Sūtra states:

When living beings see me as extinct
And make offerings to my relics far and wide,
All cherishing longing adoration,
Thirsting in their heart to seek me out,
Thus, all living beings surrender in their faith,
Upright in character and gentle,
Wholeheartedly wishing to see the Buddha,
Not sparing their body and life,
Then together with all the Sangha,
I once again appear on the Sacred Eagle Peak.

"We are the messengers of the World Honored One. And, amidst a multitude, having nothing to fear, we will assiduously preach on the Dharma. May the Buddha abide in tranquility."[3]

---

2 Varahagiri Venkata Giri [1894–1980], commonly known as V. V. Giri, was India's fourth president from 1969-1974.

3 Chapter XIII of the Lotus Sūtra, *Exhortation to Hold Firm*. Both citations are the translator's rendition.

21

Inaugural Speech of the Kalinga World Peace Pagoda

November 8, 1972
Bhubaneswar, India

Na Mu Myō Hō Ren Ge Kyō

The 8th Stone Dharma Edict[1] of Ashoka the Great[2] reads as follows:

> Kings in the past have long went on pleasure tours and relished hunting and other pastimes. However, ten years after his consecration,[3] the Beloved of the Gods advanced towards sambodhi [supreme bodhi, supreme enlightenment]. From that time the practice of Dharma tours began, during which time he visited mendicant monks and Brahmans [Hindu priests], and bestowed alms, met with elderly masters and distributed money. He also met with the people in rural areas, inculcated them on the Dharma and provided appropriate counsel on the teachings. The Beloved of the Gods in the latter half of his reign derived more pleasure from this than from anything else.[4]

---

1 Fourteen major edicts and 2 separate edicts were found at sites in Kalinga, and they are referred to as Ashoka's Major Rock Edicts. The 8th Rock Edict was issued in 256 BCE.

2 Ashoka the Great [304-232 BCE] was an Indian emperor of the Mauryan Dynasty who ruled from 273-232 BCE. He is cited as one of India's greatest emperors. His name means "without sorrow" in Sanskrit. In his edicts, he is referred to as Devānāmpriya, "Beloved of the Gods," and Priyadarshi or "Regarded with joy."

3 潅頂. Translation of a Sanskrit term *abhisecana*, a rite of pouring water from the four great seas over the crown on coronation.

4 Translator's rendition based on text Guruji relied on, which is the Chinese translated version. Research indicates that the English rendition for *sambodhi* in some sources is "Bodh Gaya" or "the tree of enlightenment," the place of Buddha's Enlightenment, and other sources translate it as "became enlightened" or "attained supreme wisdom."

From ancient times, those considered great kings of foreign lands took for granted privileges that come with the throne, reveled in splendor, wallowed in carnal pleasures of the five desires[5] and indulged in debauchery. Occasional excursions outside castle walls were opportunities to flaunt their power as great monarchs. To amuse themselves, they rode deep into the mountains and over the plains, killing hordes of birds and animals in season for banquets attended by civil and military officers alike.

However, eight years after ascending to the throne and following his conquest of the Kalinga dynasty, the Beloved of the Gods was struck suddenly by the criminality and savagery of conquest through war. He came to embrace Buddha Dharma, becoming an upāsaka[6] by taking the oath of the Three Refuges and Five Precepts.[7] Victory was to come only through the Dharma by winning the hearts and minds of the people. He personally renounced meat-eating to demonstrate his belief in the merit of the precept against taking life, abolished hunting, ended the practice of royal banquets and prohibited killing throughout his dominion.

Buddhism teaches emancipation through three vehicles, and two of the vehicles[8] of śrāvaka [one who hears the voice] and pratyekabuddhas [cause knower] are referred to as Theravāda. The Mahāparinirvāna Sūtra[9] describes the Theravāda practice as follows:

> Bhikshus! If you wish to seek the comfort of tranquility, free from delusions and the vicissitudes of birth and death, leave

5 Desires that arise in connection with the five senses of form, sound, scent, taste and touch. Also desires for wealth, sex, food and drink, fame and sleep.

6 優婆塞. A male lay devotee of the Buddha. Originally the term applied to the followers of the Buddha who were not ordained as bhikshus.

7 *Sanki-gokai* 三帰五戒. At the time of initiation, one first takes the oath of the Three Refuges and then that of the Five Precepts. The Three Refuges are: taking refuge in the Buddha, Dharma and the Sangha [the Buddhist order]. The Five Precepts are: not to kill, not to steal, not to commit adultery, not to tell lies and not to take intoxicants.

8 Two kinds of teaching apply to śrāvaka, a follower of Theravāda who contemplates the principle of the Four Noble Truths to attain Nirvāna, and to pratyekabuddhas, self-enlightened hermits.

9 There are various extant sūtras both in the Theravāda and Mahāyāna canons under the broad category of the generally known Nirvāna Sūtra, or Mahāparinirvāna-sūtra, which depicts the significance of Buddha Śākyamuni's Parinirvāna. Guruji is citing from 仏垂般涅槃略説教誡経 [Bushi hatsu nehan ryakusetsu Kyōkai Kyō] or in short, 遺教経 [Yuigyō-kyō] The Sūtra of the Deathbed Injunction, translated by Kumārajīva. The Sūtra of the Deathbed Injunction was translated into Chinese during the transition period to Mahāyāna and is one of the sūtras that focuses on Buddha's last preaching before entering Nirvāna at Kushinagara. The only extant version of this sūtra is a Chinese translation.

> clamor and distraction to reside in quiet solitude. Those who dwell undisturbed in a quiet place receive respect from Indra and the various gods. For this reason, leave the company of all to live in solitary serenity and contemplate on eliminating the root of suffering.

The Mahāyāna practice is portrayed in the chapter *A Parable* of the Lotus Sūtra as:

> If there are living beings who, following the Buddha, the World Honored One, hear the Dharma, receive and keep it, diligently practice and zealously advance, seeking the complete wisdom, the wisdom of the Buddha, the natural wisdom, the wisdom without a teacher, and the knowledge, powers and fearlessness of the Tathāgata, who take pity on and comfort innumerable creatures, benefit gods and humans, and emancipate all, these will have the vehicle named the Great Vehicle. Because the Bodhisattvas seek this vehicle they are named Mahāsattvas.

The Dharmapada says, "To save beings accommodating their desires is not the Path; to save the world far and wide and to keep it unharmed is the Path."[10] Salvation that accommodates the individual is the practice of Theravāda, which seeks the comfort of tranquility and nirvāna. Emancipation of the world far and wide is to take pity on and to comfort innumerable creatures, to benefit gods and humans and to emancipate all. This is *anuttara-samyak-sambodhi* [supreme enlightenment], the teaching of Mahāyāna. Ashoka the Great became a practitioner of the Mahāyāna Bodhisattva Way ten years after his coronation. This is what he meant by "advanced towards *anuttara-samyak-sambodhi*." Once becoming a practitioner of the Mahāyāna Bodhisattva Way, one cannot be content with seeking serenity

10 Translator's rendition of the Japanese. The Dharmapada cited is originally from Chinese. 法句比喩経. Fa-kheu-king-tsu [Ch]. Hokkuhiyu-kyō [Jp]. Dharmapada with Accompanying Narratives. Within the vast canon of Chinese Buddhism, there are four translations of the Dharmapada. Although the best known version of the Dharmapada is a Theravāda sūtra translated from Pali, the version of the Dharmapada cited here differs from the Pali version with the addition of 13 sections, hence the name "Accompanying Narratives." It was brought to China in 223 and translated during the Tsin Dynasty [265-589].

and comfort alone in a quiet place. Sympathy and concern for living beings motivates the practitioner to emancipate all. Ashoka the Great's Dharma circuits originated from this concern. It is recorded that on his Dharma tours, he visited mendicant monks and Brahmans to bestow alms, and elderly masters of learning and virtue to distribute money. Mendicant monks, Brahmans and elderly masters are spiritual teachers, respected in society. These are people who embrace and believe in profound teachings, who make plain the ancient scriptures. What prompted Ashoka the Great to take time out from the hectic affairs of a great country and to go out of his way to visit mendicant monks, Brahmans and elderly masters in all directions? The chapter of *Devadatta* in the Lotus Sūtra says:

> For the sake of the Dharma, I left the throne, deputed the administration of the domain to the crown prince, and sought the Dharma in all directions, beating the drum and proclaiming openly: "Whoever is able to expound to me the Great Vehicle, I will provide for him and be his footman for the rest of my life."

The Mahāyāna practice of a Bodhisattva is to run about in all directions in search of the Dharma of the Great Vehicle, beating the drum and proclaiming: Who is able to expound for me the Great Vehicle? It is not to sit in serene comfort in forests under a tree or to be absorbed in study in schools or monastic academies. The great king's practice in visiting mendicant monks, Brahmans and elderly masters was to offer alms and distribute money. The Mahāyāna Bodhisattva practice consists of satisfying the six pāramitās.[11] The first of the six pāramitās is the practice of almsgiving. Neither Mahāyāna Dharma nor practice exists when almsgiving is absent. Emperor Ashoka purposely recorded that he bestowed alms and distributed money. This valuable record

11 波羅蜜. *Haramitsu* is translated as *do* 度, "crossing over, salvation" and *tōhigan* 到彼岸, "reaching the other shore," i.e., Nirvāna. These are practices of a Bodhisattva in attainment of emancipation. The practice consists of six kinds and is called *roku-haramitsu* 六波羅蜜. The six kinds are: *fuse-haramitsu*, 布施波羅蜜, practice of almsgiving [consisting of offering of money and material goods, offering of fearlessness, offering of Dharma]; *jikai*, 持戒, unwavering observance of precepts; *ninniku*, 忍辱, perseverance under insult and persecution; *shōjin*, 精進, assiduity in devoting body and mind to the realization of the other five practices; *zenjō*, 禅定, quieting the mind and contemplating truth; and *chie*, 智慧, wisdom, the practice to be versed in all Dharma, to sever delusion in order to see the truth.

attests to the significance that Ashoka the Great designated to this practice of a Mahāyāna Bodhisattva. The practice of almsgiving is expounded extensively in the *Devadatta* chapter. Almsgiving starts with offerings consisting of money and treasures. Ashoka the Great's Dharma edict indicates exactly that practice. *Devadatta* is a Jataka tale of the previous life the World Honored One, Buddha Śākyamuni, who became a great king and sought the Lotus Sūtra, and the tale chronicles how thoroughly he practiced almsgiving during his Bodhisattva stage to advance into *anuttara-samyak-sambodhi.*

Seeking the Lotus Sūtra without indolence is a practice of almsgiving. Likewise, disseminating the Lotus Sūtra far and wide is nothing but the practice of almsgiving. Those incapable of bestowing the Lotus Sūtra are those who do not practice almsgiving. Likewise, those who cannot spread the Lotus Sūtra are those incapable of practicing almsgiving. The great king's Dharma edict says, "He also met with the people in rural areas, inculcated them on the Dharma and provided appropriate counsel on the teachings. The Beloved of the Gods in the latter half of his reign derived more pleasure from this than from anything else." Emperor Ashoka's Dharma circuit was the enterprise of a Mahāyāna Bodhisattva who visited mendicant monks, Brahmans and elderly masters in all directions to bestow alms. The great king met with the people, became their teacher and filled them with the true significance of Buddha Dharma, counseling them on their understanding of Buddha Dharma. The great king's edicts were not empty teachings on formalism.

Everywhere he went, Ashoka the Great entered the hallowed place of practice of a Bodhisattva where he sought both his own spiritual advancement and to lead others to the Dharma.[12] Great kings from ancient times went on pleasure tours to satisfy their five desires, and each time they amused themselves in hunting, slaying of creatures and holding elaborate banquets. However, Ashoka the Great, ten years after his coronation, advanced toward *anuttara-samyak-sambodhi* and initiated Dharma tours, in which he found satisfaction and joy through his assiduous Bodhisattva practice of self-advancement while at the same time leading others to the Dharma. This is precisely the reason he is called Ashoka who knows the Dharma.[13]

---

12 自行化他. *Jigyōketa*.

13 Dharmāsoka in Sanskrit.

Ashoka the Great conquered the world by renouncing the sword. In other words, his conquest came through Dharma. He observed the precept against taking life, built peace in the world and brought prosperity to all people. It was the victory of the Dharma.

Humanity is now in an era when the world will be destroyed and the people doomed to annihilation unless the doctrine of the sword is cast aside and the precept against taking life embraced and upheld. The single beacon able to eradicate the terror shrouding modern humanity is the Bodhisattva practice of Ashoka the Great's Dharma tour. The chapter on *Exhortation to Hold Firm* of the Lotus Sūtra says,

> Whether in villages or cities,
> Whenever there are those who seek the Dharma,
> We will all go to them and
> Expound the Dharma bequeathed by the Buddha.

When I first stepped out into the world at the age of 33 as a practitioner of the Lotus Sūtra, I gave my life and body to this single passage of the *Exhortation to Hold Firm* chapter: "We will all go to them and expound the Dharma bequeathed by the Buddha." The latter half of Ashoka the Great's reign, ten years after ascending to the throne, is distinguished by the Dharma circuits he embarked upon. Among the various Mahāyāna sūtras, *Devadatta* and *Exhortation to Hold Firm* inspired the faith and ardent practice of Ashoka the Great and led to his conception of the Dharma tours. The passages of *Devadatta* and *Exhortation to Hold Firm* were reflected flawlessly in Ashoka the Great's 8th Stone Dharma Edict. Not only do the phrases of these sūtras and the edict echo each other, they also, in fact, chronicle Ashoka the Great and the effort he made as a practitioner of the Lotus Sūtra.

Na Mu Myō Hō Ren Ge Kyō

Nichidatsu

22

Land Purifying Ceremony of the Lumbini Peace Pagoda

February 25, 1973
Lumbini, Nepal

Na Mu Myō Hō Ren Ge Kyō

The Lumbini Grove in Nepal is the sacred nativity site where the Great Sage, Buddha Śākyamuni, blessed the *sahā* world approximately 2,600 years ago by coming forth from Maya Devi's womb, assuming human form—an accommodative manifestation[1] for the sake of bringing peace and tranquility to all sentient beings—and revealing the significance of his birth. Upon birth, Lord Buddha raised his right hand, pointed to the azure sky and with his left handed pointed to the earth, uttering the following *gāthā* with a voice like a lion's roar[2]:

> In all heaven and earth,
> I alone am the Honored One.[3]
> For the threefold-world[4] is a realm of suffering,
> From which I shall emancipate all beings.[5]

He took seven steps in each of the four directions and proclaimed the reason for which he had now appeared in this world[6] by enunciating

---

1 Please refer to *Wondrous First Connection with Lord Buddha's Relic*, footnote 59, p.27.

2 A lion's roar is often used to describe the Buddha's preaching of the Dharma. One of the epithets of the Buddha is "Lion of the Dharma" meaning fearlessness in teaching the Dharma.

3 This proclamation reveals the purpose of the Origin Buddha, whose emanation appeared in the form of the accommodative body as the historical Buddha.

4 *Sangai* [三界] *trayo dhātava* [Sk]. The three realms of the world of transmigration where the unenlightened cannot escape from the cycles of birth and death. They are the realms of desire, form and non-form.

5 天上天下　唯我独尊　三界皆苦　我当度此. Mahāparinirvāna Sūtra.

6 According to Chapter XVI of the Lotus Sūtra, *The Eternal Duration of the Life of the Tathāgata*, the primordial Eternal Preceptor, Buddha Śākyamuni, is forever present,

the *gāthā*. On this day, 32 wonders manifested between heaven and earth, one of which was the miracle that no voice of grief could be heard in the three-thousand great thousandfold world,[7] where all sentient beings were suffused with joy.

Where Buddha Śākyamuni visited in the state of unfettered enlightenment to preach the Dharma, people later erected stūpas in profound adoration and yearning, paying homage and making offerings to them. Among the sacred sites, the following are known as the four major sacred sites: first, the birthplace at Lumbini Grove; second, the site under the Bodhi tree in Bodh Gaya where enlightenment was attained after subduing Māra; third, the site of the first Dharma *chakra*[8] [first discourse] at Deer Park[9] in Sarnath, as well as in Rajgir, where Buddha gave discourses on his true intent for appearing in this world; and fourth, under the sal tree in Kushinagara, where Buddha entered Parinirvāna. However, with the elapse of time, after the thousand years of the Era of Genuine Dharma and the thousand years of the Era of Semblance Dharma, once entering into the ten thousand years[10] of the Era of Final Dharma, the grace and merits of the sacred teachings of the Tathāgata have gradually diminished.[11] Distorted views have fueled tempests of varying degrees, which are fomenting the great conflagration of perpetual strife and hostility,[12] and it is about to destroy the era in which humanity has been sustained. More than enough is at hand to reduce the entire Dharma

---

providing the divine benefits of teaching and salvation in the past, present and future. The divine benefit of teaching and salvation offered from time without beginning until the advent of Buddha Great Universal Wisdom Excellence is known as *kako-yakumotsu* 過去益物, divine benefit of the past; the benefit by the historical Buddha Śākyamuni over 50 years is known as *genzai-yakumotsu* 現在益物, divine benefit of the present; and the eternal preaching and salvation by the Eternal Buddha subsequent to the Parinirvāna of the historical Buddha is called *mirai-yakumotsu* 未来益物, divine benefit of the future.

7 Used to describe the whole universe. See *Excerpt from the Warda Diary*, footnote 12 on p. 42.

8 *Shoten-pōrin* 初転法輪. The first turning the wheel of the Dharma, Buddha's first discourse.

9 Rokuyaon 鹿野苑, Mṛgrdāva.

10 *Mappō-mannen* 末法万年 literally means 10,000 years of the Era of Final Dharma; however, in this context, *mannen* means an infinite or extremely long period of time. It is the era into which are born people who are unaware that they are children of the Eternal Buddha.

11 A reference to the teachings delivered by the Buddha prior to the Lotus Sūtra, but does not include the Lotus Sūtra, which is the teaching to bring deliverance in the Era of Final Dharma.

12 *Tōjō-kengo* 闘諍堅固.

Realm[13] to ash, including the realms of non-sentient beings,[14] sentient beings and the five aggregates.[15] Tests for human annihilation have already taken place regionally, starting with the atomic bombings of Hiroshima and Nagasaki and the recent atrocious bombings of North Vietnam as examples. Whether the war is invasion based on the pretext of self-defense or cloaked in morality or religion, warfare where bombs are used to counter bombs, machines used to counter machines, will not cease short of the ultimate tragedy of humanity's annihilation.

Adopting the demeanor of *tangyō-raihai* as the model of conduct and standing firm in the conviction of the precept against taking life, humankind must bring enlightenment to the ignoble in its search for a way to avert annihilation in order to build a peaceful, tranquil world where the spiritual force of nonviolence prevails over the violence of murderous, destructive wars. Neither machines nor bombs can achieve this end. Acceptance of and faith in the teachings of Buddha Śākyamuni are the only means to achieve it. Humanity has now entered an age in which the significance of the advent of the Preceptor, Buddha Śākyamuni, must once again be closely examined.

For just such a time, former UN Secretary-General U Thant proposed in 1967 a plan to restore Buddha's sacred birthplace, the Lumbini Grove. The 12-nation Lumbini Development Committee was set up in the UN headquarters, and a draft restoration plan was drawn up consisting of the following:

1. Construction of a road connecting Lumbini Grove and the Bhairahawa Airport.
2. Construction of a village for tourists.
3. A green belt.
4. A monastic zone set aside for construction of temples and monasteries by various Buddhist countries.
5. A sacred garden zone.

Based on this master plan, a resolution was passed prohibiting the construction of any structure within a 2.5-mile radius of the Ashokan

---

13 *Hokkai* 法界, *Dharma-dhātu*. i) The realm or sphere of the ultimate reality; ii) The whole universe.

14 *Kokudo-seken* 国土世間. The physical domain, the environment in which sentient beings reside.

15 *Goon, goun* 五蘊, *pancaskandha*. The five constituent elements of all existences: i) matter or form; ii) perception; iii) conception; iv) volition; v) consciousness.

pillar,[16] located at the center of the planned sacred garden [No. 5 on the list]. This resolution required the construction of the stūpa be outside the 2.5-mile radius of the Ashokan pillar. However, an archeological excavation in 1933 and 1934 unearthed stūpas,[17] a brick foundation of a monastery and a pedestal for a statue of the Tathāgata. These archeological discoveries show that the ancient Lumbini Grove structural plan comprised of stūpas, the Caityas Hall,[18] a Buddha statue and monastery. In comparison to the layout of the ancient Lumbini Grove, the restoration and development plan by the committee lacks the great stūpa that should come with the pedestal for the Buddha statue, a great Buddha hall and monastery. This would undermine the significance of the restoration.

Instead, ideas for new development, such as a green zone and a village for pilgrims, are added. These new features are rather secondary in the work of restoring Buddha's birthplace, Lumbini. Does not the approach of incorporating a village for pilgrims and prohibiting the construction of a stūpa set the restoration and development of the Lumbini Grove on the wrong track? Nestled at the foot of the Himalayas, Lumbini is endowed with an abundance of green foliage. Fierce tigers still appear occasionally around the farmers' villages. If the farmers within the three-mile radius are relocated to create a greenbelt, wild animals might make it their habitat. Whether it is the Ashokan pillar seen as the core of the sacred garden or the Maya Devi temple containing the sculpture of the nativity scene of Buddha Śākyamuni, they both fall into the category of monuments. Several Ashokan pillars also exist in India, but they are not objects of veneration and offering by Buddhists. The Maya Devi temple could be deservedly

---

16 The pillars of Ashoka are a series of columns erected throughout the northern India subcontinent during his reign in the 3rd century BCE. Many of the pillars are carved with proclamations reflecting Buddhist teachings. Ashoka the Great is said to be one of the greatest emperors in Indian history. During his reign, he attempted to annex Kalinga [present day state of Orissa] to expand his vast empire. He won the Kalinga War, one of the bloodiest, which claimed the lives of as many as 100,000 people. Ashoka could not the bear the horrendous slaughter caused by the war and took up the path of nonviolence and become an avid Buddhist practitioner. He is said to have built 84,000 stūpas, which enshrine the sacred relics of Buddha Śākyamuni, across his empire, including 10 in Kalinga. India's national emblem after independence was taken from the Ashoka Pillar at Sarnath.

17 The building of stūpas in Lumbini started in the 3rd century and continued until the 8th century. Three stūpas were excavated.

18 *Butsuden* 仏殿, a sanctum with an altar with a Buddha statue enshrined and a hall for worship by monks and the congregation.

The Land Purifying Ceremony of the Lumbini Peace Pagoda, February 25, 1973.

considered an object of Buddhist veneration and offering in Lumbini; yet the temple is only big enough to accommodate ten or so worshippers. I wonder what the rationale is for not including the expansion of the Maya Devi temple for new development. It is imperative to build a grand Maya Devi temple, properly adorned. The restoration and development plan that Buddhists now wish to see includes the following: first, reconstructing the great stūpa; second, casting a Buddha image and constructing a Caityas Hall; and third, reconstructing the monastery.

The Eternal Duration of the Life of the Tathāgata, the quintessence of the Lotus Sūtra preached by the Preceptor, Buddha Śākyamuni, during eight years atop Grdhrakūta, strictly taught people in the ages to come after his extinction:

> When living beings see me as extinct,
> And make offerings to my relics far and wide

Because of these words, upon Buddha's Parinirvāna in Kushinagara, each king of the eight major kingdoms brought back Buddha Śākyamuni's relics and without delay built stūpas in their kingdoms to make offerings. Two hundred years later, Emperor Ashoka divided the relics from these eight stūpas and erected 84,000 stūpas as the principle object of veneration to create peace in the world. Since then and to this day, Buddhists have sought after Buddha's relics, built stūpas and revered them as the principle object of veneration and offering.

Let me next touch on Buddha images. Carving Buddha images began in the days of Buddha Śākyamuni. Out of gratitude for his mother, Maya Devi, Buddha Śākyamuni ascended to Trāyastrimśa [the heaven of the 33 gods][19] to preach the Dharma there to her. King Udayana,[20] out of his longing for Buddha Śākyamuni, commissioned Viśvakarman[21] to create Buddha's image in red sandalwood. Legend has it that this Buddha image ascended to Trāyastrimśa to bring Buddha Śākyamuni back to this world. Buddha statues are created to resemble the person of Buddha Śākyamuni and to display his august features, including the 32 attributes and 80 minor attributes of physical excellence, thus gracing the realm of sentient beings. A latter addition to the Mahāparinirvāna-sūtra [The Sūtra on the Great Extinction][22] teaches that Buddha images in wooden sculptures or pictures equal the merits of Buddha in human form. The Buddha images in Lumbini Grove are the only objects of veneration which commemorate the birth of Prince Siddhārtha in human form.

---

19 Tōriten 忉利天, also known as Sanjūsanten 三十三天. "The heaven of the 33 gods." One of the heavens in the realm of desire, located on the top of Mount Sumeru. At each of its corners there is a peak where eight gods dwell, and in the palace lives the lord of the heaven, Taishaku 帝釈, Indra.

20 Udendaiō 優填大王. The king of Kauśāmi and a patron of Buddhism.

21 Bishukatsumaten 毘首羯摩天. A subject of Taishaku [Indra] who is in charge of architecture and craftsmanship.

22 Kōbun-nehan-gyō or, formally, Daihatsu-nehan-gyō-kōbun 大般涅槃経後分. A two-fascicle version translated into Chinese by 曾寧 of Tang, China with Jnānabhara 人若那跋陀羅 consisting of 4 chapters. There are 11 extant Chinese translations of sūtras on the subject of Buddha Śākyamuni's passing into Nirvāna, including both Mahāyāna and Theravāda sūtras. The 40-fascicle Mahāparinirvāna-sūtra, a Mahāyāna account translated by Dharmakshema, [曇無識 Don-mushin] from 414 to 421, is the most extensive and important. This sūtra also expounds on the eternal presence of the Buddha and the inherence of Buddha-nature in all beings. Kōbun-nehan-gyō was translated more than 250 years after Dharmakshema's passing.

All religions enshrine the object of veneration and offering. Among the objects of veneration, none more than the revered images of the Preceptor, Buddha Śākyamuni, brings greater joy and tranquility to those who behold them in their augustness and dignity. The revered images of Buddha Śākyamuni are symbols of a peaceful world. That is because Buddha images are attempts to represent the Buddha of *ichinen-sanzen*[23] as an object of veneration. This is the Buddha within our own heart and mind, waiting to be manifested since the beginning of time. In other words, the sculptures and Buddha images are a response to, representations of and the desire within the depths of our heart and mind to seek peace and tranquility. This is why Buddha images are made and venerated.

Buddhism was introduced to Japan during the reign of Emperor Kinmei[24] approximately 1,400 years ago. The Emperor was enraptured when he first beheld the august and dignified attributes of the Buddha statue, causing him to extol that the statue was unrivalled by anything he had seen before. The transmittal of Buddhism in Japan first came as a Buddha image. Buddhism in modern-day Japan, for the most part, takes the form of visiting temples to appreciate the Buddha images. The Great Buddha of Nara, the Great Buddha of Kamakura and others are Buddha images visited by foreign tourists as symbols of Buddhism in Japan.

Stūpas, which enshrine the relics of the Buddha, the Caityas Halls that enshrine Buddha statues and scriptures, and the Sangha[25] that serves stūpas and Buddha statues as well as reciting sūtras, are the three prerequisites for the restoration of the Buddha Dharma. Even if Buddha statues and scriptures exist, without the Sangha jewel to serve, study and disseminate the Buddha Dharma, it will not flourish and be spread through the Era of Genuine Dharma, the Era of Semblance Dharma and the Era of Final Dharma. The Sangha jewel is likened to firewood, and the benefits of the Buddha Dharma are like fire. Without the Sangha jewel, stūpas, Buddha statues and canons of scriptures cannot benefit the

23 一念三千の仏. The Buddha of *ichinen-sanzen* is the Eternal Origin Buddha, who attained Enlightenment in time without beginning, as revealed in *The Eternal Duration of the Life of the Tathāgata* chapter, and whose single-minded wish of bringing emancipation to all permeates the 3,000 states of existences, encompassing the universe.

24 According to *Nihonshoki* 日本書紀, the first Buddha image brought to Japan from Kudara 百済 [southwest Korean kingdom] in the reign of Emperor Kinmei [539-571] was a gilded bronze statue.

25 Monastic community, 僧伽.

people. Similarly, the Sangha is akin to the earth, and stūpas, Buddha statues, and sūtras are like trees and grass. Without the Sangha jewel, Buddha Dharma will not be able to provide its benefit to sentient beings. The three jewels combined—the Buddha, the Dharma and the Sangha—are referred to as the one and inseparable Triple Jewel. When the Triple Jewel is one and intact, Buddha Dharma becomes eternal and ever present. This is taught as The Ever Present Triple Jewel.[26] The Ever Present Triple Jewel is an assurance that no matter how great suffering and affliction may be in the human world, no matter how imminent the threat of humanity's extinction may be, the power to extricate ourselves will always be there. The means to bring refuge will always be there, and human beings instrumental in bringing refuge will always appear.

Immediately after arriving alone in India in the Western Heavens in January 1931, I set forth on a pilgrimage to Buddhist holy sites. Starting with Grdhrakūta in Rajgir, I paid homage to Bodh Gaya, Deer Park [Sarnath], Kushinagara, and made my last stop at the Lumbini Grove in February. Among these sacred sites, Grdhrakūta and Lumbini Grove were in a particularly deplorable state of ruination. As Buddha's disciple, I was heartbroken and could not hold back my tears. Grief moved me to vow to restore these sacred sites. Since Lumbini Grove is located in Nepal, I submitted to the Nepalese government a petition with a plan to restore the Lumbini Grove. It could not be expected that the government would readily approve a petition from an obscure foreign monk, therefore, more than 40 years passed without bearing fruit.

On the other hand, in India, the first prime minister of free India, Jawaharlal Nehru, himself formed and chaired the Rajgir Restoration Committee. I also sat on the committee. After many arduous years, I was finally able to build a stūpa atop Ratnagiri Hill, Rajgir.[27] Since then, in the past four to five years, there have been anywhere from several hundred to a thousand pilgrims visiting daily. Following Rajgir, another stūpa was dedicated in Kalinga in the state of Orissa[28] in November last year, and we have embarked on the endeavor to erect a stūpa in Patna this year.

I hereby proclaim my vow to restore Lumbini Grove in the tradition

---

26 *Jōjyū-sanbō* 常住三宝.

27 Guruji dedicated the Rajgir Stūpa on October 25, 1969.

28 Located near the site of the Kalinga war of 261 BCE that led Emperor Ashoka to embrace nonviolence and the teachings of Buddha.

of the ancient construction evidenced by the ruins: first, constructing a stūpa; second, sculpting and casting a Buddha image; and third, building the Caityas Hall and monastery. When learning of my aspiration, the Nepalese Buddhist association was jubilant and unanimously offered cooperation. The Nepalese government indicated a willingness to accommodate our effort, issuing instructions to relevant agencies to help materialize the vow and provide guidance to the local people. As a result of this aspiration, we were able to greet today's joyous occasion of the ground-breaking ceremony of the Lumbini Grove Stūpa, finally taking the first step in restoring the Lumbini Grove, an aspiration waiting for fruition for many years. May the restoration of Lumbini Grove become the beacon of restoring the teachings of Buddha in the modern age, thus serving as the votive light to illuminate the path to peace in the world!

Na Mu Myō Hō Ren Ge Kyō

On the 43rd anniversary of Gyōain-Nisso Daihōni's passing
February 25, 1973
Fujii Nichidatsu

23

To My Disciples: Nipponzan Will Not be Daunted by State Power

April 30, 1973
Kathmandu, Nepal

The Nichiren School commemorates its origin with a special service on April 28. On that very day, Nichiren Daishōnin descended Mount Kiyosumi, never to set foot on it again. On April 28, Nipponzan Myōhōji's mission to spread the Dharma in Nepal, including the construction of the stūpa, was suspended [by the government of Nepal]. I immediately sent a disciple to Lumbini instructing that construction be halted. On April 30, three additional disciples were sent to Lumbini to help clean up the work site. Once this is over, every Nipponzan disciple will return to Kathmandu for the time being. This incident will not set back Nipponzan's mission in Nepal. We shall proceed forward dauntlessly amidst the three hindrances and four *māras*.[1] It is preached that *māras* vie in their attacks to impede whenever the true Dharma is practiced. These hindrances attest to the truthfulness of the Dharma practiced. The honor of Buddha Dharma of Japan shall become evident through these hindrances. Buddha Dharma which cannot overcome *māra's* hindrances is not worthy to be proclaimed and disseminated far and wide. Buddha Dharma meant to be proclaimed and disseminated far and wide throughout the world in the latter 500-year period[2] following the Parinirvāna of Buddha Śākyamuni shall

1 *Sanshō-shima* 三障四魔. Three hindrance and four māras that impede the practice of Buddha Dharma. *Sanshō* 三障, the three hindrances, are: *bonnōshō* 煩悩障, evil passions; *gōshō* 業障, evil karmas; and *hōshō* 報障, the painful retribution of being reborn in hell, the realm of hungry spirits, etc. *Shima* 四魔, the four māras, are: *bonnōma* 煩悩魔, inimical passions which torment one's mind and body; *onma* 陰魔, the five constituent elements of one's existence [*goun*] which produce various pain; *shima* 死魔, death; and *takejizai-ten-shima* 他化自在天子魔, Lord of *māra* in the *Takejizaiten* Heaven, who tries to thwart one's attempts to do good.

2 The fifth of the 500-year periods after Buddha's Parinirvāna, *go-gohyakusai* 五五百歳. The 2,500 years following Buddha's Parinirvāna is divided into five 500-year periods. The time meant for the dissemination of the Lotus Sūtra is the fifth 500-year period, the ignoble era in which Buddha Dharma is about to perish.

Receiving Guruji at Hanada Airport, Tōkyō, upon his return from Nepal, 1974.

overcome state power incited by the army of the Lord of *Māras.*

Nipponzan will not fear power. Nipponzan will not bow to power. Nipponzan will not compromise with power. Nipponzan will not fight with power.

We will clad ourselves in the armor of meekness and perseverance and endure all hardship for the sake of expounding this sūtra. We will bring to realization the following golden words of the Buddha:

> I will manifest four kinds of devotees:
> Bhikshu, bhiksunī, men and women of pure faith,
> And dispatch them to make offerings
> So that they may lead all sentient beings
> And assemble them to hear the Dharma [from a teacher
> of the Dharma].[3]

3 Chapter X of the Lotus Sūtra, *The Teacher of the Dharma.*

If these words of the sūtra are not false, Nipponzan's mission in Nepal shall, without doubt, bear fruit. In the 100 days since February, the satisfactory progress of the Dharma-work is owed entirely to the endeavors of the Nepalese devotees who have awakened to the Buddha Dharma of Japan [The teaching of Na Mu Myō Hō Ren Ge Kyō]. They have worked without sleep or rest. These people, the like of whom we have not encountered in Japan, India or any other place, appear to be the incarnations of deities sent by Lord Buddha on his behalf, assuming human form to render protection and help to those who expound the Dharma. These people have come to me indignant. Seeing me joyful, expressing my joy with smiles,[4] they seem not to understand why.

On November 1, 1271, when our great master Nichiren Daishōnin was taken to a desolated shrine called Sanmaidō in Tsukahara on Sado Island, the first words he uttered were, "Oh, what joy!" He wrote, "I, Nichiren, was born into the Era of Final Dharma and have been persecuted for propagating the five characters of Myō Hō Ren Ge Kyō."[5] The single phrase, "Oh, what joy!", now spontaneously passes through my lips. The disciples who attend to me have gradually come to smile as well. Smiles do not come easily to the devotees, but that is to be expected. They urge us to do whatever we can to turn the situation around. However, the situation we face is gratifying as it is. It is likewise gratifying if the situation can be improved, if it is meant to be.

Nichidatsu

4 The original term used here is *hagan-mishō* 破顔微笑, breaking into a smile expressing the deepest joy in a state free from delusion.

5 Reference found in 種々御振舞御書 *The Various Conducts of the Master*, 1275.

24

Jataka Tale of Prince Satya

June 20, 1973
Public Hall, Tansen, Nepal

I spent about a month in Banepa[1] before coming to Tansen. Fifteen miles south east of Banepa stands a mountain called Namo Buddha. I visited this mountain on the 3rd of June. In ancient times, that area was known as the Kingdom of Hanshara.[2] The World Honored One, Buddha Śākyamuni, once visited this country with a host of disciples. As the multitude of disciples watched, Buddha Śākyamuni pressed his hand to the ground. The earth split open and a stūpa adorned with seven precious gems emerged. Buddha Śākyamuni instructed Ānanda to open the door of the stūpa of seven treasures and to retrieve a jeweled container of seven gems. Buddha Śākyamuni took out a single relic from within for his disciples to bow to and venerate, and he himself paid homage to this relic. That is how Buddha Śākyamuni's Jataka story[3] came to be told.

In the distant past there was a great king in the country whose name was Mala Rath.[4] One day, he visited Mount Namo Buddha with his three sons on a pleasure trip. The three princes, absorbed in amusement, made their way deep into the mountain. They lost sight of their father, lost their way and wandered into a dangerous and frightening thicket. Two of the princes found their way out, but the third prince was left behind. This was Prince Satya.

Before long an emaciated tigress appeared accompanied by her five cubs. Famished and weary, she was no longer able to nurse her cubs. Seeing her predicament, Prince Satya resolved to offer his own flesh to the starved

1 A small town located east of Kathmandu, Nepal.
2 *Hanshara koku* 般遮羅國.
3 *Honshōtan* 本生譚. A collection of stories on Buddha's past lives during his Bodhisattva practice.
4 Dasha 大車.

tigress and willingly sacrificed his body and life. The relic enshrined in the stūpa was that of Prince Satya. Buddha Śākyamuni revealed that he was able to promptly attain *anuttara-sammyak-sambodhi*[5] owing to the grace of the Bodhisattva practice when he was Prince Satya, whose relic remains. Lord Buddha thus venerated the relic.

The theory of evolution, a basic school of thought in modern civilization, subscribes to the law of survival of the fittest, the law of the strong devouring the weak. The European conquest of countries in Asia, Africa, the Americas and Australia in the 19th century, and the present U.S. war against Vietnam all reflect a misplaced credence in the myth of survival of the fittest. According to the theory of evolution, what happened when the child came face to face with the tigress in Prince Satya's Jataka tale is typical in a world where the strong devour the weak. In a material civilization, history is interpreted through a materialistic lens, and human history is regarded as little more than the struggle for food. First and foremost, a man must eat. To eat, he must produce. He who produces is called a worker. He who does not work shall not eat. In this way, life is nothing more than a process to produce in order to eat, and to eat in order to produce. Moral and spiritual progress is not a consideration. Every tragedy of modern humanity originates from this false notion. When we examine communism in the context of Prince Satya and the tigress, people who subscribe to the idea that "one must first eat" as an overriding truth are the tigress, not Prince Satya. If we are to pass judgment on communism from the perspective of the Jataka tale of Buddhism, we must say communism is yet at the state of the tigress, governed by the law of beasts. For the sake of emancipating all beings from the sufferings of the world, we must put aside the law of the tigress, namely, the proposition that one must first feed oneself, and revert to a religious view towards life which entails sacrificing our lives to serve others, namely, the law of Prince Satya.

---

5 *Anokutara-sanmyaku-sanbodai* 阿耨多羅三藐三菩提. The highest, perfect enlightenment.

25

Single Word of Mystery

June 5, 1974
Washington D.C. Dōjō Dedication

Na Mu Myō Hō Ren Ge Kyō

In performing this dedication ceremony of a Japanese Buddhist Sangha, I am deeply honored by the presence of His Excellencies, the Ambassador of Nepal, the Ambassador of Thailand and the Ambassador of Bangladesh as well as representatives on behalf of their Ambassadors from the Sri Lankan Embassy, the Indian Embassy, the Embassy of Gabon Republic and the British Embassy.

In particular, it would have been impossible to lay the foundation of the Buddha Dharma of Japan here in Washington D.C. if not for the immense support by the Sri Lankan Embassy. Over many years the Buddhist *vihara* of Sri Lanka has made offerings that sustained the lives of us Japanese bhikshus, freeing us to fully exercise our faith, practice and spread the teachings. Today's dedication ceremony in Washington D.C., by our Japanese Buddhist Sangha was made possible owing entirely to the support of the Sri Lankan Embassy and Sangha. I offer my heartfelt gratitude.

The World Honored One, Buddha Śākyamuni, was born over 2,500 years ago in the Lumbini Grove in present day Nepal. His father's name was Śuddhodana, a great king of Kapilavastu. His mother was Queen Māyā, and the World Honored One's childhood name was Siddhārtha. On the day of Siddhārtha's birth, 34 wondrous omens and signs appeared, one of which was the star Visakha[1] descending and taking a human form to serve the young Prince. Gods, deities and sages from eight directions brought offerings of treasures to the Prince. Poisonous insects went into

1 In Indian Vedic astrology, Siddhārtha was born under the star Visakha [alpha libra, in western astronomy].

Dedication Ceremony of the Washington, D.C. Dōjō, June 5, 1974.

hiding, and evil creatures aroused goodness in their hearts. Various evil deeds, including killing and theft, ceased altogether and transformed into compassion; voices of grief ceased to be heard in the three-thousand great thousandfold world.[2] These are some of the good omens described in the Lalitavistara Sūtra.[3] The omens at the time of Jesus Christ's birth in Bethlehem bear some resemblance. As such, the Prince was born amidst these auspicious signs. On his own he took seven steps in the four directions, pointing to the heavens with his right hand and to the earth with his left hand, and said in a voice like a lion's roar:

---

2 Used to describe the whole universe. Please refer to *Excerpt from the Wardha Diary*, footnote 12, p. 42.

3 Fuyō-kyō 普曜経 [Ch: Puyao jing, The Lalitavistara Sūtra]. The sūtra depicts the life of the Buddha according to Mahāyāna accounts. It is considered an early translation of the Fangguang da zhuangyan jing 方廣大莊嚴經 translated by Dharmaraksa 法護 [Hōgo] of the Western Jin 西晉 in 308 into Chinese, in eight fascicles and thirty-three chapters.

In all heaven and earth,
I alone am the Honored One.
For the threefold-world is a realm of suffering,
From which I shall emancipate all beings.

The life he lived proved the truth of this four-phrase *gāthā*. In *A Parable* [4] of the Lotus Sūtra it says:

Now this threefold world is
All my domain;
All living beings therein
Are my children.

But now this place
Abounds with various suffering and distress;
And I alone
Am able to save and protect them.

In his 50 years of expounding the Dharma, the Lotus Sūtra was preached during Buddha Śākyamuni's last eight years as the definitive, ultimate sūtra. His declaration in lion-like dignity at birth was reenacted and brought full circle.

This threefold world, the heaven earth and underground, is where all creatures reside, and their life is filled with endless suffering and distress, sorrow and anguish. Whether it is killing, theft, deception, living, illness, aging or death, we are not free from anguish. Human beings discovered religion as a refuge from these afflictions. Religion is not held by any animal form other than human beings. Likewise religion does not exist for humans who are not conscious of afflictions in their lives.

The Eternal Duration of the Life of the Tathāgata[5] of the Lotus Sūtra says:

Even when all the living see, at the kalpa's end,
The conflagration burning,
Tranquil is this realm of mine,
Ever filled with celestial beings

4 Chapter III, Lotus Sūtra.
5 Chapter XVI, Lotus Sūtra.

This passage of the sūtra prophesizes a future time of crisis which has arrived in the 20th century when all living beings face imminent extinction due to modern scientific weapons. It preaches of a time when all sentient beings, the entire biological world, are at risk of being consumed by the great conflagration, making survival on this Earth impossible. It is a reference to acts of war that abuse explosives where atomic and hydrogen bombs play a pivotal role. However, this is a crisis that can be averted if we so desire. Buddha Śākyamuni gave his unequivocal word in this unmistakably clear passage of the Lotus Sūtra that he would see to it that we avert this danger and protect humanity from the catastrophe of annihilation. Indeed, these words reveal the true purpose of Buddha Śākyamuni's advent in this world.

In the *Nyorai metsugo gogohyakusai shi kanjin-honzon-shō*[6] Nichiren Daishōnin wrote:

> *The Teacher of the Dharma*[7] states, "[This sūtra, while the Tathāgata is still here, has aroused much enmity and envy;] how much more after his extinction?" *The Eternal Duration of the Life of the Tathāgata*[8] states, "This good medicine I now leave here." *Discrimination of Merits* references, "In the non-virtuous Era of Final Dharma." *The Bodhisattva Medicine King*[9] states, "In the latter five hundred years after my extinction, proclaim and spread it far and wide throughout the *Jambudvīpa*."[10] The Nirvāna Sūtra says, "Suppose a couple has seven children, one of whom falls ill. While the parents love all their children equally, their concern would be particularly great for the ill child."
>
> ... In surmising Buddha's true intent based on the crystal mirrors of these passages, Buddha's advent in this world was not for those who were present during the eight years when he delivered the Lotus Sūtra at the Sacred Eagle Peak, but was for the people during the following Eras of Genuine Dharma,

---

6 Please refer to *Nuclear Technology and the Future of Humanity*, footnote 26, p. 94.

7 Chapter X, Lotus Sūtra.

8 Chapter XVI, Lotus Sūtra.

9 Chapter XXIII, Lotus Sūtra.

10 In Buddhist cosmology, *Jambudivīpa* generally refers to the Indian sub-continent. It also means "our world."

Semblance Dharma and Final Dharma.[11] More specifically, he did not appear for the people in the Eras of Genuine and Semblance Dharma following the two thousand years after the extinction of the Buddha, but for people like myself, living at the beginning of the Era of Final Dharma. "The sick child" in the Nirvāna Sūtra is a reference to those who slander the Lotus Sūtra after Buddha's extinction. "I now leave here" is in reference to those who "do not consider this medicine with fine color and fragrance to be as such."

. . . At this very time, the Bodhisattvas Who Emerge From the Earth appear for the very first time in the world to administer the medicine of the five characters of Myō Hō Ren Ge Kyō to the infants.[12]

. . . This is what is meant by "even if they revile the true teachings and fall into the evil paths, they are nevertheless graced with the Dharma, thereby creating cause for eventual attainment of Buddhahood." My dear disciples take this to heart!

In essence, the true purpose of Buddha Śākyamuni's taking birth in this world was to save the lives of the people from extinction by weapons of science and to protect the natural environment from total destruction by

11 The three periods after the Buddha's demise. i) Genuine Dharma 正法 is the period where Buddhist doctrines, practices and enlightenment all exist as when the Buddha was alive; ii) Semblance Dharma 像法 is the period when the practices and doctrines still exist but are only a resemblance of the true teachings; iii) Final Dharma 末法 is the age of decline of Buddha's teaching. Nichiren Daishōnin taught that Buddha Dharma appropriate for the specific era would spread, namely, Hīnayāna teachings 小乗 in Era of Genuine Dharma; the expedient Mahāyāna teachings 権大乗 and Trace Teaching 迹門 of the Lotus Sūtra in the Era of Semblance Dharma; and the Origin Teaching of the Lotus Sūtra, which is the true Mahāyāna 実大乗 in the Era of Final Dharma. Tendai Daishi and Dengyō Daishi, who contributed greatly to the dissemination of the Lotus Sūtra, appeared in the Era of Semblance Dharma, but because it was during the Era of Semblance Dharma, they spread the Trace Teaching of the Lotus Sūtra and three-thousand realms in a single thought-moment [*ri-no-ichinen-sanzen* 理の一念三千: refer to footnote 69 in *Wondrous First Connection with Lord Buddha's Relic*, p.29], a practice of meditation and contemplation predicated on the Trace Teaching. Nichiren Daishōnin appeared in the Era of Final Dharma and spread the Origin Teaching of the Lotus Sūtra, [*ji-no-ichinen-sanzen* 事の一念三千], the three thousand realms in a single thought-moment of the Origin Teaching of the Lotus Sūtra, the Single Dharma of Mystery of Na Mu Myō Hō Ren Ge Kyō.

12 Infants are analogous to the unenlightened people ignorant of the Dharma in the Era of Final Dharma.

industries of science. Fifty years of expounding the Dharma and offering guidance—including the eight years of preaching the Lotus Sūtra—plus the innumerable merits accrued by Buddha Dharma in bringing tranquility to the lands and filling society with joy after Buddha's demise 2,500 years ago were simply precursors to the true purpose of saving humanity and the world from the horrific conflagration and profound anguish of the modern times.

During the fifty years of the Tathāgata's life in this world, and during the 2,500 years that followed the Nirvāna of the Tathāgata, the afflictions, sufferings and illnesses of the peoples in the sixteen major nations in India and the world were still mild and localized.

However, the tribulations in the present non-virtuous Era of Final Dharma are widely prevalent, from which no one can escape. Its all-inclusiveness causes destruction from mountains to oceans, where grasses and trees wither and no body of water remains unpolluted. Out of great compassion, the Tathāgata left the Essential Dharma contained in the single phrase to be enunciated consisting of the five and seven characters of Na Mu Myō Hō Ren Ge Kyō.[13]

The first chapter of the Gospel according to John says:

> In the beginning there was the Word and the Word was with God, and the Word was God. The same was in the beginning with God. All things were made by him; and without him was not any thing made that was made. In him was life; and the life was the light of men. And the light shineth in darkness; and the darkness comprehended it not.[14]

This Word is the life of humanity; this Word is the light of life. The Gospel according to John expounds on the mystery of the Word. Chapter XXI of the Lotus Sūtra, *The Transcendental Powers of the Tathāgata*, says:

> In essence, every Dharma at the disposal of the Tathāgata, every unhindered, transcendental power of the Tathāgata, every arcane, essential core treasury of the Tathāgata, and every fathomless achievement of the Tathāgata, is, without

13 Please refer to *Nuclear Technology*, footnote 31, p. 96.

14 The Bible, New Testament, King James version.

> omission, proclaimed, displayed, revealed and explicitly expounded in this sūtra.[15]

The transcendental powers of the Tathāgata that liberate all sentient beings, and the arcane, essential core treasuries of the Tathāgata for creating the Pure Land, are all contained in the five and seven characters of Na Mu Myō Hō Ren Ge Kyō. This single phrase of Na Mu Myō Hō Ren Ge Kyō is expounded in the Lotus Sūtra as "This good medicine I now leave here," encouraging us to "take it and have no fear of not being cured."

Nichiren Daishōnin states in *Nyosetsu-shugyō-shō*:[16]

> . . . when all the people of the world forgo the various vehicles for the One Buddha Vehicle with only the Sublime Dharma burgeoning throughout the lands, the people of the world at that time will come to chant Na Mu Myō Hō Ren Ge Kyō in one voice. The wind will no longer buffet the branches to scatter leaves, and the tempered rain will no longer break the clods of soil. The world will prosper as in the times of Fu Hsi and Shen Nung[17] with crops abundant. Ominous calamities in this life will be dispelled, and the means to longevity acquired. Let you all discern the aforementioned. The time shall come when the truth of the imperishability of the Person and the Dharma is evinced. Doubt not the veracity of the [Lotus] sūtra, which assures peace and tranquility in this actual world . . .

Fujii Nichidatsu
Japanese Buddhist Bhikshu

---

15 The rite in which the Origin Buddha Śākyamuni confers the essence of the Lotus Sūtra, the Odaimoku, as the remedy for emancipating the Era of Final Dharma to Bodhisattva Superior Practice [the disciple of the Origin Buddha] is depicted in *The Transcendental Powers of the Tathāgata* chapter. This passage comprises the core of the transmission and is called *kechiyō-fuzoku* 結要付嘱, conferment of the bundled essence.

16 如説修行鈔 *Practice Thus as Taught by the Buddha* was written on the fifth month of the tenth year of Bun'ei [1273].

17 Fu Hsi 伏義, mid-2800s BCE, is the first of ancient China's three mythical sovereigns is credited with bringing the Chinese people out of the evolutionary stage of the hunter and gatherer and into the new agricultural age. The discovery of herbal remedies is ascribed to legendary emperor Shen Nung 神農 [2696 BCE]. These two legendary emperors reigned over ideal societies in ancient China.

26

Blasphemy[1]

June 5, 1974
Washington D.C. Dōjō

The modern civilization is called the civilization of science. The civilization of science originated in Europe around the 16th century and as it developed spun out of control. The consequences of the havoc it has wreaked now threaten humanity's survival and the destruction of the natural environment. The original intent and purpose of science is not to annihilate humanity nor destroy the environment. These acts are carried out by military institutions and big business in their use of science. In turn policies set by the modern state and carried out by the military and big corporations result in human annihilation and environmental destruction. State power, then, authorizes and executes these policies. In the final analysis, state power is nothing less than the sum of the thoughts and beliefs of the people who comprise the nation. And the thoughts and will of the people is guided by what we call religion.

The purpose of opening a dōjō for the Buddha Dharma of Japan in Washington D.C., the capital of the United States of America, is to contribute in whatever way we can towards building global peace and tranquility, the aspiration of humankind, by questioning war policies enforced by the state, particularly its invasion of Asia, and by questioning the faith of the American people in Christianity.

In the Old Testament, the Book of Genesis, it says[2]:

> In the beginning God created the heaven and the earth.
> [Genesis 1:1]

---

1 This manuscript was prepared by Guruji for the dedication of the Washington D.C. Dōjō in June 1974, but he was counseled not to use it by a Christian friend, who feared it would be too controversial.

2 King James Version.

> So God created man in his own image, in the image of God created he him; male and female created he them. [Genesis 1:27]
> Thus the heavens and the earth were finished, and all the host of them. [Genesis 2:1]
> And the Lord God formed man of the dust of the ground, and breathed into his nostrils the breath of life; and man became a living soul. [Genesis 2:7]
> In the sweat of thy face shalt thou eat bread, till thou return unto the ground; for out of it wast thou taken: for dust thou art, and unto dust shalt thou return. [Genesis 3:19]

A believer in the Bible has faith in and accepts the preceding account of God's creation of humankind. This view cannot be made light of since it forms the basis towards one's perspective on life. If man became a living being when God, who created man in his image, fashioned him from the dust of the earth and breathed into his nose the breath of life, it seems to suggest that humans are creatures made from a kind of soil. In this case, a man labors to produce food, eats to stay alive and then ceases to exist, returning to the dust from which he was made. It is an existence silent on the issue of life after death. It is a life view no different than what modern materialists hold.

But the quality that makes us human is not because we are made of dust; not because we breathe, work, produce food and eat; nor because we return to dust when we die. What makes humans unique is the ability to embrace a spiritual dimension that extends to life after death. It is religion that contemplates these issues. The Lord God's creation was limited to the creation of physical beings, not metaphysical beings. Why was the heart and mind of God not breathed into humanity at the time of creation? This grave omission by the Lord God at humanity's creation destined the human race to view life as degraded and corrupt. Another error in the Lord God's creation of humanity was the violent and cruel manner in which women were created.

> And the Lord God caused a deep sleep to fall upon Adam, and he slept: and he took one of his ribs, and closed up the flesh instead thereof; And the rib, which the Lord God had taken from man, made he a woman, and brought her unto the man. [Genesis 2:21-22]

This creation of women is equivalent to the vivisection practiced in modern medicine. The heartless human history written in the blood of professed Christians may be traced to this reckless opening of a living man in order to gouge out a rib after causing him to fall into unconsciousness so that he would feel no pain. God's removal of his rib lies at the root of endless international wars waged by European powers and is the underpinning of the modern states that grew out of Europe to become the great powers engaged in the arms race. For the most part men have committed the murders and wars in human society while it is the women who aspire for peace. Women, the messengers of peace, ought to have been created by picking a flower.

The fourth chapter of Genesis says:

> And God saw that the wickedness of man was great in the earth, and that every imagination of the thoughts of his heart was only evil continually. And it repented the Lord that he had made man on the earth, and it grieved him at his heart. And the Lord said, I will destroy man whom I have created from the face of the earth; both man, and beast, and the creeping thing, and the fowls of the air; for it repenteth me that I have made them. [Genesis 4:5-7]

To wipe all living beings from the face of the earth in one fell swoop is truly a terrifying curse of God, a horrendous act by God. Just as medicine exists because of illness, teachings for enlightenment exist because people err, and salvation exists because humans suffer. When God saw that human wickedness prevailed on earth, before planning for their annihilation, why did God not provide teachings to lead all to enlightenment? People will never cease to do wrong on earth no matter how much time passes. It is the reality of human society.

If [God] were to annihilate everyone based on this reason, humanity would forever be subject to the curse of annihilation. Is killing and the elimination of all living beings not a crime when it is committed by God? If murder and annihilation are not crimes when committed by God, then likewise murder and annihilation are not crimes when done by the hands of humans. God's curse to annihilate humanity has wholly passed down to the United States of America, a self-professed Christian nation.

The atomic bombs dropped on Hiroshima and Nagasaki in Japan at the end of WWII were only the first step. Since then the United States has fallaciously called atomic bombs "guardians for peace," and dedicated the nation's resources to an all-out effort in the development and stockpiling of nuclear weapons. Eventually they will be the tools for human annihilation.

A Vietnam veteran testified to the U.S. war of genocide.

> We have brought wondrous tons of ordnance, hundreds of thousands of men, Dr. Strangelove weaponry. We have used an air force against a country that has none. We have used a navy against a country that has none. And it still wasn't enough, and still the war goes on, and still the Vietnamese fight. It has been called a war of attrition. All wars are wars of attrition.... In a nonindustrial society—in an agrarian society—such as Vietnam, when you talk of a war of attrition, you're talking only of one thing. You're talking about destroying the means to resist—that is killing people. Our country has set out very systematically to kill whatever number of people are [sic] necessary in Vietnam to stop them from resisting whatever it is we are trying to impose on that country. This, I think, is policy.[3]

The Old Testament, Genesis Chapter 6 says:

> The earth also was corrupt before God, and the earth
> was filled with violence. And God looked upon the
> earth, and, behold, it was corrupt; for all flesh had
> corrupted his way upon the earth. [Genesis 6:11-12]

"The earth was filled with violence" exactly describes the social conditions in the United States today. It is not difficult to see how God's curse of collapse and total annihilation has fatefully returned to haunt the United States. Let me site some statistics of crimes committed in New York in 1969 as a prime example of this phenomenon in the United

3 Closing statement by Don Duncan at the Winter Soldier's Investigation on February 2, 1971 at Detroit, Michigan.

States. There were 54,405 robberies, a daily average of 150, which is 157 times that of Tōkyō. To cope with this reality, New Yorkers simply make plans to replace what is stolen rather than worry about protecting their personal belongings. The number of homicides was 904, a daily average of 2.5 murders. Police often are not even called in cases of murder or when sounds of gunfire are heard. Because many cases of murder or the disappearance of individuals go unreported, the actual number of homicides is higher than the statistics show. There is no telling which is more dangerous—Vietnam in wartime or New York in peacetime. It is common knowledge that police officers are possible suspects when someone is killed. It is not unusual for the murdered to not receive justice while the murderers escape punishment and are free to kill again.

There were 1,840 cases of rape, an average of 5 women raped every day, a rate 6 times that of Tōkyō. [Incidentally] there are also books written on the rape of Japanese women by soldiers of the occupation forces after the war. There are far more beggars on the streets of New York than war refugees in Saigon. In sheer number of crimes, New York ranks highest in the United States while the United States ranks the highest in the world. From its inception United States has been steeped in lawlessness and perpetual violence as exemplified by its history in the opening of the West. Even after gaining prominence on the world stage, this paradigm never changed rather, if anything, became more pronounced.

America today is experiencing a spiritual, moral, ethical and economic breakdown as a result of having unleashed abroad a level of violence unprecedented in human history. Its invasions in Southeast Asia are proving to be the ill omen foreshadowing the collapse of the United States of America.

Chapter 6 of Genesis says:

> And God said unto Noah, The end of all flesh is come before me; for the earth is filled with violence through them; and, behold, I will destroy them with the earth. [Genesis 6:13]

The God who brought the Deluge was undoubtedly the God of judgment, not the God of salvation. When and where does salvation come for living beings, particularly the people, drowned to death instantly in the Deluge? Is seeing evil, passing judgment and drowning life the ultimate work of God? In general, religion promises salvation in the world to come. If life is eternal, any god who fails to promise salvation in the world to come is disqualified from the standpoint of religion. Seeing and destroying those who commit evil is no different than the devil's work where life is destroyed and annihilated.

The God of judgment is a God who will destroy this modern era overrun with atrocities, and absolutely not the God who will bring it salvation. It is the God who curses modern times, not the God who illuminates the path through teachings.

The God who emancipates the modern times must be the God who transforms evil into good, the God who exercises the wondrous noumenal principle of non-duality of good and evil. It must be the God who prohibits violence and killing, the one who adheres to the single precept against violence and killing.

Some may say my words are blasphemy. However, I say God in the Bible blasphemes humankind.

Japanese Buddhist *Shamon*
Fujii Nichidatsu

27

The Power of Perseverance

August 1, 1974
On the Dedication of the Tōkyō Stūpa
At the peak of Mount Ōdera,[1] Tōkyō

Today we were able to perform this auspicious dedication of the stūpa in the Tōkyō metropolis. Congratulatory messages were offered by the various representatives gathered here including India, Nepal, Soviet Union, Mongolia, Sri Lanka and Vietnam. I am deeply grateful for your extremely generous words of commendation.

This stūpa is by no means small compared to other stūpas in the world. I won't say it is the largest, but it is one of the larger stūpas. Dr. Ōoka Minoru[2] traveled to India on several occasions and through research reproduced an ancient design,[3] although the original no longer exists.

The land where the stūpa is built is part of the watershed of the Tamagawa River, the source of drinking water for the Tōkyō metropolis. An ancient temple once stood here, and it was the local people's wish to use the land for the betterment of the world. That is how the construction of a stūpa was decided. This land does not belong to Nipponzan, but an understanding with the local residents enabled us to build the stūpa.

---

1 大寺山. Mount Ōdera is situated on the border of Tōkyō metropolis and Yamanashi prefecture, on the farthest edge of Lake Okutama where the Tamagawa River splits into Tanba River and Kosuge River.

2 大岡実. Dr. Ōoka Minoru [1900-1987] was an author and architect of traditional Japanese building as well as a professor at Nihon University. He was also a member of the Ministry of Education's Council on Preservation of Cultural Treasures. Beginning with the Kushiro Stūpa dedicated in 1959, more than half of the stūpas built by Nipponzan Myōhōji throughout the world were his design. The New Delhi Stūpa, which was dedicated in November 2007, incorporates 80 percent of the design of the Rajgir Stūpa, another design by Dr. Ōoka.

3 This design was reproduced from relief works and miniature stūpas, including images found in the cave temples at Ajanta, India.

No access roads existed when the stūpa was being built.[4] A helicopter brought me here today, but some of you came up by foot. The road you took was built by the same people who built the stūpa. After the stūpa's completion, they constructed the road for your convenience to participate in today's ceremony. Throughout the construction of the stūpa, the monks commuted every morning and evening up and down a trail from the village at the foot of the mountain. It was merely three, four or five disciples who took on this extraordinary construction. It was they who labored and took on the responsibility of making today's dedication ceremony possible. I made the vow to erect the stūpa, but my appreciation goes to my disciples for bringing it to fruition. Had it not been for these disciples, the stūpa would not have emerged. These handful of disciples, merely four or five of them, truly put their lives on the line and shouldered the hardships. While I made the vow, I traveled to the Western Heavens [India], and was occupied with matters that took me back and forth between India and Nepal. I did not contribute to the building of this stūpa. To begin with, I was not even responsible for procuring construction materials. How much hardship they must have endured to build this stūpa! I trust they are gratified by your compliments. The dedication ceremony concludes the work here. But I am confident that awakened people from abroad who visit Tōkyō, those who wish to see the symbol for peace in Japan, shall climb this mountain.

Some climb mountains for the scenery, but no one climbs mountains to create peace in the world. Everything people do is for their own pleasure. Young lives are risked and lost on recreation. People throw away their lives like rubbish in mountains, rivers, roadside, beaches and oceans. Because they lose their lives for no significant purpose, the lost lives do not serve to create peace in the world. The challenges met by these disciples here shall be a ray of light in the hearts of those who seek peace in the world.

The origin of my vow to build stūpas began with a karmic connection when I visited Ceylon,[5] the present day Sri Lanka. In Sri

---

4 The translator heard from Rev. Ninomiya Taisen 二宮大仙, one of the disciples who built the stūpa, that a bulldozer was disassembled to be carried up the mountain to clear the land. The access road was built from the top down.

5 The residing monk at the monastery in Ginigathena village, Ven. N. Piyaratna Thero, was the first donor who presented Guruji with Lord Buddha's sacred relics on August 25, 1933.

Lanka, stūpas are built in each village, and the people pay homage to them. The kind heartedness I felt upon my visit there surpasses any other place in the world. I, who do not speak the language, felt their warmth in my heart. The merit of Buddha Dharma has been passed down in this way.

Sri Pada is a mountain located in the heart of Sri Lanka. At the foot of Sri Pada, where Lord Buddha is said to have expounded the Lankāvatāra-sūtra,[6] is a village called Ginigathena. I was offered a night of shelter at the humble monastery of Venerable N. Piyaratna Thero. Wondrously, Venerable Piyaratna offered Buddha Śākyamuni's relic to a mendicant monk who took a night's shelter. He asked that I build a stūpa in Japan to enshrine this relic. I was unable to fulfill Venerable Piyaratna's wish for a stūpa in Japan while he was still alive. However, I did not make a false promise when receiving Buddha's relic. Today, Venerable Piyaratna's disciple has paid homage to this stūpa. Venerable Piyaratna must also be pleased. Since I am well into my latter years, I made the vow to build a stūpa on Sri Pada next year while I am still alive.

Among our guests today are also monks from the Soviet Union. Buddhists constitute a small minority in the Soviet Union. The vast majority are Christians professing faith in the Russian Orthodox Church. While churches flourish with visitors, only a handful of Buddhists exist. Yet, I have great expectations for the Buddhist clergy and the Buddha Dharma in the Soviet Union to rise to the occasion and spearhead a movement to mobilize the nation for world peace. The work by the reverends with us today will exert tremendous power on the Soviet Union's endeavors to create peace in the world. We also intend to do everything in our power to spread the Dharma in the Soviet Union. Were I younger, I would take on the mission to the Soviet Union myself. My present condition does not allow it. Yet, I have an unshakable faith that my disciples will bring this mission to fruition.

I also had an opportunity to visit Mongolia. Not only does the country contain treacherous mountains, it is sparsely populated and covered in snow and ice. Vegetation grows only during a couple of summer months. A small number of people lead a nomadic life, herding cattle and goats. Tibetan monks journeyed to Mongolia to edify the people on the Dharma and laid the foundation of Buddhism that thrives today. I was deeply moved on my visit to Mongolia when I

6 Ryōga-kyō 楞伽經.

Arriving at a Tibetan temple in Ulan-Ude, Buryatia in Russia on May 18, 1972.

reflected on the monks, with no food, lodging or clothing to shield them from the bitter cold and snow, bearing heavy sūtras on their backs to spread the teachings in the vast and sparsely populated land. This mountain is also treacherous without a decent access road, but the hardships we encountered fade in comparison with what was endured by ancient sages and monks of virtue in transmitting the teachings to Mongolia or Siberia. Our hardship is not even worth mentioning. This power of perseverance amid hardship is what brings salvation to the people.

Both in Siberia and Mongolia, I was taken aback when I saw the gold-inscribed sūtras on display in museums and libraries. Certainly sūtras are highly esteemed in Japan, but today, at best, they are merely inscribed with ink made of charcoal. Chrysographed scriptures on paper dyed in indigo[7] are a thing of the past. In these times, the

7 *Konshi-kondei* 紺紙金泥. Thick paper dyed in navy with ruled lines in silver and lettered with distempered powdered gold, a method of copying sūtras employed since the Nara period [710-794].

teachings of Lord Buddha receive little regard. The aspiration behind gathering gold in Mongolia or Siberia to handwrite the sūtras will be the power which moves the Soviet Union today. The sūtras thus preserved will be the source of salvation for humanity across the ages. What a good thing they did! Gold tucked away in treasuries serves no purpose. Gold turned into the letters of the sūtra transmits to us today the truly invaluable aspirations of those who came before us.

There is much more I would like to say, but I will end now. Although it rained today, being wet in the rain is of no consequence. What we are to accomplish is something far greater. Whether in rain or fire, we will forge ahead.

Na Mu Myō Hō Ren Ge Kyō

28

Buddha Dharma of Japan

May 8, 1975
Paris Dōjō Dedication

Na Mu Myō Hō Ren Ge Kyō

It is estimated that some three billion people currently inhabit the Earth. What goals do these three billion people have, and what kind of work are they engaged in? Observing the current state of the world suggests that, whether consciously or not, people are killing each other through murderous wars, which will eventually bring the human race to extinction, building war arsenals and engaging in round-the-clock research and training solely to prevail in war.

Three billion people constitute nation states of varying sizes. Without exception, states are armed regardless of size. No state is without a military. The military is a group of people that operates like a machine with the sole function of using humans to kill humans. Generally speaking, what is called the modern state is, in essence, nothing more than a massive organization for committing murder and war. Now why must human beings kill or make war?

All life on earth is said to be governed by the natural law of "the survival of the fittest," meaning "the fittest" is the species that has prevailed over others in the struggle for existence. In the outcome of the struggle for survival, the strong always prevail and the weak always lose. This phenomenon is the tragedy of "the strong preying upon the weak, the law of survival."

Snakes devour frogs. Frogs croak to no avail. Tigers prey on deer, cats catch mice, and whales swallow sardines. Any one of these might strike us as tragic, but the law of survival appears inescapable. Human beings, the supreme victors in the law of survival, eat fowl, pigs, goats, cows, fish and insects. Of all living creatures, humans are the most rapacious, consuming everything that can be consumed. Humans think nothing of it, as if this privilege is deserving of the victor in the arena of the struggle for survival. Man eating cows or whales may be merciless and without virtue, yet these acts require no arsenal of arms. To that extent, the gravity of the crime is not as great. The only reason arms are needed by human beings is to execute war, the act of humans killing other humans. War is the tragedy of the powerful devouring the weak, which has become an integral part of human society.

History unquestionably attests to the innumerable wars fought by humanity from ancient times, regardless of era, ethnic group or country. Every war is an act of barbarity, where the mighty kill and dominate the weak. Never have the weak and small waged wars against the mighty and the strong. Every war is a war of invasion; every war is a grave crime.

Humanity comprised of three billion people is compelled to live in the "Western civilization." The civilization of the West is that of science, machines, murder and war. Europeans developed the civilization of science, and wherever they went invasion, war, conquest and domination pervaded the land. How many of the world's hundred plus nations, large and small, existing today has not been subjected to European invasion and domination?

The civilization of science has not only driven the Europeans to frenzied invasion and conquest, but their belief in the supremacy of economic development has also resulted in wrecking irrevocable destruction on the natural environment. Everything from air to water has been contaminated, rendering the environment harmful and unfit for sustaining life, and underground natural resources have been depleted through unsparing exploitation. The civilization of science is after all a civilization of violence. Regardless of the progress, it has not made any contribution in advancing human spirituality in morality or religion, but, on the contrary, has caused spiritual degeneration and turmoil. The civilization of science is a cursed civilization.

Along with the law of survival, there exists the law of "preservation of the species." Be it tigers, lions or wolves, parents are mighty and their cubs weak. Nevertheless, parents do not prey on their young. On the contrary, they are reared at the breast, fed and nurtured. This nurturing proves that even beasts are not inclined towards violence exclusively, but that a benevolent, spiritual function of love and compassion also exists in their heart and mind. This innate quality is the cornerstone of religion or

Dedication Ceremony of the Paris Dōjō, May 16, 1975.

morality. It is called nonviolence.

When the caring heart and mind that feeds milk and food to the weak and small is extended to those we know and they in turn pass it on to others they know,[1] with the growth of this sphere of sentiment, that

1 Chapter XVIII of the Lotus Sūtra, *The Merits of Joyful Acceptance* tells about the merits of transmitting the teachings to another, then that person transmits it to another and so on until the 50th person hears it. The merit of the 50th person who hears and rejoices upon receiving the teachings are immeasurable, more than a great almsgiver whose offerings benefited innumerable beings. If that 50th person received so much merit, how much more the first person who heard, rejoiced and transmitted the teaching.

species prospers just as one's child grows with nurturing. Mighty species that depend predominantly on violence naturally decline. The number of tigers and wolves on earth has been declining. In contrast, weaker species who do not resort to violence and are not endowed with weapons, whether they are goats, chickens, sparrows or crows, are thriving and living side-by-side with human beings throughout the world.

Religion emerged with the advent of humanity. It is referred to as the mythical age or the age of gods. Religion has spread wherever human beings settled. In mountains shrines are dedicated to mountain deities and in the ocean to the gods of the seas. Religion is the one characteristic that sets humans apart from other animals. No other animal has religion.

What does religion teach human beings? It teaches to bow in veneration. Bowing in veneration is the rite and deportment for honoring others. Bowing in veneration is not a mechanical gesture, but one that requires seeing in others the Sacred One worthy of veneration. The first thing religion provides is the entity, the esteemed object to be commonly venerated by all people. They are, for instance, the various Buddhas and Bodhisattvas in Buddhism or God in Christianity. This is then applied to societal life, and reverence towards others is taught. First parents are revered, then teachers, elders and leaders. We then venerate those who we meet every day and those who are far away. We are ultimately to venerate the bad or ignoble no matter how egregious they may be.

Harmony in the family and between couples begins with mutual respect and veneration. The security of a nation starts from respect and veneration between the government and the people. Peace in society starts from mutual trust and veneration between the young and the old. As such, all peace and happiness begins with mutual veneration. More than anything else, mutual veneration sustains the human race and enables it to flourish. This is called *tangyō-raihai.* Anything that claims the name of religion but fails to teach veneration towards others is not a religion capable of emancipating the modern times.

With our body that bows in veneration, our mouth utters admiration towards others, stating the reason for reverence. Veneration expressed by our bodies cannot be sustained at all times and at all places, yet the oral practice of commendation can be done anywhere, whether in sleep or awake, sitting down or as we walk, whether those who are the subject of our reverence are present or not. The sūtra expounds on this as,

". . . always spoke thus."[2]

The praise in Tathāgata Śākyamuni's Era of Final Dharma is the five and seven characters of Na Mu Myō Hō Ren Ge Kyō. In the past infinite, boundless, inconceivable and asamkhyeya[3] kalpas, during the Era of Semblance Dharma of Tathāgata Majestic Voice King,[4] the praise consisted of the twenty-four [kanji] characters,[5] "I deeply revere you. I dare not slight or despise you. For you will all go about and practice[6] the Bodhisattva way and are to become Buddhas." These twenty-four characters explicitly elucidate the reason for not slighting or holding others in contempt but rather to deeply revere them. The quintessential practice of the Lotus Sūtra is taught to be represented by these twenty-four characters. The five and seven characters of Na Mu Myō Hō Ren Ge Kyō and the twenty-four characters may be different in length, yet are identical in spirit.

The chanting of the five and seven syllables of Na Mu Myō Hō Ren Ge Kyō through one's mouth is an act that believes in the Buddha-nature in the hearts and minds of others that is to be honored; that prays, encourages and exhorts the rapid manifestation of this Buddha-nature to become the ultimate perfected Sacred One. The chanting of Na Mu Myō Hō Ren Ge Kyō through the mouth is the easiest of all practices and yet the most vital among all modes of religious practice. This practice is called *tanshin-kushō*.[7]

The heart of a tigress that nurtures her cub by feeding milk and food is at the core of what preserves the species. Not only is it in common with the benevolence of a human mother caring for her child, but it is also in common with the boundless compassion of the Buddhas and

---

2 Chapter XX of the Lotus Sūtra, *Bodhisattva Never Despise*.

3 Incalculable; indication of a huge number.

4 Ionnō-nyorai 威音王如来. Chapter XX of the Lotus Sūtra, *Bodhisattva Never Despise* says: "After the extinction of the first Tathāgata Majestic Voice King, and after the Era of Genuine Dharma which followed immediately after his extinction, in the Era of Semblance Dharma, bhikshus of arrogance gained prominent power. At that time there was a Bodhisattva bhikshu named Never Despise. Great Power Obtainer! For what reason was he named Never Despise? Because every time he sees bhikushus, bhiksunīs, upāsakas or upāsikās, he bowed in veneration and commended them as thus, 'I deeply revere you, I dare not slight or despise you, for you will all go about and practice the Bodhisattva way and are to become Buddhas.' "

5 The twenty-four Chinese characters, 我深敬汝等 不敢軽慢 所以者何 汝等皆行菩薩道 當得作仏.

6 行. Specifically referring to practice engaged on a spiritual path.

7 但信口唱. The single-hearted practice of oral chanting of Na Mu Myō Hō Ren Ge Kyō with faith.

Bodhisattvas. This heart, whether belonging to a beast, wrongdoer or anyone else, is a heart that is to be revered. This heart and mind is called Buddha-nature, which is innate in all sentient beings. The Nirvāna Sūtra preaches that "Buddha-nature exists in all sentient beings; no matter how wicked a person, Buddha-nature exists." When Buddha-nature develops and manifests, it can become the various Buddhas and Bodhisattvas or God who are the ultimate objects of veneration. It is therefore truly to be revered.

The Buddhas, Bodhisattvas or God who are offered as the object of veneration and praise by religion cannot be seen nor felt. They are a revered presence that can only be contemplated within one's heart and mind. What we can see, then, are meditative images. Theism holds true for those who wish to see God, and likewise, atheism holds true for those who have doubts or do not wish to see God. In either case, the heart and mind of a person can neither be seen nor touched. While the human heart and mind cannot be seen nor touched, their workings are capable of achieving anything, both good and evil. The Buddha-nature in one's heart and mind brings about the Pure Land, and, by the same token, malevolence harbored in the heart and mind creates the great conflagration of the hell of incessant suffering.

Anger towards others is born out of the heart and mind, so are contempt and malice. That same heart and mind can engender tender emotions in a child toward his or her mother, as well as a mother's benevolence towards her child. It is the same heart and mind that causes a person to see God or, likewise, to harbor doubts about God. Humans create anger, contempt and hatred in the heart and mind. We experience it daily and hear and see it in others as well. Similarly, the heart and mind have created modern weapons and war. These states of the mind and heart are not worthy of respect. The mind creates for itself the flames of hell of incessant suffering, hunger and thirst of hungry spirits, and brute savagery.

The heart and mind that wish to see God are the heart and mind that aspire to approach the Kingdom of God, the mind that seeks to gain an understanding of God's justice. This kind of heart and mind is to be revered. They are what provide the moral foundation in human life and inspire us to elevate our spirituality. It is what guides humans to peace and happiness.

> The Jigage[8] in *The Eternal Duration of the Life of the Tathāgata* of the Lotus Sūtra says, "Wholeheartedly wishing to see the Buddha, not sparing their body and life. . ."[9] This passage is the Buddha realm in [my] Nichiren's own heart and mind.[10] That is because this single passage of the sūtra is what impelled me to realize the teaching of *ichinen-sanzen*[11] revealed in the chapter of *The Eternal Duration of the Life of the Tathāgata* through the practice of the Dharma of Three Great Mysteries.[12] Do not preach it injudiciously; do not preach it injudiciously.
> . . . I, Nichiren, believe that "whole" in wholeheartedly is *myō* 妙, sublime; "heart" is *hō* 法, Dharma; "wish" is *ren* 蓮, lotus; to see is *ge* 華, flower; Buddha is *kyō* 経, sūtra.[13] It takes not sparing one's body and life to spread these five characters. Wholeheartedly wishing to see Buddha means the heart with the sole desire to see the Buddha, this wholeheartedness is the Buddha.[14]

What is meant here is that the heart and mind wholeheartedly aspiring to see the Buddha is the Buddha and Bodhisattvas who are to be venerated and extolled. This unwavering single-mindedness is called

---

8 自我偈. A reference to the *gāthā* in *The Eternal Duration of the Life of the Tathāgata* chapter in the Lotus Sūtra that starts with 自我得仏來 "Since I attained Buddhahood" and goes until "And speedily attain the Buddha-body?" Buddha Śākyamuni reveals his eternal nature in this *gātha*. The first two characters 自我 *jiga* is taken and in short called *jiga-ge*.

9 一心欲見仏.

10 This Buddha Realm is the realm in which Buddha Śākyamuni's true desire is inherited, as stated in Nichiren Daishōnin's *Kanjin-honzon-shō*, "Śākyamui's two Dharma of causal practices and resulting merit are inherent in the five characters of Myō Hō Ren Ge Kyō. When we embrace these five characters, the merit of his cause and effect will be naturally transferred to us." He goes on to state, "This *sahā* world is the realm where the Origin Buddha without beginning attained Enlightenment, the Pure Land where he forever resides, free from the three calamities and confinement of the four kalpas."

11 Please see *Wondrous First Connection with Lord Buddha's Relic*, footnote 69, p. 29.

12 *Sandai-hihō* 三大秘法. It consists of *honmon-no-honzon* [principle object of veneration] revealed in the essential section of the Lotus Sūtra [Origin Teaching]; the *Daimoku* [Na Mu Myō Hō Ren Ge Kyō] of the Origin Teaching of the Lotus Sūtra; and the *kaidan* [precept dais] of the Origin Teaching of the Lotus Sūtra.

13 Nichiren Daishōnin explicates that the five kanji characters of Myō Hō Ren Ge Kyō are, in essence, the five kanji characters of 一心欲見仏 "Wholeheartedly [with a single heart] wishing to see the Buddha."

14 *Gijō-bō-gosho* 義浄房御書. *Letter to Gijō-bō.* Written by Nichiren Daishōnin on May 28, 1273 to Gijō-bō 義浄房, who was his senior disciple under Dōzen-bō 道善房 of Seichō-ji temple 清澄寺.

Myō Hō Ren Ge Kyō. In reverence and praise of this wholeheartedness, it is saluted as Na Mu Myō Hō Ren Ge Kyō. Nichiren Daishōnin wrote:

> Buddha Śākyamuni, Buddha Prabhūtaratna and all the Buddhas in manifestation in the worlds in ten directions are the Buddha Realm intrinsic in our heart and mind. That is to say, we are in their footsteps and inherit their merits[15]. . . . Buddha Śākyamuni, who dwells in our heart and mind, is the ancient Buddha[16] without beginning, manifesting himself in three Buddha-bodies,[17] and it is he who attained Buddhahood in the eternal past described as 500 dust-particle kalpas ago.[18]

A single thought-moment in our mind is not a fleeting function of physical existence. Just like the open skies, it has no beginning or end in terms of time, spatially boundless and ubiquitous. When viewed this way, it can be said that Buddha, Bodhisattvas or God has existed in the single thought borne in our heart and mind from the eternal past with no beginning. This God, this Buddha, at one time and place was called Jehovah or assumed the human form and appeared as Buddha Śākyamuni in India. This God or Buddha is the God and Buddha who dwells in our hearts and minds. We now must bow to the Bodhisattva, Buddha residing in our hearts and minds in veneration to once again invoke its manifestation as Jehovah or Buddha Śākyamuni. Religion exists to realize the advent of the Sacred One.

Myōraku Daishi[19] wrote, "Let it be known that both our bodies and the land on which we live are the results of our heart and mind containing three-thousand states of existence in a single thought-

---

15 The understanding here is that this inheritance comes when we embrace and recognize the Buddha seed in us and work to achieve the vow of the Origin Buddha to emancipate all.

16 *Kobutsu* 古仏. Ancient Buddha is a reference to the primordial Buddha without beginning, the source of all emanative Buddhas, as distinguished from finite Buddhas. The Eternal Buddha Śākyamuni is also referred to as *Honbutsu* 本仏 Origin Buddha.

17 The three bodies of Buddha are *hosshin* 法身 Dharma-body, *hōjin* 報身 reward-body, and *ōjin* 応身 accommodative-body. Please refer to footnote 59 in *Wondrous First Connection with Lord Buddha's Relic*, p. 27.

18 *Kanjin-Honzon-shō*. See *Nuclear Technology*, footnote 26, p. 94.

19 妙楽大師. Grand Master Miao-le Ta-shih, also known as Tannen 湛然 [Ch. Chan-jan 711-782], a Chinese T'ien-t'ai [Tendai] monk. The fifth patriarch of the T'ien-t'ai school.

moment. Therefore, at the time when the Origin Buddha attained Enlightenment,[20] according to this ultimate truth of 'three-thousand existences in a single thought,' his body and thought permeated the entire universe [reality-realm]."[21] As an existence with a heart and mind that holds thoughts, we have a body that houses them. In turn, our body requires land on which to live.

Nichiren Daishōnin said:

> When the hearts and minds of the people are defiled, so is the domain defiled. When the hearts and minds of the people are pure, so is the domain pure. What is called the Pure Land or the Defiled Land is not distinct one from another, but is made different by the good or evil in our mind.[22]

Our body and the domain in which we live are manifestations of the single thought we bear within our heart and mind. Modern politics and economy pay scrupulous attention to superficial issues that meet the eye, but fail to address intangible, fundamental issues of the heart and mind. Endless confusion results.

Humans can be sustained physically on bread alone, yet joy and gratitude are absent in a life based primarily on needs and wants of the flesh. Dissoluteness leads to a chaotic society, giving way to ferocious brute and animal-like indolence, a society marked by robbery, rape and murder. New York and other major cities in the United States are prime examples. Courts and jails are of no use. Eventually pervasive crimes would require entire cites or the whole country to be turned into a prison. Every place is a potential crime scene and every person a potential criminal, making life extremely dangerous with no effective countermeasure. Success in traveling to outer space or building submarines to explore the seabed will

---

20 The Enlightenment of the Origin Buddha exists in the realm of realization that one's mission is to emancipate all sentient beings who are also one's children. The *gāthā* in *The Eternal Duration of the Life of the Tathāgata*, "in the same manner, I am the father of the world who heals all misery and afflictions" is a reference to this. Enlightenment of an ordinary mortal comes when this is comprehended.

21 摩訶止観輔行伝弘決. An annotation by Grand Master Miao-le on the *Discourse on Mahāyāna Meditation and Contemplation*, written by 天台大師 Tendai Daishi [Chih-i 智顗 538-597].

22 *Isshō-jōbutsu-shō* 一生成仏鈔. *On Attaining Buddhahood in This Life*, written by Nichiren Daishōnin in 1255 in Kamakura to Toki Gorō Jōnin 富木五郎常忍.

not bring peace to America. These phenomena reflect spiritual degeneracy coming from the heart and mind of Americans.

The fundamental flaw in Western civilization is its incessant research of external matter, which likewise treats humans as one such matter. Even spiritual activities that should be intrinsically esteemed are considered a function of matter, resulting in a failure to discriminate right from wrong, good from evil. Its outcome is a view towards life and living in which humans, animals, rubbish, feces and urine, are all regarded more or less the same as far as matter goes. No wonder slighting or even murdering others is almost inconsequential, not considered a grave crime. Others who ought to be spoken of with regard are disparaged. "Gooks" used by Americans and "yellow peril" by Germans[23] are examples of slurs coined to disparage others.

To protect and emancipate humanity from the terror caused by the conflagration, war and bloodshed of the non-virtuous modern age and to bring tranquility, every person must be taught of the presence that is intrinsically to be venerated. It exists in the heart and mind of humans. It is what engenders respect towards others in our heart and mind. It is called *Kanjin-honzon*. To actualize the heart of respect towards others, our body bows in reverence. This is called *tangyō-raihai*. To express the heart of respect towards others, we utter the words of praise through our mouth. This is called *tanshin-kushō*. These constitute the Dharma of the Three Great Mysteries[24] of the Buddha Dharma of Japan. The Dharma of the Three Great Mysteries of the Buddha Dharma of Japan teaches that people are the very ones who are intrinsically sacred. The discovery of the four kanji characters of "intrinsic reverence 本来尊重" is the one and only religion that can emancipate the anguish of modern humanity.

Na Mu Myō Hō Ren Ge Kyō

Nichidatsu

---

23 The term is said to have originated with Prussian Kaiser Wilhelm II in 1895. A footnote in John Toland's *The Rising Sun* [p.69] relates: "He had a revelation of oriental hordes overwhelming Europe and made a sketch of his vision: a Buddha riding upon a dragon above ruined cities. The caption read: *"Die gelbe Gefahr,"* which translates to "The Yellow Peril." Several copies were made and presented to royal relatives all over Europe as well as every embassy in Berlin.
24 *Sandai-hihō* 三大秘法.

29

On the Dedication of the Great Sri Pada Stūpa

February 25, 1978
Sri Pada, Sri Lanka

Na Mu Myō Hō Ren Ge Kyō

Here at Seetagangula, mid-way up Sri Pada,[1] Buddhism's supreme sacred grounds, a magnificent stūpa was built to enshrine the relics of Buddha Śākyamuni. A grand inaugural ceremony is taking place with people from all walks of life and from near and far attending, clergy and laity alike. Upon hearing my vow to build a stūpa on this most holy ground, the elders of the Sri Lankan Buddhist Sanghas responded immediately with jubilation and support. The Honorable President of Sri Lanka himself performed the land purifying ceremony in recognition of the stūpa as the principle object of veneration in prayer for world peace. The people of Sri Lanka, men, women, young and old, have paid homage to the great stūpa with offerings and veneration, exulting in the auspicious omen of Buddha Dharma blossoming.

The sacred origin of Sri Pada goes back to the visitation and preaching of Buddha Śākyamuni in the distant past. The Sūtra on the [Buddha's] Entering of Lankā[2] states:

> Thereupon, Rāvana, the Lord of Lankā, sang this in the measure of the *gāthā*:
>
> After the expiration of seven days,
> the World Honored One left the abode in the ocean,

1 Sri Pada, also known as Adam's Peak, is an ancient sacred mountain in Sri Lanka. It is a conical mountain 7,360 feet high, soaring above the surrounding mountain ranges. It is not only a sacred mountain to Buddhists, but to Hindus, Muslims and Christians alike.

2 Ryōga-kyō 楞伽経 Lankāvatāra-sūtra.

the palace of the Sea Serpent King,
and emerged on the shore in absolute tranquility.
Rāvana, owing to the transcendental powers of the Buddha,
came forward and announced his name to the Buddha.

"I, who have come to pay homage to you,
am Rāvana, the ten-headed king of the Rākshasas.
May the Lord graciously accept me
and all the residents of the Lankā Kingdom.
The innumerable Buddhas in the past
all made the palace at the peak of this gemmed mountain their abode and expounded the Dharma they acquired.

"I humbly implore the World Honored One to do the same.
May you sojourn in this mountain adorned with precious stones,
surrounded by various Bodhisattvas,
and expound the pure Dharma.

"I plead to you, World Honored One, Buddha,
have compassion on us Yaksas,
and enter the palace of precious stones
to expound the ineffable Dharma.
This wonderful Lanka palace is adorned with various gems
its walls are not made of stone or earth;
the ornamental laceworks that are hung are also of precious jewels.
I implore Buddha to accept this palace as your abode."

Thereupon the World Honored One said,
"King of Yakshas, this mountain of precious stones
was visited by various great teachers in the past
who took pity on you and accepted your wish.
They came to this mountain of gems
And expounded the Dharma they acquired.
The Buddhas of the future shall also do the same.

This is the abode of those who engage
in the profound essential practice

Inaugural Ceremony of the Sri Pada Stūpa, February 25, 1978.

of seeking Buddha's true heart,
and manifest the self-enjoyment of bliss in the Dharma.
I and the various Bodhisattvas shall accept your wish
out of our compassion for you.[3]

Perusing these passages of the sūtra in reverence brings us to the understanding that not only is Sri Pada a sacred ground where Buddha Śākyamuni had turned the wheel of Dharma, but also a sacred ground where numerous Buddhas in the past turned the wheel of Dharma, and shall be a sacred ground where the innumerable Buddhas to come likewise will turn the wheel of Dharma. As such, Sri Pada is a sacred ground where the Buddhas of the past, present and future turn the wheel of Dharma. It is a holy mountain made of various precious stones, a sacred mountain adorned with gems, a sanctified mountain forever protected by gods and ascetics with transcendental powers.

"This is the abode of those who engage in the profound, essential practice of seeking and accepting Buddha's true heart, and manifest the self-enjoyment of bliss in the Dharma, at which time the celestial drums spontaneously resound." Is not this passage of the sūtra a precise prophecy of our life here? Is this not an abode of those who reside on this mountain of precious jewels pursuing the profound practice of *Kanjin-honzon* [the practice of the Dharma of Three Great Mysteries], manifesting the state of self-enjoyment immersed in the bliss of the Dharma [becoming one with and taking the vow of the Eternal Buddha] in the non-virtuous era 2,500 years after the demise of the Buddha, a time when all sentient beings are faced with the horror of annihilation by the great evil of pervading strife and hostilities? The young men and women who presently reside at Sri Pada all have been designated and prophesized 2,500 years ago by the golden words of the Preceptor, Buddha Śākyamuni, to engage in the ineffable practice of *Kanjin-honzon*, revealed for the first time in the fifth five-hundred year period following the demise of the Tathāgata, for the sake of emancipating all sentient beings in the Era of Final Dharma. How could they not be deeply moved when awakening to their mission, owing to the virtuous acts accumulated in past lives?

---

3 Translator's rendition from the Japanese text of the sūtra cited by Guruji.

This grand stūpa was built by Viśvakarman.[4] Viśvakarman resides in the heavens and does not descend to Earth, yet he bestowed the skills for building the stūpa on the young men and women of Earth. The young men and women on Earth do not ascend to the heavens, yet they received the skills to erect the stūpa. Precisely for this reason, the legion of young people, inexperienced in the building of a stūpa, were able to complete this grand stūpa and dedicate it in merely 10 months time, using nothing but primitive methods. This great stūpa is unparalleled in the history of stūpas in the speed of its completion.

We now offer it to the World Honored One. May you show compassion and graciously accept it.

Shamon of Nipponzan Myōhōji
Gyōshōin Nichidatsu

4 Bishukatsuma-ten 毘首羯摩天. A deity and a subject of Indra who is in charge of architecture and craftsmanship.

30

The Significance of Birth

May 6, 1978
Atami Dōjō, Japan

We recently held a festival to commemorate Buddha Śākyamuni's birth. A *hanamidō*[1] was made, adorned with flowers, and sweet tea poured on Buddha's birth image to celebrate. Legend has it that immediately upon birth, Buddha Śākyamuni took seven steps in each of the four directions, starting with the east, then to the west, south and north. He raised his right hand pointing to the heavens, his left hand pointing to the earth and uttered a single *gāthā*. "In all heaven and earth, I alone am the Honored One." He declared that none surpassed him in reverence. "For the threefold world is a realm of suffering from which I shall emancipate all beings."[2] From this perspective, there seems to be no mistake that Buddha is the supreme honored one in heaven and earth.

Religion is a quest for the sacred. The sacred, the Honored One, in some religions is called God. The Native Americans call it the Great Spirit. Jesus Christ, the son sent by God in heaven, is considered the sacred being in Christianity. In Buddhism, Buddha Śākyamuni is considered to be God in the heavens who took birth in human form. These are varying views on the sacred being among the different religions.

Buddha Śākyamuni says he is the Honored One. Why is he honored? There is what is known as the threefold world. The world can be roughly divided into three realms;[3] the realm of celestial beings, the realm of those who live on earth, and the realm of those who live underground or in water. The entire threefold world is the world of

1 *Hanamidō* 花御堂. A small shrine to house the nativity statue of Lord Buddha.
2 天上天下　唯我独尊　三界皆苦　我当度此. Mahāparinirvāna Sūtra.
3 The threefold world, or the three realms of the world of transmigration, i.e., the realm of desire [*yokkai* 欲界], the realm of form [*shikikai* 色界] and the realm of non-form [*mushikikai* 無色界]. The realm of desire comprises hell, the state of existence of hungry

suffering. The Buddha is revered, because he will extricate all the living from the sufferings of the threefold world. It is said that on the day he was born, Buddha proclaimed that he will remove all the sufferings permeating the threefold world. I don't know whether this occurred or not, but what a marvel. This is what is handed down.

Let us consider birth. Every human being experiences birth. In the beginning we are all babies. The significance of our birth must be honorable. The reason for our birth should not be trivial nor should it be to do wrong. When we aspire to save the world from suffering, the significance of our birth becomes esteemed.

Religion is the work to free the world from suffering. It is also called the Bodhisattva practice. For one to single-handedly shoulder the task of emancipating all the suffering that exists in the world is of the highest virtue. Some may think the way to command esteem is to rise to power, become the sovereign ruler, but a single rebellion quickly changes esteem into disgrace. We know of countries today where the sitting president was executed in a coup d'état. Attempts to win esteem through power or the like are short-lived. Oda Nobunaga was killed by Mitsuhide's coup d'état during Japan's *sengoku* period.[4] Even if one is not killed, what is won through power and might eventually perishes. The imperishable is what truly serves others, what emancipates them. This is what religion teaches.

Birth—one is born to do good. The greatest good is to emancipate the multitudes from suffering. Lord Buddha declared that to be the mission he was born to. What missions are we born to? Perhaps not too many can readily say that they are born with an esteemed mission. When we do wrong instead of good, we cannot honestly say that we are born with an esteemed mission. An honest, close examination of our life reveals to us the significance of our birth.

---

spirits, animals, fighting spirits and human beings, and part of heaven. Beings of this realm have, among other things, sexual desire and other appetites. The realm of form comprises of heaven, where beings have neither sexual desire nor other appetites, and there are only five types of matter. The realm of non-form comprises of part of heaven, where no material element exists and brings only joy in meditative states. Here Guruji explains the threefold world in terms of spatial universe, based on the three-thousand great thousandfold world.

4 *Sengoku* period. The Warring States period [1467-1568] was a time of civil war between various *daimyō* [feudal warlords] seeking to achieve political power and unification of the country. Oda Nobunaga 織田信長 [1534-1582] was one of the warlords seen as most promising in uniting the nation. He was forced to commit suicide when one of his generals, Akechi Mitsuhide 明智光秀, attacked his quarters at Honnōji temple 本能寺 in Kyōto.

The most precious thing a person has done and will do is to save others. It has nothing to do with physical strength, like lifting heavy objects. First we must contemplate the root of suffering, which affects all people, and remove it so that suffering ceases. Religion teaches this power, the inexplicable power of religion. Buddha Śākyamuni lived his life in mendicancy and peacefully passed away under the shade of a tree. He led an extremely simple life as a human being. Nevertheless, his teachings have emancipated multitudes from suffering throughout the past 2,500 years. This is the power of religion. It is nothing like physical power or academic prowess.

There is a limit to what we can do on our own when aspiring to save others. Given the history over time and space in which Buddha emancipated the people from their suffering, we cannot deny the power exerted by Buddha. It is a fact that people were saved. It is a fact that everyone rejoiced. The best thing we can do within our own reach is to carry on Lord Buddha's legacy and transmit his teachings to all. Ososhi-sama ponders the significance of his own birth in *A Letter to Jakunichi-bō*.[5] He believed that encountering the Odaimoku and ultimately becoming its practitioner, chanting the Odaimoku every day, is only possible for those who made offerings to ten thousand billion[6] Buddhas in the past. We know nothing of our past lives. However, the Lotus Sūtra teaches that those who made offerings to ten thousand billion Buddhas in the past will be reborn in the non-virtuous age to preserve and practice the teachings of the Lotus Sūtra. Ososhi-sama was joyous that owing to the good deeds of making offerings to ten thousand billion Buddhas in the past, he was able to encounter the Buddha and to preserve the Odaimoku. We do not know of our past lives, but this is what is taught. Like Ososhi-sama, when we believe in the sacredness of the Odaimoku, our past also becomes revered. We must be able to emulate Ososhi-sama's joy, believing that we owe it to the merit of making offerings to ten thousand billion Buddhas in the past. While you currently chant the Odaimoku, you do not seem to truly appreciate how fortunate you are because you fail to see its invaluableness. Lack of appreciation for the sacredness of the Odaimoku and lack of wanting to do esteemed work obscure the meaning of your birth.

---

5 *Jakunichibō-gosho* 寂日房御書, written in 1279 in Minobu.

6 *Jūmanoku* 十万億. Oku generally means a hundred million, but here it is used as a translation of the Sanskrit term *koti*.

What else is more precious than the Odaimoku? One who does not appreciate its invaluableness would not be able to understand it. With such a mindset there is nothing one could feel grateful for be it parents, teachers, politicians or neighbors. Couples fight without appreciating each other. Parents do not appreciate their children. No one seems to be worthy of gratitude. It would be a shame to end our life thinking that it was worthless. If we are to make our life worthy, we need to find a pursuit that is sacred. We must bring ourselves to live a revered life. In such a life lies the significance of our birth.

Where is the Honored One? It exists nowhere else than in our own heart and mind. Nichiren Daishōnin was the only person who believed in the reverence of his life. No one else shared his view. In the eyes of the politicians of his time, Nichiren Daishōnin was a felon sentenced to execution. The general public's view was much the same. This very person, so despised and detested, believed he made offerings to ten thousand billion Buddhas in the past. And from this, what did he believe he was born into this world for? The sūtra says:

> Just as the light of the sun and moon
> Can dispel the darkness,
> So this person where he goes about in practice,
> Shall disperse the gloom of the living.[7]

Because Nichiren Daishōnin believed he was born by Buddha's mandate to illuminate the darkness of the world—a world steeped in ignorance, illusion and delusion, which are the root causes of suffering—he felt his life was invaluable. Even if no one respected him, even if they despised him, his life was radiant with this belief.

You might say that you cannot find the Honored One in others. The Honored One is not found in others, but in ourselves. If you fail to find reverence in your own heart and mind, you cannot find reverence anywhere else, no matter where you look. This is the malaise of today's world. You cannot honor your parents, children, friends or anyone else because you fail to see the Honored One in your own heart and mind. Hence, the significance of life is lost on many.

---

7 Chapter XXI of the Lotus Sūtra, *The Divine Transcendental Powers of the Tathāgata.*

It is taught that when Buddha Dharma is violated, filial piety ceases to exist in the family. Unfilial children do not honor their parents. A modern education that gives priority to science and technology teaches needless things and does not teach the importance of honoring one's parents. Children who do not respect their parents cannot respect their neighbors. Finding nothing to revere makes them irreligious. Religion, faith, teaches us to seek the sacred. Without faith, one cannot find the revered.

Sri Lanka is a small island country and a Buddhist nation the size of Kyūshū.[8] It is not an affluent country, and not many have the opportunity for higher education. However, Buddhism flourishes, and people greet others bowing in veneration with joined palms. The pilgrims from Japan were deeply impressed and joyous over the unexpected respect paid them by the people of Sri Lanka. A visit abroad would not have been joyful had they been made light of or mocked. The people they met were all strangers, but even children greeted them respectfully, bowing with palms together. How could anyone greeted like that slight these children? Mutual fondness develops.

The illness of modern times is in not being able to find the Revered One in one's heart and mind. Color blindness might be an analogy. It allows you to see, yet hinders the discernment of color. One cannot distinguish red from blue or any other beautiful color. The eyes cannot discern colors. It is an issue of the eyes. If you see the sacred that deserves veneration in your own heart and mind, you will then offer reverence to others.

One Bodhisattva who appears in the Lotus Sūtra is Bodhisattva Never Despise, and he practices its teachings. He bows in veneration to everyone he meets with palms pressed together. He is a monk, but does not read sūtras. More than anything else, he bows and venerates others. When Buddha Dharma has declined and the hearts of the people are hardened and dissolute, lecturing others based on academic learning does not provide the cure. Sophistry cannot persuade people. The only act Bodhisattva Never Despise performs is to bow in veneration and utter the meaning of his veneration. "I deeply revere you. I shall never slight or despise you, for you shall eventually become Buddha." When hearing these words and receiving veneration, perhaps

8 The southernmost island of Japan's four major islands.

Enshrining of the Buddha Image and Opening Ceremony of the Pokhara [Nepal] Dōjō, November 28, 1973.

one in a thousand might start to think whether he or she has something deserving of veneration, the seed of Buddhahood. There is no other way to bring emancipation. If we refuse to venerate others because they do not venerate us, nothing good comes of it. Most likely there will be a spat. We must find the sacred in our heart and mind if we seek to lead a revered life. When our eyes are opened to seeing the sacred within our own hearts and minds, everyone we see becomes sacred. Everyone becomes the object of veneration. That is when peace will prevail in the world.

Birth—birth as a human. "Among the heavens and earth, I alone am revered. The triple world is filled with suffering. I shall relieve all." If we are taught this from birth and bear it in mind from morning to night, then our eyes will be opened to the sacred. That means you and I also aspire to free others from suffering. Sacredness exists in freeing others from suffering, to know the sacredness of others and to emancipate them. This becomes possible when our hearts and minds awaken to what is sacred.

31

THE LONGEST WALK

July 16, 1978
Washington, D.C.

HERE AT WASHINGTON, D.C., IN NORTH AMERICA, the great gathering of The Longest Walk is taking place today. This walk began on February 11th this year from a small island in the San Francisco Bay. The walkers braved uninhabited deserts, slept in snow-covered mountains at 12,000 feet, trudged through strong gales and pelting rain. Despite overwhelming odds, they have finally arrived in Washington, D. C., covering 30 to 80 kilometers a day without a single dropout. The ancestors of the Native Americans were repeatedly forced to march westward by the violence of the European refugees who landed on the East Coast. Every single one of these forced marches left a trail of tears, a trail of blood. Women and children were slaughtered, and many died of starvation and exposure in the harsh weather. Some 20 million people are said to have been sacrificed. In an abuse of state power, the United States of America legislated and continues to attempt to legislate a series of unjust laws aiming to annihilate the surviving Indian population. The Indian people have appealed their just cause to the world community at large in a truly spiritual way to defend their right to survival. They have organized The Longest Walk to push aside the violence of the US government with nonviolence.

Historically, the modern state is built on the myth known as the *raison d'état* [for the good of the country]. Its highest principles are determined by what is needed to sustain and what is convenient for the status quo. In this case, the state can disregard various laws and statutes, morals and religion if they are not in the interest of state preservation and fortification. All laws, statutes and social morals have value only to the extent that they preserve and fortify the state. The sovereign power of the state is upheld as sacred. The Machiavellian realism in politics, which is craftiness, duplicity and manipulation, allows laws to be disregarded and deliberately misinterpreted.

Another characteristic of the modern state is the use of Christian missionaries, who should be advocates of peace, as proxies of state power in igniting countless wars. The defiled reputation of Christian missionaries was earned through their association with the state power that they served. The use of nuclear weapons is even condoned under the myth of *raison d'état,* the fallacious belief in the sacredness of the sovereign state. Ever since it first used nuclear weapons in Asia, the United States of America, without compunction, has blackmailed the rest of humanity repeatedly and overtly threatening their use under this rationale. If there is land White America needs, everything native must evacuate. Just as hares and snakes are driven away, so are the people who reside there. This is what is known as the "American pioneering spirit." This notion, based on the mythical notion of state sovereignty, leads to violent acts. Ethnic dignity and self-determination of the Native American nations were denied by the violence of state sovereignty. How could these people, whose very survival is at stake, not see this state as their sworn enemy?

On November 24, 1961, the United Nations General Assembly presented "The Declaration on Banning the Use of Nuclear Weapons." It states:

> Believing that the use of weapons of mass destruction, such as nuclear and thermo-nuclear weapons, is a direct negation of the high ideals and objectives which the United Nations has been established to achieve through the protection of succeeding generations from the scourge of war and through the preservation and promotion of their cultures, declares that the use of nuclear and thermo-nuclear weapons would exceed even the scope of war and cause indiscriminate suffering and destruction to mankind and civilization and, as such, is contrary to the rules of international law and to the laws of humanity; the use of nuclear and thermo-nuclear weapons is a war directed not against an enemy or enemies alone but also against mankind in general, since the peoples of the world not involved in such a war will be subjected to all the evils

> generated by the use of such weapons. Any state using nuclear and thermo-nuclear weapons is to be considered as violating the Charter of the United Nations, as acting contrary to the laws of humanity and as committing a crime against mankind and civilization.

On August 6, 1945 in Hiroshima, and on August 9 in Nagasaki, humanity experienced the very first catastrophes of the atomic bomb. None other than this country, the United States of America, unleashed these bombs. The then commander-in-chief, General MacArthur, praised the achievements of the nuclear bombing, claiming that they hastened the end of the war. He later explained that the use of nuclear weapons was necessary to protect the lives of young American soldiers. No one in the United States acknowledged the criminality of the use of nuclear weapons. Recklessly intoxicated with the ecstasy of victory and lauding nuclear weapons as guardians of peace, the United States feverishly devoted itself to the development, production and stockpiling of nuclear weapons after the war. Despite the enormous disaster that they cause humanity, rather, precisely because of it, nuclear weapons were self-righteously hallowed for the sake of "national security" and "in the interest of the people."

At the 32nd General Assembly of the United Nations in 1977, Dr. Kurt Waldheim, Secretary General of the United Nations, called for the opening of the United Nations Special Session on Disarmament, saying, "The threat of self-destruction by nuclear war is the greatest danger confronting the world. The enormous amount of stockpiling and accuracy of nuclear weapons are further enhancing the danger of the final annihilation of mankind. It has become more evident that effective security cannot be obtained by the expansion of arms. The very basis which can eliminate the cause of tension and conflicts, and establish reciprocal international cooperation, can be found in disarmament."

The United States of America has already used nuclear weapons. Not a single soul will praise a victory thus won. History shall eternally condemn the criminality of the atomic bombings by the United States. First, the United States of America violated the UN Charter. Second, it committed crimes against humanity. Third, it is an enemy to humanity that could bring calamity to the whole of humankind. Fourth, it is a criminal capable of destroying civilization. But world affairs need not be looked at only in the context of the current pessimistic circumstances. The state of affairs constantly changes and is by no means static. Today with the extreme development of nuclear weapons and humanity's knowledge of them, the only way to prevent humanity from the catastrophe it faces is to eliminate war itself. We must work with all our might for general and complete disarmament. General and complete disarmament is not a cerebral exercise, but the most realistic solution. The era of war, the era of violence, the era of murder and destruction is about to be put to rest.

No measures taken in anticipation of future conflicts or war will enable us to build true peace. The foremost issue in creating genuine peace is removing fear and mistrust between discordant nations. Elimination of fear and mistrust is a purely spiritual issue, which religions have consistently taught from ancient times. Fear shall disappear when we believe in the almighty God. We believe in the omniscient, omnipotent God to dispel our fear. We fear others when we suspect they are evil. When we believe in the goodness of others, we no longer fear them. We do not believe in God because we have seen his omnipotence. We seek to see God's omnipotence by believing in him. We do not believe in the goodness of others because we have seen their goodness. When we believe in the goodness of others, we can dispel our own fear and become capable of amicable associations with them. Believing in the omnipotence of God, who we cannot see, cultivates the mind and heart to believe in the goodness of others, though it might not be readily apparent.

Once we reject the belief in absolute state sovereignty, and after we eliminate all weapons, including nuclear weapons, and completely bring an end to war, we must create a new civilization, an era of ever-lasting peace. However, the people of this new era will be the same ones who depended on self-defense through arms. It is most critical for these people to act on conscience as human beings in order to create a spiritual foundation for disarmament. Scientific development built a materialistic civilization yet brought on the crisis of human annihilation. The abiding myth of absolute state sovereignty is another spiritual ailment, a consequence of heightened arrogance and avarice. No matter how much systems or ideas change, mutual fear and mistrust can never be dispelled unless people open the gate to spiritual change. Spiritual transformation comes without disgrace. Buddha Dharma teaches that when we free ourselves from delusions, we become enlightened.

The civilization of the new era, the era of perpetual peace, will be the spiritual civilization. The civilization of religion is the universal center of the spiritual civilization. Nichiren Daishōnin called this *Risshō-ankoku* [give rise to the True Dharma to bring peace and tranquility to the land]. The religious faith that Native Americans have carried to this day will be the source for forging lasting peace in times to come. No one visits the graves of General MacArthur or Harry Truman today, yet tens of thousands of people gather and mourn the sacrifice of Hiroshima and Nagasaki each year.

The Longest Walk started in Alcatraz, San Francisco Bay on February 11, 1978 and ended in Washington, D.C. in July of that year. Eighty tribes and more than 600 Native people participated in the walk and run to promote the rights of their people.

32

Nipponzan's Disgrace

December 12, 1978
Sri Pada, Sri Lanka

Okamoto Kōji sensei,[1]

The announcement of the Nehru Award by India was extraordinary news, a totally unexpected surprise. I have accepted it with gratitude. The fact that Gandhiji's granddaughter[2] and her husband nominated me made it all the more cherished.

Be it the Nehru Award, Lenin Award or the Nobel Prize, all are instruments for fame and recognition. People of faith should steer clear of them on principle. While one of the merits of the Bodhisattva practice is "reputation universally heard,"[3] it is a merit that comes without being sought. The Nobel Peace Prize awarded to Satō Eisaku[4] is an example of honor bestowed on one who sought after it. I wonder if any critic speculates that awarding me has undermined the value of the Nehru Award. Yet, I feel humbled and grateful.

---

1 Okamoto Kōji 岡本光司 [Kōkichi 幸吉] [1924–1994] became the second editor of the monthly *Sarvodaya* magazine, published by Japan-Bharat Sarvodaya Mitrata Sangha, after the passing of Rev. Maruyama Gyōryō 丸山行遼, in accord with Guruji's wishes. Sensei 先生 is a title used to refer to or address teachers, professors and other professionals such as lawyers, doctors, politicians and clergy. He and his wife, Kazue 一枝, taught children at Shinobu-juku 忍塾, an afterschool program that offered spiritual guidance as well as tutoring, while dedicating 18 years [1964-1985] to publishing the *Sarvodaya* magazine. Mr. and Mrs. Okamoto spent their life's savings to rebuild the Buddha Hall and stūpa at the Walukaramaya Temple, Moratuwa, Sri Lanka. Notification of the first Kakasaheb Kalelkar Award for his tireless work in the Sarvodaya movement in Japan reached his wife right after Mr. Okamoto's funeral.

2 Mrs. Sumitra Kulkarni and Mr. Gajanana Kulkarni.

3 *Myōshō-fumon* 名称普聞. Phrase found in Chapter I, *Introductory*, and Chapter II, *Expedients*, of the Lotus Sūtra,.

4 佐藤栄作 [1901-1975]. Prime minister of Japan 1964-1972, and the longest serving prime minister in Japan's history. He shared the 1974 Nobel Peace Prize with Sean MacBride in recognition of Japan's signing of the Nuclear Non-Proliferation Treaty.

Starting with Nichiren Daishōnin and the six elder monks, no one from the order has been acknowledged in the chronicles of the time as a Buddhist master. It is quite alright. Nipponzan's conduct ought not to be mixed up in the fame and recognition pursued in the secular world. Nipponzan's honor does not exist where fame and recognition are sought. Have I, too, in my efforts, been unconsciously motivated by a desire for fame and recognition? If so, I have disgraced Nichiren Daishōnin. It is possible the Nehru Award might be used to impress the foolish. If this should happen, I would be less guilty had I declined the award.

Everything at Nipponzan must be done in the spirit of "May the Buddha know our hearts."[5] Believing in the light shed by the Buddha and his compassionate watch over us, the realization of the single phrase of "I [the Buddha] shall be pleased"[6] is the goal we constantly strive for. Pursuit of mundane fame and recognition is Nipponzan's disgrace, which must be absolutely avoided. It is more dreadful and corrosive to Nipponzan than intoxicants or drugs. Let us be mindful and conduct ourselves in a way that is free from the pursuit of secular fame and recognition.

Nichidatsu

5 Chapter XIII of the Lotus Sūtra, *Exhortation to Hold Firm.*
6 Chapter XI of the Lotus Sūtra, *Beholding the Stūpa of Treasures.*

33

The Seal of Fearlessness

January 19, 1979
Acceptance Speech for the Jawaharlal Nehru Award
for International Understanding
New Delhi, India

Na Mu Myō Hō Ren Ge Kyō

I would like to extend my profound appreciation for being favored with the Nehru Award for International Understanding from India here this day. I reached 95 years of age this year. Reflecting on my long relationship with India, I feel as though there were no other life for me besides that in India

In the center of Kyūshū, located in the western end of the Japanese archipelago, is the world's greatest volcano called Mount Aso. I was born in a sparsely populated remote area surrounded by mountains called Sakanashi, a basin that was once a crater of Mount Aso.

Buddhism, which originated in India, was introduced to Japan by way of China and Korea more than 1,400 years ago. Since the dawn of history, the Japanese believed in an indigenous religion known as Shintoism. Whether or not to accept Buddhism was deliberated. In due time, Shōtoku Taishi [Crown Prince Shōtoku][1] rose and favored Buddhism as the national religion. His Seventeen Article Constitution proclaimed the national policy of a peaceful nation and declared reverence for the Buddha Dharma a prerequisite towards that end. Since then, Japan became a nation of Buddhists irrespective of one's social status. Notwithstanding the many transitions in the political system, no attempts were made to expel Buddhism during the ensuing 1,300 to 1,400 years. It was as if the national character of the Japanese people and Buddhism

1 Please refer to *The Purpose of Erecting a Stūpa and Making Offerings*, footnote 10, p. 58.

were one and the same and could not be separated.

However, the Meiji Restoration, a political revolution to build a modern state, took place approximately 100 years ago. "Modernization of the state" was a dominant state policy from Europe to counter the influence of the religious civilization by favoring a civilization led by science. It culminated in the founding of a communist state. Similarly, the revolution of the Meiji Restoration in Japan launched a campaign to expel Buddhism, a religion embraced by the people. State-sponsored Shintoism took its place. Politics and Shintoism were integrated, and the slogan "the unity of church and state" coined. Under the unity of church and state, the figure at the center of politics inevitably became the essential object of veneration as the central actor in religious rites. The deification of the Japanese Emperor was the inescapable outcome of the unity of church and state.

I was born in the 18th year after the Meiji Revolution. It was a time when the momentum to drive out Buddhism finally took root among the people. Yet, fortunately, since my birthplace is a remote area nestled in the mountains situated in the western corner of Japan, people still led a life of Buddhist faith. I was blessed to be born into a life of Buddhist faith. My relationship with India thus goes back to the times of my ancestors long before my birth.

There were hardly any sports in my childhood. Life in the country offered no entertainment throughout the year. I was quite busy helping with farm work even as a child. Recreation was a visit to the temples or attending celebrations at shrines. We woke with the sunrise and were in bed at sunset. It was life lived with nature. The impoverished life in the country was a happy life, free from temptations.

By the time of my secondary education, I gradually awakened to issues of life. To be a politician and ruling the people or to be a general and winning victory are both seemingly brilliant careers. Yet, their glory is short-lived, their influence limited. On the other hand, religion does not perish since it is a quest for the eternal. It is also a search for a path that is universally embraced; therefore, it spreads to the worlds in ten directions. Religion cannot be monopolized by anyone, but is commonly shared by all.

Religion defines good and evil. It forbids evil and nurtures good. Good and evil are indistinguishable where religion does not exist, and where good and evil are indistinguishable, life in peace cannot exist. For

Accepting the Jawaharlal Nehru Award for International Understanding, New Delhi, January 19, 1979.

this reason, we must first seek religious faith in life.

By the time I completed my secondary education at the age of seventeen, I aspired to seek the Dharma and became a bhikshu. That is to say, I became Buddha's disciple and entered a unique way of life detached from ordinary society. To become Buddha's disciple means to lead a life as the disciple of the World Honored One, Buddha Śākyamuni, the founder of Buddhism in India, notwithstanding the vast expanse of the ocean and a lapse of 2,500 years. My body was born in Japan, yet my mind and heart were given birth to in India.

I started reading the sūtras after becoming a bhikshu. In the Lotus Sūtra *Introductory* Chapter I it says, "Thus have I heard. Once the Buddha was staying at Rajgir on Mount Grdhrakūta with a great assembly of great bhikshus, in all twelve thousand."

Mount Grdhrakūta in Rajgir is indeed the mountain where the supreme teaching of humankind was preached, the mountain where the World Honored One revealed the true purpose for taking birth in this world, the mountain where the religion that emancipates the suffering of the modern ill world was preached. The Lotus Sūtra sets forth:

"I, ever dwelling here, by my transcendental powers, cause living beings with distorted views, not to see me though I am nearby."

Although Lord Buddha cannot be seen, the Sacred Eagle Peak [Mount Grdhrakūta], the eternal abode of Lord Buddha, still stands as it did in the past. It was my heart's desire to pay homage to the Sacred Eagle Peak, believing in the eternal presence of Lord Buddha. This is not merely a wish of my own, but one shared by all Japanese people. India and Japan are connected by Buddhism, and thus are closely tied to each other.

I left Japan and came to India over fifty years ago. I was determined never to return to Japan and vowed to devote the rest of my life to India. I called this mission of mine *Saiten-kaikyō*[2] [Returning the Buddha Dharma to India]. Indeed, I was able to exert myself in my mission centering on India for 50 years since that time. Joy overwhelms me day and night thinking of the fortune of having become Buddha's disciple.

The Congress Party, a political organization, was formed in India and planned a political revolution for independence and self-rule. I was born in Japan the year the Congress Party came into being. I grew up together with the expansion of the Congress Party movement, and became aware of its activities. In time, Mahatma Gandhiji appeared to lead the Congress's movement.

In the first half of the present century, political revolutions took place in various countries of the world. Vladimir Ilyich Lenin of the Soviet Union, Benito Mussolini of Italy, and their like sought to overthrow old forms of government and establish new political powers. Violence was condoned to achieve that end. India's revolutionary movement did not rely on military force or machinery, but on a primitive means of spinning cotton yarn or boiling seawater to produce salt. There is no precedent in human history of a successful political revolution that overthrew the existing government by spinning cotton or producing salt. Not a single soul in the world could have even fathomed it. It was deemed to be nothing short of Gandhiji's daydream.

Gandhiji and his disciples were committed to jail for their crimes of spinning yarn and producing salt. In prison Gandhiji proclaimed that God's judgment is near. Gandhiji was pursuing his vision alone in the depth of his "dreamland."

---

2 西天開教. Please refer to *Shishin-kaku*, footnote 21, p. 5.

I was astounded to see pictures of Gandhiji on the Salt March or spinning yarn. I felt I was witnessing something incredible unfold: at this time of modern scientific civilizations, a genuine revolutionary movement that does not rely on science or machines, which is, in fact, completely contrary to them, had been launched. Can such a movement overcome the solidly fortified institution of the modern state and create a different world, a world of nonviolence? Even if it does not succeed, I thought it to be a fine plan with extraordinary insight. Spinning yarn or salt making are things even a disciple of the Buddha like myself can be part of and make a contribution. I decided to immediately leave for India to pray for the success of Gandhiji's revolutionary movement.

The heaven and earth of India are sacred to Buddhists, the domain of the Tathāgata's eternal presence. The people of India, believing in the Tathāgata's precept of not taking the lives of living beings, were attempting to apply it to a political revolution. The theater of my religious activities as Buddha's disciple had indeed opened up for me in India.

Three years had passed since I had landed in India. I still had no followers nor had I been able to meet Gandhiji. For most of that time, Gandhiji and his people were incarcerated. My first opportunity to meet Gandhiji came on October 4, 1933 at the ashram in Wardha. Our meeting lasted only 15 minutes, and there was hardly any time to speak on matters of substance. We met the following day and the day after that, but unfortunately I could neither speak English nor Hindi. I therefore submitted an English translation of my views to Gandhiji. This is how it came to pass that I found residence in the Wardha ashram.

In the meantime, the state of the world was turning ominous. A war between Japan and China broke out. Its fire gradually expanded. Japan, Germany and Italy concluded a Tripartite Axis Pact that eventually led to World War II. My country, Japan, was the source of fire. What would become of Japan? I felt it more urgent to prevent Japan's ruin before I could help in India's freedom movement, and left India alone for Japan.

Upon my return I met with leaders of the army and navy; I ran about battlefronts praying for a peaceful resolution to the war. However, my effort was in vain. On August 15, 1945, Japan surrendered to the Allied Forces, which brought an end to World War II. On August 15, 1947, India had succeeded in the nonviolent revolution and became a free and autonomous nation.

Jawaharlal Nehru became India's first Prime Minister and visited

Japan to console the people of a defeated nation. With the utmost consideration, he presented an elephant to the children of Japan. In May 1951, the Allied Forces held the International Military Tribunal for the Far East in Tōkyō and executed seven top-level Japanese leaders. Judge Radhabinod Pal of India rendered a sole dissenting opinion of not guilty.[3]

On September 9, 1951, a Treaty of Peace was signed. At this conference the representatives from the Allied Forces unanimously accused the Japanese military of committing a war of aggression. Because of this, India did not send a representative to this conference, and Sri Lanka stood alone and asked that generous measures be adopted toward Japan in accordance with the teachings of Buddha.

Immediately following independence, Indian leaders gathered at the Sanchi Stūpa and determined the principle policy of India, which was to establish a peaceful nation. A resolution was passed to restore Buddhism, a religion of peace, in the interest of building a peaceful nation. As an initial step to restore Buddhism, a committee to reconstruct Rajgir was organized [1956]. Prime Minister Nehru himself headed the committee and five members were appointed. Despite my being a foreign national, I became a member of this committee in my capacity as a disciple of the Buddha. The erection of the Rajgir stūpa and a stūpa in Kalinga are some of the works by this committee to restore Buddhism. Restoration of Buddhism is not only a spiritual movement within India, which is requisite to establish a peaceful nation; it is also the most vital spiritual movement in establishing universal peace in today's world. India's nonviolent revolution is not merely a mark of her political honor, but a compass that points towards the future policy of all nations of the world.

The reason for restoring Buddhism in India and disseminating Buddha's teachings throughout the world is to bestow the

3 Judge Radhabinod Pal did not believe international law justified a guilty verdict against the Japanese defendants. Furthermore, he believed that war crime indictments should be equally applied to both the victor and the vanquished, but that did not happen, and as an example in his dissent he pointed to the atomic bombing of civilians in Japan as a case which should have been tried as a war crime. Although he did believe some of the defendants were guilty of Class B and C war crimes, because of this unequal application of international law he did not believe they were guilty of the Class A war crimes for which they stood trial before the Tōkyō International Military Tribunal. More on Judge Pal is written in *Requisition of Land*, footnote 17, p. 72.

seal of fearlessness on a humanity menaced by murderous weapons of destruction, capable of repeatedly annihilating life in this *sahā* world.

Fear not, "The various Buddhas and saviors exist with great sovereign, transcendent power and reveal their innumerable divine powers to please living beings."[4]

There is a power that destroys this world: it is called the power of machines. There is a power of the ones who emancipate this world: It is called *dai-jintsū-riki*[5] [the great, sovereign, transcendent power]. The power of machines is nothing more than materialistic power. *Dai-jintsū-riki* is spiritual power. Civilizations of any age will perish when materialistic power supersedes spiritual power. If humanity hopes to avert its doom, a spiritual power that surpasses material power must manifest. The exertion of a spiritual power is preached as *kai-butt-chi-ken*[6] [to gain access to the wisdom of the Buddha to comprehend the truth of the Dharma]. The various Buddhas and the World-Honored Ones appear in the world in order to let living beings, sunk in the sea of suffering, gain Buddha's wisdom. This is expounded as the most important cause for which Buddha appeared in the world.[7] The attainment of self-rule and independence by India is material proof of spiritual power prevailing over material power.

Should humanity exert its spiritual power in quest of peace and tranquility, nuclear weapons, Trident missiles, space weapons and the like will not be able to fulfill their role. The precept of not taking life is a solemn precept laid down by the Preceptor, Buddha Śākyamuni, the World Honored One, in his lifetime. It is the true law of nature, which gives birth to life and nurtures heaven and earth. No great demon can ever defeat it. Fear not, the seal of fearlessness has already been bestowed in our hands.

Na Mu Myō Hō Ren Ge Kyō

4 Chapter XXI of the Lotus Sūtra, *The Divine Transcendental Powers of the Tathāgata.*
5 大神通力.
6 開仏知見.
7 *Ichidaiji-innen* 一大事因縁.

34

Petition to the Indian Government

January 30, 1979[1]
Sri Pada Dōjō, Sri Lanka

To His Excellency Morarji Desai,[2]
Prime Minister of India

Na Mu Myō Hō Ren Ge Kyō

The Nehru Award I received during your incumbency as Prime Minister of India was the greatest honor ever conferred on me. I am deeply grateful.

Restoration of Rajgir, the principle vow of *Saiten-kaikyō* [returning Buddha Dharma to the Western Heavens], had borne its initial fruit as a stūpa through your Excellency's thoughtful attention, and the time is now ripe to embark on its full-scale restoration. Your Excellency's sincere interest in seeing the restoration plan executed despite your hectic responsibilities for the affairs of the state as Prime Minister can only be understood as a karmic blessing. Reminiscent of the glorious reign of the great King Bimbisāra,[3] your karmic virtues give cause to rejoice, and I pray for the health and longevity of your Excellency, who strives day and night to attain the ideals raised at the time of India's independence.

Pursuant to our meeting on January 19th and 20th, I am submitting the following three items:

1. Restoration Plan for Rajgir—original and a copy with

---

1 It is believed that Guruji chose the anniversary of Gandhiji's assassination, January 30, to write this letter.

2 Morarji Desai [1896-1995] was the fifth prime minister of India [1977-1979] and an Indian freedom fighter. He was the first prime minister who did not belong to the Indian Congress Party; rather he was elected representing the broad Janata [Hindi for "the people"] coalition.

3 A great king [558-491BCE] of the Magadha Empire and a protector of Lord Buddha.

drawings attached.

2. Application for the construction of the New Delhi Stūpa—original and a copy.
3. Requests regarding pending issues related to the Darjeeling Stūpa with the attachment of relevant documents.

It would be a supreme honor if we could see these three matters quickly realized through your Excellency's profound appreciation and decision.

Fujii Nichidatsu
Founder of Nipponzan Myōhōji

Rajgir Restoration Plan

The following are the plans for a phased full-scale restoration of Rajgir.

1. Phase One:
   a. Restoration of the Venuvana Vihar[4] in the ruins of the Bamboo Grove. Drawings attached.
   b. Restoration of the Ajātaśatru stūpa.[5] Plan attached.
   c. Restoration of the Ānanda[6] stūpa. A grand garden will be built around it.
   d. Construction of a clinic offering acupuncture and Ayuvedic

4 Venuvana Vihar, or Bamboo Grove Temple, was the first temple built for Buddha Śākyamuni and his Sangha. The land and temple were offered by King Bimbisāra. The temple was restored by Nipponzan Myōhōji in 1981.

5 Ajātaśatru was King Bimbisara's son who incarcerated and left his father to die of starvation after falling under the influence of Buddha Śākyamuni's antagonist Devadatta. He latter repented and embraced Buddha's teachings and became a protector of Buddhism. After Buddha's passing Ajātaśatru built a stūpa in Rajgir as an offering to Buddha. The foundation of the Ajātaśatru stūpa remains in front of the old Nipponzan temple in Rajgir.

6 Ānanda was Buddha Śākyamuni's attendant as well as his cousin and disciple. His ability to memorize many of Buddha's discourses earned him the reputation as one who "heard much." Shortly after Buddha's Parinirvāna, the First Buddhist Council was convened. Ānanda was called upon to recite many of the discourses that later became the Sutta Pitaka of the Pāli Canon. Legend has it that after the Parinirvāna of Buddha, he became revered by the two kingdoms of Magadha and Licchavi, located on either side of the Ganges. Concerned that the two countries would fight over his relics after his nirvāna, he rowed a boat out to the middle of Ganges, rose into the air, entered samādhi and attained nirvāna at the age of 120. He then divided his relics into two and dropped a portion on either shore. The two kingdoms then each erected a stūpa enshrining Ānanda's relics. One stūpa was erected in Rajgir, the capital of Magadha, and the other which still exists, in Vaishali, the capital of Licchavi.

treatments. Initially, part of the new Venuvana Vihar would be utilized as a clinic.

2. Phase Two:
   a. International Buddhist University modeled after Rabindrinath Tagore's original school founded at Shantiniketan.[7]
   b. Establish the Jivaka[8] charitable hospital. Development of this plan will depend on responses to Ayurvedic[9] and acupuncture treatments, which will be closely observed and evaluations made.
   c. Cultivation of herbs.
   d. Construction of lodges with the development of hot springs. This matter is currently awaiting advice from experts in Japan.

Together with Nipponzan Myōhōji I will endeavor to bear necessary expenses for the completion of the abovementioned Rajgir Restoration plan. For the time being, we do not intend to request financial support from the Indian national government or the Bihar state government. However, we solicit appropriate guidance from relevant ministries and agencies with regard to transfer of land and issuance of construction permits. The State of Bihar has already purchased 84 acres of land based on its Rajgir city restoration plan. I consider the Rajgir Restoration Plan a virtual success if this land can be made available to the Rajgir Buddha Vihar Society.

Given my age, I am eager to proceed with the aforementioned Dharma works without delay. For this reason, it is my heartfelt wish that

---

7 Nobel Laureate Rabindranath Tagore formed Shantiniketan [Abode of Peace] as an International University intended to be a place where the cultures of the East and the West could meet and mingle.

8 Jivaka Kumarabhacca was the most renowned physician and healer in the time of the Buddha during the reign of King Bimbisāra of the Magadha Kingdom. He is regarded as the Father of Medicine, a knowledgeable source about the healing powers of plants, minerals, massage, among other things. He is said to have performed the first brain surgery in the world. He provided free medical care to the Buddha and his order and donated his mango grove at Rajagriha for use as a monastic community named Jivakarama.

9 Ayurvedic medicine is an ancient system of health care indigenous to the Indian subcontinent. The word "Ayurveda" is a compound of the word *āyus* meaning "life," "life principle," or "long life" and the word *veda*, which refers to a system of knowledge. Ayurveda is concerned with measures to protect *ayus*, which includes healthy living along with therapeutic measures that relate to physical, mental, social and spiritual harmony.

Your Excellency would be available to perform the cornerstone ceremony of Venuvana Vihar on March 25th [as I travel from Sri Lanka] on my way to London. I would be most obliged for your due consideration of this matter.

Gasshō [With palms together]

Fujii Nichidatsu
Founder of Nipponzan Myōhōji

Addendum: Application for Construction of the New Delhi Stūpa

I extend my deep appreciation for the kindness of the Indian government in conferring the 1978 Jawaharlal Nehru Award for International Understanding on an ordinary Buddhist bhiksu from Japan. It is the greatest honor in my life.

When Buddhism was transmitted to Japan 1,400 years ago, it immediately became spiritual sustenance for the Japanese nation, the flesh and blood of Japanese culture, and it effectuated a peaceful country, a rarity in world history. For this reason, the Japanese people have held boundless esteem and love for India, the country of Buddha Śākyamuni.

Reflecting back, I came to India 50 years ago and plunged into Mahatma Gandhiji's freedom movement. Likewise, my disciples remained at Sevagram ashram and continued to pray for the successful attainment of independence by chanting the ineffable Dharma condensed into the single phrase of Na Mu Myō Hō Ren Ge Kyō.

This karmic connection led to the emergence of the Rajgir Stūpa followed by the Kalinga Stūpa. Without Gandhiji's profound love and astute insight, I may never have become what I am in India today.

If I am favored with five acres of land between Rajghat[10] and Shanti Vana,[11] I wish to erect a stūpa, where I can watch over and serve the cremation sites of Gandhiji and Nehruji with offerings and prayers. At the same time, it will be a place where everyone—Buddhists and non-Buddhists alike—can pray for world peace. The prize of the Nehru Award will be the seed money for this sacred work. I submit this matter for Your Excellency's profound understanding and consideration.

---

10 Rajghat is the site where Mahatma Gandhi was cremated on the west bank of the Yamuna River on January 31, 1948. An open platform is inscribed with the words, "Hē Ram," [O God], Gandhiji's last words.

11 Shanti Vana mean "the forest of peace." It is the cremation site of Jawaharlal Nehru, the first prime minister of India and Indian freedom fighter.

35

On the Occasion of the 50th Commemorative Filial Service For the Late Maha Bhiksunī Gyōain Nisso[1]

February 25, 1979
Atami, Japan

Na Mu Myō Hō Ren Ge Kyō

Nichiren Daishōnin's *Response to the Wife of Gyōbu Zaemonno-jyō*[2] says:

> Those who wish to practice filial piety for their parents shall offer the recitation of the Lotus Sūtra. Buddha Śākyamuni, our Preceptor, expounded the Lotus Sūtra for the sake of his parents. While belated, I, Nichiren, in utter repentance for going against my mother's wishes too often in her life, probed into the entire sacred canon of the Tathāgata in his lifetime [to determine which sūtra he expounded was for filial piety] to serve filial piety to her. At such time, I identify with all who perform filial services to their mother as if they were my other-self. I have written this letter in brief for not being able to contain my joy. Without doubt, the holy soul shall immediately be released from the defilement of the six states of existence[3] and arrive at the Sacred Eagle Peak, the abode of the Tathāgata, the Pure Land.

There are various aspects to the significance of Nichiren Daishōnin's

1 The Dharma name received by Guruji's mother upon ordination.

2 Written by Nichiren Daishōnin in the third year of the Kōan period [1280] at Mount Minobu.

3 *Rokudō* 六道. "The six paths" are the six lower states of existence, i.e., hell, and the realms of hungry spirits, animals, *asuras*, human beings and celestial beings. Becoming free from the defilement of the six states of existence means to be freed from the sufferings of undergoing cycles of transmigration between these realms.

Maha Bhiksunī Gyōain Nisso, 1929.

methodical elucidation on the entirety of the sacred teachings delivered by Lord Buddha in his lifetime, as well as his critical comparative analysis on the existing eight schools of Buddhism.[4] However, the greatest significance lies in the fact that he did all this out of filial piety toward his mother. Among eminent monks of great virtue and knowledge in the three lands,[5] Nichiren Daishōnin is unparalleled in embracing filial piety in his heart. It seems that throughout his life, not a day passed without repenting his inadequacy of filial piety toward his parents.

On August 6th in the 18th year of Meiji [1885], I was born at the foot

4 Kusha, 倶舎; Jyōjitsu 成実; Ritsu 律; Hossō 法相; Sanron 三論; Kegon 華厳; Tendai 天台; and Shingon 真言.

5 India, China and Japan.

of one of Japan's celebrated mountains, Mount Aso. My mother was 37 years old.

> Who can complain the sweltering heat?
> When reflecting on maidens weeding grass
> Out in small paddy fields
> Laboring under the scorching sun.
> –Emperor Meiji

In the farm work of rice cultivation, weeding grass is the most backbreaking job of all. My mother weeded grass in the fields until the day of delivery. She returned home a little ahead of others to prepare supper and went into labor as she was boiling water on the stove. She gave birth to me with the help of my grandmother. The hot water on the stove became my first bath. Her diligence and hard life is more than I can imagine.

I was weak as a young child and often suffered from roundworms and the like. One day, I fell seriously ill and lost consciousness. When I was finally on my way to recovery, mother said through her tears: "Oh, Yoshi, should you die, mother would not live!" She was prepared to take her own life when I became unconscious. How terribly unfilial it is for a child to precede his parents in death. I am truly grateful that I did not die then. How dreadful that would have been! Mother placed *manjū* [sweet bean cake] and *mochi* [rice cake] at the side of my pillow and eagerly urged me to take them. Since my appetite had not yet recovered, I resisted saying, "Not now. Please let me have them later when I want them." Not knowing what to do, she promised, "All right. You can have them later when you feel like it." However, this promise was left unfulfilled after my recovery. Except for *mochi* on New Year's Day and *manjū* during Urabon, sweets were a rarity throughout the year, yet I did not miss them. It was to be expected of a country life, the sadness of a life of poverty.

The house I was born in was situated on the side of a brook in a valley, completely isolated from others. It was a small, narrow house of a single room. At dusk, the solitude was particularly piercing. I would first kindle a small light called *tōmyō* [votive light] on the altar for the Buddha and family ancestors and another for the local guardian deities. When mother returned from fieldwork, she was pleased to see the house well lit and praised a job well done. This work of lighting votive candles was the early growth of my faith.

Whenever I fell ill, my parents were extremely concerned. The village doctor was called to examine me, but when the condition was serious, that did not suffice. They prayed to every Buddha and deity they had ever heard of. They vowed in their prayers, "Please heal this child's illness. If he recovers, we will take him to pay homage." When I recovered, I was busy visiting temples and shrines here and there to thank the Buddhas and deities. Some were as far as 30 kilometers away. I had to walk these great distances with straw-woven sandals tied around my small feet in my convalescence. Although a road had been opened, there were no houses at the skirt of Mount Kujū-zan[6] along the way. It was mother's pleasure to take me to temples and shrines for thanksgiving. Along the long journey, she tirelessly retold edifying stories on faith. She would say, "Your life was spared by Buddha and other divine beings. You must be thankful." My recovery from illness attested to the relationship of my life with the Buddhas and gods. These pilgrimages of thanksgiving were the gate to my life of faith.

The social climate in those days honored civil servants and slighted people outside the government. Those who worked for the Meiji Government were called *kanri* [government official]. Anyone from the old class system of samurai, farmers, artisans and merchants was able to become a government official. Yet, schooling and examination were required to enter the ranks of either a civil or military officer. Entering school and passing the examination for civil servants became a common aspiration of children. Despite their indigence, my parents sent me to school. I went off to school far from home elated, reciting a verse to inspire myself: "Once a man leaves his hometown with an aspiration, never shall he return, even in death, unless learning is achieved."

However, immediately upon graduation, instead of becoming a civil servant, I entered a Buddhist temple and became a novice monk, a profession most despised in society due to the anti-Buddhist policy enforced by the Meiji Revolution. All my relatives were indignant over this; my teachers at school were also against it. Yet, my mother alone believed in me and stood by me to honor my aspiration. She appeased the opposition of the relatives.

I stepped out on my mission abroad to disseminate the Buddha

---

6 九重山. A generic name for the volcanic belt in Ōita Prefecture that is part of the Aso National Park between Kumamoto Prefecture and Ōita Prefecture.

Dharma far and wide at the age of 33. In 1919 when I was 36 years old, I founded Nipponzan Myōhōji at Dalian, Manchuria. Since my father passed away in North Korea the same year, I welcomed my mother to the Dalian Dōjō. Life at the dōjō to spread the Dharma abroad was unrelentingly severe for my mother. The temperature drops to -20° Celsius in the winter. A stove was provided yet was seldom used. We lived bare-footed. A devotee, unable to bear seeing this, offered my mother a pair of *tabi* [Japanese split-toe socks]. Yet, in order to maintain the discipline of the dōjō life, I had to request her not to wear them. This is how my mother's life of religious practice began.

On September 1, 1923, a major earthquake struck the entire Kantō region[7] of Japan. It occurred on the heels of a succession of other natural calamities. At that time, I took the Siberian Railway to Harbin with the intention of spreading the Dharma in the Soviet Union, the land of communist revolution. I was in Harbin when the news of the great earthquake in Japan reached me. In the light of the cloudless mirror of *Risshō-ankoku-ron*, this natural calamity seemed to signify the total ruin of Japan. At a time when Japan may be facing imminent doom, I felt all else, be it my mission to the Soviet Union or the Western Heavens [Indian subcontinent], was of lesser urgency. I immediately returned to Japan and initiated my prayers of *Risshō-ankoku* [To give rise to the True Dharma for peace and tranquility of the land].

Starting with Tōkyō, Numazu, Nikkō, Shiobara, Nasu and the like,[8] we went wherever the Emperor stayed to pray. Not a single Nipponzan dōjō existed in any of these locations. We were compelled to live like *nobushi* [wandering warriors living in fields and mountains] or *yamabushi* [monks who practiced in mountains]. We were regarded with serious suspicion by the then Special High Police,[9] who interfered and obstructed our prayers. In the midst of all this, as soon as a Nipponzan's dōjō came about in Tagonoura, my mother became tonsured and wore the robe, becoming ordained to serve the Tathāgata. She was 77 years old. However, occasional arguments between me and the Special Higher Police agents, who were constantly shadowing me, made her anxious.

7 Mainland Japan's largest plain and most densely populated region surrounding Tōkyō, consisting of seven prefectures.

8 These are locations of the Imperial Palace and villas.

9 *Tokubetsu-kōtō-keisatsu* 特別高等警察, known as *Tokkō* for short. A civilian counterpart to the military police whose main function was to monitor and arrest those subversive to public order. Those who were deemed to have "dangerous thought" were all targeted.

I felt something must be done and, therefore, built a humble cottage as a dōjō in her birthplace, Hanaokayama, Kumamoto, and requested her to move there where I would visit from time to time. On each visit, I found her aging and becoming weaker. I immediately decided that I could not leave her there and brought her back to a dōjō in the Kantō region.

In the course of moving from one dōjō to another in the Kantō region, we were eventually welcomed by Mr. Ishiwatari Shichigoro, a resident of Nishikigaura, Atami. Initially a tool shed in the citrus field was our dōjō. Mother assisted the disciples by picking bracken, searching for mushrooms and making porridge with rice and vegetables to support their practice. We had neither miso nor soy sauce. Salt was the only seasoning. Not able to afford even a coarse tea, we drank hot water. Her health declined from old age in this life of austerity, and she left this world. She was 82 years old. I cannot but regret my inadequacy in filial piety as a son. To erect a stūpa at a place of her passing, to adorn the dōjō and to hold memorial services for her is the least expression of my heartfelt apology.

Mother, aware that her death drew near, left me her final vow one night. "I will pass on like a big tree that naturally falls. Yet, wherever the Reverend may go, I will be with you and will not fail to protect you." Her last vow was not an empty one. For 50 years since she left this world, I have believed in her divine protection and have never yielded to any adversity, even defeating the Demon King of the Sixth Heaven.[10] Not only was I able to fulfill my vow to disseminate Buddha Dharma in the Western Heavens, I now am truly at the forefront to spread the Dharma far and wide into the *Jambudvīpa* [the entire world]. Three events took place last year [1978] as final testament to the veracity of my mother's last vow. First, a great stūpa was dedicated on the mountainside of Sri Lanka's sacred mountain, Sri Pada. The dedication was on February 25, the anniversary of my mother's death. Second, on October 10, the [Milton Keynes] Development Corporation approved construction plans for a stūpa by Nipponzan Myōhōji in the evergreen paradise of Milton Keynes as the crowning touch to England's development of this new city. Third, on November 14, after a review, the Republic of India announced the recipient of the 1978

10 *Dairokuten* 第六天. The realm of desires. It is called *Takejizaiten* 他化自在大, *Paranirmitavaśavartin* [Sk], meaning "having power over [enjoyments] magically created by others [in the lower realms]." The palace of the Demon King is in this heaven. The Demon King of the Sixth Heaven also signifies persecution by state power.

Jawaharlal Nehru Award for International Understanding. To my great surprise, the honor was conferred on me. Every one of these events is a wonder. They were major Dharma works that no one, not even those close to me, could ever imagine. They were indeed the materialization of my mother's last vow.

Looking back on my life in this human world, I feel both fulfilled and grateful. Considering both life's joys and sorrows, it was truly a joyous, fleeting dream. "Long may a human life be; yet it does not exceed a hundred years. Everything in that time is but a fleeting dream."[11] I was blessed with the rare occurrence to be born human and to encounter the Buddha Dharma, most especially the Daimoku of the Lotus Sūtra. Even rarer, a blessing was to become its practitioner. Truly, truly, I must have paid homage to and made offerings to ten thousand billion Buddhas over incalculable eons in the past to be blessed with such a life. The time is drawing near when I will awaken from this transitory dream. Upon my awakening, I shall make haste to the Sacred Eagle Peak, the Pure Land, to call on Nichiren Daishōnin and, in the presence of the three Buddhas,[12] I shall surely see Maha Bhiksunī Gyōain Nisso.

For fifty years since the passing of my mother
I beat the Celestial Drum in the Western Heavens in solitude
The peace award conferred by India
Reverently offered to her spirit
As a requital of gratitude for her boundless benevolence

Fujii Gyōshōin Nichidatsu
Nipponzan Myōhōji

February 25, 2523 BE [1979]

---

11 松野殿御返事. *A Reply to Lord Matsuno*, written by Nichiren Daishōnin at Mount Minobu on December 9, 1276.
12 Buddha Śakyāmuni, Buddha Prabhūtaratna and Buddhas of the realms of ten directions emanated from Buddha Śākyamuni.

36

The Dawn of World Peace

April 8, 1979
Foundation Laying Ceremony of the
Milton Keynes Peace Pagoda
Milton Keynes, England

Na Mu Myō Hō Ren Ge Kyō

From the dawn of history to this very day, the record of humanity is marked by innumerable wars. What's held in common by these countless wars of varying scale throughout all ages and countries is that war is an agglomeration of every conceivable vice committed by humankind, a monument of bloodshed and tears.

As is suggested by the verse, "The glory of a commander rides on the deaths of innumerable soldiers,"[1] behind the glorious victory attributed to a politician who plans a war, or a general who commands it, are tens and hundreds of thousands of innocent men, women and children of all ages, who are injured, maimed and killed. Their corpses are left to rot in fields and mountains, their riches despoiled, their houses destroyed, and those who survive are enslaved. To appease the grief and resentment of those victimized by war, politicians and generals cloak the act of war, which is nothing more than murder and destruction, under a religious guise of "sacred" or "patriotic" and falsely bestow upon it the moral honor of being "just" and "valiant." Through the endorsement of war as a sacred, patriotic, just and valiant act, as though it were fundamental for human survival, the history of humanity has become a history of war.

War is not an act of ancient barbarians; it has been an act most frequently committed by so-called modern civilized men. Nations that pride themselves on the highest level of civilization in the world are those

1 From 亥歲詩 by late-Tang Dynasty poet Cao Song 曹松 [830?-901] written in 879.

who lavish a large percentage of their gross national product on war schemes under the pretext of national defense. The United States is ranked highest, followed by the Soviet Union. Japan is under constant pressure from the leaders of the United States to increase its military spending.

Will there ever come a time when war will cease? Yes, eventually there will come a time when war is no longer. How long will it take for us to get there? Nuclear physicists estimate that the era when war ends is will likely come by the end of this century, which is within the next twenty years. This will be called World War III. Under what conditions will war cease to exist, according to their scenario? Worldwide nuclear proliferation, escalation of greed, together with a sense of entitlement, make the use of nuclear weapons easier than ever, as if such use were a lawful right to be exercised. This would result in exterminating all existence on earth, including human civilization.

The atomic bombing of Hiroshima, Japan, on August 6 and Nagasaki on August 9, 1945 were warnings to be heeded; they were a ghastly prelude to the extermination of humanity to be expected in World War III. Once the mass destruction and carnage by atomic bombs were reported to the world, the scientists who developed them were jubilant to learn that the "scientific truth" they discovered brought about unprecedented and far-reaching results in its application. It was deemed a victory for science. The scientists did not believe that any crime was committed in developing the atomic bomb. They rationalized that the politicians and military officers, who used nuclear bombs in war, were the ones to be held accountable for the crimes of murder and destruction. The modern civilization of science is, as such, frivolous and reprehensible.

As might be expected, Albert Einstein, the authority and leading scientist whose work helped develop the atomic bomb, and Bertrand Russell, the philosopher, adopted a resolution out of concern for the potential tragedy of annihilating humanity by nuclear weapons. It reads, in part:

> In view of the fact that in any future world war, nuclear weapons will certainly be employed, and that such weapons threaten the continued existence of mankind, we urge the Governments of the world to realize, and to acknowledge publicly, that their purpose cannot be furthered by a world

> war, and we urge them, consequently, to find peaceful means for the settlement of all matters of dispute between them.[2]

In response to this resolution, the scientists of the world gathered in an obscure village in Canada called Pugwash and warned world leaders by presenting them with the above mentioned resolution. Successive meetings have taken place since, and scientists have repeatedly warned world leaders with this resolution. In spite of this, contrary to what they hoped for, the development, production and sales of nuclear weapons are even more widespread in the world. What has become obvious is that there is no way to salvage the civilization of science from being destroyed by its own inventions. The modest remedy provided in the scientists' warning already exists in the age-old moral code and is not anything new. If it were effective, there would not have been any war in the first place. It is of no use. And yet, the warning of possible human annihilation becomes all the more compelling.

Several thousands of years before the scientists issued their warnings, there was one who foresaw the threat of human annihilation, who not only warned of it but who also left behind a way to extricate humanity from it, namely the spiritual civilization. Without the spiritual civilization, humanity would have perished in the remote past due to greed, arrogance and war. More specifically when referring to the spiritual civilization, the World Honored One, Buddha Śākyamuni, the Preceptor of Buddhism, expounded in *The Eternal Duration of the Life of the Tathāgata* of the Lotus Sūtra:

> Even when all the living see at the kalpa's end,
> The conflagration burning,
> Tranquil is this realm of mine
> Ever-filled with celestial beings.

The catastrophe of humanity's annihilation is referred to here as the great conflagration, which means the explosion of man-made weapons,

---

2 Einstein-Russell Manifesto issued July 5, 1955. Einstein had signed it earlier in the year, before his death in April. The manifesto decried the likely spread of nuclear weapons and called for the great powers to renounce war as a means of resolving disputes in light of the unthinkable consequences that nuclear weapon use would bring.

the atomic and hydrogen bombs, also called the "second sun." The era of potential human obliteration is prophesized to take place 2,500 years after the passing of Buddha Śākyamuni, that is, in the fifth half-millennia of the five times five-hundred years after the demise of the Buddha.[3]

However, the *sahā* world, this very world in which we live, is a place where life is born and nurtured. It was never meant to be a place where all creation is reduced to ashes. "This realm of mine" is inherently tranquil. Humankind born in this world, by nature, seeks joy and aspires to create peace. We were not born to seek ruin or commit murder and destruction. This nature is what makes a spiritual remedy efficacious.

Fear created by nuclear weapons is, after all, a product of atrocious machines contrived by a few scientists. These horrendous machines cannot trigger deadly explosions on their own; they require a human hand. A human hand does not move on its own volition. It moves at the command of the human mind. A multitude of evils are committed by the human mind, yet it is not completely stuck in evil. The human mind works day and night engaging in activities that are called "good" by morality, "love" by Christianity, and "compassion" by Buddhism. Current human society on earth attests to the workings of goodness in the mind, which has enabled this society to survive and flourish and ever prevail over evil. The development of scientific truth is neither good nor evil. When scientific development is abused by the evil in the mind, the crisis of potential human extermination follows. Animals, in general, do not judge between good and evil, neither are they given guidance on compassion and love. Brute force is what they rely on. Animals that prosper, to some extent, are those species that lead a life more akin to compassion and love than violence.

I believe in the possibility of uniting the minds of billions of people in goodness. Couples create the foundation for humanity's survival when they are able to love each other and stay together for life, raising offspring. The principle of building world peace is found here. When humanity awakens to the wondrous marvel of the forces of heaven and earth, the unrestricted free power of nature, then humanity comes to appreciate the limit of its power. This is where animism originates. With

3 Please refer to *To My Disciples: Nippozan Will Not Be Daunted by State Power*, footnote 2, p. 194.

the awareness of the wondrous activities of the human mind comes faith in spirituality, religion.

Religious teachings are given to sustain religious faith. Putting religious teachings into action is called *shugyō* [practice]. Religious practice needs to be in its simplest form to allow it to be easily performed. That is, to place palms together, bow with the body, chant Na Mu Myō Hō Ren Ge Kyō through the mouth and embrace veneration in the heart and mind. The fervent desire of the World Honored One, Buddha Śākyamuni, to provide spiritual deliverance is achieved through such minute actions by us sentient beings. If the spiritual, religious lessons from the heavens and earth, the universe, were applied to human society, and if people mutually respected one another, where would there be room for war to occur? After all, the root cause of war, nuclear war, is a lack of mutual respect and veneration. It is a human catastrophe incurred by the civilization of science where spirituality, religion and faith are absent.

A civilization of science lacks moral value because it assumes human existence depends upon prevailing in competition, a notion void of spiritual dignity. This notion can be seen in the importance placed on athletic games, such as the Olympic Games. Its authoritative belief in "survival of the fittest" predicated the development of nuclear weapons and the intensification of war. When abolition of nuclear weapons and war is sought in the human mind, human beings can embrace spirituality, follow religious teachings and act on their beliefs with effortless ease. First and foremost, we must embrace and adhere to the precept of "not to take life," as laid down by the World Honored One. To deprive others of life requires skill and instruments. Neither skill nor equipment is required to not take life. The only requirement is to embrace and adhere to the precept of not to take life.

When the precept of not to take life is embraced, nuclear weapons will be abhorred and war rejected. Then the future of humanity will be free from fear, abounding with life and prosperity. To mark the fall of the civilization of science at this most beautiful site in the newly-created peace city of Milton Keynes, England, I reverently perform the foundation laying ceremony of the stūpa, out of my wish to usher in the dawn of world peace by enshrining the genuine relics of the World Honored One, Buddha Śākyamuni, who bestowed upon us the precept

At Milton Keynes, U.K., 1981

against taking life for the sake of bringing an end to war and to deliver humanity from the crisis of annihilation.

With deep veneration,

Nipponzan Myōhōji
Fujii Nichidatsu

37

Look Up to the Heavens, Bow to the Earth and Pray

May 19, 1979
Yumeno-shima, Tōkyō

Na Mu Myō Hō Ren Ge Kyō

I have come to join you on this occasion that marks the beginning of the great national peace march. I was somehow able to take a few steps with you until last year, but this year I am not even able to do that. Instead, I have come to see the marchers off.

Today, the peace walk, this movement against nuclear weapons, is taking place throughout the globe. A protest rally was held at a nuclear weapons manufacturing facility in the United States. I am told that fifteen thousand people participated in the event. Among them were Native Americans, whose presence was not seen before in demonstrations against nuclear weapons. In England, a cross-country peace walk was launched in mid-April, passing by various military bases and nuclear weapon sites. This walk will continue until the beginning of June.

The people of the world are now aware of the nuclear threat. The issue facing humanity today is how to dispel potential disasters by nuclear weapons. We walk to resolve this very issue. It appears that everyone is walking. We look up to the heavens, bow to the earth and pray. One day when this becomes a force so compelling that it moves heaven and earth, nuclear weapons would have no place in the world. We walk for that day.

Venerating the walkers as they begin the Tōkyō to Hiroshima Peace Walk, May 19, 1979.

38

Kanjin-Honzon

August 31, 1979
Atami Dōjō, Japan

We are said to have become human through gradual steps of nature. As such, we are born with the nature of beasts. However, we were born as human beings so that we may realize God who dwells within our hearts. This is the basic distinction between the beasts and us. Realizing God is the privilege given to us.

This can happen only when we voluntarily give up the use of physical force and when we become aware of the nonviolence which lies dormant in our hearts. We can only realize God through faith.

(From the *Precept to the Gandhi Seva Sangh*)[1]

According to the theory of evolution, human beings evolved from one variety of apes. Bestiality is said, therefore, to be inherent in humans. However, what characterizes the evolved human is not bestiality but rather the ability to reflect upon, control and free oneself from physical desire and beastliness along with a yearning to discover and venerate the sublime God, which is invisible and dormant, in one's mind. This act is called faith. Spiritual acts make human life unique. Such acts are not seen in any animal other than human beings.

---

1 English rendition by the translator based on a Japanese translation of Gandhi's words that Guruji cites. The original English text by Gandhi is as follows: "I am ready to believe that we are evolved from the animal into the human state. But we are born as human beings in order that we may realize God who dwells within our hearts. This is the basic distinction between us and the beasts. This can happen only when we voluntarily give up the use of physical force and when we develop the nonviolence which lies dormant in our hearts. It can be awakened only through real strength."

Portrait of Guruji from behind.

Depth of yearning to discover God and truth is what distinguishes progress and development in human society. Gandhiji said discovering God and worshipping God become possible through a faith steeped in the spirit of nonviolence and pursuit of truth, all of which lie dormant in the heart and mind.

Buddha Śākyamuni is the most highly esteemed being in the human world. He was born, lived and died in the human world. He is revered for attaining the Buddha-body of peerless dignity while living his life like anyone else. In every person's heart and mind there equally exists an innate quality that enables her or him to attain the Buddha- body just like Buddha Śākyamuni. It is called the Buddha-nature. Buddha Śākyamuni preached in the Mahā-Parinirvāna Sūtra that all living creatures possess Buddha-nature. Buddha Śākyamuni is the fullest embodiment of the Buddha-nature in a human body.

The *Kanjin-honzon-shō*[2] cites *The Eternal Duration of the Life of the Tathāgata* of the Lotus Sūtra to prove the existence of Buddha-nature.

> *The Eternal Duration of the Life of the Tathāgata* states, "It has been infinite, boundless hundreds of thousands of myriads of kotis of nayutas[3] of kalpas since I attained Buddhahood." This means that Buddha Śākyamuni, who dwells in our heart and mind, is the ancient Buddha[4] without beginning who manifests in three Buddha-bodies and attained Buddhahood in the eternal past described as 500 dust-particle kalpas ago.

Although called Buddha-nature, it does not imply that there is a Buddha within our hearts and minds waiting to become complete. It is a fully perfected Buddha immemorial whose transcendental powers and light are yet to manifest in the human mind and heart. When we believe in the presence of the ancient Buddha who resides in our hearts and minds, the purpose of our lives becomes dignified. We then dare not be arrogant towards any one and can only venerate them. The ancient Buddha in our

---

2 . Please refer to *Nuclear Technology*, footnote 26, p. 94.

3 *Nayutas*. A unit of number in India representing 100 billion.

4 *Kobutsu* 古仏. Ancient Buddha is a reference to the primordial Buddha without beginning, the source of all emanative Buddhas, as distinguished from finite Buddhas. The Eternal Buddha Śākyamuni is also referred to as *Honbutsu* 本仏Origin Buddha.

mind and the ancient Buddha in the minds of others are one in the same. When the Buddha in our minds worships the Buddha in the minds of others, in turn the Buddha in the minds of others worships the Buddha who resides within us. When we bow in veneration towards the mirror, our reflection bows back. This is known as the veneration free of the perception of duality of oneself and others.[5] Reverence between oneself and others becomes one and inseparable. That is when peace becomes a reality, and war ceases to exist. The voice of the ancient Buddha, who resides in the heart and mind of others and in our own, was recorded in 84,000 discourses expounded through the mouth of the World Honored One, Buddha Śākyamuni.

However, the modern civilization cannot hear or see a single phrase or *gātha*. Here lies the grief and agony of the modern civilization.

> Wholeheartedly wishing to see the Buddha,
> Not sparing their body and life. . .[6]

This half *gātha* is the origin of spiritual civilization. Human beings are not animals of mere physical existence. The undivided heart and mind ardently wishing to see the invisible God, the ancient Buddha who has no beginning, the truth of peace, becomes God, the Truth and the ancient Buddha. Nichiren Daishōnin taught that the Buddha exists in the fervor to see the Buddha. The earnestness of the heart and mind to see the Buddha is the privilege of humans that Gandhiji referred to. This working of the spirit is faith.

---

5 *Jita-funi-no-raihai* 自他不二の礼拝.
6 Chapter XVI of the Lotus Sūtra, *The Eternal Duration of the Life of the Tathāgata*.

39

The Unity of Life

June 17, 1980
Excerpts from conversations with Bill Wahpepah
of the American Indian Movement
Kiyosumi Dōjō, Japan

A troop of monkeys came here this morning and spent a long time playing, climbing the tree next to the altar room while we were having our morning prayer practice. The monkeys, too, seemed to like our prayer. This dense mountain, I'm told, is a habitat for about 50 Japanese monkeys.

There is a delightful story about monkeys handed down in Kamakura. Nichiren Daishōnin had a thatched hut in Kamakura, and those of a different sect plotted a raid.[1] They conspired to set his hut on fire in the middle of the night and beat him to death as he ran to escape. On the evening of the planned assault, monkeys came and tugged Nichiren Daishōnin's sleeve and ushered him up the mountain. Before long, his hut was on fire. A temple now stands there.

All beings, creatures and humans, are meant to create a world of joy and comfort together. Failure to understand this relationship led to killing and being killed. Unable to appreciate each other, we parted ways out of fear and animosity. This was not limited to humans and animals. Enmity between human beings has incurred today's threat of nuclear war. People have come to kill each other over differences in thinking. Instead of conceiving ways to coexist, people think of ways to kill each other. This is the impasse bred by the irreligiousness of modern times.

Religious life teaches to live and allow others to live, a way of life where people, monkeys, birds and other forms of life live amicably together. In the modern civilization, what developed was the

---

1 Persecution at Matsubagayatsu 松葉ヶ谷の法難, 1260.

January 1974,
Pokhara, Nepal.

art of killing. If humanity hopes to survive in the future, we must revert to seeing life from a spiritual point of view. Then mountains, rivers, snakes, monkeys and everything else become our friends. We no longer hold enmity against them, rather they complement our lives.

Judaism, Christianity and Islam teach that creation, including heaven, earth and human beings, came from God. That much I understand. However, when human beings, God's creation, did wrong, God regretted the force of evil pervading the earth and decided to destroy creation. God planned to destroy everything except for a pair of each animal. The Old Testament relates this to us as Noah's Ark and the Deluge.

However, the very idea of destroying the wicked can be exploited by the wicked. Who are the wicked anyway? Religion was handed down in the world to transform the wicked to good rather than to destroy them. In Buddhism, the Buddha appeared to reveal this teaching, and monks will also appear to carry and spread the Buddha's teaching against taking life.

This is what Buddha Dharma is about. Buddha Dharma prohibits the taking of life, and there are festivals in which people bring fish and even domestic animals from their households to set them free. This tradition is known as *hōjōe.*[2] It means to release life from captivity, to free them. Such a teaching is woven into our festivals.

I have come to know the Native Americans during my visits to the United States, but never have I heard from them that the Creator uses power to destroy all life. They are also taught that life is to be nurtured and protected. This is what we have in common.

We seek peace in our lives. So how can we create a peaceful life? *Ankoku* means to create a peaceful world. *Risshō* means to embrace the truth, the genuine teachings, to hold them in high esteem above anything else. The root issue has nothing to do with the tangible, but with truth. Truth may sound abstract and intangible; in essence, it gives primacy to the true teachings of sages. Without it a peaceful world cannot be built. *Risshō-ankoku* is an issue of the heart and mind. Its core concerns the heart and mind. To give you an analogy, *ankoku* [peace of the land] is like a shadow cast by *risshō. Risshō* is its substance. *Ankoku* is a manifestation of *risshō.* The world established on modern day materialism attempts to create peace without *risshō.* Deadlocks are seen everywhere we go due to the absence of true spiritual teachings, as in China or the Soviet Union where revolutions were based on materialism. Vietnam is a recent example. The prevailing principle that guides nations is a materialism focused solely on *ankoku*, providing comfort, such as feeding the nation, but disregarding the essential truth upon which a nation stands.

After Japan's defeat in the war, I believed it essential to once again give rise to the teachings of the Buddha in restoring the nation. I built stūpas for that reason. It requires tremendous amounts of material, yet I embarked on this plan with nothing. The government has yet to subsidize a penny towards any of the stūpas. Even prefectual governors rarely showed up. Nevertheless, Buddha Dharma has finally been restored in the hearts and minds of the people. We have built more than fifty stūpas in Japan. They are symbols of peace, which will unite the entire world. The nations of Asia are primarily Buddhist, and their people joyously make homage to the stūpas.

---

2 A Buddhist custom of releasing creatures to accumulate virtue and to admonish the taking of life. This custom eventually spread to Shintō shrines, and the tradition lives on.

40

The Turning Point of the Civilization of Science

September 21, 1980
On the Dedication of the Milton Keynes Stūpa
Milton Keynes, England

THE 30TH PUGWASH CONFERENCE was held over six days starting on August 20th of this year at an old castle in Brueken, a suburb in Utrecht, the Netherlands. Its final declaration stated, "Unless prompt and effective steps are taken to reduce and eliminate the tendency to arms proliferation, we foresee a major catastrophic nuclear war before the end of this century." It continued by declaring, "In these circumstances, our duty as human beings and scientists is clear—we must opt for survival." Dr. Yukawa Hideki of Japan sent a message to the Russell and Einstein Manifesto Session of the Pugwash Conference stating that scientists cannot evade responsibility for creating the present situation. His is a voice of conscience.

The six-day Pugwash Conference was attended by Nobel Peace Prize laureates and people of wisdom and learning from East, West, South and North, and yet, lamentably, it was practically ignored by the West European press. This silence by the press points to the grave issue faced by the Pugwash Conference. The scientists attending the meeting are keenly aware of the impending total human catastrophe should nuclear proliferation continue, yet, they are overcome by a sense of powerlessness because they are unable to eradicate this crisis. However, Dr. Joseph Rotblat,[1] a professor from London who attended the Pugwash Conference in the Netherlands on his way back from an August 6 conference in Hiroshima, noted that while both pessimistic and optimistic views exist,

---

1 Sir Joseph Rotblat [1908–2005] was a Polish-born, British-naturalized physicist. His experience with the Nazi takeover of his native Poland led him to work on an atomic bomb in England and later with the Manhattan Project at Los Alamos. However, his increasing qualms over the use of a nuclear weapon led him to be the only physicist to leave the Manhattan Project on the grounds of conscience. After World War II, he became a tireless

Inaugural Ceremony for the Milton Keynes [U.K.] Peace Pagoda, September 21, 1980.

---

advocate for nuclear disarmament, and his work on nuclear fall-out was a major contributor to the agreement of the Partial Test Ban Treaty. A signatory of the Russell-Einstein manifesto, he was secretary general of the Pugwash Conferences on Science and World Affairs from its founding in 1957 until 1973. In conjunction with the Pugwash Conferences, he received the Nobel Peace Prize in 1995 for efforts towards nuclear disarmament.

all is lost if we become pessimists. Up to this point I have been citing excerpts from an article in the Asahi Newspaper on September 2 entitled *The Prevailing Powerlessness Among Scientists.*

[Albert] Einstein was alarmed by the potential danger of Nazi Germany developing nuclear weapons and recommended to the then American president [Franklin Roosevelt] that the U.S. develop its own, cooperating in the effort. The United States detonated the world's first nuclear explosion on July 16, 1945 at a test site in Alamogordo, New Mexico. Three weeks later, on August 6, the second nuclear detonation devastated Hiroshima. In quick succession, the third nuclear explosion carried out by the United States on August 9 razed Nagasaki. The brutal destruction was unprecedented in the entire history of war.

Upon arrival in Tōkyō, General MacArthur immediately declared that the use of atomic bombs brought an early conclusion to the war and saved the lives of many American soldiers, although he admitted that Japan was no longer capable of even producing bullets. He gave no hint of reflecting in the slightest on the atrocious ravages of the atomic bombing. An American first lady [Eleanor Roosevelt] subsequently came to Japan and visited cities ruined by war. She, likewise, showed no sign of regret regarding the atomic devastation. The only American penitent of the crime of the atomic bombing was an airman [who flew a reconnaissance plane in the Hiroshima bombing]. He later suffered from mental illness and since has passed away.

Had Hitler developed nuclear weapons he could not have used them in a crueler way than Truman. Regardless of who uses them, the catastrophe is no different. The root cause of the atrocity is in the development of nuclear weapons. It lies in the advancement of the civilization of science because the truth discovered by science is unrelated to human morality. Technology developed by science has nothing to do with the survival of humankind. We are told that the American scientists clapped their hands in jubilation upon hearing the reports of the detonated atomic bombs and the utter destruction of Hiroshima and Nagasaki. How woeful are the scientists. Cursed are the scientists.

Like any human being, scientists who developed nuclear weapons assert that they have a duty to present a path for survival amidst the crisis created by these weapons. Sadly, no path for survival is available in the civilization of science—not in its politics, economics, military or anywhere else. The pervading powerlessness among scientists accurately acknowledges this fact. If they wish to opt for survival, they might still be able to find a single path. Promptly and without hesitation, they must abandon their profession as scientists, sever themselves from employment with the government or military-industrial complex and run over hill and dale crying out their desire to survive. They may not know where to find the path to survival, but the foremost prerequisite for survival is to believe that it is there. Faith in an inscrutable power that enables us to survive is essential, to believe that there is One who manifests immeasurable transcendental powers for the sake of rescuing us. A firmly-rooted faith shall immediately dissipate the scientists' sense of powerlessness like smoke vanishing in thin air. In that very moment, scientists become people of faith. Because they know the harm wreaked by the civilization of science, they possess the greatest potential to become people of faith.

War is the most direct harm inflicted on society by the civilization of science. Those who make war their trade are called soldiers. Said military personnel prevaricate by calling themselves members of the self-defense force instead of murderers or members of killing squads. All anticipate war to result in a clear-cut victory. Nuclear weapons, weapons of mass slaughter, are prized because they can secure this certain victory. Nuclear weapons cannot be eliminated so long as soldiers exist.

The adverse effect of the civilization of science lies in the abuse of power. Those who seize power are called politicians. Power is amassed through military might. Therefore, military officers frequently become politicians. So long as politicians exist, there is little hope of abolishing nuclear weapons.

In his State of the Union address, President Nixon stated that ranking second among world powers is not an option for the United States. The intent behind a statement like this by a political leader is to compel research and development of weapons that will prevail in a nuclear war and to keep on course with the nuclear arms race. President Eisenhower issued a warning in his last message to the nation to "guard against the acquisition of unwarranted influence, whether sought or unsought, by the military-industrial complex." Scientists, too, have joined in this work, and nuclear development goes on. They know it must be stopped, but are at a loss where to start.

In the final analysis, the civilization of science is a civilization of war, a civilization of violence and a civilization of murder and destruction. The tragedy of killing and destruction is caused by ignorance regarding the true nature of existence and afflictions[2] in the human heart and mind. Ignorance and afflictions originate in suspicion, jealousy and mistrust. Like claws of a beast or fangs of a poisonous snake, they are not innately essential for survival. The necessity to sharpen claws and fangs arises from suspicion and mistrust of other animals. Dogs and cats are also beasts, and cobras are poisonous snakes. Nevertheless, once domesticated, they grow gentle, and their trust and allegiance to their caretaker makes the use of claws and fangs unnecessary.

It is reported that the European press completely ignored this conference to assess the dangers posed to human survival, held from August 20 by world intellectuals at an old castle in Brueken, Netherlands. But this is nothing new. Although Einstein urged that deliberation on the crisis confronting the survival of humankind be given top priority, only a handful of scientists held a gathering. A year before the atomic bombs were dropped on Hiroshima and Nagasaki, Niels Bohr,[3] a Danish physicist, presented a memorandum to President Roosevelt and Prime Minister Churchill stating, "The fact of immediate preponderance is, however, that a weapon of an unparalleled power is being created . . . Unless, indeed, some agreement about the control of the use of the new active materials can be obtained in due time, any temporary advantage, however great, may be outweighed by a perpetual menace to human security."[4] Roosevelt and Churchill heard this plea but failed to heed it.

On June 26, 1945, the United Nations Charter was signed in San Francisco. Maintaining international peace and security was declared to be one of its main purposes and principles. The same year, on August 6 and August 9, atomic bombs were dropped on Hiroshima and Nagasaki. By the time the UN Charter became effective on October 24, 1945, disarmament was already a significant challenge. The UN Security Council was faced with the urgent task of regulating production and use

---

2 *Bonnō* 煩悩, mental functions which disturb and pollute the mind and body; earthly passions.

3 Niels Henrik David Bohr [1885-1962] received the Nobel Prize for physics in 1922 for his contributions to the understanding of the atomic structure and quantum mechanics. He was a member of the secret Los Alamos physicists' team working on the Manhattan Project. He organized the first Atoms for Peace conference in Geneva in 1955 and was a recipient of the 1957 U.S. Atoms for Peace Award.

4 Bohr memorandum of April 2, 1944 cited in his letter to the United Nations. *Impact of Science on Society*, Vol. I, No.2, 1950, pg. 68, Open Letter dated 9 June 1950.

of nuclear weapons by setting up a mechanism to bring nuclear weapons under international control, and the United Nations Atomic Energy Commission was established in January 1946.

In 1961, the Soviet Union and the United States collaborated in submitting a plan for general and complete disarmament to the United Nations. This important document provides landmarks and guidelines for disarmament today. Disarmament negotiations began in 1961, and the Committee on Disarmament held meetings. Although various agreements were reached, the comprehensive measure of general and complete disarmament was forsaken. In this way, the fact that the very existence of nuclear weapons constitutes the greatest crime ever was lost. Subsequent disarmament negotiations were wasted on discussions of partial measures. The long history of failure to reach an effective agreement on disarmament may suggest that establishing any significant measure in this area is impossible. However, we cannot give in to despair.

The arms race is an absurdity. The more advanced the weapon, the more inhumane. The more recent the war, the more brutal. Wars have occurred everywhere since ancient times, yet there existed laws governing conduct in war in accordance with the times. In modern warfare, rules of war were accepted as international law. In spite of this, nuclear war ruthlessly trampled existing laws of war underfoot. How could there be hope for any law to effectively regulate a war that does not even fear the appalling risk of wiping out the human race? The military, industrial and scientific circles are fully aware of the absurdity and immorality of war and the arms buildup. Notwithstanding this knowledge, the arms race is perpetuated, driving to despair even those who champion optimism on the issue of human survival. The general public, then, is ostensibly left helpless and doomed.

What rescues humans from despair is religious faith. There is an existence that instills faith in resurrection and hope for rebirth for those who seem destined to perish in nuclear war as a consequence of progress in the civilization of science. It is the One with absolute spiritual authority, called God or Buddha in religion. Those who commit the grave crime of human holocaust are called demons. Demons wear a human face and live among us as scientists, soldiers, politicians and the like.

One who offers resurrection and restores humanity from the brink of extinction is not a concept of meditation or delusion, but likewise had a human face, took a human form and lived among us. He liberated himself from doing wrong, and has extricated humans from suffering, brought peace to societies, caused cultures to blossom, taught the dignity of life, inspired mutual veneration and expounded on the true nature of cause and effect. This person called Buddha, the World Honored One, lived a finite life as a person. Yet his true being is eternally present and never perishes. The sūtra describes the promise he made to forever rescue and protect humankind. Believing in this promise, the sacred relics of Lord Buddha were sought, and the stūpa was built and offerings made to honor the Buddha here at the lakeside of North Willen Lake, Milton Keynes, England.

What a phenomenal wonder! How auspicious were the omens that accompanied the stūpa's emergence! When news spread that a stūpa was to be built in the newly developed peace city of Milton Keynes, England, a European country with hardly any Buddhists, people representing 24 different nationalities came with food and sleeping bags to offer their service and labor. Some stayed for several days, others several tens of days. With the exception of the nine-ring ornamental spire and the roof over the dome of the stūpa, the main body of the stūpa was completed by a mere ten or so monks and nuns of the order!

What a phenomenal wonder! The completed stūpa has started to blow a fresh breeze of peace into the hearts and minds of the European people, starting with the British, and people from far and near have come to its inaugural ceremony. Representatives of Asian Buddhist countries have also gathered in jubilation. People from North America and the Soviet Union are here, too. Perhaps this is the greatest ceremony in Buddhist history, maybe even in the history of religion. The great transcendental powers to liberate humanity are manifest from the eternal and ever present World Honored One, Buddha Śākyamuni, an auspicious prelude to free humanity from the menace of nuclear weapons.

So at the pinnacle of the civilization of science, the scientists issue warnings and the Committee for Disarmament signs agreements, and yet the arms race continues to develop nuclear weapons. Humanity seems to have no choice but to despair. If humanity desires to survive, it must abandon the civilization of science and create a different civilization, namely, a spiritual civilization. A spiritual civilization is a civilization of faith. By civilization of faith I am specifically referring to a civilization of Buddhist teachings.

A Buddhist civilization teaches the Three Refuges and the Five Precepts.[5] In order to cause human beings to honor, venerate and make offerings to everything from the distant universe to the heavens and earth and to human society closer at hand, the three jewels of Buddha, Dharma and Sangha are chosen as representatives for veneration. Destruction and wars occur when they are not held in esteem.

The Five Precepts teach that there are two types of deeds—good or evil—and encourages a person to do good instead of evil. What is a good deed? The greatest good is to protect the lives of all living things. What is an evil deed? The greatest evil is to take the life of any living being. However, the reality of the world we live in is conducive to one form of life sustaining itself by feeding on other forms of life. This predicament makes killing unavoidable. We know this law as "survival of the fittest." This phenomenon is widely seen in the animal world. Prohibiting it is not the purpose of the precept against taking life. Humans, likewise, kill other animals for food. To prohibit this practice, the precept against taking life widely encourages the observance of a Buddhist rite called *hōjōe*[6] [a ceremony to release animals from captivity]. The precept against taking life starts by prohibiting the killing of life for sustenance, yet the true essence of the precept is to ultimately and absolutely forbid humans from killing each other.

The harsh punishment for violating and destroying the fundamental precept against killing is this modern terror, the menace of the civilization of science and the horror of nuclear weapons. If we are to explore a path for survival in modern times, that path is not found in the optimism of a scientist nor in agreements that emerge from disarmament conferences, rather it is found by believing in the merit and adhering to the foremost of the five Buddhist precepts, the precept against taking life.

Why are we not to do evil? Why must humans do good? The truth of causation is expounded in Buddha Dharma in order to answer this question. An iniquitous act begets the fruit of suffering. Good acts bear the fruit of comfort and joy. All humans seek to avoid suffering and desire peace and comfort. It is a natural urge. If so, one must do good to first create a good cause. The law of causation is irrefutable and cannot

---

5 *Sanki-gokai* 三帰五戒. The Three Refuges are taking refuge in the Buddha, Dharma and Sangha. The precepts are prohibitions against murder, lust, theft, lying and intemperance.

6 放生会.

be changed. To willfully do evil and expect comfort and joy is called a delusion. Those who commit wrongs never think of the inevitable result of pain and suffering that follows. It is called the distorted view that rejects the just law of causation.

The civilization of science created the modern state. A state is an institution to protect material interests, and a state exercises its sovereignty in order to preserve those interests. Since countries compete in their interests, rivalry and wars occur. Only victory or defeat matter in war; good or evil is never an issue. To prevail in war, the question of good or evil is ignored. No peace and comfort can exist where the issue of good or evil is disregarded. Let us say a country was to wage war to preserve its interest and security, and that country uses nuclear weapons to prevail. The use of nuclear weapons becomes the cause that brings on the result of nuclear destruction and ends up shattering the very interest and security of the nation for which it went to war.

Until the mid-1940s, the United States was unconcerned about losing a war from an overseas attack. First, it was blessed geographically. Secondly, it had military might. In 1945, the United States won the war after completely destroying Hiroshima and Nagasaki and exterminating their citizens by the nuclear weapons it developed. The United States never considered the use of nuclear weapons a grave crime against humanity; on the contrary, it valued them as guardians of peace and furiously developed, produced and stockpiled them.

This weapon build-up caused the Soviet Union to develop their own nuclear weapons. By the mid-1950s, the Soviet Union had an arsenal sufficient to kill millions or even tens of millions of Americans in a single day by use of nuclear weapons and long range delivery systems. By the late 1960s, it had developed the capacity to destroy every city in the United States and annihilate the entire American population within an hour. Presently, the United States has absolutely no available means to prevent total destruction by Soviet missiles.

On the other hand, the United States can also completely destroy Soviet cities, and no means exist for the Soviet Union to prevent it. The cities and people of both the United States and the Soviet Union are exposed to unlimited danger. The evil cause made when the United States of America completely destroyed Hiroshima and Nagasaki has yet to result in complete destruction of its cities and citizens. Just as cucumbers grow from cucumber seeds and eggplants from eggplant seeds, the outcome and the cause is preached to be of the same kind according to the law of causation. Consequently, averting evil and doing good will bring the desired result of protecting the nation's interest and security.

When we believe in the just truth of the law of causation, we must completely abolish arms, not only nuclear weapons but all tools of killing and destruction and all means of war. Then, for the first time, the Buddhist precept against taking life is embraced and held. When the precept against killing is embraced and held, for the first time we become Buddhist. When the people of the world become Buddhists, true peace will materialize in the world. In the chapter of the *The Eternal Duration of the Life of the Tathāgatha* of the Lotus Sūtra it says:

> Even when all the living see, at the kalpa's end,
> The conflagration burning,
> Tranquil is this realm of mine

In the *Nyosetsu-shugyō-shō* Nichiren Daishōnin states:

> . . . when all the people of the world forgo the various vehicles for the One Buddha Vehicle with only the Sublime Dharma burgeoning throughout the lands, the people of the world at that time will come to chant Na Mu Myō Hō Ren Ge Kyō in one voice. The wind will no longer buffet the branches to scatter leaves, and the tempered rain will no longer break the clods of soil. The world will prosper as in the times of Fu Hsi and Shen Nung[7] with crops abundant. Ominous calamities in this life will be dispelled, and the means to longevity acquired. Let you all discern the aforementioned. The time shall come when the truth of the imperishability of the Person and the Dharma is evinced. Doubt not the veracity of the [Lotus] sūtra, which assures peace and tranquility in this actual world . . .

Preserving the precept against taking life taught by Buddha is the assurance of peace and tranquility in this world. Violation of the Buddhist

7 Please refer to *Single Word of Mystery*, footnote 17, p. 205.

precept against taking life would ultimately bring about the great calamity of humanity's annihilation. Out of ignorance the civilization of science did not recognize murder and destruction by humans as the inviolable great evil and failed to prohibit them. There are no ethics in science's development. There is no distinction of right and wrong in truth discovered by science. Only mathematical calculations exist. If the numbers add up, any horrific killing or destruction is committed. Its anti-religious logic, the result of ceaseless development of nuclear weapons, brought on the irredeemable fear of nuclear weapons in the modern age. The menace of annihilation of the human race is neither God's wrath nor a calamity brought by the heavens, but a tragedy manifested by the delusion of the civilization of science.

In closing I must mention one more miracle: today's weather. The forecast was rain continuing from yesterday. England is known for rain, particularly at this time of year. The beautiful weather that blessed us today is a noteworthy miracle in England of late. This could be said to be a miracle that the heavens sent, but there is an old Christian church nearby. Prayers are offered daily by people who gather there. Word came to me that the people at the church all prayed for a fine weather on the 21st for the dedication of the stūpa. We are witnesses to the wondrous power of the heart and mind of the people that moved the heavens.

41

We Are Messengers of the World Honored One

December 31, 1980
Kiyosumi Dōjō, Japan

This was truly an auspicious year, a year that can be said to mark the beginning of Nipponzan's effort to spread the Dharma throughout the *Jambudvīpa*.[1] Tomorrow we greet the first day of the year that commemorates the 700th anniversary of Ososhi-sama's[2] passing. I feel the coming year will bustle with activities worthy of the arrival of the time for the Dharma to be spread far and wide. Nipponzan has chosen this Kiyosumi Dōjō as the location for the grand ceremony of the 700th anniversary.

At the age of 12, Nichiren Daishōnin entered this mountain and was also later ordained here.[3] Likewise, it was at this mountain where he first chanted Na Mu Myō Hō Ren Ge Kyō, the Buddha Dharma of Japan. From this mountain, we can see the stūpa at Kominato,[4] built to memorialize his birthplace. I would think that around age 12, he must have gazed towards the heaven and earth of Kominato, longing for his parents. Such is the karmic significance of this mountain. This dōjō was built out of my wish to commemorate the 700th anniversary at this mountain. Though time was limited, fortunately it was realized. I would like to invite leaders of the world peace movement and of religious circles to this mountain to

---

1 *Ichien-budai* or *enbudai* 一閻浮堤、閻浮提. The world of humans, the entire world.
2 御祖師様. Founding master of the school, Nichiren Daishōnin.
3 In 1233 Nichiren Daishōnin, then called Zennichi-maro 善日麿, entered Mount Kiyosumi at the age of 12 and became a disciple of Dōzenbō 道善房. He was formally ordained and shaved his head at the age of 16 in 1237, with the ordination name Zeshōbō Renchō 是聖房蓮長.
4 Kominato 小湊 is a small fishing port in the current southern Chiba Prefecture that faces the Pacific. Nichiren Daishōnin was born here and was later ordained at Seichōji Temple, also called Kiyosumi Temple [different pronunciation of the same kanji characters], located at Mt. Kiyosumi. Guruji is referring to a stūpa erected at Nichiren Daishōnin's birthplace in Kominato village by Nipponzan Myōhōji on October 10, 1972.

resolve the impending danger threatening modern humanity.

Buddha Dharma of Japan, as embodied in *Risshō-ankoku-ron*, which Nichiren Daishōnin advocated throughout his life, is the creed upon which he founded a new school after his awakening as the reincarnation of Bodhisattva Superior Practice,[5] Lord Buddha's disciple sent to emancipate the Era of Final Dharma. For the most part, Buddhism in Japan was studied and introduced from Korea and China. Even Dengyō Daishi[6] traveled to T'ang,[7] China. The same is true with Kōbō.[8] Likewise, Zen Masters Eisai[9] and Dōgen[10] traveled to China, studied Buddha Dharma and brought it back. The Nenbutsu teachings developed in China.[11] In Japan, a scholar monk at Mount Hiei[12] named Genkū[13] perused a book[14] and started to chant and spread "Na-mu Amidabutsu," but this was a teaching he inherited that had already spread outside Japan. Nenbutsu is the teaching of transmigration to the Western Pure Land in the life after death. That is not true with the Zen School. The Zen School teaches that perceiving the truth with clarity in the mind[15] is Buddha Dharma. All

---

5 *Jōgyō-Bosatsu*, 上行菩薩. In Chapter XV of the Lotus Sūtra, *The Bodhisattvas Who Emerge From The Earth*, when Maitreya [who is assured to succeed Buddha Śākyamuni] and other Bodhisattvas asked the Buddha to entrust them with the task of spreading the Lotus Sūtra after Buddha's Nirvāna, Buddha halted them by saying "Enough, good sons!" and called out innumerable Bodhisattvas, headed by Bodhisattva Superior Practice, who emerged from openings in the earth. They were disciples of the Origin Buddha from innumerable kalpas past, who are then commissioned with the task after his passing in the Era of Final Dharma.

6 Dengyō Daishi [伝教大師 Great Teacher Dengyō] is a posthumous title given to Saichō 最澄 [767-822], founder of the Japanese Tendai School.

7 Ancient Chinese Dynasty 唐 [618-907].

8 Kōbō Daishi 弘法大師 is a posthumous name and title of Kūkai 空海 [774-835], the founder of the Japanese Shingon School, esoteric Buddhism.

9 栄西 [1141-1215], founder of the Japanese Zen School.

10 道元 [1200-1253], founder of the Japanese Sōtō School, disciple of Eisai.

11 Buddha Śākyamuni's The Triple Pure Land Sūtras 浄土三部経 provides the basis of the Pure Land School teachings. The three Chinese masters T'an-luan 曇鸞, Tao-ch'o 道綽, and Shan-tao 善導 systemized the Pure Land thought.

12 Reference to the monastery built by Dengyō Daishi atop Mount Hiei.

13 源空, also known as Hōnen-bō Genkū 法然房源空 [1133-1212]. He was the founder of Jōdo School during the Kamakura period that developed the Japanese version of the Pure Land Buddhism with the exclusive practice of chanting nenbutsu, or calling on the grace of Amida Buddha for salvation [*senshū-nenbutsu* 専修念仏].

14 *Kanmuryōgikyō-sho* 観無量義経疏 [*Annotations on The Meditation on the Buddha of Infinite Life Sūtra*] written by Zendō 善導 [613-681], Shan-tao [Ch.]. The third of the five Pure Land masters and the fifth of the seven patriarchs in the tradition of the Jōdoshin School.

15 Perceiving the existence of Buddha Mind in one's mind through meditation is considered the state of enlightenment in Zen Buddhism, therefore it is also known as the Buddha Mind School [Busshin-shū 仏心宗].

these teachings promote salvation of the individual. On the other hand, Nichiren Daishōnin's creed is not focused on the individual. No matter how one seeks personal salvation, peace of mind cannot be attained amidst a world of turbulence and unrest. Arriving at the Pure Land in the after life is also questionable because one's state in this life is passed on to the life hereafter.[16] Nichiren Daishōnin denounced as fallacious the premise that a teaching which could not address the issues of present life could bring salvation in the world to come.[17]

What are we to do to eliminate the immediate suffering we see everywhere in this world? There is a limit to what can be done to expound the Dharma to each and every person. Since there exists an organization of the state to govern a nation, Nichiren Daishōnin sought to guide the government so that it would walk the right path together with him.[18] This is what *Risshō-ankoku-ron* was about. *Ankoku*, to bring tranquility and security to a nation, is thought to be the work of politicians. Yet, in reality, when politics or government afflicts the people, someone needs to remonstrate towards the government. Someone needs to correct the government's wrongs. The authority of religion stands outside the influence of state power to show a correct, spiritual path. Despite this mission for the clergy, many clerics, subservient to state power, accommodate the teachings to the government's whims. The sūtra describes them as "monks of flattery and deviousness."[19] They bend Buddha Dharma, their faith and everything else. It is an inescapable challenge religion faces at any age. If we are to refuse to bend to the will of government, we must be prepared to collide with state power like Nichiren Daishōnin.

---

16 The law of causation, according to the Lotus Sūtra, is to reap what is planted, good cause bringing good results [Chapter V, *The Parable of the Herbs*], whereas the Pure Land School teaches to "shun the defiled land and seek the Pure Land." 厭離穢土　欣求浄土.

17 Nichiren Daishōnin's criticized Pure Land teachings that encourage the chanting of the name of Amida Buddha and teach followers to resign themselves for salvation only in the afterworld. Nichiren Daishōnin believed that "the merit of a day's practice in the defiled land surpasses that of a hundred years of practice in Amida's Pure Land of Utmost Bliss." [極楽百年の修行は穢土一日の功徳に及ばず.]

18 Governance through the spirit of the Lotus Sūtra would allow the nation to achieve "peace in the world and tranquility of the land." *Risshō-ankoku-ron* was a treatise of remonstration submitted to the Kamakura shogunate. Should the government accept Nichiren Daishōnin as spiritual master together with a governance inclusive of the people, "peace in the world, tranquility and security in the land" based on the spirit of the Lotus Sūtra would be realized.

19 *Tengoku-no-sō* 諂曲の僧. Literally, monks who flatter and bend themselves.

The *gāthā* in Chapter XIII, *Exhortation to Hold Firm*, which we just recited, starts out with, "Be pleased to be without concern." The succeeding phrase is, "After the Buddha's extinction, in the dreadful evil era." It is an era in which humanity is exposed to fear, and evil is rampant. In such an era of terror and evil, "We will expound [the Dharma] far and wide." The verse proclaims that we will transmit this Dharma for the sake of the multitude, and thereby assures the Buddha to, "be pleased to be without concern." This is how the 22-line *gāthā* in *Exhortation to Hold Firm* chapter begins. What follows when we expound the Dharma far and wide?

The worst that could happen is the appearance of the three formidable adversaries.[20] Those who slander the practitioners of the Lotus Sūtra appear. Some resort to force; even worse, monks without virtue appear. The worst of the three adversaries are monks who wear the patched garment[21] live in seclusion and conceitedly think they are properly practicing the Buddha Way as a monk. This is the demon that emerges from within the Buddhist order at the very end, bringing on the woeful destruction of the Dharma.

I caution you, too, to be mindful of this. These are monks clad in a monk's patched robe, who spend their whole life living quietly in temples doing nothing true to their calling. Convinced that they are practicing the Buddha Dharma, they look down on and belittle monks who work. They say things like, "Those inferior monks walk around, beating the drum because they are incapable of making a living in temples." There may be some truth to that, but in light of all these hindrances, what can be done to truly spread the Way?

"In the dreadful evil era . . . we will expound [the Dharma] far and wide." I agonized over this passage. I was ordained and studied the doctrines until 33. Not being too smart, I read writings by past sages and

---

20 三類の強敵. The three adversaries are: i) lay men and women who slander and revile, beat and assault those who practice the Genuine Dharma; ii) perverse monks who incite lay men and women to harm or slander those who practice the Genuine Dharma; iii) monks with a high reputation which commands reverence and who act saintly, but cause state power to persecute those who practice and spread the Genuine Dharma.

21 *Nōe* 納衣. A monk's robe in the days of Buddha Śākyamuni was made of discarded cloth, offered or found, of various sizes sewn together and dyed in the earth, achieving a color like saffron, a moderate orange to orange-yellow. Every offering of cloth, regardless of size and color, was thus treated equally by Buddha. A monk's robe today is still made of patches of cloth, following this tradition.

studied everything there was to study, yet I wrestled mightily with what I must do after completing my learning. Since I learned from books, shall I teach? Shall I write for newspapers or magazines? Shall I go around giving discourses and sermons? It seemed to me that these were the things people with scholastic training did. Another possibility was to become a *genja*,[22] a monk who performs incantations and faith healings. Somehow I had to find a way to spread the Dharma in this non-virtuous age as described in the *gāthā*, "In the dreadful evil era . . . we will expound far and wide." Nevertheless, I could not decide which choice was right.

Once I step forward, if I step to the east, I would no longer be heading west. If I face west, it may be only a single step in that direction at first, but I would end up going west. Joining the faculty at a school didn't seem to be much of an accomplishment. Faith healers claim they can cure illnesses, but they come to no good.[23] Suffering displayed by faith healers in their final hours is proof.[24] It is an undisputed fact. I have seen it with my own eyes. This was not an option. Torn by this issue, I practiced under different waterfalls, fasted and did everything possible to reach a resolution. Since I was training at Hōrūji Temple[25] in the country of Yamato[26] at the time, I visited various ancient sacred sites in Yamato where Dharma seekers practiced. One such place was a cascade called

---

22 *Genja* 験者 is short for *shugenja* 修験者. Originally it was a reference to monks practicing mystical rites of esoteric Buddhism deep in the mountains. Incantations, faith healing and exorcism started among monks of esoteric Buddhist factions of the Tendai and Shingon Schools in the Heian Period [794-1185], and they were also called *genja*. During the Edo Period [1603-1867], esotericism made its way into the Nichiren School and *genja*, properly called *shūhosshi* 修法師, appeared engaging in religious activities that went against the Buddha Dharma taught by Nichiren Daishōnin.

23 Faith healers tend to be more interested in performing healing or exorcism for material gain, taking advantage of people who are vulnerable. From the standpoint of salvation based on the Triple Jewel of the Buddha, Dharma and Sangha, this practice contravenes each of them.

24 Faith healers who willfully engage in religious activities that go against the Buddha are said to manifest the sufferings of falling into hell at the hour of death. Buddha ought not to be used as a tool, and faith healing or incantations to satisfy desires create karma rather than leading to emancipation.

25 In 1911 Guruji studied *yuishiki* 唯識 [the "consciousness-only" doctrine] and trained under Most Venerable Saeki Jōin 佐伯定胤 [1867-1952] 103rd Chief Abbot of Hōryū-ji. Hōryu-ji Temple 法隆寺, the principle temple of the Shōtoku School 聖徳宗, is the oldest completely preserved temple complex in Japan. The same year Guruji also studied *The Discourse on the Repository of Abhidharma Discussions* under Most Venerable Saeki Ryōken 佐伯良謙 [1881-1963] who later became the 104th Chief Abbot.

26 Present-day Nara Prefecture.

Momonoo. Temples stood there in ancient days where monks of high virtue and knowledge had resided. No trace of these temples remained, just a couple of small, remnant shrines.[27] I secluded myself for a week, practicing under the waterfall. This was when I arrived at the ultimate conclusion. I experienced a miraculous vision.

It may sound as if I was in a sort of dream, but I actually saw a person come up the hill, beating the drum and chanting the Odaimoku, carrying a baby on the back.[28] I asked who this person was. The response came, "I am Bodhisattva Superior Practice." I then asked who was being carried. "The World Honored One, Buddha Śākyamuni." That was all that was said, and we parted. The vision brought me to the ultimate realization that the practice for the Era of Final Dharma was to carry Lord Buddha, the Lord Buddha at the time of birth,[29] on my back, and walk throughout the world beating the drum.

From there I went to the Myōken waterfall in Nose.[30] There are 16 head temples [in Kyōto].[31] Among them is a major head temple called Honkoku-ji,[32] which used to stand adjacent to Hongan-ji Temple.[33] A humble dwelling Nichiren Daishōnin had in Matsubagayatsu, Kamakura, was relocated [to Kyōto] in the Ashikaga period.[34] It is a major head temple with many affiliate temples. I paid homage at this temple.

It was already cold wintertime, and I was circling the temple praying, with only sandals on my bare feet. A friend of mine, who graduated

---

27 *Odō* お堂. Here it is a reference to a hut-like shrine without incidental facilities that a temple would have, the size where one person can barely fit in to lie down.

28 In Japanese, there is nothing to distinguish gender here.

29 A reference to Lord Buddha proclaiming, "In all the heavens and earth, I am the Honored One. For the threefold world is a realm of suffering from which I shall emancipate all beings."

30 A historic waterfall located in Nose, Ōsaka frequented by those with faith and where a 19th century Nichiren School high monk, Honmyō Nichirin 本妙日臨, also practiced.

31 *Honzan* 本山. These head temples are known as the 16 Nichiren head temples in Kyōto, *Kōyōto-jūroku-honzan* 京都十六本山.

32 本圀寺. In 1253, Nichiren Daishōnin named his humble dwelling in Matsubagayatsu the Hokkedō. In 1263, it became Daikōzan-honkokuji 大光山本圀寺, the first temple founded in the order connected to Nichiren Daishōnin after his banishment to Itō, Izu. With the fall of the Kamakura shogunate, it was transferred to the new capital, Kyōto, by imperial command. In 1971 it was transferred to the current location in Yamashina, Kyōto.

33 Built in 1272, Hongan-ji Temple 本願寺 is the headquarter of the Jōdoshin School.

34 Also called the Muromachi period [reign of the Ashikaga clan] with a shogunate in Kyōto [1392-1573]. Sometimes the Nanbokuchō period [1336-1392] is included in the first half of the Muromachi period.

from Ōsaki[35] around the same time as I, was administrative head of the temple.[36] When he saw me he said, "I always wondered how distinguished Fujii-kun[37] would become after many years of study and practice with various Buddhist traditions since Ōsaki. What a pity that he's fallen to become a vagrant monk living like a *sengaji*."[38] *Sengaji* are those who leave home to make pilgrimages to sacred sites, praying for health and longevity or recovery from incurable illness. Of course he didn't say this to my face. The dismissive comment was made to the nuns of affiliated temples in Kyōto. It eventually reached my ears.

I also did research at the Shingon School[39] and befriended scholar monks. On my visit to the residences of these faculty monks, they mentioned that this same administrator of Honkoku-ji Temple criticized Shingon doctrine for its theory of *daisan-keron*.[40] In contrast, they inquired what brought me to study the Shingon doctrine despite the differences [between the Nichiren and Shingon schools]. In addition to studying Shingon doctrine, I was giving lectures at a Shingon university, as well as another Buddhist school.[41] The administrator must have thought that what I ended up doing after all the learning was senseless, especially when he saw me barefoot in sandals, walking about beating the drum.

---

35 The Ōsaki campus of present day Risshō University was founded 130 years ago as a religious institution of the Nichiren School.

36 *Shitsuji* 執事, a monk with responsibility for administering the temple on behalf of the Chief Abbot, considered to be a position of importance.

37 Fujii-kun is used here by the former classmate and indicates the informality in their relationship. Fujii is Guruji's family name combined with kun, a male diminutive in Japanese. Also, people socially higher or older might use kun, especially for a boy or young man.

38 千箇寺,千箇寺参り. A mode of practice or the practitioners who make pilgrimages to temples, a term unique to Nichiren School that started in mid-Edo period [1603-1867]. It is the practice of a lay person in prayer to attain a personal wish. The pilgrims are vested in white clothing with inscriptions of Odaimoku or mandala on the back, make homage to 1,000 Nichiren School temples, beating the drum and chanting.

39 In 1912 Guruji was admitted into the Shingon School University attached to Tōji Temple and studied under Venerable Hase Hōshū 長谷宝秀.

40 法華第三戯論. While the supremacy of the Lotus Sūtra as the ultimate teaching of Buddha Śākyamuni is generally accepted, Kūkai 空海 was an exception. He asserted that the Mahāvairocana-sūtra is the highest sūtra, followed by the Garland Sūtra and then the Lotus Sūtra, a mere third rank, thus belittling the Lotus Sūtra's teaching as *keron*, meaningless and insignificant. Nichiren Daishōnin refuted Shingon mysticism and its collusion with state power with the phrase "Shingon brings ruination to the nation." [*Shingon-bōkoku* 真言亡国].

41 In 1915 Guruji lectured on the four major Tendai doctrines at institutions with Hokke-ji Temple 法華寺 and Chōmyō-ji Temple 頂妙寺 in Kyōto [Nichiren School] as well as Aisen-ji Temple 愛染寺 [Shingon School].

Standing in front of Gṛdhrakūta [Sacred Eagle Peak], where Buddha Śākyamuni preached the Lotus Sūtra. 1936.

I presume many disciples in Nipponzan today hold a view on the practice at Nipponzan similar to the administrator of Honkoku-ji Temple. "What good would walking about the streets beating the drum do?" When we walk about, we must be prepared to go without shelter at night. Even a single blanket adds to the load on the back, so I cut a white blanket in half and placed it on top of the wooden box I carried. I started out on my mission prepared to sleep in the open air wherever I went. It was in the dead of winter. No shelter was offered. I could have taken the blanket out to keep warm, but I didn't. There were times I awaited the dawn shivering. It's not that I did that all the time, but I still cannot forget those experiences. I remember looking for a faucet to bathe at dawn, but when I found one, the frozen faucet would not budge.

This was how I walked about. On the back of the wooden box in which I carried sūtras and a change of clothes, I placed a wooden plaque on which I inscribed Na Mu Myō Hō Ren Ge Kyō in the center and a passage from the sūtra[42] on both sides of the Odaimoku:

> Whether in villages or cities,
> Whenever there are those who seek the Dharma,
> We will all go to them and
> Expound the Dharma bequeathed by the Buddha.

I believe this wooden carrying case is still kept at Aso.[43] "Whether in villages or cities, whenever there are those who seek the Dharma, we will all go to them and expound the Dharma bequeathed by the Buddha." This passage has now been put into practice. Starting from the Nipponzan Myōhōji dōjō in Milton Keynes, England, the disciples are presently walking about different parts of the globe, and along the way have come across people seeking the Dharma. One such person is a lady who I hear escaped Auschwitz from an outhouse. I understand she is now a mayor, I believe, in Poland. These people have expressed their desire to gather here next year.[44] People who share an aspiration for world peace will converge here in the coming year. "Whether in villages or cities, whenever there are those who seek the Dharma, we will all go to them." I urge you to follow suit. We must bring ourselves to those who seek the Dharma. "We will all go to them and expound the Dharma bequeathed by the Buddha." This is what we must realize. We are finally seeing this work take root in Milton Keynes.

As one of the retinues numbering as great as the sands of sixty thousand Ganges, and as followers of Bodhisattva Superior Practice reincarnated, the disciple of the Eternal Buddha Śākyamuni, those who walk about to expound the Dharma after the demise of the Buddha in the evil and dreadful era will engage in the practice described in *Exhortation*

---

42 Chapter XIII of the Lotus Sūtra, *Exhortation to Hold Firm.*

43 The Aso temple in the region where Guruji was born.

44 Guruji convened a World Religious Workers Conference for Disarmament on the 700th anniversary of Nichiren Daishōnin's passing at the Kiyosumi Dōjō.

to Hold Firm chapter as heirs of Ososhi-sama's teachings. It is long past time for anyone to remain secluded in temples and make monkhood merely a livelihood. "After the Buddha's extinction, in the dreadful evil era, we will expound [the Dharma] far and wide." How far have you gone to expound the Dharma? Our calling is to expound the Dharma far and wide. To expound far and wide, we must walk about far and wide. No matter how many times you visit the same group of devotees to perform memorial services or funerals, it amounts to very little. There is nothing far and wide about that. Only a handful in Nipponzan expounds the Dharma far and wide. The rest are living off the virtues of these few. Do not make the mistake of thinking that you are making a living owing to your own virtues. When those who expound the Dharma are no longer, there is no way you would be able to sustain yourselves.

Compared to me, you are all still young. It's not too late. From here on, I urge you to go out and walk about far and wide, beating the drum and chanting the Odaimoku. "Whether in villages or cities, whenever there are those who seek the Dharma, we will all go to them and expound the Dharma bequeathed by the Buddha." Then for the first time you can proclaim: "We are the messengers of the World Honored One."

42

The Time Has Come

April 22, 1981
Delivered at the Opening Plenary Session
of the World Assembly of Religious Workers
Tōkyō

Na Mu Myō Hō Ren Ge Kyō

The time has come. The time has come when we can no longer sit or stand idle but are compelled to rush out of the confines of our homes. The time has come to look up to the heavens, bow to the earth, voice our concerns to one and all and share our grief. This is what the great peace march[1] is about, what the World Assembly of Religious Workers is about.

Nichiren Daishōnin states in the *Chie-bōkoku-gosho*,[2] "Great evil heralds the coming of great good. When the *Jambudvīpa* is in turmoil, there is no doubt of [Na Mu Myō Hō Ren Ge Kyō] disseminating far and wide throughout the *Jambudvīpa*." What is great evil? It is a great global war capable of obliterating humanity, completely destroying cities and wiping all of civilization from the face of the earth. It means not merely a great war, but a great war fought with the nuclear weapons developed in modern times. The great global nuclear war has yet to occur. But preparations are underway, namely, the nuclear arms race. The global

---

1 The World Peace March was initiated in Kiyosumi, Japan on April 28, 1981 by Guruji in commemoration of the 700th anniversary of the passing of Nichiren Daishōnin. It had five separate courses on three continents, all to convene in New York City for the Second Special Session on Disarmament at the United Nations in June 1982. This special session drew the largest anti-nuclear demonstration ever when 1 million people gathered in Central Park in NYC on June 12, 1982. Guruji was invited to the stage to say a few words. Instead of making a speech to the great crowd, Guruji decided to chant and drum with his disciples on stage.

2 智慧亡国御書 *Without Wisdom the Nation Shall Fall.* Written by Nichiren Daishōnin in 1275 at Mount Minobu.

At the start of the World Peace March in Kiyosumi, Japan, April 28, 1981.

nuclear war can occur only once.

When it breaks out, the surface of the earth, sky and underwater will become uninhabitable. A single atomic bomb killed approximately 100,000 Japanese citizens in an instant when the United States dropped it on Hiroshima at the end of World War II. Presently stockpiles equivalent to one million Hiroshima bombs exist in the combined arsenals of the United States and the Soviet Union. In the event of an all-out nuclear war, some estimate the killing capacity would take the lives of 100 million people.

About 50 million people died during the six years of World War II. Just a second would suffice to kill 50 million people in an all-out nuclear war. There seems little prospect of halting the development of nuclear weapons and their delivery systems short of a massive global catastrophe within the next twenty years.

Risshō-ankoku-ron[3] prophesized, "Two of the three calamities[4]

3 Please refer to *Shishin-kaku*, footnote 5, p. 1.
4 *Sansai* 三災. Wars, pestilence and famine.

foretold in the Great Collection Sūtra[5] have already manifested leaving the third to follow, namely, the calamity of war." The United States of America was the first to develop nuclear weapons, weapons capable of annihilating humanity. The United States of America also was the first to use nuclear weapons in war. Furthermore, the United States of America mythologizes nuclear weapons as guardians of peace and continues feverishly to develop, produce, stockpile and sell them, acts which threaten and terrorize the whole of humanity. Not a single president nor General MacArthur has ever reflected upon or repented the grave crime committed by the United States, which opened the gate of inferno for human annihilation. The world has yet to condemn this crime or pass judgment on it. The Allied Forces of World War II and conscientious people of the world alike stood aghast but remained idle bystanders. They are complicit in today's mounting threat against humanity's very survival.

In the name of national security or under the guise of protecting a nation's lives and assets, governments spend a percentage of the gross national product on the nuclear arms race, which, in turn, brings about violence that kills and maims people and destroys cities. Meanwhile, the number of people dying from lack of food, clothing and shelter rises. Accepting violent criminal acts of murder and destruction against other nations and people simply because the government ordered them adversely affects young people's outlook on life. They soon believe the use of violence is an integral part of life, and the general population is gradually desensitized to acts of violence as well. When the morality of the nation grows numb and the foundation of social order collapses, serious crimes including murder, robbery and rape occur openly in broad daylight regardless of how many police, courts and prisons are employed.

We see a prime example of such agony in the United States. Presidents are assassinated and elected officials murdered. Even clergy and passersby are killed. Murder is committed indiscriminately. Money, personal belongings and everything else are stolen, and women are raped. Crimes once prevalent only in major cities like New York have gradually spread to rural areas, leaving no safe haven in the country. Voices lament the unfortunate state of the union with the record breaking number of felonies committed. From government leaders down to the general public,

---

5 Daishū-kyō also known as Daihōdō-daishū-kyō 大集経, Mahāsannipāta-sūtra.

nowhere is safe, leaving the state of the nation doomed.

I prepared this manuscript on March 30th at 2 p.m. in Japan. I learned that on March 30th at 2:00 p.m. [in Washington, D.C.], President Reagan was shot by a student in the capital city of Washington D.C. Is this coincidence or fate? The spiritual depravity of the United States is evident not only in the shooting of the president but also in its defeat in the Vietnam War. Another example closer to home is the hit-and-run incident of a Japanese freight vessel, Nisshō-maru, by the U.S. submarine George Washington off the coast of Kagoshima.[6]

Let us now turn our eyes to Japan. Japan not only aided numerous U.S. war policies through the Japan-U.S. Security Treaty, but now we hear an increasing number of arguments defending the Self-Defense Forces as constitutional along with calls to amend [Japan's] Peace Constitution. The number of reported domestic violence cases involving juveniles beating their parents to death alone exceeds one thousand. Students inflict injuries on their teachers, and even distinguished commencement ceremonies cannot go forth without police security. These are examples of school violence. These juveniles grow up and join the Self-Defense Forces, which deems violence almighty. Emergency legislations are enacted to allow a single commander to arbitrarily decide to take Japan to war against other nations. The United States constantly urges Japan to build up its weapons arsenal. Notwithstanding all this, the great evil manifested in the United States can be regarded as an auspicious omen of its deliverance if we heed the golden words, "The great evil heralds the coming of great good."

The shooting of the president could be retribution for the crimes of fueling the arms race to achieve military superiority and pursuing world domination through wars of aggression. Defeat in the Vietnam War came from factors both at home and abroad, namely, the widespread, popular anti-war movement, the refusal of U.S. servicemen to fight and the case brought by conscientious people of the world to the International

---

6 On April 9, 1981, the USS George Washington surfaced underneath the Nisshō-maru. The 2350-ton Japanese freighter sank in about 15 minutes. Two Japanese crewmen were lost; thirteen were rescued. The accident strained U.S.-Japan relations, and Japan criticized the U.S. for taking more than 24 hours to notify Japanese authorities and demanded to know what the submarine was doing surfacing only 20 miles outside Japan's territorial waters. Neither the submarine nor the patrol aircraft overhead made any attempt to rescue the Japanese crew.

Guruji praying before one million people at Central Park in New York City, June 12, 1982.

Criminal Court, whose condemnation of the United States inspired the Vietnamese people in their moral effort of to save their homeland.

The Soviet Union and the United States, who competed fiercely to come out the undisputed victor in the event of a great global nuclear war, finally realized that both face unimaginable dangers due to their own acts. They then hatched a plan to recognize each other's territory as sanctuaries, committing not to use strategic nuclear weapons against the other, instead limiting nuclear war to territories of lesser satellite counties. This became known as the limited war strategy.

The Soviet Union and the United States, the authors of limited war, consulted and devised a strategy to assure the security of their homelands as sanctuaries, while leaving smaller, weaker countries to ruination. Still, it is more likely that before lesser and smaller countries are destroyed, the sanctuaries of the two nations will be reduced to ash by their nuclear weapons.

To begin with, the nuclear arms race originated in the Soviet Union's mistrust of the nuclear weapons possessed by its ally, the United States. Suspicion and fear directed against the United States led to the development of Soviet nuclear weapons. On the other hand, fueled by fear of the Soviet nuclear development, the United States spent exorbitantly on its military to increase the kill-effectiveness of its nuclear weapons. In a polarized world, how could nuclear weapons, accumulated in this manner, be stockpiled forever without being detonated in a confrontation between the two superpowers? We cannot predict the origin of the next world war, but the greatest likelihood is a conflict between the Soviet Union and the United States where massive nuclear weapons are stored.

The perilous nuclear war policies of the United States and Soviet Union must shift if we are to forestall imminent global war and eliminate nuclear arms. To accomplish that goal, the arrogance of world domination held in the minds of the people of the two countries, first and foremost, must be transformed into peace. This conversion towards peace within the two nations requires an example set by other countries to unilaterally forsake the concept of national defense through arms, to disarm, to abandon nuclear weapons, renounce the right to war and to abstain from violence in any international conflict, instead seeking peaceful solutions and maintaining domestic social order through law enforcement. With such governments in the lead, the voices of conscience and religious faith of the awakened people must unite to ring the bell of warning to the peoples of the United States and the Soviet Union.

> Promptly mend thy trivial faith and immediately embrace the single Truth of the Genuine Vehicle. Then the entire triple world is one and inseparable from the Buddha Realm; how can the Buddha Realm ever decline? The worlds in the ten directions are without exception, the Jeweled Land. How can the Jeweled Land ever be destroyed? When our land is free from decline and the world free from destruction, our bodies will be safe and our hearts and minds tranquil. Believe in these words and revere them.[7]

Na Mu Myō Hō Ren Ge Kyō

---

7 Citation from *Risshō Ankoku-ron.*

43

Sanctuary

April 28, 1981
700th Anniversary Commemoration of Nichiren Daishōnin
Kiyosumi Dōjō, Japan

Na Mu Myō Hō Ren Ge Kyō

Sanctuary is a term bandied about in recent days by the proponents of the nuclear arms race. It is a term generally reserved to describe consecrated grounds. However, the word "sacred" is non-existent in the vocabulary of materialism, not to mention the jargon of the military, whose profession specializes in murder and destruction. It is the very antithesis of the military nature and cannot coexist with such a profession. Words like sanctity describe the quintessence of spirituality, particularly in a religious and moral society. It is what imbues life to such society. No religion or ethics is devoid of the concept of sanctity.

The president of the United States declared: "No power on earth is stronger than the United States of America. None will be stronger than the United States of America in the future. This is the only national defense posture which can ever be acceptable to the United States."[1]

[In Alva Myrdal's *The Game of Disarmament*, she states], "Initially, the Soviet Union started from a position of inferiority, but it has gradually advanced towards equality in the gross kill-effect of nuclear weapons deployed or in production."[2]

[In the same source, Herbert F. York is quoted], "If the Soviet leadership, for whatever reason, or as a result of whatever mistaken information, chose to destroy America as a nation, it is unquestionably

---

1 Richard Nixon in his address to a joint session of Congress, June 1, 1972, immediately on his return from Russia after SALT I talks. [Strategic Arms Limitation Talks].Cited in *The Game of Disarmament* by Alva Myrdal, p. 25.

2 Myrdal, p. 26.

capable of doing so in less than half an hour, and there is literally nothing we could now do to prevent it. The only thing we could do is to wreak on them an equally terrible revenge. And, of course, the situation is the same the other way around."[3]

Both the Soviet Union and the United States aim to come out victorious in an all-out nuclear war and could be nothing short of alarmed by the ever-mounting danger posed by nuclear weapons. This was the motivation to formulate a policy of limited nuclear war. Limited nuclear war is predicated on the understanding that the two countries abstain from using their strategic nuclear weapons against each other in order to keep their homelands intact, thus referred to as "sanctuaries." Nuclear war is to be limited to territories of lesser, weaker nations. Although cause of future wars cannot be predicted, the most likely scenario is a conflict between the Soviet Union and the United States.

In total nuclear war, the sanctified territories of the Soviet Union and the United States may temporarily remain intact. But inevitably, the security of these sanctuaries will vanish like a fleeting dream. This mindset of distrust, suspicion, fear and hatred, held mutually by the two countries, is the root cause of the nuclear arms race, particularly in the case of strategic nuclear weapons. A world completely polarized between the United States and the Soviet Union at each extreme heightens the conflict between the two and threatens an inevitable showdown. No question nuclear weapons are utterly criminal instruments, capable of obliterating humanity. So while they competed in the development, stockpile and deployment of these weapons, the Soviet Union and the United States devised a way to avert danger and disaster by calling their homelands sanctuaries. Sanctuary is what all countries and people of the world fervently aspire to. But in this case, it became nothing more than the self-interest discussed and agreed upon by the leaders of the two countries. This leaves smaller and weaker non-nuclear nations with the task to meet and explore ways to discover sanctuaries.

The Soviet Union and the United States appear pleased and satisfied with sanctifying their homelands. Are they likewise content and pleased at the deplorable situation of ruination and devastation faced by smaller and weaker non-nuclear nations? If the Soviet Union and the United

---

3 Myrdal, p. 27. Herbert F. York, an expert at a 1973 Conference organized by the Center for the Study of Democratic Institutions in Santa Barbara, CA.

States were willing to be content and pleased at making the entire world a sanctuary, it could be easily and immediately accomplished. All that is required is to resolve never to use the nuclear weapons they have developed and stockpiled. Humanity at large could then live in happiness and with peace of mind. Why cannot the Soviet Union and the United States find contentment and joy in making the entire world a sanctuary?

Aspiring to and arriving at sanctuary is a pursuit common to all religions. At times it is called the Pure Land while others call it heaven. Yet, the world we live in is replete with the five cardinal sins[4] and the ten evil deeds,[5] and neither the Pure Land nor heaven is anywhere to be found. Nevertheless, the undeterred and continued longing for the Pure Land, heaven, without giving in to despair, caused humans to seek to arrive there in the hereafter.

The teaching of *Risshō-ankoku* expounded by Nichiren Daishōnin, however, does not seek for a sanctuary in the next world but in this world.

> When the hearts and minds of the people are defiled, so is the land defiled. When the hearts and minds of the people are pure, so is the land pure. What is called the Pure Land or the Defiled Land is not distinct, one from another, but is made different by the good or evil in our mind.[6]

In the *Treatise on Protecting the Nation*:[7] Nichiren Daishōnin states:

> *The Eternal Duration of the Life of the Tathāgata* chapter, the essence of the Lotus Sūtra's twenty-eight chapters, states, "All this time I have always been present in this *sahā* world," and "I shall forever be here." It further states, "Tranquil is this realm of mine." Given that these words are true, the

4 Killing one's father, killing one's mother, killing a saint, injuring the body of Buddha and causing disunity in the community of monks.

5 Killing, stealing, committing adultery, lying, using immoral language, slandering, equivocating, coveting, anger and false views.

6 *Isshō-jōbutsu-shō* 一生成仏鈔. *On Attaining Buddhahood in This Life* was written by Nichiren Daishōnin in 1255 in Kamakura to Toki Gorō Jōnin 富木五郎常忍.

7 *Shugo-kokka-ron* 守護国家論. Written by Nichiren Daishōnin in 1259.

> Eternal primordial Buddha, the origin of all Buddhas in manifestation, the One who attained full Buddhahood in time without beginning, resides in this world. Why should one wish to abandon this world for any other? Thus, know that the Pure Land is where the practitioner of the Lotus Sūtra resides. Why should one seek for another dominion? That is why *The Divine Transcendental Powers of the Tathāgata* states: "Be it in a garden, in a grove, at the foot of a tree, in a monastery, in the house of a white-clad layman, in a stately building or in a mountain, in a valley or in the wilderness . . . be it known that it is the very place to practice the Dharma." The Nirvana Sūtra states: "Good men, wherever this ineffable and profound sūtra—the Mahā-Parinirvāna-sūtra—spreads, is in itself indestructible as a diamond, and the people therein are likewise imperishable as a diamond." Those who embrace and practice the Lotus and Nirvāna sūtras should not seek the Pure Land anywhere other than in the very place where the believers of this sūtra reside.

According to Nichiren Daishōnin, sanctuary, in other words the Pure Land or heaven, is everywhere in this physical realm we live in. It is in the mountains and valleys, wilderness, gardens, forests, temples and stately buildings. This is based on his uncompromising faith in the following *gāthā* of the Lotus Sūtra:

> Even when all the living see
> At the kalpa's end
> The conflagration burning
> Tranquil is this realm of mine

Embracing this *gāthā* of the sūtra frees us from dismay or despair and instills a belief indestructible as a diamond that protection and salvation will prevail no matter how ominous the threat of nuclear weapons. Without ever resorting to wars of destruction, harm and murder, we shall work unremittingly to transform the hearts and minds of the people of the Soviet Union and the United States toward peace. Building global peace is ultimately a spiritual issue.

Yet we must hear the criticism directed towards religious workers:

> The religious movements have not as yet had much of an impact for creating peace or against preparations for war . . . I have painted a sad and not very promising picture of public apathy. How can this unfortunate passivity of peoples, popular movements, organizations, political parties, and finally governments be changed into realistic and rational concern?[8]

Religion's propensity to focus on spiritual matters like inner fears, suffering and grief, causes it to be naturally inclined away from matters of the external world. During the reign of the Kamakura shogunate, the religious community failed to see the value of *Risshō-ankoku-ron* presented by Nichiren Daishōnin, and the same remains true today. This failure is the cause of stagnation of contemporary religious movements, which turn a blind eye to the world's realities. Mahāyāna Buddhism expounds that a single thought-moment encompasses the entire Buddha Realm, and all phenomena are manifestations of one's heart and mind. Accordingly, all external phenomena are one and inseparable from the Dharma mind.[9] The Dharma mind cannot be found anywhere else than in phenomena of the external world. Any attempt today to ensure one's own safety while failing to prevent the perils and calamities posed by nuclear weapons is nothing but a dream within a dream. It is imperative for all religious workers to awaken to this.

The modern civilization is called a civilization of science. "Some 400,000 scientists and engineers, nearly half of the total engaged in research and development work, are employed in military pursuits in industrialized countries. Estimates gauged the total manpower involved directly or indirectly in military purposes at 50 million people, also a staggering figure."[10] Nuclear weapons are developed one after another to support the affluent lifestyles and privileged status of these people. They are totally indifferent to and irresponsible towards the magnitude of the calamities that these nuclear weapons bring upon humanity. The disregard

---

8 Myrdal, p. 321.
9 *Shinpō* 心法 *citta-saṃtāna*.
10 Myrdal, p. 13.

these scientists have for the consequences of their actions outstrips the incompetence of the clergy.

Risshō-ankoku-ron teaches that the "*sahā* world[11] is one and inseparable from the Land of Tranquil Light."[12] The *sahā* world is permeated with impurity and evil, a place where the three calamities[13] and seven disasters[14] occur in succession. The Land of Tranquil Light is filled with purity, a place of tranquility and joy. It does not mean that the impurities and evils that abound in this world are themselves pure. It means that any impurity or evil becomes pure when transformed. "Is one and inseparable from" as in "the *sahā* world is one and inseparable from the Land of Tranquil Light," means that without a doubt we can achieve this transformation. The work of religion is an experiment to realize this sense of "one and inseparable from."

Mount Kiyosumi is a sanctuary. Nichiren Daishōnin entered this mountain at the age of twelve. This was his first step in making it a sanctuary. At the age of sixteen he was ordained under his master, Dōzenbō. This was his second step in making it a sanctuary. "One who aquires and practices the Buddha Dharma should always bear in mind his debt of gratitude to his parents, master and nation. How could I possibly requite my great debt of gratitude to them without attaining the Buddha Dharma and become a man of wisdom?"[15] This was the great vow Nichiren Daishōnin made in front of the image of Akasagarbha Bodhisattva,[16] [the Bodhisattva of wisdom], the principle object of worship enshrined at Seichōji temple. This was the third step he took in making it a sanctuary. On April 28, 1253, Nichiren Daishōnin stood facing the rising sun from the Pacific Ocean at a corner of Mount Kiyosumi called Asahinomori, and for the first time chanted Na Mu Myō Hō Ren Ge Kyō without sparing his voice. In this way he initiated the Buddha Dharma of Japan as expressed by his words, "Not a single person ever chanted Na Mu Myō Hō Ren Ge

---

11 *Shaba* 娑婆. The land of endurance, a reference to this world where people must endure various afflictions and pain.

12 娑婆即寂光.

13 *Sansai* 三災. War, pestilence and famine.

14 *Shichinan* 七難. There are different versions, but the Benevolent Kings Sūtra, Ninnō-kyō, 仁王経 cites loss of brilliance of the sun and moon, loss of brilliance of constellations, fire, floods, strong winds, droughts and hostilities.

15 報恩鈔 *Requital of Gratitude*. Written by Nichiren Daishōnin on July 21, 1276.

16 Kokūzō-bosatsu 虚空蔵菩薩. Known as the Receptacle of Void because his wisdom is said to be boundless as space itself.

Kyō during the 2,220 years after the demise of the Tathāgata. I, Nichiren, was the first to chant Na Mu Myō Hō Ren Ge Kyō, Na Mu Myō Hō Ren Ge Kyō, without sparing my voice."[17] This was the fourth step taken to make Mount Kiyosumi a sanctuary. On the heels of his proclamation of founding his school of Buddha Dharma, Nichiren Daishōnin was compelled to escape from Mount Kiyosumi due to the wrath incurred from local authorities. There was never another opportunity to return to Mount Kiyosumi for the rest of his life.

However, Nichiren Daishōnin's heart forever resided at Mount Kiyosumi. More than 400 of his writings are compiled. His first treatise is the *Kaitai-sokushin-jōbutsu-gi*.[18] Below the title and above his signature are the words "resident of Mount Kiyosumi," something not seen in any of his other writings. In *Tripitaka Master Śubhākarasimba*,[19] he wrote, "I, Nichiren, was a resident of Mount Kiyosumi in Tōjō Village in the Awa province." All the above illustrates how a sanctuary was created at Mount Kiyosumi by Nichiren Daishōnin.

Seven hundred years have elapsed since the passing of Nichiren Daishōnin. This time precisely marks the era in which strife and hostilities reign. Summits of word leaders are held here and there. They are nothing but meetings to conspire and talk about war. Mount Kiyosumi, a sanctuary, is the ground where the greatest Japanese cedar grew. Recently, a magnificent white stūpa emerged from the earth soaring into the blue. A temple was built and the most superb Honzon in the *Jambudvīpa* that will shed light on the darkness of the Era of Final Dharma was enshrined.[20] Celestial umbrellas, canopies and banners adorn the altar, and incense, flowers and votive lights are offered. These are all enchanting representations of the Pure Land, transforming the fields and forests of the *sahā* world, a beginning in the transformation of the entire world into a sanctuary.

---

17 *Requital of Gratitude.*

18 戒体即身成仏義. *Embodying the Spirit of the Lotus Sūtra Through Conduct is the Path to Enlightenment* was written in 1242.

19 善無畏三蔵鈔. *Zenmui-sanzō-shō* was written in 1270 to Jōken-bō 浄顕房 and Gijō-bō 義浄房. *Zenmui* is Śubhākarasimba [637-735], said to be a prince in central India who abdicated the throne and went to Nalanda where he learned esoteric Buddhism. He went to Chang-an in 716 with Sanskrit scriptures and, under the patronage of Emperor Hsüan-tsung, translated basic esoteric texts.

20 The mandala and stūpa with the inscription of Na Mu Myō Hō Ren Ge Kyō flanked by two Tathāgatas.

At this very time, on the occasion of the 700th anniversary of the passing of our founding master, Nichiren Daishōnin, representatives of the world's religious communities, leaders of peace organizations from around the world, and men and women who take a stand against nuclear war have congregated to explore ways and means to eliminate nuclear weapons and realize general and complete disarmament. Through this effort we aspire to sanctify the entire globe, to realize the transformation of this *sahā* world that is in itself the Land of Tranquil Light, and to bring about peace and tranquility through the rise of the Genuine Dharma for the sake of all nations. We shall transform the seemingly omnipotent violence while at its height into what serves to sustain human life.

Will violence, nuclear weapons, materialism prevail? If so, humanity shall perish. Will nonviolence, religion, morality, veneration, offerings, spiritualism prevail? If so, humanity shall witness tranquility in this world we live in rather than in the life hereafter. Should the compassion of our founding master, Nichiren Daishōnin, be immeasurable, then enable us to transform the already manifested great evil, which has brought us to the edge of human annihilation, into the great good of human survival. Na Mu Myō Hō Ren Ge Kyō.

All the Buddhas, saviors of the world,
Who abide in your great transcendental powers,
For the sake of bringing joy to all living beings
May you manifest your immeasurable divine powers.[21]

Na Mu Myō Hō Ren Ge Kyō

21 Lotus Sūtra, Chapter XXI, *The Divine Transcendental Powers of the Tathāgata.*

44

Dedication of the Bamboo Grove Monastery

October 24, 1981
New Venuvan Vihar Monastery
Rajgir, India

Na Mu Myō Hō Ren Ge Kyō

Some 2,500 years ago, King Bimbisāra, the great ruler of Magadha Kingdom, built a majestic monastery on a sacred site adjacent to the hot springs in the vicinity of ancient Rajgir where his castle stood. King Bimbisāra built the monastery as a means to fulfill his five vows.[1] He offered it to the Preceptor of Buddhism, the World Honored One, Buddha Śākyamuni, and his disciples to reside and named it Venuvan Vihar [the Bamboo Grove Monastery]. It was the first *vihar* built for Buddha Śākyamuni's order. Venuvan Vihar served to spread the newly-founded Buddhism far and wide. Buddhist orders flourished throughout the five regions of India.

With the passage of time, Buddhism reached countries outside India, creating peaceful nations wherever it spread, and nations embraced Buddhism. In particular, Emperor Ashoka, who appeared 200 years after the Parinirvāna of the Buddha, spread Buddhism extensively throughout the world during his time. Asian nations continue to profess faith in Buddhism to this day.

As Buddhism declined towards the end of its one thousand years in India, so did India; and with the Muslim invasion, Buddhism became extinct in India. However, in the early part of this century, India once again established a great nation of complete independence and autonomy through the nonviolent movement led by Mahatma Gandhi. She hoisted

1 The vows were: i) To become king; ii) To see the Buddha in his kingdom; iii) To serve the Buddha; iv) To receive Buddha's preaching directly; v) To understand Buddha's teachings and attain enlightenment.

the banner of a peaceful nation and pledged to restore Buddhism as a guiding policy. India's first Prime Minister, Jawaharlal Nehru, became the chair of the restoration committee, and five committee members were appointed. The initial project planned by the committee was restoration of Rajgir, and reconstruction of Venuvan Vihar its intended first step.

Nichiren Daishōnin, the initiator of Na Mu Myō Hō Ren Ge Kyō, Buddha Dharma of Japan, proclaimed that restoration of Buddhism in India was the mission of the Buddha Dharma of Japan. This year marks the 700th anniversary of the passing of Nichiren Daishōnin. In this auspicious year, Venuvan Vihar was restored with grandeur through the vow of the Sangha of Buddha Dharma of Japan at a site adjacent to the ruins of the original, and its dedication ceremony is taking place today with the presence of the honorable President of India.

As a descendant disciple of Nichiren Daishōnin, I was awakened to the mission of Buddha Dharma of Japan and came to India. For over fifty years I have engaged in the mission of *Saiten-kaikyō* [mission to restore Buddha Dharma in India]. It is indeed solely the fruit of India's independence through a nonviolent movement that allowed the unhindered dissemination of the Buddha Dharma of Japan in India today. Had India not become a free nation, the Buddha Dharma of Japan would have been persecuted and expelled. The presence of His Excellencies—the President of India and both the Governor and Chief Minister of the State of Bihar—attests to India's unparalleled understanding and favor towards the Buddha Dharma of Japan, for which I am deeply grateful.

Buddha Dharma of Japan is founded on the Saddharma-pundarīka-sūtra [the Lotus Sūtra.]. The Preceptor, the World Honored One, Buddha Śākyamuni initiated the preaching of the Saddharma-pundarīka-sūtra at the age of seventy-two here at Mount Grdhrakūta, Rajgir and completed it after eight years. The true intent of Buddha Śākyamuni's advent in the *sahā* world was fully revealed during those eight years. Buddha Śākyamuni descended from Mount Grdhrakūta at the age of eighty for his journey to Parinirvāna.

The Saddharma-pundarīka-sūtra is a sūtra of prophecy. Thus, Nichiren Daishōnin states,

> The advent of the Buddha was not for those present during the eight years atop Mount Grdhrakūta, but for those who followed in the Eras of Genuine Dharma, Semblance Dharma

and Final Dharma.[2] More specifically, it was not for those living during the two thousand years of the Eras of Genuine Dharma or Semblance Dharma, but for those, like myself, living at the beginning of the Era of Final Dharma. Those referred to as affected with illness are those who slander the Saddharma-pundarīka-sūtra.

The Saddharma-pundarīka-sūtra chapter of *The Eternal Duration of the Life of the Tathāgata* states,

Even when all the living see, at the kalpa's end,
The conflagration burning,
Tranquil is this realm of mine,
Ever filled with celestial beings
Gardens, forests, and various temples and stately buildings
With every kind of gem adorned.

This passage of the sūtra is a precise prophecy of the modern times. "When all the living see/ at the kalpa's end/ the great conflagration burning," is the time that is to come when all life cannot be sustained, whether in the sky, on earth or in the water. The great conflagration is said to consume all life. In the past, this great conflagration was interpreted to be flames that would erupt from the earth. No one fathomed that it could be flames made by human beings that would consume all forms of life.

However, the atomic and hydrogen bombs, nuclear weapons developed during World War II, were indeed the great conflagration capable of totally destroying all forms of life. Excessive nuclear weapons that proliferate throughout the earth are more than enough to consume the world repeatedly. Some think they could be detonated by the end of this century. This is the significance of the passage: "When all the living see/ at the kalpa's end/ the conflagration burning." Nichiren Daishōnin construed that the true purpose of the World Honored One, Buddha Śākyamuni's advent in the *sahā* world was not for the sake of guiding the people of his time toward the Dharma nor for the salvation of the people in the ensuing Eras of Genuine Dharma and Semblance Dharma,

2 Please refer to *Single Word of Mystery*, footnote 11, p. 203.

1,000 years and 2,000 years, respectively, following the Buddha's demise. Rather, it was to liberate the people affected by the five impurities of the Era of Final Dharma, 2,500 years after the Parinirvāna of the Buddha.

The Eternal Duration of the Life of the Tathāgata of the Saddharma-pundarīka-sūtra says, "I leave here this good medicine. Take it and do not fear of not being cured." The good medicine that was left in the *sahā* world is the good medicine that cures today's spiritual delirium. It is the five and seven characters of Na Mu Myō Hō Ren Ge Kyō.[3] We are taught not to doubt that chanting this single phrase extracted from the sūtra would ever fail to extinguish the great conflagration about to engulf the length and breadth of the earth; doubt leaves only despair, our concern unanswered. Chant Na Mu Myō Hō Ren Ge Kyō without doubt but with faith in it; rest assured that the great conflagration will be extinguished.

Nichiren Daishōnin exhorted us saying that when the people of the land come to chant Na Mu Myō Hō Ren Ge Kyō in one voice, the ominous calamities in this life will be dispelled, the means to longevity acquired; likewise, the state will manifest where both humans and the universe are liberated from death and disease by unnatural causes, which deprive all forms of life of their given life span. "Doubt not the passage of the sūtra, which assures of peace and tranquility in this actual world."[4] The passage of the sūtra, "Tranquil is this realm of mine/ ever filled with celestial beings. Gardens, forests, various temples and stately buildings/ with every kind of gem adorned," is the prophecy for the 21st century.

No means are available in the modern times to quell the great flames of a nuclear holocaust. The nuclear catastrophe is a paroxysm caused by spiritual delirium of humans who develop and use nuclear weapons. Once this spiritual delirium is cured, nuclear weapons cannot detonate voluntarily and bring catastrophe to the human world. It is expounded in the sūtra that humans "lost their right minds taking the other poisonous medicine." "The right mind" alludes to the innate spirituality that befits humans and exists in every human being from birth. Parents killing their children; the fetus deemed the unborn enemy of a parent; children killing parents; parents regarded as enemies by the children who plot to steal the throne and family possessions; adultery that results in husbands killing wives or vice-versa. These are all dreadful acts no ferocious animal or poisonous snake would even do. These acts are not the workings of a heart

3 Please refer to *Nuclear Technology*, footnote 31, p. 96.
4 *Nyosetsu-shugyō-shō* 如説修行鈔 *Practice Thus As Taught by the Buddha*.

and mind befitting human beings, in other words, the right mind. They are all violations of morals and ethics. Yet, those who engage in such acts can be restored to their right minds through teachings. Morality was spread for this purpose.

Even the terrible acts of stealing the throne or treasures or wallowing in carnal pleasures are not disasters that could spread to cause human annihilation. The brutal and inhumane act committed by Ajātaśatru[5] in Rajgir is but such an example. Yet, the tragedy of humanity's extermination will occur with the next nuclear war. A consortium of a massive military, the munitions industry, scientists and politicians is what executes war. Their desire for power and wealth, in other words, the avaricious mind, is the motive of war. Buddha Dharma preaches that war arises from greed, and restraint of the covetous mind is the most important discipline in human life. In violation of this basic teaching, covetousness was encouraged and euphemistically redefined as raising the standard of living. When the nation believes war's purpose is to enhance the standard of living, war is no longer considered a crime. Killing or destruction then becomes as mundane as eating a meal or drinking tea. This is the sign of the times when human beings have lost their "right mind" as a result of "taking the other poisonous medicine."

In the modern civilization, humanity has come to glorify war and to enthusiastically propagandize the causalities and the merciless devastations of cities. The modern civilization, the civilization of science, has no inherent power to eliminate war. That is why it is "the other poisonous medicine." The modern civilization is a material civilization and a civilization of machines. Development of machines culminated in nuclear weapons. They are of no benefit; rather, they threaten the survival of humanity. Humans have built them; humans, likewise, must eliminate them. Once we liberate ourselves by awakening from the myth of the civilization of machines and revert to the innate principles of life taught by the spiritual civilization, nuclear weapons immediately are laid to rest for good. When human delirium is cured, nuclear weapons can be eliminated without any difficulty.

Out of the whole wide world, the cradle of the spiritual civilization

---

5 Ajātaśatru was the son of King Bimbisāra who imprisoned and killed his father under the evil influence of Devadatta. The astrologers predicted while he was in the womb that he would become his father's enemy, thus his given name Ajātaśatru, meaning "unborn enemy." Later he repented and became Buddha's devout follower.

Guruji drums and chants at 2 a.m., October 24, 1981 as the final check is made for the Venuvan Vihar [Bamboo Grove Monastery] dedication ceremony.

is here, at Venuvan Vihar. The restoration of Venuvan Vihar came out of the wish to offer the good medicine to arrest the poisonous medicine, which is the material civilization bringing delusion and agony to modern humanity. Our friends who have gathered here from the worlds of ten directions[6] are all advocates of disarmament working toward the elimination of nuclear weapons and general and complete disarmament. This Venuvan Vihar was built to be utilized for the purpose of attaining your lofty goals. Venuvan Vihar is a place to apply Buddha's teachings to the modern times, not a place to indulge in interpreting or researching classics. Neither is it a dōjō for performing funerals or memorial services for the dead. It is where the prayers for global peace and tranquility of the nations are to take place, a place to build world peace. The true intent in restoring Venuvan Vihar is *Risshō-ankoku,* to give rise to the True Dharma to bring peace and tranquility to the nations of the world.

Na Mu Myō Hō Ren Ge Kyō

---

6 Coinciding with the dedication of the new Venuvan Vihar, Nipponzan Myōhōji convened an international forum for the abolition of nuclear weapons with people of faith.

45

Greetings to the East German Peace Committee

September 17, 1982
East Berlin

I am deeply grateful for the peace medal presented to me by the leaders of the East German peace movement gathered here today.

The time is now for humanity to radically transform the way in which we live from what has gone on in the past. Until now, competition has largely informed human existence and prosperity, particularly when it comes to force and violence. Such a stage in human development was inevitable. For example, Japan sought to ascend to the height of world power 100 years ago through military power in a political revolution known as the Meiji Restoration. From top to bottom, the entire nation became soldiers. The emperor was commander-in-chief. Although ordained a monk, I, too, was conscripted simply because I passed a physical. Japan's experience shows how military power received sanction at every level: from the people, the state and the world. Drawn to this power, it became commonplace to engage in reprehensible practices of oppression and invasion by those with military means against those without. This practice continued throughout World War II. Japan, seeking to lead the world through military power, joined hands with Germany and together they sought to guide the world through force. Italy, too, joined in. That was the war. It was to be humanity's last war.

Yet that was not the case. Nuclear weapons, developed by the end of World War II, were first used on Hiroshima and Nagasaki. Their astounding kill force and destructive power have rapidly progressed until they now amass a brute force so compelling that not only can they obliterate humanity, they can utterly change the earth and universe as we know them. The preparation has been completed; preparation has been completed to annihilate humanity several tens of times over. It is now apparent that for humanity to survive, not only war policies but science itself must be reexamined to avert a catastrophe from befalling humankind. The question then arises whether humans can successfully sustain society without resorting to force, without possessing weapons of murder like firearms, cannons or bombs. Without doubting whether it's possible, we must believe we can.

Grounds for our belief can be found in the independence movement of India before World War II, a movement without a single soldier, without a single bullet fired from beginning to end. It sought only to correct the wrongs of the British invasion and rule over India. The world was incredulous that such a movement could achieve a political revolution for independence and self-rule. History lacked any precedent, yet Mahatma Gandhi believed it to be the sole path if humanity were to continue to live in the future. He declared the heavens themselves would render judgment, and a time was coming when this aspiration would bear fruit. He immersed himself in prayer morning and night. He traveled on speaking engagements throughout the country, largely for the purpose of praying wherever he went. I was fortunate to be at his Wardha ashram in the midst of all this. His prayer did bear fruit for not one Indian civilian was sacrificed for war, not a single enemy killed. Immediately after World War II, India attained unconditional independence and self-rule. It was indeed an awesome undertaking.

It is said that Germany lost 6 million of their countrymen and women in World War II. Japan also lost some 3 million of its own citizens to the war, including victims of the atomic bombings of Hiroshima and Nagasaki. Furthermore for the first time in its 2,600-year history, Japan endured the humiliation of defeat and ruination in war. The Peace Constitution was founded on the belief that a nation cannot exist through military power and war, rather the survival of a nation is assured only through faith in others and peaceful reciprocity. The Constitution renounced the right to war, and Japan disarmed. Rapid national growth followed, and the people thrived.

Currently the United States relentlessly presses Japan to prepare for war. The rationale cited is the Soviet threat. Until recently I have had several occasions to visit the Soviet Union. I attended every meeting of the Asian Buddhist Conference for Peace held there. I made an offering of the relics of Buddha Śākyamuni and proposed a plan to build a stūpa in Moscow to key government officials. They promised that if this is a wish shared by the people of Asia, they will build a stūpa in harmony with the aspirations of the people. This is the relationship we have with the Soviet Union. The origin of this karmic connection goes back even further.

Before Mahatma Gandhi, in an era when the world accepted the right to war without question, Leo Tolstoy emerged in Russia. His literary works were widely translated into Japanese. These works lead me to believe that Russia's Tolstoy was this era's first torchbearer for peace. One of Tolstoy's writings is *Nichiro-Sensō* [*Russo-Japanese War*].[1] It is a piece on the war between Japan and Russia. Manchuria, China was a major battlefield. A Russian soldier, who was a pacifist, sent Tolstoy a letter on his commitment to this ideal. He wrote that he was conscripted by the government and will be sent to the battlefield, but that he goes unwillingly for he cannot escape. However, he vowed not to kill a single Japanese soldier with his firearm. Any suspicion harbored towards these people can fill us with terror. Yet, when we believe in them, we find the foundation for world peace deep in the hearts of the people of the Soviet Union.

Political restrictions prevented me from visiting East Germany before now. The disciples of Nipponzan Myōhōji walked throughout East Germany in a peace march. They needed food as well as shelter at night as they walked. Word has reached me that the people of East Germany were gracious in offering hospitality. I am deeply grateful. Although this is my first visit to your country, I profoundly believe the people of East Germany will rise and take on a significant role in eliminating nuclear weapons. I express my heartfelt appreciation for this unexpected kindness and hospitality extended to me today.

---

1 The translator is not certain if this is a reference to *Bethink Yourselves: Tolstoy's Letter on the Russo-Japanese War* carried by the London Times on June 27, 1904.

46

Our Mandate

October 9, 1982
Milton Keynes, England

On the surface, every Dharma-battle Ososhi-sama engaged in was a defeat. None of his admonitions were heeded. Not only was he not heard, each time he remonstrated those in power he was harshly persecuted, incurring harm on his own person. It is indeed remarkable. Ososhi-sama never despaired. *Risshō-ankoku-ron* is said to be his last discourse to the disciples in his final hour. His parting discourse on *Risshō-ankoku-ron* in the hour of death must be understood as his mandate to the disciples who would appear in ages to come. We must be thorough in examining *Risshō-ankoku-ron* and fulfill the mandate vested in us by Ososhi-sama. "Peace in the world and tranquility of the land", are what religion should be about. "When the domain is free from decline, and the land free from destruction, our bodies will be safe and our hearts and minds tranquil."

Our mandate waiting to be fulfilled is to emancipate all sentient beings. This is the mission we are entrusted with. Building temples or stūpas are expedients toward that end. Our ultimate goal is the realization of a world where people's bodies are safe and their hearts and minds tranquil. Temples and stūpas are of no use unless facilitating this goal and would not bring joy to the people. The physical safety of an individual does not exist without the safety of the non-sentient realm [physical environment] we live in. Likewise, the physical safety of an individual does not exist without the safety of the realm of sentient beings we are part of. Our sphere of work is to bring peace among the people, adorn the domain and free this world from strife. We must turn it into a place where all find profound spiritual joy. That is what the building of stūpas is about, what adorning temples is for.

47

HAKUJYU[1]

NEW YEAR'S CELEBRATION TO MARK TURNING 99 YEARS OF AGE

January 2, 1983
Tama Dōjō, Tōkyō

I EXTEND TO YOU JOYFUL GREETINGS OF THE NEW YEAR. Of all life forms, I was blessed to be born human, which is said to be rare. Despite the anguish that accompanies birth, death and life's impermanence, I have been blessed with a longevity spanning 99 years. During my long life of 99 years, I have been able to live in comfort with relatively few illnesses and afflictions. I have been moving constantly back and forth, circling the globe without weariness.

It is also said that it is likewise rare to encounter Buddha Dharma. Yet I was born into a country where Buddha Dharma had spread and encountered it by birth. Among all the teachings taught by Buddha, I encountered the Daimoku of the Lotus Sūtra and consequently became a practitioner of the Daimoku. The Lotus Sūtra states that to be born in the iniquitous Era of Final Dharma following Buddha's extinction and to become a practitioner of the Lotus Sūtra is owed to the merits accumulated from past lives of closely serving and offering to ten thousand billion Buddhas as a Bodhisattva practice. It is hard to fathom how overwhelming Nichiren Daishōnin's joy must have been when he read this passage and realized the rewarding fruit of his past had brought him the fortune of becoming a practitioner of the Lotus Sūtra. My shallow faith does not afford me as great a joy when reflecting on my merits from past lives. Nevertheless, looking back on my life as a practitioner of the Lotus Sūtra I feel only joy.

I became ordained, which granted me a life of complete freedom.

---

1 *Hakuju* 白寿. The ceremony to mark turning 99. *Haku* 白 is a single brushstroke less than *hyaku* 百, a hundred. One Japanese tradition holds that the New Year's marks the addition of another year to a person's age rather than the actual birthday. Therefore, Guruji marked his 99th year in January of 1983, although his birthday was August 6.

It is a life with no sovereign authority above nor servitude of subjects below. It is a life unencumbered by the worry of earning a living, unaffected by age differences, nor discriminating between kith or kin and stranger. With no attachment to the temptations of the five dusts and the six desires,[2] I came and went where I pleased. Where I visited, I left my footprint; and built stūpas where I stayed. Mine was a life resembling white clouds blown by the wind. Yet, when closely examined, it has been a life treading a single path, the life of a monastic. Among the life of various monastic practices, mine was a life of missions abroad to disseminate the Dharma. Of all the places abroad, it was a monastic life with the mission of *Saiten-kaikyō*. And among the Western Heavens, it was a mission to restore Buddhism to India. The work to restore Buddhism to India has taken root, sprouted leaves and is about to blossom and bear fruit. Out of the whole wide world, it was in India that the Buddha Dharma of Japan spread and Buddhism restored.

The spreading of the Buddha Dharma of Japan in India does not mean that Japanese nationals simply built stūpas and temples. Rather, the Indian people themselves came to chant Na Mu Myō Hō Ren Ge Kyō. "The moon shifts from the west to east, the sign of the Buddha Dharma of India spreading to the east. The sun orbits from east to west, an auspicious omen of the Buddha Dharma of Japan returning to India [the country of the moon]."The prophecy by Nichiren Daishōnin in *Kangyō-Hachiman-shō*[3] has indeed proven true 700 years after his passing. What an unparalleled splendor! *Kangyō-hachiman-shō* says:

> Dim is the light cast by the moon. Buddha's preaching of [the Lotus Sūtra] was limited to eight years during his lifetime.[4]

---

2 Please refer to *Nuclear Technology and the Future of Humanity*, footnotes 9 and 10, p.87-88.

3 *Admonishing Bodhisattva Hachiman* 諫暁八幡抄. Written by Nichiren Daishōnin in 1280 at Mount Minobu.

4 The Dharma preached by the Buddha for the salvation of all, the Lotus Sūtra, was offered eight years only preceding Buddha's Nirvāna. In contrast, the sūtra's quintessence, the Odaimoku, is to spread for an indefinite period of time through the disciples of the Eternal Buddha, the Bodhisattvas Who Emerges From the Earth, for the emancipation of sentient beings in the Era of Final Dharma. Nichiren Daishōnin uses the simile of the sun and the moon to make this distinction, the shorter period of eight years shedding more limited light [like the moon] than the indefinite period that the Odaimoku is to spread [the sun]. Also, Nichiren Daishōnin uses the countries' names to reinforce the simile: Gasshi, 月氏, Land of the Moon, is an ancient name for India; Nihon 日本, the name for Japan, literally means Land Where the Sun Rises.

> Light emitted by the sun outshines the light of the moon, an auspicious omen of the Buddha Dharma of Japan illuminating the prolonged darkness of the era starting in the fifth five-hundred-years.

Reply to Lord Shijō-kingo[5] says:

> We are now indeed in the latter fifth five-hundred-year period, the beginning of the Era of Final Dharma. It is likened to the sun on May 15th and the moon on August 15th.[6] T'ien-t'ai and Dengyō were born too soon.[7] At the same time, those born hereafter will regret not having been born sooner. The adversary's main contingent has been defeated. The remnants are of no consequence. Now is the time following the demise of the Buddha, in the beginning of the Era of Final Dharma,the fifth five-hundred-year period, when persecution of those who expound this sūtra is predicted to be even greater than during the time of the Buddha. If there is no falsehood in Buddha's words, then would not a sage have surely appeared within the *Jambudvīpa*? An outbreak of the greatest battle in the *Jambudvīpa* is preached as a sign of the sage's advent. The battle has already begun,[8] thus a sage would have inevitably made his appearance within the *Jambudvīpa*.

Saiten-kaikyō might be perceived as a religious sectarian endeavor. India's independence may sound like a political enterprise.

---

5 *Shijō-kingodono-go-henji* 四条金吾殿御返事. Written by Nichiren Daishōnin at Minobu in 1279.

6 According to the lunar calendar, the sun on May 15 is at the summer solstice, the peak of its strength. August 15th is the mid-autumn full moon, the harvest moon. Both are analogies to the maturation of time, ripe for the spreading of the Lotus Sūtra as prophesized by Buddha.

7 Meaning the time before the time the Lotus Sūtra was prophesized to spread.

8 A reference to the Mongolian domination of the world and invasion of Japan. After two failed attempts demanding tribute from the Hōjō regency, Kublai Khan, Genghis Khan's grandson, sent a massive Mongolian and Koryō fleet. Troops of over 30,000 invaded in 1274 and over 140,000 in 1281, where the battle took place in Kyūshū and its surrounding islands. However, in both instances, heavy wind, most likely typhoons, caused catastrophic damages to the fleets anchored in the ocean resulting in major Mongolian defeats.

However, Nichiren Daishōnin's tenet of *Risshō-ankoku* [giving rise to the Genuine Dharma for peace and tranquility of the land] is a teaching in which *Saiten-kaikyō* and India's independence are one and the same. His words in the *Risshō-ankoku-ron*: "Promptly mend thy trivial faith and immediately embrace the single truth of the Genuine Vehicle. If so, the entire triple world is the Buddha Realm; how can the Buddha Realm ever decline?" are synonymous to the remonstration by Gandhiji to the British Viceroy in India. *Saiten-kaikyō* was nothing other than India's independence. To see it as anything less, trivializes it to mere business by monks who turn religion into a profession. Nipponzan's *Saiten-kaikyō* was India's freedom movement.

Once *Saiten-kaikyō* was accomplished, what is to follow? Nichiren Daishōnin states in *Kangyō-hachiman-shō*, "Light emitted by the sun outshines light of the moon, an auspicious omen of the Buddha Dharma of Japan illuminating the prolonged darkness of the era starting in the fifth five-hundred-years." He also states, "We are now indeed in the latter fifth five-hundred-year period, the beginning of the Era of Final Dharma. It is likened to the sun on May 15th and the moon on August 15th. T'ien-t'ai and Dengyō were born too soon. At the same time, those born hereafter will regret not having been born sooner. The adversary's main contingent has already been defeated. The remnants are of no consequence." The iniquitous era of terror repeatedly alluded to in the chapter *Exhortation to Hold Firm* in the Lotus Sūtra, is "the prolonged darkness of the fifth five-hundred-year period" referred to by Nichiren Daishōnin. It is the time he believed was specified for the world dissemination of the seven characters of Na Mu Myō Hō Ren Ge Kyō, the heart of the Lotus Sūtra, with the advent of the Bodhisattvas Who Emerge From the Earth.

Exhortation to Hold Firm in the Lotus Sūtra states: "We shall indeed widely expound this sūtra, in the iniquitous era of terror after your extinction." Therefore, Nichiren Daishōnin determined that the dissemination of the Lotus Sūtra was to happen in the iniquitous era of terror. *The Eternal Duration of the Life of the Tathāgata* chapter of the Lotus Sūtra preaches such time to be "when all the living see, at the kalpa's end, the conflagration burning."

Nichiren Daishōnin's *Risshō-ankoku-ron* states:

> Five of the seven calamities prophesized in the Scripture of the

> Master of Healing[9] have come to pass, leaving two waiting to occur: foreign invasion and domestic disturbance by mutiny. Moreover, two of the three calamities foretold in the Great Collection Sūtra[10] have already manifested, leaving just one to be fulfilled: disorder by military feud.

Fear of eradicating all life stems from war and its destructive fires. The gargantuan institution of the state together with its military allies perpetuates war and its destructive fires. This is what is meant by "iniquitous era." War and its destructive fires are created by those who are aware of what they are doing—such as the military, governments, scientists, engineers, workers, merchants of death—but also unwittingly embroils ordinary citizens, who are unconscious of their involvement. This is what is meant by "prolonged darkness." Buddha Dharma of Japan is the light which illuminates the protracted darkness of the fifth five-hundred-year period. What rolled back the rock covering the entrance to the cave where the Sun Goddess hid to bring light once again to the world[11] were *Saiten-kaikyō* and India's independence, both of which embodied nonviolence and the practice of *tangyō-raihai*.

Reply to Lord Shijō-kingo states:

> Now is the time following the demise of the Buddha, in the beginning of *Mappō*, the fifth five-hundred-year period, when persecution of those who expound this sūtra is predicted to be even greater than during the time of the Buddha. If there is no falsehood in Buddha's words, then would not a sage have surely appeared within the *Jambudvīpa*? An outbreak of the greatest battle in the *Jambudvīpa* is preached as a sign of the sage's advent. The battle had already begun, thus a sage inevitably would have made his appearance within the *Jambudvīpa*.

---

9 Yakushi-kyō 薬師経 Bhaisajyaguru-sutra [Sk] contains the 12 vows of Yakushi-bosatsu [Master of Healing Bodhisattva] also known as Medicine Master of Lapis Lazuli Radiance or King of Healers.

10 Daishū-kyō 大集経 is a translation by Dharmaksema in 60 fascicles. The full title is Daihōdō-daishū-kyō 大方等大集経.

11 An analogy to rolling back the rock that covered the cave where the Sun Goddess Amaterasu, the goddess from which all light emanates, had hid herself. According to Japanese mythology, removing the rock brought light back to the world which had been plunged into darkness.

> . . . Nichiren's [my] heart and mind are not at all like that of a messenger of the Tathāgata, for I am an unenlightened mortal. However, the two banishments I experienced through the rancor of the three kinds of mortal enemies make me akin to the messenger of the Tathāgata.[12] While I am an unenlightened mortal with my heart and mind deeply affected by the three poisons,[13] when I enunciate Na Mu Myō Hō Ren Ge Kyō through my mouth, do I not bear a resemblance to the messenger of the Tathāgata?

To quell the greatest conflagration of war that is to occur in the *Jambudvīpa* at the beginning of the Era of Final Dharma, the latter fifth five-hundred-year period following the demise of the Buddha, and to eternally protect the lives of all sentient beings, Buddha Śākyamuni taught, "I leave here this good medicine. Take it and do not fear of not being cured." He sends a messenger home to encourage the taking of this good medicine. T'ien-t'ai in China and Dengyō in Japan both propagated the Lotus Sūtra well, yet they were born before the Era of Final Dharma and could not become the prophesized envoys of the Buddha. Nichiren Daishōnin determined that the messenger of the Buddha to be born in the Era of Final Dharma "while possessing the body of an unenlightened mortal, when enunciating Na Mu Myō Hō Ren Ge Kyō," that one will "bear a resemblance to the messenger of the Tathāgata."

In recent years, we have seen a ground swell of great universal peace marches, great mass rallies and great movements rejecting nuclear weapons, war and armaments throughout Europe and North America. Each one is a movement of nonviolence, a movement of *tangyō-raihai*. When examined closely, they are also outcries proclaiming the Genuine Dharma with the reverberations of the drum and major enterprises to manifest the emergence of stūpas.

The mission to spread the Dharma in Europe had been delayed but was finally initiated in recent years. Vows were made to build stūpas, and construction has begun or will in various European countries starting

12 The chapter of *Exhortation to Hold firm* in the Lotus Sūtra describes the hardships to be endured by the emissaries of the Tathāgata who transmit the teachings of the Lotus Sūtra in the in the iniquitous era of terror after the Buddha's extinction.

13 *Sandoku* 三毒. Greed, anger and ignorance.

with the U.K., followed by Vienna, the capital of Austria, Helsinki, capital of Finland, Athens in Greece, Dresden in East Germany, Berlin, West Germany, Verdun in France, Venice, Italy and elsewhere. They remind us of bamboo shoots popping up from the ground one right after another.

It is nothing short of a marvel that Buddhism's principle object of veneration—the stūpa enshrining the relics of the Preceptor, Buddha Śākyamuni—is widely welcomed and dedicated in European countries where Buddhism had not spread historically. This phenomenon corresponds to the Golden Words of the Buddha that the Lotus Sūtra will spread far and wide at the beginning of the Era of Final Dharma, the latter fifth five-hundred-year period following the demise of the Buddha. Even in traditionally Buddhist countries of Asia, the emergence of a stūpa is a rare Dharma-work in recent times.

The beginning of our mission in the United States of America goes back more than 20 years. Regardless of the many vows made, stūpas are yet to be built. The first such example is San Francisco followed by Los Angeles, and, third, Seattle. The United States of America is the country that developed nuclear weapons—lethal weapons that can annihilate humanity—and employed them in war wiping out civilian populations. This is the country frantically preparing for nuclear war, which threatens human genocide. What it fears the most is peace, world peace. So how can we expect peace pagodas to be readily approved for they enshrine the relics of the World Honored One, Buddha Śākyamuni, as the principle object of veneration of a faith that works to build global peace. But mark my words; the Buddha Dharma of Japan will build stūpas. I say this because I believe in the divine transcendental powers of the Tathāgata to protect all living beings in this iniquitous era of terror at the beginning of the latter five-hundred-year period.

Let me introduce to you one such example, a legal proceeding on the proposal to construct a peace pagoda across from the front gate of the Trident submarine base [near] Seattle.[14] The Kitsap County Board of Commissioners had denied permission to build a peace pagoda, and a complaint challenging that decision was filed in neighboring King County. State law allows for decisions by a county board of

14 Kitsap County, Bangor, Washington.

commissioners to be reviewed by an adjacent county's Superior Court. On November 29, 1982, King County Superior Court Judge Frank Sullivan issued an oral opinion saying it was unjustified to suspend construction of the peace pagoda at Ground Zero Center for Nonviolent Action. He further stated that the Kitsap County Board of Commissioners had no right to stop the construction. Judge Sullivan found that Kitsap County Board of Commissioners had disregarded the report by the Hearing Examiner, who recommended approval of the peace pagoda construction based on an initial public hearing. He concluded that the court found no substantial evidence for the county's unilateral denial. When this decision was handed down, the 30 or so peace workers present held hands and shed tears of joy.

Religious and sectarian barriers could also pose obstacles in building Buddhist stūpas. In Europe and the United States, there are no Buddhists or Buddhist temples. Therefore, stūpas have not materialized in Los Angeles or San Francisco. However, since Nipponzan's great World Peace March commemorating the 700th anniversary of the passing of Nichiren Daishōnin,[15] sudden sweeping changes have been felt throughout the world in the spirit of people, who welcome efforts to build stūpas and embrace our practice on the streets of chanting the Odaimoku to proclaim the Dharma while the beating of the drum. For example, a major Catholic church in Los Angeles held a large gathering for Nipponzan Myōhōji and offered the use of ten acres of land to erect a stūpa. A sister of the church participated in the *rōhachi-sesshin*[16] practice at Nipponzan's temple last December. Just as the wind meets no obstacles in the open sky, the Buddha Dharma of Japan is reaching wide and far into countries in Europe and different parts of North America. The facts I have cited are in exact concordance with the *gāthā* in *The Divine Transcendental Powers of the Tathāgata* of the Lotus Sūtra.

So far I have spoken on Nipponzan's activities. Let me give you other examples from America. The bishops of the Catholic Church, who in many cases acquiesced to military actions and U.S. foreign policy in the past, assembled in Washington, D.C., in mid-November and

---

15 Please refer to *The Time Has Come*, footnote 1, p. 300.

16 *Rōhachi-sesshin* 臘八摂心, practiced by Nipponzan Myōhōji, is a week of fasting without water or food, chanting the Odaimoku from daybreak to dusk during the week leading up to the day of Buddha Śākyamuni's Enlightenment, celebrated on December 8 in Japan.

deliberated on a draft pastoral letter.[17] The draft letter condemns the use of nuclear weapons on cities and townships as immoral and opposes their first use. They were profoundly skeptical of the doctrine of nuclear deterrence, which claimed to afford protection under the nuclear umbrella. The letter also urged resistance to the MX missile, the intercontinental ballistic missile system to be deployed in Europe. The National Conference of Bishops supports the freeze movement opposed by the Reagan Administration. This was a watershed moment in the history of the modern Catholic Church. At the bishops' conference, the Reagan Administration expressed its opposition to the pastoral letter though a lengthy letter signed by National Security Advisor William Clark. This letter was distributed to all 285 bishops attending the conference. Only six bishops sided with the government's point of view. The remaining 279 bishops endorsed the anti-nuclear draft. In the event the draft pastoral letter is adopted at the next National Conference of Catholic Bishops in Chicago come May, it will become a guide in the daily life of 50 million American Catholics. It underscores the supremacy of religious conscience saying, "As citizens we wish to affirm our loyalty to our country and its ideals, yet we must also hold to the universal principles proclaimed by the church." Herein lies its awesome power.

The anti-nuclear movement in Japan has held annual conferences and great peace walks for more than 30 years. Yet, the primacy of religious and moral conscience is not only de-emphasized, but, to some degree, political partisanship prevented the nuclear abolition movement from growing into a major national popular movement. The draft pastoral letter urges workers in nuclear weapon production to leave their jobs as well as well as calling on the government and military to honor the conscience of the individual. The draft pastoral letter has been examined and worked on for the last two years. Two years ago in spring, Nipponzan sponsored the World Religious Workers Conference for Peace where a resolution against nuclear weapons, war and armaments was unanimously adopted. The Japanese government portrayed this conference as "an undesirable gathering" to the outside world, similar to the position taken by the Reagan Administration towards the National Conference of Catholic Bishops in America. And yet, the White House

17 The annual meeting of the National Conference of Catholic Bishops deliberated on the draft pastoral letter, "The Challenge of Peace."

was shaken by the political impact of the conference. Additionally, the resistance of Native Americans and nonviolent opposition movements by African Americans are coming together and are about to transform U.S. military policy.

Nichiren Daishōnin's words, "The adversary's main contingent has been defeated. The remnants are of no consequence" is the prophecy about to be fulfilled by the Buddha Dharma of Japan and those who embody it, heralding a new direction in U.S. policies for world peace. I am pleased to introduce these auspicious events befitting of the beginning of the New Year.

The Letter on the Inception of Spring[18] written by Ososhi-sama two to three years before his death has been handed down to this day. While I comfortably sing the blessings of peace and tranquility on New Year's, let us ponder on the letter of our founding master, Nichiren Daishōnin, which celebrates a New Year greeted in his latter years at Mount Minobu. Na Mu Myō Hō Ren Ge Kyō.

> I extend the joys of the beginning of spring.[19] Just like flowers blossom on trees and fresh blades of grass cover the mountain, I and others share the joy on the arrival of spring [the New Year]. Now, I have been favored with the offerings of your journal, a straw sack of rice, a straw sack of salt, thirty pieces of steamed rice cakes and a straw sack of taro. Deep in the mountain here, snow has accumulated three meters in the yard over the past three days. Vales have risen like ridges, and ridges soar like ladders to the heavens. Birds and deer enter our hermitage to take refuge; lumber jacks no longer set foot into the mountain. Clothing is thin, and food depleted. At night I am no different from *kankuchō*.[20] The thought of descending the mountain to human settlement occupies my

18 *Haru-no-Hajime-no-Goshōsoku* 春初御消息. Written at Mount Minobu to a devotee, Lord Nanjō Tokimitsu, also referred to by Nichiren Daishōnin as Lord Ueno, taken from the name of his fiefdom. The date it was written is not clear. Possible dates are the first year of Kōan [1277] or fifth year of Kōan [1282].

19 Here Nichiren Daishōnin is referring to New Years. According to the lunar calendar, spring includes January, February, March.

20 寒苦鳥. A legendary bird said to be living in the snow-capped mountains in India [the Himalayas] that suffers the cold at night and sings of its intention to build a nest come dawn, but the warmth of the morning sun makes it forget the agony of cold.

> mind during the day. The [my] voice reciting the sūtra has faded, and the mind of contemplation weakened. At a time when I was grieving on the prospect of receding in the practice of the Way, thus plunging into the eternal cycle of transmigration over the next five hundred to three thousand-dust-atom *kalpas*, the alms delivered reinvigorated my life. I am delighted that I may be able to see you again.

This letter depicts Nichiren Daishōnin's life, snowbound in the deep mountain, unvisited by a soul. "Clothing is thin, and food depleted." There were no clothes to layer, and after several days without food, he was debilitated to the extent that his voice reciting the Lotus Sūtra had faded. His mind to explore the profound truth of Buddha Dharma through contemplation was weakened, biding the moment of death from starvation and cold in the snow. The thought of descending the mountain to human habitation frequently occupied his mind during the day. The bitter cold of night was unbearable, and he mused on finding a way to warm up with daybreak. Afflicted by cold and pangs of hunger day and night, Ososhi-sama expressed his grief of an unlikely enlightenment in the world hereafter should his life come to an end like this, and thus he would be compelled to repeat transmigration among the six worlds of suffering.[21]

Ososhi-sama had offered his precious body to such extremes of cold and hunger to set an example for his disciples and devotees who would be willing to take on the dissemination of the Lotus Sūtra in the turbid Era of Final Dharma caused by the five defilements.[22] In comparison to such a master, I, as his disciple, am waited on at this banquet celebrating the New Year. Rather than being cold, I am covered in layers. How can I possibly avoid divine retribution?

Na Mu Myō Hō Ren Ge Kyō

---

21 The six worlds of suffering out of the ten realms of existence are hell, the realms of hungry spirits, animals, asuras, humans and heavenly beings. They are the realms of delusion.

22 Please refer to *Wondrous First Connection with Lord Buddha's Relic*, footnote 52, p. 26.

48

True Neutrality[1]

September 21, 1984
Atami Dōjō, Japan

Question: What are your thoughts on Japan's doctrine of unarmed neutrality?

Guruji: Japan's doctrine of unarmed neutrality falls short of the prerequisites. Unarmed neutrality posits neither enemy nor ally. Only those seeking genuine peace can claim it. Possession of arms assumes potential enemies, and talk of demilitarization rings hollow when arms are allowed. Weapons are totally useless unless potential enemies are anticipated. Some political parties in Japan advocate demilitarization, but in reality we are already armed in the name of national defense, sanctioning the Self-Defense Forces because we hypothesize enemies on one hand while collaborating with allies on the other. Under these circumstances, unarmed neutrality is not viable. This is why I say Japan's doctrine of unarmed neutrality fails to meet the prerequisites. We must be willing to first cast aside arms to create a world of genuine unarmed neutrality. Arms become a necessity only when enemies are assumed. The first and foremost prerequisite is to shed the notion of "the enemy". Neutrality follows.

Japan's first misstep was to side with one of the two global adversaries. Despite our own renunciation of war, we are in an alliance with one of these adversaries, whose intrigue opened the door to the great war of human annihilation. Not only is Japan exploited militarily, but now the Self-Defense Forces are about to be used for the purpose of war. This kind of unarmed neutrality will never hold water. Japan is not neutral. True unarmed neutrality is predicated on not conjuring up enemies and

1 Excerpt from an interview with Asahi Newspaper.

requires us to forsake the notion of a military response, even in the worst case of an attack by a hostile nation. If we employ a military response, war is inevitable. The notion that we will be killed without a military response is a fallacy. Being unarmed is not what gets us killed. Aligning with one side or the other is what will kill us.

When we recognize the potential for human annihilation and refuse to take sides, genuine unarmed neutrality becomes viable. On his visit to India, Britain's Lord Brockway[2] spoke on this very issue in a response to questions from reporters, following a meeting with Indian officials, including Prime Minister Indira Gandhi. Lord Brockway told of an opportunity he had to speak closely with [Mahatma] Gandhiji. They must have met on the occasion of Gandhiji's participation in the London Conference.[3] Lord Brockway wondered whether Gandhiji's view of unarmed neutrality was a demonstration of Jesus Christ's edict of "Love thy enemy." In his movement for peace and nonviolence, Gandhiji replied, "I have no enemies. Therefore, the question of loving and hating does not at all arise."[4] This is not a quote from the Bible. He spoke to the essence of the peace movement in the modern times.

If today's movements for peace are to uphold unarmed neutrality, the notion of "the enemy" must first be rejected. When we declare that no enemies encircle Japan, peace movements, movements calling for neutrality, become viable for the first time. Regardless of which political party rises to power in Japan, they will maintain a minimum level of arms and troops in the name of self-defense. If anyone should attack, this army claims it can do the job. Therefore, Japan's doctrine of unarmed neutrality, in the real sense of that term, does not hold water. Because it does not hold water, Japan had to unabashedly join hands with the United States and sign the Japan-U.S. Security Treaty which states that while

---

2 Archibald Fenner Brockway [1888-1988] was born in Calcutta during the British colonial reign of India and became a socialist, pacifist and political writer who campaigned for Indian independence and championed African nationalism. His passion and convictions led him to serve five prison terms, two of which were for his militant pacifism during World War I, one of those terms included hard labor.

3 Gandhiji participated in the Second Roundtable Conference convened by the British government in 1931 as the sole representative of the Indian National Congress.

4 Original quote found in *Mahatma Gandhi Letters to Americans* in an essay by its general editor, Shri S. Ramakrishnan, whose close association with Gandhi led him to become the director general of Bharatiya Vidya Bhavan, an educational trust established with Gandhi's blessing.

Japan will not use nuclear weapons, it will be protected by the United States who would. Under this agreement, the nation came to believe it was safeguarded from the Soviet Union. This is dangerous. And the strange variety of demilitarization currently offered by the Liberal Democratic Party is being advocated only by a negligible fraction of that party.

The world in modern times has seen the emergence of the non-aligned nations. Their number has grown substantially. Initially it emerged at the time of the Indian independence. Today even India has become a nuclear power. Nevertheless, India still leads the peace movement of the non-aligned nations. Essentially, non-aligned nations do not align with either of the two military superpowers, but simply walk their own path without resorting to force to keep the peace. The number of such countries is now quite a few. Many of these nations do not have military forces and seem to help each other based on trust. This is a viable way of life. If a country joins a military alliance, it creates enemies on the other side. It is inevitable. It would be good for Japan to take the position of non-alliance like the many non-aligned nations. However, since Japan follows the United States and assumes a posture of countering the Soviet Union's military strength, any talk of demilitarization or neutrality lacks credence.

Alarmed by the great earthquake that hit Kamakura, Nichiren Daishōnin wrote the prophetic treatise of *Risshō-ankoku-ron*, his first remonstration of the government. Similarly, a major earthquake hit the entire Kantō region[5] on September 1, 1923. I was also startled by the earthquake and in fear that it might be a prelude to Japan's fall in light of the clear mirror of *Risshō-ankoku-ron*, I immediately returned from my journey of spreading the Dharma abroad. The moment I set foot in Japan, I started to walk alone through Tōkyō in the ruble of the earthquake's aftermath, praying every day. A devotee of the Lotus Sūtra, Mrs. Matsudaira Toshiko,[6] joined in with me with her two daughters. No one paid attention to a party of four walking around the streets of Tōkyō, beating the drum. Therefore, I went to a busier main street where people gathered in front of Shirokiya,[7] and told the crowd that the earthquake

---

5 The earthquake damage was far-reaching including Tōkyō, Kanagawa, Chiba, Saitama, Ibaragi, Shizuoka, and Yamanashi prefectures, affecting 3.4 million people including 100,000 fatalities.

6 松平俊子 [1890-1985]. Chairwoman of Risshō Women's Association, Dean of Shōwa University and author of *Celebrating the Lotus Sūtra* 法華経禮讃.

7 白木屋. Once a major department store in Japan.

is an alarm, warning us of dangers facing Japan. Mrs. Matsudaira spoke in the same vein. As I feared, Japan later experienced the greatest ruin in its history. Recently, a series of earthquakes are again rocking Japan. The areas affected comprise much of the central area of mainland Japan. Seismologists cannot discount the possibility that the series of earthquakes are precursors to a catastrophic earthquake. There is danger of a major earthquake that would rock the entire country. What do these earthquakes tell us about Japan's future? The heavens forewarn of Japan's total destruction under U.S. leadership. Japan is being led by a man who vows to make Japan an unsinkable aircraft carrier.[8] The risk of Japan being totally destroyed by nuclear weapons is real. I hope this concern is totally unfounded on my part, yet if it happens, it will be too late for regret. The general public must bear this in mind.

Q: What are the future challenges to the religious community?

Guruji: The religious community possesses the power to transform the civilization of science in today's world. Above all, nuclear abolition will be realized when Christianity and Buddhism join forces. It is starting to manifest as a movement in America. It is an exquisite concept that renders all of America's murderous weapons, including nuclear weapons and missiles, useless. As a Christian nation and as followers of the teachings of Jesus Christ, Christians are resolutely speaking out against the abuses of the civilization of machines. In fact, Christian priests and ministers are playing a leading role in the peace movement, and their followers are gaining ground in making nuclear abolition a reality. Buddhists are falling behind in comparison. However, what's at work at the root of this movement comes from the core essence of Buddhism. The unification of Buddhism and Christianity in realizing nuclear abolition creates a spiritual civilization. The movement to spread the teachings that let others live instead of killing them is about to be fulfilled.

Arnold Toynbee, a British historian, once made a prophetic remark that when looking back on the 20th century, the event of greatest significance and note will not be man going to the moon, not the development of nuclear weapons and the wars fought with them, but the encounter of Christianity and Buddhism. His prophecy is about to

8 At the height of the Cold War in 1983, then Prime Minister Nakasone Yasuhiro [b. May 27, 1918] declared in an interview with the Washington Post that "the whole Japanese archipelago...should be like an unsinkable aircraft carrier...against the infiltration of the Backfire bomber."

come true. Christians are constructing the Buddhist essential object of veneration—the stūpa—without any reservations; and Buddhists are likewise building stūpas in Christian nations with no hesitation and spreading Buddhism. This is fact. What we are seeing is neither conventional Christianity nor conventional Buddhism, but the realization of Nichiren Daishōnin's Dharma of the Three Great Mysteries expounded and revealed for the sake of the Era of Final Dharma.

Nichiren Daishōnin's Dharma of Three Great Mysteries consists of first, the *honmon-no-honzon*[9] [the principle object of veneration revealed in the Origin Teaching of the Lotus Sūtra] as signified by the stūpa that emerges in mid-air of the *sahā* world. Next is the Daimoku, Na Mu Myō Hō Ren Ge Kyō, the teaching of religious prayer. It neither depends on violence nor explanation, but is a word of prayer chanted by one or chanted by a multitude. It is to be chanted in jail, amongst people, in the midst of war or anywhere and at any time. Na Mu Myō Hō Ren Ge Kyō, the Daimoku, the second aspect of the Dharma of Three Mysteries, manifests the *honmon-no-kaidan*[10] [the precept dais of the Origin Teaching of the Lotus Sūtra]. The precept dais revealed in the Origin Teaching of the Lotus Sūtra is not a physical structure. It could be anywhere in the *sahā* world in which we live, just as it is in the water where fish swim, the sky where birds fly, forests where creatures dwell, and the streets where humans reside. All these places are intrinsically seen and known as Pure Land. This is what the precept dais of the Origin Teaching of the Lotus Sūtra is about. The entire world is our precept dais. The manifestation of the spiritual Pure Land where Lord Buddha dwells is the precept dais of the Origin Teaching of the Lotus Sūtra. We are not talking about going to Heaven or the distant Pure Land. We do not leave this world. The world we live in, as it is, must be seen in the new light as the Pure Land where Lord Buddha dwells. This understanding becomes the power to create peace. The principle object of veneration and the precept dais of the Origin Teaching of the Lotus Sūtra are bundled in the Odaimoku, the five and seven characters of Na Mu Myō Hō Ren Ge Kyō, so that we can easily keep it today. This is what the Daimoku of the Origin Teaching of the Lotus Sūtra is. The Dharma of the Three Great Mysteries is the Single Great Dharma of Mystery[11] of Na Mu Myō Hō Ren Ge Kyō.

---

9 本門の本尊.
10 本門の戒壇.
11 一大秘法.

49

Eternal Life

September 24, 1983
Vienna, Austria

A stūpa will emerge next in London. I believe the London Peace Pagoda will be my last. I will see to it that it is completed. "Long may a human life be; yet it does not exceed a hundred years. Everything in that time is but a fleeting dream." I am about to awaken from my dream in the *sahā* world. It appears that the time is upon me. However, the footprints I have left throughout my life will not disappear in all eternity. Political movements disappear with the passing of a generation. Once the light of Buddha Dharma enters Christian nations, enters Europe, enters America, it will never go out. I am forever living through it.

London Peace Pagoda

Tributes

Bruce Kent, *Vice President of Movement for the Abolition of War* (UK)

Many times I saw and heard Fujii Guruji here in England—at Milton Keynes and at Battersea in London. Many times, too, in places all around the world, I have heard the beating of the drum and knew at once that somewhere near one of Fujii's monks or nuns was witnessing to peace and justice.

As I read his writings and remember his speeches, I have always felt his partnership with the greatest spiritual leaders of my [Christian] tradition, St. Francis of Assisi, in particular. Francis, too, challenged power, status and violence. He, like Fujii, was a global person. St. Benedict, founder of Western monasticism, would have applauded Fujii's warning to his followers of the dangers, even in religious life, of seeking power, security or comfort under the guise of faith. It was always an inspiration to hear what he had to say. His words were ever a challenge.

We Christians in our churches are too often used to soft words, gentle piety and unthreatening ideas. Fujii knew well how to describe the world as it really is—a place of violence dominated by the worship of the state. He never minced his words when talking about the violence of the politically powerful.

He believed, above all, that what was needed was a profound spiritual change. Only that will drive out the fear of "the other" and bring us to appreciate the goodness of God that is in us all. Quakers, in particular, would warm to that.

He was a very old man even when I first met him. But to the end there was a passion and a power in his words that never failed to inspire. God worked and works wonders in and through him still.

Dennis Banks, ***cofounder of the American Indian Movement, Native American elder from the Anishinaabe Nation***

I first saw Guruji in 1956 at Sunagawa, [Japan]. Although I was unaware of who he was, he was praying, chanting Na Mu Myō Hō Ren Ge Kyō. It was an unfortunate meeting as he along with many Buddhist monks and nuns of Nipponzan Myōhōji and tens of thousands of farmers, students and community people were demonstrating against the expansion of the U.S. Air force's runway in Sunagawa. I was a member of the U.S. Air Force then, but what I witnessed that day convinced me to leave the U.S. military. [The police attacked the monks and nuns.]

I came face to face with Guruji at Atami 22 years later, listening to his words, teaching the disciples of Nipponzan Myōhōji. I later traveled with him to India and Sri Lanka, drawn to the humbleness and wisdom of this spiritual man. He became my mentor until he passed into the Spirit World on January 9, 1985. Sadly I could not attend his service because I was in a South Dakota prison. [He was sentenced to 18 months in prison for his organizing work with AIM.]

Once released from prison I knew I had to follow in his footsteps. Like a message tattooed on my heart, Guruji left me a great path to follow. And I shall carry his message the world over. I felt honored to have met Guruji, and I have placed his memory next to the Great Spirit.

Dr. A.R. Kidwai, ***Governor of Haryana State, India and former governor of Bihar and West Bengal states***

Guruji had seen a picture of Mahatma Gandhi leading the Dandi March in a Japanese newspaper. He also learned how Mahatma Gandhi's unarmed soldiers used the weapon of nonviolence against the armed British rulers. This made Guruji an instant admirer of Mahatma Gandhi. He came to India and spent quite some time at his Ashram where he saw nonviolence and Satyagraha [Truth Force] being successfully used for India's Independence and was convinced that the philosophy of truth and non-violence has to be spread far and wide to curb the violence and exploitation of mankind.

Guruji often referred to the concept of one world. "Vasudhaiv Kutumbakam" or "all belonging to one global family" has been an integral part of Indian psyche since Vedic times. During the 1st century BCE, the wanderer monk, Ashwaghosha, tread this path and later Huien Tsang and Fahien followed it. Fujii Guruji was of the same tribe. He never confined himself to the boundaries of his monastic discipline and strived for a global society and undertook a mission to set up Peace Pagodas all over the world to promote peace and harmony in the global society. The Peace Pagoda at Rajgir, designed by renowned Buddhist artist and architect Upendra Maharathi, is the most important monument built by Guruji in modern India at the behest of Pandit Jawaharlal Nehru, prime minister of India.

Guruji was a man of peace and religion with a vision of truth and concern for the future of the mankind. He realized that if humanity is to survive and grow, concerted effort is needed to mold people and nations towards mutual understanding and peace. Nations have to be more trusting towards each other for peace and goodwill to prevail on earth. For this he chose the eternal celestial sūtra, "Na Mu Myō Hō Ren Ge Kyō," which also became permanent feature of the prayers at Mahatma Gandhi's Ashram. Guruji once remarked, "When I look back on my long relationship with India, it seems that there was no other life besides that in India."

Shelley Douglass, ***cofounder of Ground Zero Center for Nonviolent Action in Bangor, WA, USA, and of Mary's House, a Catholic Worker house in Birmingham, AL***

In 1980 we were part of a small group that had bought 3.8 acres of land sharing fence with the Trident Nuclear Submarine Base being built at Bangor, Washington. We were a rag-tag group of visionaries without much clout.

One member of our rag-tag group was a Japanese man named Katsumi Suzuki. He belonged, we knew, to some kind of Buddhist order. Suzuki would appear at Ground Zero for meetings or events and to beat his drum and chant. He had a dream about building a peace pagoda at Ground Zero. We made encouraging noises, but we really knew very little about Suzuki's order, Nipponzan Myōhōji, or his peace pagoda idea.

In the fall of 1980 Suzuki told us excitedly that the founder of his order, Guruji, would be traveling to New York for a special session of the UN. Suzuki would go to meet him and report on his experiences in the United States and Canada. It was Suzuki's hope to bring Guruji to Ground Zero. "Sure," we said, "That would be fine." It really didn't occur to us that such a thing could actually happen.

Imagine our surprise, then, when Suzuki phoned from New York one day in early November to say, "Get ready! You must get ready! Guruji and thirty monks and nuns arriving Ground Zero on Tuesday!" Tuesday—which also happened to be Election Day—was very close, and we had to prepare our rustic center for prestigious visitors, and invite other people to help us welcome them. No small task to do so quickly—but the dye was set!

Guruji and his monks and nuns did indeed arrive, jolting into our back yard at Ground Zero and gathering with our own members, friends from local churches and prayer groups, our Kitsap Affinity Group, and whoever else wanted to pray for peace as Ronald Reagan was elected President. With Guruji came a whole new chapter in our lives, and a deeper understanding of hope and nonviolence.

Guruji was like no one we'd ever met. An elderly man, he walked with difficulty and seemed to be in pain. He was very frail, yet he undertook arduous journeys, fasts, and was involved in every facet of his order's work. He had the joyous, innocent smile of a baby, the same smile we had seen in movies of Gandhi. Guruji seemed to take most delight in the simplest things, yet he clearly understood the monstrous violence of nuclear weapons threatening us all. His innocent joy stood in contrast to the horror of nuclear war, which he opposed with all his being.

Guruji was a follower of the Buddha and of Nichiren; he was also a Gandhian. He recognized immediately what we were trying to do at Ground Zero, and not only gave his support to the campaign, but agreed with Suzuki that this was the best place for an American peace pagoda. He believed this not because we were big or important in the peace movement, but because he saw a small group dedicated to nonviolence and willing to suffer and go to jail. This, he felt, was the best response to overwhelming violence: community, commitment, suffering—and the joy that comes out of them.

During the years that followed we labored to gain permission to build the pagoda. Our request became a release valve for much war-time hatred, racism, and violence. Guruji and the monks and nuns of Nipponzan Myōhōji were always a beacon for us, showing great patience and praying constantly for world peace and disarmament. Even now the pagoda remains an ongoing process, a dream to be fulfilled when we have made enough peace.

We saw Guruji a number of times before he died. His body became steadily weaker and more frail so that eventually he had to be carried from place to place. His joy, however, seemed only to grow. His practice had hollowed him out so that he seemed full of a clear light that shone from his smile.

In Christian art an icon is not just a picture. It is a window to Reality, an opening through which we approach more closely to the Infinite. Guruji has that kind of place in my life. Certainly, he is an example of disciplined adherence to Practice, of putting the ego to death, of selfless commitment to Truth. His words are full of wisdom and we would do well to study them. We could go on with many things that are admirable about Nichidatsu Fujii. But simplest and most important of all, I think, is the window of his smile, a direct entry into the profound joy at the heart of the universe.

James W. Douglass, ***cofounder of Ground Zero Community and author, most recently of*** **JFK and the Unspeakable: Why He Died and Why It Matters**

Great teachers are a gift of God.

Guruji was our teacher. Guruji taught us how sacred a place Ground Zero was, because its people were willing to go to jail for peace. He taught us to see the Buddha in ourselves and in our Gandhian campaign, in which people were willing to sacrifice. Guruji gave us in a new way the vision of nonviolent transformation that might one day culminate in a Peace Pagoda.

Jesus is Shelley's and my first teacher. ...Knowing Gandhiji in spirit and Guruji in both spirit and flesh has been deeply liberating to me as a Christian, for these two great teachers had a practice of suffering violence into love much like that of Jesus. Neither Gandhiji nor Guruji was a Christian, yet both have taken us into a deeper understanding of Jesus, for whom God is Love. Our Hindu and Buddhist teachers, Gandhiji and Guruji, have taught us in their own special ways to transform violence into love.

Na Mu Myō Hō Ren Ge Kyō

John Schuchardt, ***attorney, former Marine Corps officer and member of the Plowshare Eight and Avco Plowshares, is cofounder of the House of Peace in Ipswich, MA.***

It was in the summer of 1976 that The Most Venerable Nichidatsu Fuji sent his ordained monks to participate in The Continental Walk for Peace and Social Justice, from San Francisco to Washington, D.C. For 30 years I have vividly remembered my first meeting with the monks at the Pentagon in October. Completing their 3,000 mile walk, the monks approached with prayer drums the Pentagon, the world's most violent institution, which directs an offensive war budget greater than the other 94 percent of the world combined. With joy and reverence, they continued to pray, and then to bow. "I deeply respect you. I dare not be arrogant. For you will achieve enlightenment."

Guruji knew that only an awakening of the people could avert the impending catastrophe of global nuclear holocaust. He knew that neither analysis nor mere political movement could bring radical change. With insight which seemed astounding for a mendicant foreign monk, Guruji identified the twin roots of evil in American history, the evil of genocide against Native Americans, and the evil of the enslaved exploitation of African Americans, both leaving open, bleeding wounds and continuing injustices. Guruji directed that the energies and devotion of his monks be especially devoted to the extirpation of these two roots of evil from the soul of Americans.

By any measure, the Most Venerable Nichidatsu Fuji is one of the greatest spiritual world leaders of the 20th century. The Most Venerable Fuji is the treasure of the East, given as medicine to the West, at a time when the West appears fatally consumed by mushrooming cancers of militarism, nuclearism, racism, and materialism.

Illtyd Harrington, ***former Chairman of the Greater London Council***

This holy man from the beginning of his priesthood looked upon the horrors of the 20th century. But he never ran away, however fearsome they were. His clarity and universality are as relevant today as ever. Often I recall how [Fujii Guruji] encouraged us to think about blending Arnold Toynbee's view of World Civilization and his own concepts of Buddhism. His broad and inclusive personal philosophy should strengthen our own personal convictions. Fujii Guruji entered the world stage void of vanity. That was what made his life a noble voyage. It is we who should be proud of what he brought to this time and those heavenly assurances in the Peace Pagodas he caused to be built. From North America to the Himalayas, they represent a force for Creative Good. A true shining example of bright hope on a high hill. But also a severe warning. In Western Europe, people are obsessed by legacies. What do we leave? Money, possessions, houses, even ideas. The legacy he handed to us is that which must be accepted with reverence and embraced.

Selected Bibliography

Sources on Buddhism:

Anesaki, Masaharu. Nichiren: *The Buddhist Prophet.* 2nd ed. Gloucester, MA: Harvard University Press, 1966.

Bays, Gwendolyn, trans. *The Lalitavistara Sūtra. The Voice of the Buddha. Vol. 1.* Dharma Publishing, 1983.

Christensen, J.A. and Nichiren Buddhist International Center. *Nichiren, Leader of Buddhist Reformation in Japan.* 2nd ed. Fremont, CA: Jain Publishing Company, 2001.

Inagaki, Hisao. *A Dictionary of Japanese Buddhist Terms.* 5th ed. Kyoto: Nagata Bunshodo, 2003.

Kato, Bunnō, Yoshirō Tamura and Kōjirō Miyasaka, trans. *The Threefold Lotus Sūtra.* 6th ed. New York & Tōkyō: Weatherhill/Kosei, 1984.

Muller, A. Charles, ed. *Digital Dictionary of Buddhism.* 26 December 2007. <http://buddhism-dict.net/ddb>.

Murano, Senchu, trans. *The Lotus Sūtra, The Sūtra of the Lotus Flower of the Wonderful Dharma.* Translated from the Chinese. 2nd ed. Tōkyō: Nichiren Shū Shimbun Co., Ltd, 1991.

The Lankavatara Sūtra. Trans. Daisetz Teitarō Suzuki. <purifymind.com/LankavataraSutra.htm>.

Writings of Nichiren Shōnin, Doctrine 1. Ed. Kyōtsu Hori. Tōkyō: Nichiren Shū Overseas Propagation Promotion Association, 2002.

Writings of Nichiren Shōnin, Doctrine 2. Ed. George Tanabe, Jr. Tōkyō: Nichiren Shu Overseas Propagation Promotion Association, 2003.

Writings of Nichiren Shōnin, Doctrine 3. Ed. Kyōtsu Hori. Tōkyō: Nichiren Shū Overseas Propagation Promotion Association, 2004.

SELECTED BIBLIOGRAPHY

Sources for Historical References:

"Article 9 of the Japanese Constitution." *Wikipedia, The Free Encyclopedia*. 24 Jun 2009. <http://en.wikipedia.org/w/index.php?title=Article_9_of_the_Japanese_Constitution&oldid=298260862>.

Banasick, S. "Globalization, Social Protest and the Militarized Landscape of Okinawa." *SpringerLink Institute: The GeoJournal Library*. Vol. 86. 16 May 2007. pp. 177-189. 5 June 2009. <www.springerlink.com/content/p60v8u3612668874>.

Bohr, Niels. "Memorandum of April 2, 1944." [Cited in open letter to the United Nations, 9 June 1950.] *Impact of Science on Society*. 2.1 (1950): 68.

Dulles, John Foster. "Indochina—Views of the United States of the Eve of the Geneva Conference." *American Foreign Policy 1950-55, Basic Documents Volumes 1 & 2*. United States. Department of State. Publication 6446, General Foreign Policy Series 117.

Eisenhower, Dwight D. "156 - Remarks at the Governors' Conference, Seattle, Washington." 4 August 1953. *The American Presidency Project at UC Santa Barbara*. 15 July 2007. <http://www.presidency.ucsb.edu/ws/?pid=9663>.

Feuerbach, Ludwig. *Essence of Christianity*. Trans. Marian Evans. 3rd edition. Kegan, Paul, Trench Trubner & Co. 1893.

Frisch, J. Kitaham. Teilhard De Chardin, *A Jesuit Explorer, His Life and Spirit*. 7 June 2009. <http://www.st.sophia.ac.jp/T.de.Chardin/ref-eng.pdf>.

Gandhi, Mohandas. "Doctrine of the Sword." *Young India*. 11 August 1920.

Harris, Sheldon H. *Factories of Death; Japanese Biological Warfare, 1932-45, and the American Cover-up*. London: Routledge, 1994.

Hooker, Richard. "The Japanese Constitution." *Ancient Japan*. 1999. Washington State University. 8 Jan 2007. <http://www.wsu.edu/~dee/ANCJAPAN/CONST.HTM>.

Ichiyō, Mutō. "U.S. Military Bases in Japan—An Overview." *People's Plan Study Groups*. Okinawa Environmental Network. 5 June 2009. <http://www.jca.apc.org/wsf_support/2004doc/WSFJapUSBaseRepoFinalAll.html>.

Itoi Shigeko 糸井しげこ. Chastity of Japan—Memoirs of Women Violated by Foreign Soldiers 日本の貞操-外国兵に犯された女性達の手記. Tōkyō: Sōjusha 蒼樹社, 1953.

Maki, John M. "The Documents on Japan's Commission on the Constitution." *Journal of Asian Studies*. 24.3 (May, 1965) pp. 475-489.

McDowell, Kevin. "Japan in Manchuria: Agricultural Emigration in the Japanese Empire, 1932-1945." *Eras Journal*. Monash University. 4 September 2007. 5 June 2009. < http://arts.monash.edu.au/eras/edition_5/mcdowellarticle.htm>.

Miki, Hideo. "Thoughts on the Military History of the Occupation of Japan." *Institute for Historical Review*. 19 January 2005. <http://www.ihr.org/jhr/v09p177_Miki.html>.

Myrdal, Alva. *The Game of Disarmament*. Manchester University Press, 1977.

Nikam, N.A. and Richard McKeon, eds., trans. *The Edicts of Asoka*. The University of Chicago Press, Midway Reprint, 1978.

Pal, Radhabinod. *In Defense of Japan's Case 1 & Case 2*. Ed. Prof. Nakamura Akira. Tōkyō: Dokkyō University, Kenkyūsha Shuppan.

"Prince Shotoku." *International Buddhist University*. 8 Jan 2007 <http://www.shitennoji.ac.jp/ibu/english/ibuprinceshotoku.html>.

Prouty, Doug. "The Race to Build the Atomic Bomb: A Resource for Teachers and Students." *Contra Costa County Office of Education*. 6 June 2009. *<http://www.cccoe.k12.ca.us/abomb/timeline.htm>*.

Russell, Bertrand, Albert Einstein, et al. "The Russell-Einstein Manifesto." 9 July 1955. *Pugwash Online*. 5 June 2009. <http://www.pugwash.org/about/manifesto.htm>.

Shimizu Ikutarō 清水幾太郎, Miyahara Seiichi 宮原誠一 and Ueda Shōzaburō 上田庄三郎. Children of the Base 基地の子. Tōkyō: Kōbunsha 光文社, 1953.

Shobō, Hara. "Nippon Gaiko Shyuyo Bunsho II." *Kajima Heiwa Kenkyujo*. Trans. Prof. Alexander Konkretny. 1983. pp. 598-599.

"Special Comfort Stations ." *Recreation and Amusement Association* 特殊慰安施設協会. *<http://d.hatena.ne.jp/keyword/%C6%C3%BC%EC%B0%D6%B0%C2%BB%DC%C0%DF%B6%A8%B2%F1>*.

"The Opening of the Nationwide Movement Against Atomic and Hydrogen Bombs in Japan: On the Signature Campaign Against Atomic and Hydrogen Bombs in 1954." *Hiroshima Peace Science*. Vol. 5. 1982. pp. 199-223. 5 June 2009. <http://ir.lib.hiroshima-u.ac.jp/metadb/up/kiyo/hps/05/hps_05_199.pdf>.

"The Question Posed by Justice Pal." *NHK Special Programming*. 14 August 2007.

Tolstoy, Leo. *Bethink Yourselves. A Letter on the Russo-Japanese War*. Trans. V. Tchertkoff. Boston: American Peace Society, 1904. Google Books Online: <http://books.google.co.jp/books?id=26cAAAAAYAAJ&dq=Bethink+Yourselves&printsec=frontcover&source=bl&ots=hd2B CBwWa2&sig=ApC_lX3j9a3My5OC1xh5Hmt5- Y0&hl=ja&ei=DgUrSrfuMpS0NZbilcgJ&sa=X&oi=book_result&ct=result&resnum=4#PPA1,M1>.

Toynbee, Arnold J. *A Study of History, Vol. 1*. London: Oxford University Press, 1934.

"Uchihara Youth Brigade Training Center for Developing Manchuria." 満蒙開拓団青少年義勇軍内原訓練所 (茨城県東茨城郡内原町内原). 3 November 2001. 7 June 2009. <http://www.eonet.ne.jp/~ssirube/travel2.htm>.

United States. Homeland Security National Preparedness Task Force. *Civil Defense and Homeland Security: Short History of National Preparedness Efforts.* September 2006. p. 9.

Ward, Robert E. "The Commission on the Constitution and the Prospects for Constitutional Change in Japan." *Journal of Asian Studies.* 24.3 (May, 1965) pp. 401-429.

Wu, Tien-wei. "A Preliminary Review of Studies of Japanese Biological Warfare Unit 731 in the United States." *Advocacy and Intelligence Index for Prisoners of War-Missing In Action.* 5 June 2009. < http://www.aiipowmia.com/731/731mnu.html>.

Sources in Japanese

『織田仏教大辞典』　織田得能、1983新訂6刷、大蔵出版（株）

『現代意譯　大般涅槃経』原田霊道、 1922、仏教経典叢書刊行會

『昭和定本日蓮聖人遺文』日蓮宗電子聖典、 2003、日蓮宗

『日蓮聖人御遺文』加藤文雅・霊艮閣版、重刻新版 1967、山喜房佛書林

『日蓮宗事典』、1981, 日蓮宗宗務院

『藤井日達聖人全集』1994–1999、隆文館

『法華辞典ー山喜房仏書林 広説仏教語大辞典』中村元著、2001、　東京書籍

『「立正安国論」管見』-近畿教区教研会議講義録-難波宏正講述、2007,　本養寺